STONEWALL JACKSON

Portrait of a Soldier

John Bowers

We know him as Stonewall—a symbol of stubborn resistance. To his men he was Old Jack, a stern yet tenderhearted leader, someone who led his soldiers on quick thirty-mile marches and then stood guard over them while they slept. He shot deserters without qualm. Old Blue Light, as he was also known, believed fervently in the Bible and served as a Presbyterian deacon. After the unholy fighting at First Manassas, one of his first communiqués went to his church in Lexington. In the heat of battle, he had forgotten to send his contribution to the Colored Sunday School (which he had founded) and enclosed a check.

On the one hand simple and straightforward, on the other secretive and mystifying (where, for instance, did his perpetual supply of lemons come from?), Thomas Jonathan Jackson was, more than anything else, deeply and everlastingly American. John Bowers, himself a Southerner whose grandfather and great-uncles fought on opposing sides in Tennessee during the Civil War, presents Jackson in the round, as flesh and blood, someone who struck terror in the Union forces and who stood tall as a hero in the South when all else turned bleak.

Relying on letters, diaries, memoirs, and eyewitness accounts, Bowers deftly and artfully unravels Jackson's puzzling character—his orphaned childhood on a frontier farm, where he was raised by a rambunctious bachelor uncle; his career at West Point; his experiences in the Mexican War with many of the future generals on both sides of the Civil War; his two marriages; and his stint as an improbable professor at V.M.I., where he couldn't

(continued on back flap)

STONEWALL JACKSON

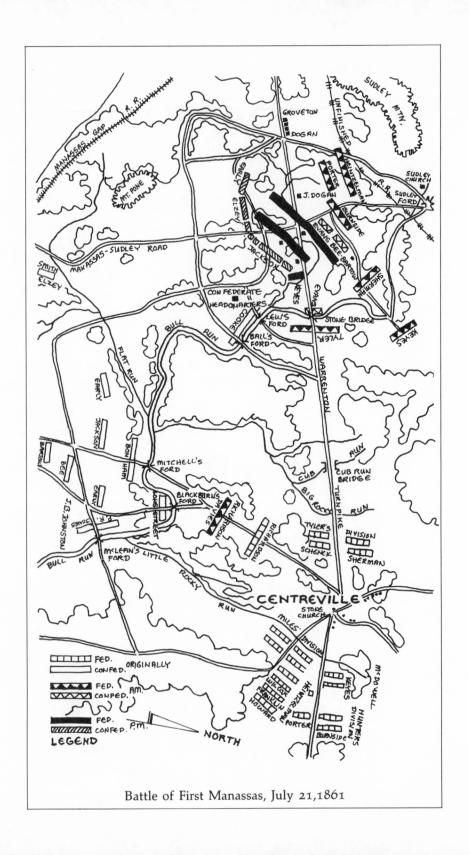

Battle of First Manassas, July 21, 1861

Also by John Bowers

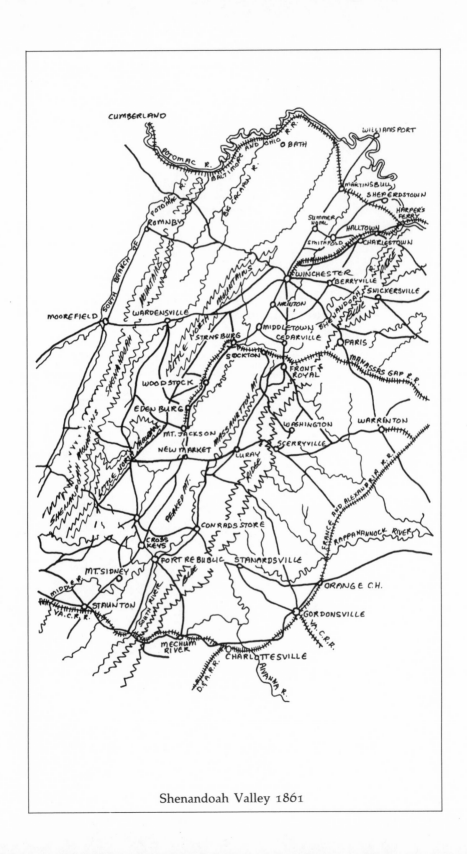

Shenandoah Valley 1861

STONEWALL JACKSON

PORTRAIT OF A SOLDIER

John Bowers

WILLIAM MORROW AND COMPANY, INC.
New York

33404

Library of Congress Cataloging-in-Publication Data

Bowers, John, 1928–
Stonewall Jackson : portrait of a soldier / by John Bowers.
p. cm.
Includes index
ISBN 0-688-05747-0
1. Jackson, Stonewall, 1824–1863. 2. Generals—United States—
Biography. 3. Confederate States of America. Army—Biography.
4. United States. Army—Biography. 5. United States—History—
Civil War, 1861–1865—Campaigns. I. Title.
E467.1.J15B68 1989
973.7'3'0924—dc19
[B]   88-37918
                                                       CIP

Printed in the United States of America

First Edition

1 2 3 4 5 6 7 8 9 10

BOOK DESIGN BY NICOLA MAZZELLA

*This book is dedicated to
William A. Bowers—Private 4th
Tennessee Cavalry Battalion, CSA
John A. Thornhill—Captain 9th
Tennessee Cavalry Regiment, USA*

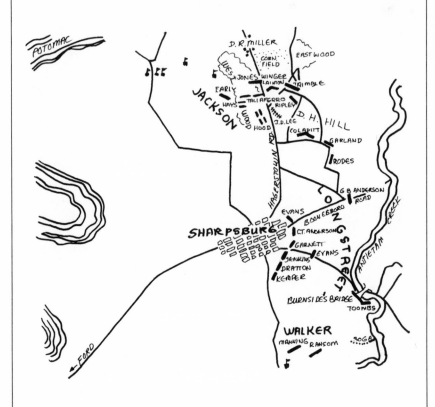

Confederate Forces at Sharpsburg

Contents

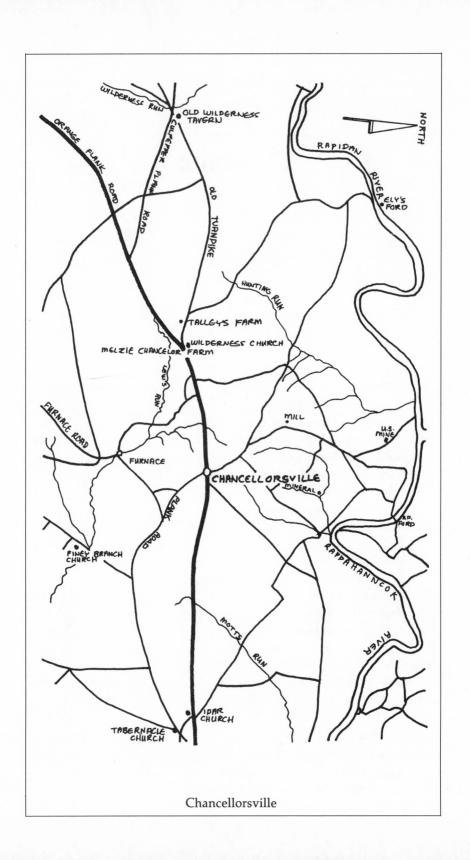

Chancellorsville

Prologue

Like more than one present-day Southerner, I fought knowing more about the Civil War than I needed to know. It was too much around me, and it didn't seem to return much dividend for all the space it took up; it was like the fundamentalist religion I grew up with—a lot of fervor that didn't seem to have much to do with real life. It didn't quite have flesh and blood (the way, say, World War II had); it filtered into my imagination only thinly, just dates and abstractions—like the "inferiority feeling" Southerners are supposed to suffer because they lost the War. Pedagogues and misfits and dotty old folk spouted off about it at the drop of a hat. It got boring—like biscuits every day. It was a dark abyss you might fall into and never be heard from again. When I wanted to meander in the past, I preferred to be in England with Charles Dickens or in Russia with Leo Tolstoy.

I was living away from the South when I idly began reading *Reveille in Washington* by Margaret Leech. (The book had belonged to my mother, Stella Swafford Bowers, a member in good standing of the United Daughters of the Confederacy. Her uncle, James Edgemon, had fought for the South. My father's uncle, John Thornhill, had fought for the North, and Thornhill's brother-in-law, my paternal grandfather, William A. Bowers, had fought as a boy for the Confederacy.) By the second paragraph of Leech's narrative of war-torn Washington I myself started to slide into that deep hole of obsession from which few Civil War buffs return. Her prose sparkled and the people came alive and were fascinating. I was lost. "In spite of his nearly seventy-five years and his increasing infirmities," Leech wrote, "the General [Winfield Scott] was addicted to the pleasures of the table. Before his six o'clock dinner, his black body servant brought out the wines and the liqueurs, setting the bottles of claret to warm before the fire. The old man had refined his palate in the best restaurants in Paris; and woodcock, English snipe, poulard, capon, and *tête de veau en tortue* were among the dishes he fancied."

My eye became alerted for Civil War material—and I found it from rich sources, likely and unlikely. I read letters, diaries, and journals from relatives who had fought in the War. Martha Joyner Miller, my cousin's wife, furnished me with unpublished journals from her grandfather, James Blackman Ligon, who had fought at First Manassas under General "Shanks" Evans and who had helped give first resistance to the seemingly invincible Federals under McDowell at Stone Bridge. Here is his description of the Federals opening fire: "When they did it, it seemed as if the earth [had] burst up. They threw cannon balls, bomb shells, canister, grape, musket balls, minié balls, and rifle balls which wrought havoc among us. The noise was awful—it was like two thunderstorms met—only worse if possible. The smoke and blaze from the guns rose above the tree tops. The groaning of the wounded and dying chilled my very soul."

I read with great pleasure *Patriotic Gore* by Edmund Wilson and the *Memoirs of Ulysses S. Grant.* I read Bruce Catton's books and then, fatally, I picked up Shelby Foote's narrative of the Civil War. It was the coup de grâce. I had passed the daunting three fat volumes many times in bookstores, and could resist no longer. I settled back one late evening in bed and began what I considered was going to be a by now familiar story. It began familiarly enough but before long took hold of me as no other account of the Civil War had. It was told through a novelist's eye. And suddenly in the narrative, in the midst of battle, one man jumped off the page at me. It was almost magical. This difficult, complicated soldier seemed not only to reveal home truths about my progenitors but to explain some essential ingredient in the character of all Americans, North and South. I had read about him often enough; Lord knows I had heard enough people extolling his steadfastness and stubbornness. Now he just appeared and seemed to say, "Write about me." For his imaginative resurrection I thank Mr. Shelby Foote, for this was Stonewall Jackson.

For several years the Civil War became, for me, Stonewall Jackson. I visited his Winter Headquarters in Winchester, Virginia; was shown around by Mrs. Marie Bowman, a local archivist, who is a fount of knowledge about the Civil War in the Shenandoah Valley. I discovered while there that the actress Mary Tyler Moore's great-grandfather, Lieutenant Colonel Lewis Tilghman Moore of the Fourth Virginia Volunteers, had lent this, his home at 415 North Braddock Street, to Jackson for his headquarters. It had been the neighborly thing to do, back in 1861, in Virginia.

I visited V.M.I. in Lexington, Virginia, and strolled through the small rooms of Jackson's modest two-story brick home there, the only one he ever owned. I walked over the battlefields where he had fought. I became acquainted with Dr. Thomas Jonathan Jackson Altizer, a professor and theologian at New York State University at Stony Brook, as eccentric in his own way as his illustrious ancestor. As Jackson's direct descendant he was invited to speak before the cadets in V.M.I.'s chapel. This namesake of the devout Presbyterian general began his sermon with "Gentlemen, God is dead."

The Civil War is not easy to understand; neither is the historic figure of Jackson. The first accounts of the War, by those who survived it, were generally grandiloquent in form and verbose. R. L. Dabney, a Christian minister who had been on Jackson's staff, wrote a life of his former commander in 1866—a most loving biography, told in flowery language. But Jackson's character comes through. Dabney pointed out that Jackson did not believe in taking prisoners of war. "[The Civil War] was not," he wrote, "a strife for a point of honor, a diplomatic quarrel, a commercial advantage, a boundary, or a province; but an attempt on the part of North against the very existence of the Southern

States." It is well to keep in mind that this most savage war did not take place amid fine noble sentiments. Dabney wrote as one who had lived through it, not as a dispassionate scholar. *I Rode with Stonewall* by Henry Kyd Douglas, a young Maryland member of Jackson's staff, was a spritely personal account. Newspapers printed accounts of battles and descriptions of soldiering while the events unfolded. Then those who had witnessed the conflict firsthand, those who had shouldered arms with Jackson, began dying off. In 1898 George F. R. Henderson, an English military writer, brought out the classic, *Stonewall Jackson and the American Civil War.* Suddenly the War unfolds with a British cadence: "Upward and eastward the battalions [of Jackson's army] passed, the great forest of oak and pine rising high on either hand, until from the aerie of the mountain eagles they looked down upon the wide Virginia plains."

The "second generation" chroniclers took a hard, reasoned look at the conflict—and brought splendid minds and sensibilities forward. I refer to two in particular—Douglas Southall Freeman, who was associated with the Richmond *News-Leader,* and Bell Irvin Wiley, who taught at Atlanta's Emory University. They bridged the gap between the romantic nineteenth century and the harsher modern mind. I relished the way Freeman began sentences with the word "Ere." "Ere Jackson took to the turnpike . . ." I equally relished his grasp of the telling detail of character. He was quick to recognize the human failings (and occasional nobility) in these warriors. Bell Wiley pored over untold numbers of diaries, letters and news accounts and gave us the inestimable *The Life of Johnny Reb* and *The Life of Billy Yank.* He let us see how the War was fought by the common soldier.

In the present day we have fiction and near-fiction and revised estimates. I especially liked *The Killer Angels,* which made me taste the hot scalding coffee over the campfires at Gettysburg, and *The Confederates,* which forced me to consider Stonewall Jackson and all men who fought in the War as human enough to have had sex drives and the impulse, under stress, to curse a blue streak. I did not pass up any scrap of paper that might have added insight. *Stonewall Jackson Day by Day* by John W. Schildt was a most helpful guide in finding where the elusive general was at any given time. Jackson's wife, Anna, left behind valuable memoirs,

but unfortunately her husband left scant written records himself—a smattering of letters and some jottings in his notebook
journal. Two extremely insightful volumes were *Mighty Stonewall*
by Frank Vandiver and *Stonewall Jackson* by Lenoir Chambers. Vandiver was a protégé of Freeman's; Chambers is a descendant of
the minister who performed the marriage ceremony for Jackson
in North Carolina.

And so I came to write my tale of Stonewall Jackson. The
reader may well ask—is it fiction or is it fact? It is nonfiction in
the sense that it is based on a real man and a real time. Throughout I have drawn on documented evidence or the guidance of
Civil War scholars. I thank Professor Charles B. Strozier of John
Jay College, New York; Professor J. Michael Lennon of Sangamon
State University, Springfield, Illinois; and Professor Gary W. Gal-
lagher of Penn State University for looking over the original
manuscript. Their comments have proven invaluable. I have
"made up" nothing in this book out of whole cloth. The very
weather on any given day comes from Schildt's *Stonewall Jackson
Day by Day*. Some speech comes from history; at other times, in
attempting to get at the heart of a individual or circumstance, I
have imagined how some of these people might have spoken. For
instance, history books tell us that soldiers swore—in the case of
John Harmon, Jackson's quartermaster, spectacularly—and yet
the history books do not give examples. I have taken a leap
forward, with no one's permission, and imagined how it might
have sounded, as I imagined how the terrific clatter of battle
might have sounded—and in this respect, the book is fiction.

In my research I discovered that it is difficult indeed to actually find the historical "truth." Douglas Southall Freeman gave
several versions of how Jackson got his famous nickname. An
unusual one has it that General Barnard Bee was calling not with
admiration but in anger, when he said in the first battle at Manassas that Jackson was "standing like a stone wall"; he wanted
Jackson to come to his aid and Jackson wouldn't budge.

In this narrative, I have tried for the truth—truth, in part,
through how the past speaks through the present. For instance,
Jackson may seem ridiculous at times. Well, a lot of outsiders
consider all Southerners slightly ridiculous. Casual strangers
from beyond the region seldom hesitate to ask, "Where you

from? What's that accent?" They even feel entitled to try out a
Southern accent in broad form in front of a Southerner. They may
even ask, "They wear shoes down your way?" Southerners observe outsiders warily, never inquiring about their footwear or
commenting on their vowels—waiting perhaps, it seems, to ward
off another invasion, for the memory of the last one still lingers.
Stonewall Jackson faced that invasion and was a near-perfect
soldier. There have been Presbyterian deacons of greater note
than T. J. Jackson, certainly more distinguished professors, but
there have been few greater soldiers than he.

I realize now that not just Southerners but a diverse band are
drawn to Stonewall Jackson. For one, Moshe Yegar, Israel's am-
bassador to the United Nations. Like me, he has trodden the
Virginia battlefields and studied the character of the man. As a
small piece of God may be in all of us, so a little bit of Jackson
may be there, too. He does not belong to rednecks waving a
Confederate flag and yelling "Dixie." He speaks for those who
will not be defeated and to those who fight against all odds. It
must be admitted, too, that he speaks at times for plain craziness
and for reasons that transcend all reasonableness. He had a great
deal of ambition, which he usually kept under wraps, and more
than his share of righteousness, which he never hid, and there are
moments when he is not so likable.

I soaked up Jackson's presence as best I could and, in the end,
came to realize that I was coming to terms with the people from
whom I sprang—the Scotch-Irish of Appalachia. They can be
infuriating and hard to make peace with—as Stonewall Jackson
was. Jay Robert Reese wrote in the preface to *Latchpins of the Lost
Cove* by Malone Young, "Americans have found in Southern Appalachia the dream of ourselves at our best, and the nightmare of
us at our worst." Thus Stonewall Jackson appears to me at times.

CHAPTER I

A Man of Mystery

As Lexington's leading citizens gathered for the monthly meeting of the Franklin Society, a new face appeared: a broad forehead, dark brown hair, and a determined look; a rather handsome but somewhat peculiar figure. He sat ramrod straight, his blue-gray eyes gazing ahead, while others lounged about and familiarly draped an arm over the back of a neighboring chair. Gaslight flared. The all-male Franklin Society was considering the question: Could a heathen who had never heard of Jesus Christ be Saved? At the last meeting they had debated whether or not theatrical amusements were prejudicial to morality. Judge Brockenbrough adjusted his ear trumpet with pleasant anticipation. The Franklin Society held lively, stimulating meetings, wrestling with the most trenchant issues of the day.

Speakers fiddled with their watch fobs; they paced back and forth past the lectern, thrusting a hand into their waistcoats; they lowered their voices to a whisper to make the members of the audience lean forward, then shouted to push them back into their seats. They told jokes, wove parables, inspired tears, and made hearts race. In Lexington, it was considered a high privilege for a man to belong to the Franklin Society. It was a mark of high social approval, which was no small matter to these Southern gentlemen.

"And now for the affirmative side, that a heathen *can* be Saved without hearing about our Savior, the Lord Jesus Christ, we call on our newest member, Major Jackson. I believe he is here . . . Major Jackson, will you please come forward and give us your argument?"

The man rose smartly and there was some twittering. He seemed faintly comical. He strode forward in a long loping way, on enormous booted feet—as though he were about to mount a horse, not stand before a lectern. Then the twitter died. Jackson just stood there, gazing out over heads. Expectant smiles followed and some embarrassment. A silent plea from the group urged him to start. Wasn't he going to open his mouth? Thomas Jonathan Jackson said a word or two about Jesus Christ and His mercy; then he touched upon the question of the heathen. Then his thin straight mouth snapped shut and stayed so. He simply stood there, without yielding his turn.

"I hear that man is a professor," Judge Brockenbrough said into the silence, his voice carrying around the hall. "Why is he called a major?"

"Major Jackson served under General Winfield Scott in Mexico."

"Served with distinction. He was at the Point. Fearless, they say."

"Man's scared out of his wits up there," Judge Brockenbrough boomed. "How can those cadets at the Institute suffer him?"

"They're hardly doing that, Judge," his neighbor said in a whine, drawing snuff up a nostril. "They're skinning him up there. Dubbed him Tom Fool."

"Ha! Man seems like a fool."

The members of the Franklin Society did not go too far, though. No full-fledged guffaws came. There was something about the man that stopped them, some hint of danger if they went too far. Despite the comedy there was the aura of deep dignity in the man, some inviolate reserve that it might be best not to trifle with. Yet it was all some members could do not to roar. One man escaped by the side entrance; another shook out the latest *Lexington Gazette* and began reading. Jackson just stood there, his face now blazing, his blue-gray eyes narrowing. Some thought he might be in actual physical pain. He would not budge, would not relinquish his allotted time at the lectern even though he had nothing to add at the moment. At last he said that even savages were God's children and abruptly, determinedly, strode back to his chair. No one clapped; no one knew what to do.

Jackson came to the next debate promptly on time. He came to the one after that, and he took his turn on the side that proposed that a secession of the states would be preferable to a limited monarchy. Virginia should secede from the Union before she should ever bow to the rule of another King George. Jackson struggled with his argument but the Franklin Society began to listen. No one groaned.

And no one could ever pinpoint the moment when Jackson's name evoked delight instead of dread at the meetings. But there Jackson finally stood, face hawklike, speaking in a direct, emphatic, and convincing manner. He didn't stumble over a word. His sentences flowed. His naturally high voice rose and fell. Mysterious. It was as if he had simply willed away his awkwardness and taken on a gifted debater's style. It was also, a few thought, as if he might have memorized his lines like an actor. A reporter from the *Lexington Gazette* began showing up at the Franklin Society just to hear what the professor had to say. He had the most interesting ideas of anyone in the society, the most up-to-date theories. A very strange man.

In 1860 Major Thomas J. Jackson was among twelve hundred people who lived in closely adjoined houses in Lexington, Virginia. Lexington was bustling and getting more modern by the day. Wagons rattled in over the Old Plank Road, bringing beeswax, tallow, and feathers. Three times a week a stagecoach swayed in, on its way to Tennessee where natives still wore coonskin and leather britches. As the stage neared the town gates, the passengers vibrating as the coach's wheels ran over the road's wooden boards, the driver stood majestically, cocked a trumpet, and blew a wild sweet blast.

Visitors from the Old World often lingered in Lexington, for the town held echoes of rural England, of southern France, of

Switzerland. Europeans felt at home. The sea-colored Blue Ridge rose to the south and east—to the north you could see Hog Back and Jump Mountains; to the west, House Mountain ("Our Fujiyama," the learned called it.) This Appalachian range rose ten to fifteen miles away—close enough to fascinate, distant enough not to smother.

Major Jackson paid $3,108 for a sturdy two-story brick home on the slight rise of Washington Street for his young dark-eyed bride, Mary Anna (more often called Anna). Maybe this time, in this house, under the beneficent guidance of the good Lord, he would have better luck. His first wife, Ellie, had died in childbirth a few years before, in 1854. The infant was stillborn. In 1857 he married Anna, who, like his first wife, was the daughter of a clergyman. His dwelling had a small coach house out back, a modest vegetable garden, and a tranquilizing view of the sapphire-blue hills.

Jackson installed a wood stove, one of the first in town, in his dirt-floored basement kitchen. The curious dropped by to take a look, for nearly everyone else cooked by open hearth, with kettles and a pot hanging over a brisk fire. Jackson's lid-topped black stove captured the acrid smoke, and it kept an even temperature for simmering vegetables. During the week Major Jackson taught at the Virginia Military Institute, the new college in town, holding the Chairs of Natural and Experimental Philosophy and Artillery.

V.M.I. was the brainchild of Claude Crozet, a Frenchman who had fought under Napoleon at Waterloo. After emigrating to America in 1817, he had become associated with West Point, where he taught mathematics. He moved ever south and in Virginia designed the Chesapeake and Ohio Railroad tunnel under the Blue Ridge at Afton. In Lexington he helped set up V.M.I. in 1839 along the lines of the Academy at West Point. Uniforms of both schools were modeled after those of the French Guard. Like West Point above the Hudson, the new Institute loomed like a castle on high ground above the town. It bordered another, older seat of learning: Washington College.

Lexington supported eight popular drinking establishments, among which were Old Blue, Fancy Hill Mansion, and the Eagle Hotel. Private homes in town were also turned into unlicensed

watering holes on occasion, for there was a roving band of va-
grants, ex-convicts, and ex-soldiers who moved steadily in an
alcoholic daze from house to house. Ladies played "Flow Gently,
Sweet Afton" on the parlor piano for gentlemen after supper
while rowdies fistfought in taverns and rolled over in combat on
the street. Odors along the road and in the homes were pungent:
the lather of horses, their droppings, the sharpness of boot black-
ing and the sweetness of household sachet. Chimney smoke
curved down the streets and alleys, and the rattle of wagons and
the neighing of horses were constant.

Lexington was a town where people didn't think twice about
borrowing a bucketful of water, or a smoldering coal to start a
fire. On the street it was a familiar sight to see someone with a
burning plank or red-hot coal going from one house to another.
The more advanced, like Major Jackson, took a chance with little
blocks fastened together at the butt ends and costing 40 cents a
dozen. They were made of sulfur and were split off one at a time;
prudence dictated that one hold them far away when striking.
Candles were generally made at home.

Extremes were the norm for these people poised between the
illimitable frontier and murky complex modernity. Many homes
had private stills, and religion was of consuming concern. Pres-
byterianism found fertile soil in Lexington; the pillared Presbyterian church was the most prominent in town, on Main Street.
Major Jackson held a pew there. The Presbyterian message was
strongly Calvinistic and focused on the fall of man, the depravity
of human nature, and salvation through Jesus Christ alone. One's
fate was preordained. The custom was to hold two services on the
Sabbath, one in late morning and another in the afternoon, separated by half an hour for food and composing one's emotions.

Most of these people belonged to that group called Ulster-
Scots by the Irish and Scotch-Irish on these shores. They came
from the province of Ulster in Northern Ireland, feeling put upon,
seeking their own place in the sun, and leery of anyone in a
position to tell them what to do. In the 1720s around fifty thousand Scotch-Irish arrived in the Colonies. By the year of independence, 1776, almost half of Ulster had crossed the Atlantic and
one in seven colonists was Scotch-Irish. (Lincoln and Jefferson
Davis were Scotch-Irish; they were in fact born within a few

miles of each other in Kentucky.) The moody Scotch-Irish settled easily into the hazy dreamlike mountain setting, had a weakness for liquor and religion, and vied with the mule for stubbornness. They were dark-haired, handsome, suspicious of strangers, loyal to family, often regarded as crazy by outsiders, and tightfisted with money. They paid their debts. They expected others to do the same. They were Scots who had previously followed on the heels of Cromwell's invasion of Ireland and fled the Covenanting Wars of Scotland. They had the blood of Celts in them and forebears who had refused Latinized words and the wearing of ornate garb when the Norman Conquest came in 1066. They seemed destined, like the Jews, to be outnumbered by those around them who thought in different ways, and they eventually came to be at odds with whatever majority in whatever land they happened to settle in.

The waves of those who sailed for the New Land in boxlike warrens of pitching ships settled first in mountainous Pennsylvania. They did not prove ingratiating to those already there. The secretary of the Province of Pennsylvania wrote in 1724: "It looks as if the whole of Ireland is sending its inhabitants hither, for last week not less than six ships arrived. The common fear is that if they thus continue to come they will make themselves proprietors of the Province. It is strange that they thus crowd where they are not wanted."

They did not want to be there. They did not want to be under the thumb of anyone who would make such statements. They had received harsh treatment under William and Mary and Queen Anne—for their religious beliefs—and they were not about to bow to the Quakers in the domain of Brotherly Love. They pressed on.

In the Shenandoah Valley of Virginia they halted, believing that they had stumbled on a kind of Eden—a glorious forest primeval. They cleared the land, built church and school, and those with greater leisure made sure that their children had a taste of high culture. These Scots believed in learning—in reading, in the appreciation of music, in trying to understand what the more sophisticated considered art. Life was incomplete unless there was something to learn, some form of self-improvement. They quoted learned texts, but they did not bring charity to the subject of the Law. Transgressors should be punished, and punishment, they believed, should be swift and unmerciful. In Lexington, at the close of the eighteenth century, dire malefactors were hung by the neck till dead, the town watching. Sometimes this was not enough. The head would be removed from the body, and the poor wretch's features twisted on a spike and exposed on the highest hill in town, a signal to the weak of what awaited those who transgressed the Law. In many ways, it was a savage time.

In early colonial days a man who had made a niche for himself, a person who held some acreage and ran a household and sought some relief from the menial, took on "redemptioners." These were indentured servants, many also from Ireland, who had been convicted in England for small crimes and condemned to pay their penalty in the New World. It was the way things were done before the Revolution, before egalitarianism took hold. After their period of service these redemptioners received their freedom. Others in bondage were debtors sent abroad by creditors, poor relations, and ne'er-do-wells of various stripes that England was eager to be rid of. Before the Revolution it seemed to work to everyone's advantage. The master got cheap labor. The servant was better fed and more humanely treated than in the old country. Most servants stayed on after their obligatory service (usually five years) and became citizens, allowing succeeding generations to forget a past ancestry of petty criminals and horse thieves and profligate gamblers.

There was, of course, another system of labor that grew in favor in the heady days following the Revolution and the break with England: black slave labor. Slavery had been around from the beginning, almost from the time the first Pilgrim stepped ashore on this continent, from the sixteenth century when confused distraught natives of African villages were forcibly brought here. It became a convenient mercantile answer to a pressing consumer need. No debates were held. No commission met. No one voted on whether it was a good idea or not. The spirit of egalitarianism after the Revolution did not affect it. In 1650 there had been three hundred Negroes in Virginia. In 1721 they composed about half the state's population. Debates then began. What to do about slavery?

Liberals said the merciful thing was to send former slaves

back to Africa. By 1826 the African Colonization Society flourished in Lexington. It wished freedmen well and helped book
them passage to Liberia. The majority died soon after reaching
the far shores, confused, sick, and in deep culture shock. As late
as 1850 they were being sent to Liberia, but slavery still flourished on these shores—and most citizens came to realize that the
problem could not be exported. It could not just be sent away.

Anna Jackson later wrote, "I am very confident that [General
Jackson] would never have fought for the sole object of per-
petuating slavery. It was for her *constitutional rights* that the South
resisted the North, and slavery was only comprehended among
those rights.

"He found the institution of slavery a responsible and trou-
blesome one, and I have heard him say that he would prefer to
see the Negroes free, but he believed that the Bible taught that
slavery was sanctioned by the Creator himself, who maketh men
to differ and instituted laws for the bound and the free. He
therefore accepted slavery, as it existed in the Southern States,
not as a thing desirable in itself but as allowed by Providence for
ends which it was not his business to determine. . . . He was
strongly for the Union, but at the same time he was a firm States'-
right man. He was never a secessionist, and maintained that it
was better for the South to fight for her rights in the Union than
out of it."

There was much arguing in Virginia about slavery and states'
rights. Politicians clamored, but no statesman rose. Debate grew
heated on Main Street in Lexington where loafers brought chairs
to sit in the shade on hot days, changing to the other side when
the sun shifted. Husband argued with wife over politics. Brother
went against brother. Fathers screamed at sons. No one trusted
the new generation in Lexington. It was a fast, strident-seeming
hotbed of radicals. Those harebrains at Washington College and
the fanatics at V.M.I. wanted to *secede* from the Union! The
townspeople thought they should be drawn and quartered.
Brawls erupted in taverns. The Union dissolved? It would be the
Second American Revolution. One was enough.

Major Jackson kept to his schedule, and didn't try to change
what he knew he could never change. He was a Presbyterian
fatalist.

* * *

He arose, as was his custom, at six and knelt in prayer, in his nightdress, by his heavy four-poster. Then he sought out the small alcove where ice-cold water had been drawn. Hetty, the matriarchal servant, had already begun getting the household moving. One of Hetty's sons, Cy or George, had charge of filling a small sitz bath each morning for the major. The boys, along with their imperious mother, had joined Jackson's household when Anna married him. They had been with her family in North Carolina, and now they adapted themselves to their new master's ways. Major Jackson had to have his daily cold-water plunge, even in the dead of winter. He doffed his flannel nightdress and plopped right down, bolt upright, no second thought, roughly moving his hands over his lean body. Next he took a rapid walk, rain or shine, sleet or snow, sick or well, every day of the year. In rough weather he donned India-rubber cavalry boots and a heavy army overcoat. At seven in the morning in the parlor he held family devotions. The six servants were invited and expected to attend.

The first slave Jackson had owned in Lexington had been clean-featured, somber-faced Albert. He hadn't needed a slave then, in fact he hadn't thought of ever owning one—he was a bachelor—and then Albert had suddenly sprung out on Main Street before him. "Please, marsa, I'm in bondage. Please buy me out." Albert wanted no part of bondage, and this was his first step out. He had a mean master, a penny-pinching, oppressive man, and if this man Jackson, who was known for his kindness and fairness, would buy him, then he would pay Jackson back in annual installments and gain his freedom. What the colored man was proposing was complicated. Slavery was complicated. Jackson bought Albert and permitted him to work as a hotel waiter to pay off the debt. By the time Jackson married Anna, Albert had become bedridden and Jackson was taking care of him. Old Amy had come to him in much the same way, for she was about to be sold for debt. Then there was little Emma, a tiny orphan whom a venerable woman in town had implored the major to take in.

Jackson himself lovingly tended the vegetable garden out back, a bandanna tied around his forehead, his fingers sinking in the loamy soil. He was a gracious host who could take time to roll on the floor with children, putting on funny faces and entering their games unobtrusively. He took care of guests. He made them comfortable. He might be found late at night, after all were asleep, checking on a sick child, making sure there were enough blankets or that a high fever hadn't struck. He was the model of courtesy, understanding, and filled with good humor.

His daily routine hardly varied. At seven in the morning, after the cold bath, the half-trot stroll, he stepped smartly into the parlor and snapped the door shut. It was not a second before or a second later. Seven on the dot. He was there to lead the daily morning prayers. No one was allowed to be tardy. No exceptions. His adored Anna rounded the corner, patting her dark hair, straightening her skirt, to find the door swinging closed a few feet away. She knew enough to wheel around and head back.

Cy and George flew through prayers. Hetty's young sons had learned to count on swift retribution if they went against Jackson's will. They had learned enough about the major's ways to know that. They could count on having to broom-sweep the whole first floor or being denied time off to go fishing on a warm afternoon. They would see his blue-gray eyes flashing. He made you remember that you had missed morning prayers. Forget to shut a door upon leaving a room and he'd wait until you were down in the basement before calling you back to close it, making you remember. He could be maddening.

After morning prayers, though, the door opened and another Major Jackson emerged. Duty had been done. Now he smiled, nodding to one and all, and calling Anna his *esposita*. In Mexico, in a far different time, he had mastered Spanish. *Esposita* was his favorite endearment for Anna; he could say it, almost sing it, without embarrassment. "My *esposita*," he called her after morning prayers, even when she'd been shut out for tardiness. "My *esposita*."

He seemed so grateful to have a home, a good wife, a routine. Some of those who observed him at home wondered what sort of past he must have had to be so overjoyed with the common domestic scene. He was not quite the ordinary householder, though. According to Anna Jackson's memoirs, her husband could do the most startling yet endearing things. He could be strange and comical and formidable by turns. There was the time

he came home from an early artillery drill, dressed in full regi-
mentals, and she thought he had never looked so noble or so
handsome. He entered with sword in hand. Suddenly, unbelieva-
bly, he began mocking his military bearing, rolling his eyes and
waving his sword over her head. She drew back with a gasp, and
when he saw those large dark eyes widen even more, he flung his
sword down. *"Amor mío,* no harm will ever come to you!"

Years later, Anna described her husband in the early years
of their marriage: "His head was a splendid one, large and finely
formed, and covered with soft, dark-brown hair, which, if allowed to grow to any length, curled; but he had a horror of long
hair for a man, and clung to the conventional style, *à la militaire,*
of wearing very close-cut hair and short side-whiskers. After he
was persuaded to turn out a full beard, it was much more becoming to him, his beard being a heavy and handsome brown, a shade
lighter than his hair. His forehead was noble and expansive, and
always fair, from its protection by his military cap. His eyes were
blue-gray in color, large, and well-formed, capable of wonderful
changes with his varying emotions. His nose was straight and
finely chiselled, his mouth small, and his face oval. His profile
was very fine. All his features were regular and symmetrical, and
he was at all times manly and noble-looking, and when in robust
health he was a handsome man."

Each day Major Jackson strode the two miles to campus—
from 8 East Washington Street to the hilltop upon which the
turreted V.M.I. stood. His step long and rapid, he had the habit
of stopping every so often and raising his left hand to the level
of his eyes, palm turned out, as if shielding himself from the sun.
The sun, however, would be over his right shoulder. The gesture
was a peculiarity, another one of the major's, to which the townspeople had grown accustomed. He doffed his hat to one and all,
a pleasant reserved smile on his face. He even skimmed his hat
off to colored folk, which took some doing for the locals to
become accustomed to—but, then again, everyone knew that this
strange Major Jackson had his *ways.* "I could be no less polite than
a colored man who raised his hat to me," he explained, when
someone asked why he did it.

Jackson had his tight circle of friends. Among them was John
B. Lyle, a happy and confirmed bachelor, who ran a bookshop on

Main Street. Lyle didn't care about money. He sought to save men's souls and to lead people in song. He led the Presbyterian church choir. Lyle was flamboyant—you couldn't miss him in a crowd—and he knew how to take charge, a trait the socially shy Jackson prized. Lyle guided Jackson along, like an older brother. He recommended books; he sought to improve his mind. Jackson couldn't carry a tune, but he regularly attended Lyle's musical soirees. He became a deacon in the church.

Jackson also showed a good eye for business, and had a knack for making good investments: prudent for the most part, but striking quickly when he sensed a good thing. He was named a director of the Lexington Bank. But his oddities were never completely out of sight. He fell asleep while seated rigidly in church. He just dropped off, like a stone, his head lolling and an occasional snore reverberating through the rafters. A sermon by kindly Dr. White was sure to do it, and a bevy of V.M.I. cadets could be counted upon to lean over the balcony rail, anticipating the decisive moment. Anna took to poking him in the ribs and, as an extreme measure, jabbing him with a hatpin, but nothing quite roused him satisfactorily. "Our Father in heaven—" Dr. White called from the pulpit, and a harsh vibrato broke from between Jackson's lips. Nodding off was a malady that afflicted Jackson throughout his life—like his mysterious stomach complaint. Jackson had something congenitally wrong with his innards. His own treatment of this ailment consisted of standing bolt upright or sitting rigidly erect in order not to bend his digestive organs. He ate plain brown bread, hardly any meat, and drank only cold water. His eyesight was fading (he could not read by artificial light), and he had trouble hearing with his right ear. No one seemed to know if he was a hypochondriac or a person in deep lasting pain. And at no time did he give any indication of the stature he would assume in the coming war.

Once, according to Julia Davis Adams in her book *Stonewall,* he had an appointment with the superintendent of V.M.I., Colonel Francis H. Smith. As he sat perched at a ninety-degree angle in the superintendent's office, someone called Colonel Smith away to attend to some urgent business at another part of the campus. Colonel Smith called over his shoulder, "Sit where you are, Major. I'll be back."

The emergency took much longer than the superintendent had expected. It was onerous and demanding, and it wasn't until bedtime that he remembered Major Jackson. I'll apologize fully tomorrow. Wonder how long the poor man waited? When he entered his office the next morning, he found Jackson sitting exactly as he had left him. "My God, man! You haven't left? You've been here all this time?"

"I believe you ordered me to do so, sir."

Major Jackson expected quite a bit from himself, and did not believe in excuses. His serious eye problem, which had begun as far back as 1848, did not keep him from reading and studying. Since he could not distinguish letters by candlelight—only the full force of the sun would do—he prepared his class lectures by manipulating the day. He worked out a system. After class ended at eleven, Jackson read the next day's lecture material, standing in front of his high desk. No one knocked on his study door, an unthinkable interruption in his household. He read diligently, painstakingly, totally concentrating. His lips moved, his eyes stayed riveted. He hardly blinked. He kept one step ahead of his students. After supper he returned to his study, and for two hours sat ramrod straight in his chair, facing the wall, going over and over, word for word, the next days's lecture on Optics and Analytical Mechanics or Acoustics and Astronomy. He had no flair for either subject.

There are teachers who entertain, who pepper their students with anecdotes and theatrics. They become superior chums, jostling and merry. Characters enter academic ranks, showmen who wear two different socks to show a disregard for tradition, ever expecting the same results from two different students, unburdening themselves of personal sagas and rages, keeping students "interested" at all costs, teaching them as many truths outside the text as within. Hams. Mesmerizing lecturers. These distinct personalities are called *good* teachers. Jackson was not one of these. He was learning along with his students and didn't hide the fact. "I have no genius for *seeming*."

At the lectern, facing his class, he repeated what he had engraved in his head the day before while staring at the wall. He went through it like a trained seal. A raised hand might sometimes halt him. "Major Jackson, could you please give us an example of the speed of light? I was wondering if you knew how long it takes a light to get here from Mars?"

He backed up in his lecture, as if running a tape in reverse. He went back a couple of paragraphs and repeated, word for word, what he had just said prior to the question being asked. He drew no analogies, no parallel examples, and would not consider an alternate plan. He did not charm his students with storybook tales of his experience in the Mexican War. Some found it hard to believe that he had indeed served in battle.

The class window looked out on the hazy blue mountains in the distance. In warmish weather a scent of grass and flowers filtered in and the chirp of many birds resounded. Blackbirds particularly flocked to Lexington. No one wanted information on optics and astronomy. These were Virginia gentlemen, tested, a great number of them, in herculean alcohol bouts. They swaggered with all the pomp and arrogance they had learned from their fathers or betters. Virginia gentlemen were quick to sense an insult, too—about as quickly as they took a drink, and in antebellum days they carried bulging wallets and credentials of fine breeding and they flaunted their power. These sons of the leading families of Virginia were raised to believe in their own supremacy. And if by mischance they came from elsewhere—Georgia or Tennessee, God forbid—they quickly adapted to the aristocratic Virginia stance.

They lolled in Jackson's class. In their white pants and gray tunics they dozed off or stared at a honeybee circling the open window or thought up further strategies to pierce the batty professor's hide. Old Jack was Tom Fool. To most, his astounding dumbness was only exceeded by his ironclad idea of discipline. He was polite, courteous to a fault, but he stuck to his idiotic guns. There are yellowing textbooks today that hold these faded blue near-illegible scrawls: "Old Jack put Frank Hannum under arest [sic] today for not obeying orders." "Old Jack skinned me today. I tell you he did." They hated this hick, this overbearing Puritanical killjoy. So unlike the teacher who had come before him, Major William Gilham. "Old Gil" had moved with alacrity, buoyed by quick wit and an understanding of young blood. He had been strict, he had set boundaries, but Old Gil had been one of them. Not Jackson. As Tom Fool strode through the sally port of the barracks, in his leaping long stride, his improbable size-14 cavalry boots clomping, a brick, released from the third floor by a cadet bombardier, sailed for its target. It connected with the edge of his hat. One centimeter more to the left and we would not have had the Battle of Manassas as we know it today. Jackson did not break stride, nor look up, nor deign to show fright or concern.

One morning in class, Cadet W. H. Cox was called upon to recite. *Recite?* He looked around flabbergasted, for classmate approval and sniggers. Recite to Tom Fool? Sooner explain something to a wall or brick. "The professor, I fear," he said, in haughty, nasal cadence, "is not capable of judging anything I might say." He was court-martialed. Tom Fool did not fool around.

Before his marriage Jackson had had quarters in the brand-new barracks—the east-central tower room, third level. One evening a knock sounded on his door. "Enter, please." No further sound. He opened the door to find an unusual sight: A V.M.I. cadet, tightly bound and gagged to a chair like a robbery victim, fell backward into the room. Hee-haws bounced off the stone masonry, scampering feet, wild delighted shrieks sounded. But there was a touch of the cold icy north in Jackson. He found the culprits, had them hauled before a court-martial, and watched their slumping backs as they left the Institute abruptly and forever.

Another day his lecture on various eruptions in the galaxy wore on. Cadet James A. Walker, with clean-cut good looks and an impetuous jut to his chin, had had a bellyful. He wasn't being raised landed gentry to undergo this. His eyes darted and his tongue wagged. Someone made a noise near him—wind breaking?—and there was the customary explosion of sniggering, a blessed relief from the intolerable steady wind from up front. "Mr. Mason, do not make noise in this classroom. And . . . Mr. Walker, do not talk." The lecture was back-taped and released again. The major halted. "Mr. Walker, did you hear? You are not to talk while I am speaking."

Walker's mouth kept moving, and it didn't stop through his being booted from class and having to stand court-martial. He was white with Southern fury. Mason made the noise! I did not!

When the noise was made Major Jackson accused Mr. Mason of making it! It was a long trial, and the verdict ended Cadet Walker's career at V.M.I. His honor as a Virginian had been besmirched. At the court-martial the professor had looked on coolly, his eyes level with Walker's, a somewhat lazy, almost sleepy cast to his features. Immediately after the court's ruling Cadet Walker challenged the major to a duel, whereupon Jackson registered no more emotion than when the brick had whizzed past his cranium, as if it were nothing more annoying than the buzz of a fly. Superintendent Smith became worried, though not for Jackson; for Walker. He wrote Walker's father: "I would advise you to come up at once and take him home as I have reason to believe he may involve himself in serious difficulty."

A few years later Walker, wearing the gray tunic of an officer in the Confederate Army, paused before the flower-decked coffin in Richmond, one among the thousands who were paying their respects in soft flickering candlelight. A tear ran down his cheek, and he said, "I'm sorry."

Major Jackson had come in contact with many free blacks while soliciting contributions for the Presbyterian Bible Society of Lexington. He carefully wrote down in his ledger the little sums that were donated. In 1855 he organized a Colored Sunday School—against considerable local opposition. Resentment built: "These darkies aren't church members! Why should they come into our church?" Jackson answered, "As the Bible Society is not a Presbyterian but a Christian cause, I deem it best to go beyond the limits of our own church."

Townspeople shook their heads. The man had good intentions, but it was all harebrained, as usual with Jackson. A nigger Sunday school in a white church! There were Virginia laws against mixed racial assemblies. Jackson simply went ahead. At the first service, after bolting the door on the split second, he began—with a song. One hundred stolid black faces gazed forward, baffled for the most part, wanting to please this strange tall white man who had hauled them here, but not exactly sure how. They weren't too comfortable, and it was all confusing. Here in the biggest white church on Main Street they sat. The man's hand came down and he bellowed, off-key:

Ah-mazing Grace,
how sweet the sound
     that uh saved a wretch
like me!

Other white men got interested and taught, too. Blacks
learned Scripture, some to read and write (a precious skill kept
from many by custom and even law), and Jackson's Colored
Sunday School continued until 1884. It produced many Negro
leaders after the war, one of whom became president of Morgan
State University in Baltimore.

The Scots from whom Jackson came had a mixed bloody
history, but they had no history of slavery. There were no Pha-
raohs in their past. They had no antecedent to go by, nothing to
draw on for guidelines. The Scots had paid their way across the
ocean. These black people had been wrenched from their homes
and brought here against their will. A slave named Venture had
been exchanged for four gallons of rum on the Guinea Coast and
lived out his days in Connecticut. These slaves tried various
methods to cope with the violence done them. Frederick Douglass
escaped from bondage in a borrowed navy uniform with forged
papers and lived to advise presidents. Nat Turner, on a calm
summer night in Tidewater Virginia, intent on exorcising his
demons and evening the score, stole into sacrosanct off-limit
homes and killed, as brutally as possible, fifty-odd whites who
were slumbering in bed.

Jackson would certainly have missed a place in history if his
career had ended as a professor. His students mocked and teased
him and did not take him seriously. They certainly learned little
from him. A V.M.I. alumni committee was formed to have Jackson dismissed. Jackson himself applied for a vacancy at the University of Virginia, and had the recommendation of an army
officer named Robert E. Lee. It didn't help. He was turned down.
Yet there was a handful of people who had been captivated by
Major Jackson, who saw past his inarticulateness, through his
blue-gray eyes, into a will as strong as the Rock of Gibraltar. One
cadet saw immediately past the eccentricities. Cadet Adjutant
Tom Mumford said, "I flatter myself to have had extraordinary

advantages to learn to honor and to respect and to love . . . this grand, gloomy and peculiarly *good* man."

Cadet Mumford, who became a colonel in the War, was in the minority. So was Colonel Robert E. Lee. So were the few women who didn't mind teasing him—he could be so ridiculous!—but who loved him. To most he was a dithering and valetudinarian misfit professor. Lord, you wouldn't trust him to mail a letter! Today at V.M.I. there is a wing that houses the papers of General George C. Marshall, a graduate of the Institute and U.S. Chief of Staff during the Second World War. General George S. Patton attended V.M.I. before going to West Point and fame as commander of the Third Army in the Second World War. Patton's grandfather lies with a prominent granite marker on top of a verdant hillside in the Confederate Graveyard in Winchester, Virginia. The bones of George S. Patton of the 32nd Virginia rest a few feet from those of Brigadier General Turner Ashby, the strange mercurial cavalryman in Stonewall's troops.

But out of all those who once marched on V.M.I.'s quadrangle, out of all those who believed themselves fearless and flawless, one perhaps stands out most: Thomas Jonathan Jackson. Little Sorrel, the horse he rode in battle, has been preserved and stands behind glass in the Institute's museum. Even the rubber raincoat Jackson was wearing at Chancellorsville is behind glass. And words from his commonplace book are etched in the marble archway to the barracks:

YOU MAY BE WHATEVER YOU RESOLVE TO BE.

In the course of two short years he would leave an imprint on history that lasts to this day. Some say the Germans developed the *blitzkrieg* from studying his tactical maneuvers. He turned the tide of battle at First Manassas. If the South had lost at Manassas, blue-clads would have poured into Virginia and the Civil War might have ended that day. Our history would read differently. Many say he was the greatest general of that war. He was deeply American, a contradiction from beginning to end.

CHAPTER II

Back Where It All Began—
"Out There"

Jackson grew up on the frontier. He was not conditioned by the plantation or grand ancestral home, nor by mint juleps at sunset or endearing black mammies to look back on. Life on the western fringes of Virginia was hard. Few lived past sixty and a man rarely grew to be six feet. He had little leisure to ponder philosophical matters, and found his pleasure where he could.

The seasons and nature always held surprises and often furnished the sole entertainment. Around 1800 a meteor passed across Harrison County, Virginia, casting a brilliant heavenly light and causing tremendous explosions as if the earth were being rent. In 1816 there was no summer, absolutely none in Harrison County. Winter never ended—it went right through July, August, and September with no crops, no fruit, a frost over the land. Who could explain this aberrance of nature? How could the pioneers survive? Summers were much cooler back then, with scarcely a warm night. The pioneer cabin lay in the deep shade of a lofty forest which spread as far as the eye could see. Tall grass and weeds abounded, much taller than a man's head. At sundown the air, no matter what season, turned bone-chillingly damp. In summer the streams dried up and the mills did no grinding after the first of June. Nature—or God—determined who got through and who did not.

Thomas Jackson's people helped settle the western part of Virginia a short time before the Republic was formed. It was raw frontier and the Shawnees were often on the warpath. An incident that happened at Harbert's blockhouse in Harrison County was typical of that time and place. It was early March, the stirring of spring in the air, and some children began playing a short distance from the bunkerlike blockhouse. They spied a crippled crow near the edge of some woods and went to examine it. They saw a number of Indians tiptoeing toward them. They rushed to the blockhouse and yelled a warning. In *The History of Harrison County* by Henry Haymond, the struggle began when:

> John Murphy stepped to the door to see if danger had really approached, when one of the Indians, turning the corner of the house, fired at him. The ball took effect and Murphy fell back into the house. The Indian, springing directly in, was grappled by Harbert and thrown on the floor. A shot from without wounded Harbert, yet he continued to maintain his advantage over the prostrate savage, striking him as effectively as he could with his tomahawk when another gun was fired at him from without the house. The ball passed through his head and he fell lifeless. His antagonist then slipped out of the door sorely wounded in the encounter.
>
> Just after the first Indian had entered, an active young warrior, holding in his hand a tomahawk with a long spike in the end, also came in. Edward Cunningham instantly drew his gun to shoot him, but it flashed and they closed in doubtful strife. Both were active and athletic and sensible for the high prize for which they were contending [Cunningham's wife] and each put forth his utmost strength, and strained his every nerve to gain the ascendency. For a while the issue seemed doubtful. At length by great exertion Cunningham wrenched the tomahawk from the hand of the Indian and buried the spike to the handle in his back. Mrs. Cunningham closed the contest, seeing her husband struggling closely with the savage she struck at him with an axe. The edge wounding his face severely, he loosened his hold and made his way out of the house.

Well after the British had ceased supplying the Indians with firepower and encouragement, well after the American Revolution and into the nineteenth century, the savagery between Indian and settler continued. It was war. The settlers of Harrison County never learned the Indian names for their mountains, but they did copy the Indian dress style, outfitting themselves in buckskin and moccasins. Later, from cultivated centers, came the elegantly worded treatises on the Noble Red Man. Frontiersmen had to step over their scalped and dead children, fleeing with an infant in arms, and saw things differently. Indians lost more. They lost land, as well as their own blood. They lost forever their way of life.

There were respites and moments of peace on the frontier. There were barn raisings, prayer meetings, and nothing much to do after the sun went down. Nearly everything was made at home, and Indian corn was the staple crop. It was eaten as roasting ears, made into bread and hominy grits, and used as feed for animals as well as currency for trade. Money was exotic. In Pennsylvania the Scotch-Irish had devised a way to turn corn into spirits: white lightning. When the good Quakers made these people unwelcome, they carried their stills and know-how farther into the mountains. Anyone could make the product, nearly everyone drank it. Tom Lincoln, the father of our sixteenth president, was a distillery boss and used to take more than an ample portion of his salary in the product he turned out. His son never got along with him and never developed a taste for corn liquor.

A century and a half ago, about four generations back, buffalo roamed near Clarksburg. The last one known to be killed was in 1825. Thomas Jackson was born in 1824. Later in life he took the middle name of Jonathan to honor his father. Jonathan Jackson had a full head of dark brown hair, a sunny good-looking face, and a strong neck that fit neatly into the high white collar he wore on formal occasions; a miniature from the early nineteenth century shows him thus. Everybody liked Jonathan Jackson. They even liked him when he was the Federal Collector of the Internal Revenue for Western Virginia. They liked him perhaps better though when he was simply a lawyer in Clarksburg. He was generous, and he loved the town. He had in abundance a quality peculiar to certain small-town Americans—incurable optimism and a thankfulness toward God for setting them down right where they stood. Things might be bad occasionally, but they would get better. Progress was on the way. No greater country existed in the world. A booster, a go-getter. He formed a cavalry company and was elected first lieutenant in the War of 1812. He saw no battle, no carnage, but he was ready. His relatives had fought in the Revolution of 1776. Some had served in the U.S. Congress. His cousin, Judge John G. Jackson, was married to the sister of the beautiful Dolley Madison.

Distances were long in the country back then—and days of torturous travel stood between Richmond and the frontier settlement of Clarksburg. But a man could still drop by the White House and shake the president's hand personally if he ever found himself in Washington. A man back then might even find a tenuous claim to blood relationship with a president. President Andrew Jackson and Thomas Jackson's progenitors came from the same small parish in Ireland. There is some evidence that they may have been related.

Julia Beckwith Neale, Tom's mother, came from a family with deep roots in Virginia. In 1692 Thomas Neale was commissioned Royal Patent Postmaster of all the colonies and established the first postal service in the land. Benjamin Franklin took over the office near the start of the Revolution. The Neales helped clear the frontier, felling trees, perpetually fighting Indians, and perpetually begetting children. Julia Beckwith Neale was third in a family of eleven.

Another strain of blood that contributed to young Thomas was that of the Cummins family. Jackson's paternal great-grandmother, Elizabeth Cummins, became an orphan at an early age in England. A big raw-boned woman, of indomitable will, she was around six feet tall and as strong as a man. She came from a family of public-house owners, and she set sail across the Atlantic without friend or guardian, while still in her teens, in search of a married sister who had earlier emigrated.

After arriving in the New World with only the notion that her sister was somewhere in the teeming port of New York, she discovered, after much searching, that this beloved sister and her husband and their two young children had died of the Fever the year before. She made the best of it. She racked her brain for the name of anyone she might call upon for help, and thought of some English acquaintances down in Maryland. She journeyed down and, while there, met and married John Jackson, who—though of Protestant Irish stock—had been, as she, born in London and early left an orphan. They traveled by degrees, raising children, homesteading, until they came to the far reaches of civilization, in Clarksburg, Virginia. Elizabeth Cummins Jackson lived to be 102 years old, and, till her dying day, she held on to a few gold guineas she had brought with her from England.

There are those who minimize the importance of bloodlines, but Southerners and horse trainers are not among them. Southerners set great store by family, character, and the proper way to act. Still, they do not live in the past as much as others may think. "The glory of our ancestors belongs only to them," Stonewall Jackson said, on the battlefield. "It is up to us to make our own future."

Jonathan Jackson's firstborn child was a daughter, named Elizabeth, who came down with the Fever when she was seven. He did all in his power to bring her through the crisis. In the eighteenth and early nineteenth centuries no one knew where the Fever came from. It defied all logic. Some said it just sprang up from the soggy ground like a miasma, and this was as good an explanation as any. Doctors came on horseback, and their presence was often more a source of comfort than a medium of cure. It was a relief to see someone trot up with a bag full of bottles and pills. It was a rare doctor on the frontier who had been to William and Mary. None from Virginia in this early pioneer period had been to Northern medical schools—King's College or Harvard—and no doctor anywhere had a proper name to give this Fever or understand how to cure it.

At seven Elizabeth knew that something strange and awesome and overpowering was taking charge of her body. Typhoid fever, as we now know the disease, is an insidious enemy. It offers a variety of suffering. Some barely know they are ill; others, in unrelieved agony, die in a fortnight. Back then doctors weren't sure if it was infectious or not. They did know that it often wiped out whole families, but why was a mystery.

Jonathan Jackson changed Elizabeth's nightdress as the cloth

became drenched. He changed sheets and lifted her from one bed
to another. He listened for the hoofbeats of the doctor's horse. He
held his daughter's hand and sat by her bed during the day. At
night he lay beside it. He was still cheerful, grasping the least
optimism he might glean from a chance remark from the grave
doctor. He comforted his wife, who was in advanced pregnancy,
He wasn't able to spend as much time as usual with his middle
child, Warren, five, or the baby, Tom, three—and they knew
something was wrong. His step had always been quick, but now
he raced. Doors banged, strange pungent odors rose, visitors arrived, bedtimes went awry, meals became different, a tense atmosphere prevailed through the frame one-story house, candles
burning all night. It was March 1826. Before the month ended
both father and daughter lay dead. He had disregarded his own
swelling tongue, the terrible taste, his burning face for as long as
he could—up to the time Elizabeth stared at the ceiling, gave a
rattle in her throat, and closed her eyes. He lay down, and never
rose again. Julia Beckwith Neale Jackson, a widow of one day,
grieving and wailing, gave birth to a daughter, Laura Ann.

Jonathan Jackson had never discussed business with his
wife. Townsfolk thought him on top of the world. Darkly handsome, engaging, wheeling and dealing through Clarksburg, he
would not depart this world with nothing. But, as with many
men, particularly Americans, who put much stock in tomorrow,
the idea never took root that tomorrow might not come. Jonathan
Jackson left not one yard of ground, no house, not one cent. He
left debts. His generosity and "far-sightedness" had caused him
to co-sign many notes. It was one means a young lawyer had of
gaining a modest fortune—granted of course he lived. These were
long-term notes. Everybody had liked Jonathan Jackson. He
couldn't say no. And he liked to play cards.
His widow had been educated in the Tidewater tradition of
fine learning. She was an admitted beauty by all accounts—dark
hair, blue eyes, fair skin, a sweet smile. She knew nothing about
earning a living, and now she had two young sons and a newborn
daughter on her hands. The Masonic fraternity, of which Jonathan had been a member, helped. The widow moved into a small
cottage that was actually a glorified room. Julia took in sewing

and ran a primitive school for a few pupils in the cottage. And it was axiomatic that a pretty woman without a man in frontier Virginia would soon find a suitor. He was Captain Blake Woodson, a man much older than Julia and a lawyer like her deceased husband. He turned out to be in financial stress, too. A sense of failure clung to him—his eyes, the cut of his clothing, his lugubrious voice heralded it. The Jackson relatives opposed the match, so much so that they said they would take the children from Julia if she married Woodson. Captain Woodson was deemed to be a social notch or two beneath the Jacksons, too, but Julia stood firm. They then tried bribes and said they would contribute to her support if she would turn Woodson down. But Julia knew her mind, saw something some others hadn't seen, and married Captain Woodson.

She had certainly not discerned an enterprising, go-for-broke nature. (Perhaps she had seen too much of this quality previously.) The Woodsons moved to Fayette County where Captain Woodson secured the post of county clerk. Julia felt ill. With Captain Woodson's meager salary and Julia's fading health, her children had to be farmed out to relatives. Then, as luck would have it, Julia became pregnant again. Tom's older brother Warren—hotheaded, impulsive, domineering, the perfect model of the model older brother—had already gone to live with his uncle Alfred Neale. Now Tom, age six, and Laura, three, were told they would live with relatives at Jackson's Mill, in the real boondocks. It was a cutting, swift announcement. Laura, who had the dark hair and blue eyes of her mother, was too young to comprehend. Tom understood only too well. His father, a shadowy figure in his mind, had been taken from him. Now his mother. He hid in the woods when they came to get him.

Tom stayed in the woods, disregarding the cries and entreaties to return. Only the long shadows of night, the weird, awful noises of the woods, caused him to raise the white flag. His mother hugged him and wept. An uncle who had come to fetch him offered treats. Everyone put on a cheerful face. "Oh, won't you have a grand time on the farm! A place to fish and hunt and go swimming. Think of all the fun you can have!" After two days, he gave in. It was one of the few times in his life he did so.

At Jackson's Mill lived Tom's Grandmother Jackson along

with her three unmarried sons and two daughters. It was a happy place, but one that had been deprived for some time of the shrieks of children. These relatives made a big fuss over Tom and Laura. For the longest time, no children; now, suddenly, instantly recognizable Jacksons. Tom was wary, heartsick for his mother, but these kinfolk certainly beat staying out in a dark woods. There was bustle here—uncles who knew how to hunt and fish and act manly. The aunts were mysterious, smiling, agreeable, vastly attractive.

Cummins Jackson was head of the house. Six feet two, he could lift a whiskey barrel straight up, extract the bung with his teeth, and take a mouthful without benefit of cup. If Tom's later religious beliefs came from someone, they did not come from his Uncle Cummins. Cummins liked to race horses, and soon he had young Tom outfitted as a jockey for these gambling ventures. Tom was sturdy, willing—but no great rider, then or later. He rode with the stirrups up high, back straight, chin up, rocking awkwardly. But he was determined to please his winning, attractive uncle, and he gave it his all in various races. By his sheer will he won.

Horses, pleasure, fights, and fun—Cummins never ceased being a youth on through middle age. He dearly loved to get the best of someone in a sharp trade. He might, on occasion, act the bumpkin, feign a high enthusiasm, total lack of interest, abysmal ignorance—until the deal had been made and he ended up with the fast bay, the other party with a sick mule. No less a Jackson enthusiast than the Reverend Robert L. Dabney termed Cummins unscrupulous "in his business morals," i.e., horse trading and land speculation. He was in constant litigation. One thing no one ever caught him doing, however, was breaking his word. Law on the frontier was simple; a man's word was his bond. All honor fled when a man broke his word—if he shook your hand and said, "You have my word, sir," a sacred trust was in effect. Frontier civilization rested on it; it could not exist otherwise. When the chips were down, when the Indians were coming or a barn was burning—*real* things, not horse trading—people wanted to know whom they could count on. They could count on Cummins Jackson, a hedonistic, go-for-broke, perennial bachelor. Poorer neighbors and all his less affluent relatives depended upon him. All, except those he hornswoggled, adored his company.

Tom's mother sent word for all her children to come to her a short time after she gave birth to a son named Wirt in 1831. She was dying, and knew it. Before penicillin and X rays and CAT scans, seriously sick people knew that they were probably going to die. They liked to have loved ones around as they took leave to journey to "the other side." There were multiple good-byes and hellos for Tom in his early life—all so strange, mystifying, nearly hallucinatory. He would spend time with uncles and aunts and cousins, stay a month or two, then be whisked away some early dawn. Into one bed with a distinct musty odor, awakened at a particular hour, sent to bed at another, fed a special biscuit at one table, cornbread at another. Like a forest animal trapped for the moment, he kept his glance guarded, wary. He sought motives—what were they going to do to him, where were they going to put him?

Uncle Robinson took Tom, both on the same horse, to say good-bye to Tom's mother. Uncle Robinson was a slave who wasn't certain anymore who owned him. Once he had been owned in loose fashion by Tom's father. Now he circulated among Tom's relatives the way Tom himself did. Who owns me? Where am I to go? What bed will I lie on tonight or what meal will I eat for breakfast? He and Tom had a special bond.

Julia Jackson Woodson said goodbye to each of her four children, including two-month-old Wirt, who suckled her up to a moment before she died. Her full pallor exposed by flickering candlelight, she prayed softly as they passed before her. Ever after Tom hoarded this memory. His mother never lived to let him know how she felt about, say, the art of soldiering. He never, after seven years of age, had a mother; he had never really known his father. In such cases myths often develop. An orphaned boy keeps his mother in a hazy idealized past; he seeks his father forever.

Captain Woodson hardly played the role of father, for he could not afford to keep the children. He could ill keep himself and died two years later. Wirt, Tom's half brother, joined the migrating team of orphans, going from one hearth to another. He died, a young man, in Missouri, from the same pulmonary disorder that had affected his mother. For some reason Tom did not go back immediately to his Uncle Cummins; he undoubtedly had no say about where he went. The list of relatives who took him in reads like a litany of whistle stops. He stays for a brief while with Mrs. White—his father's sister. Later, we find him in the domicile of his Uncle Brake a few miles away.

And now comes an incident that foreshadows his legendary stubbornness. Smoke arose between young Tom and this uncle. Reverend Dabney thought the heavily work-oriented relative might have requested—or required—that Tom work on the Sabbath. It's doubtful, though, that Tom was the by-the-book Christian that he later became. But he was already someone with a nose for injustice, sticking by his guns, and not yielding an inch when he thought he was in the right and the other party shoved. There was a cousin in this family around his own age—William. Tom could have thought William was treated much better than he was, a not unlikely possibility.

In any case, matters weren't right between Tom and Uncle Brake. Uncle Brake was an exacting, rather humorless man and no Uncle Cummins. He made Tom do the hard joyless work of farming without any rewards. He assigned him to move a mule down the road, and when Tom had almost completed the task, the beast slid in mud and couldn't be uprighted. A whole path of desultory, strict, unrewarding labor lay before him in the sight of this mule who slowly and inexorably sank in the mud. Jackson never had a kind word to say for a mule after that, the animal that was the mascot of West Point and the symbol of stubbornness.

One evening, around sunset, he showed up at the home of his father's first cousin, Judge John G. Jackson, in Clarksburg. Just popped up and asked for supper. On the Western frontier you could do that—pop up after hiking fifteen miles from somewhere else. Over food, eyes fixed on his plate, he said, "Uncle Brake and I don't agree; I have quit him, and shall not go back anymore." The judge was judgelike. It must be a misunderstanding—Brake was a responsible man; he was supposed to take care of Tom and Tom was supposed to obey him. "No; Uncle Brake and I can't agree; I have quit and shall not go back anymore." He would not even stay with Judge Jackson that night. He kept traveling, ending up with a favorite female cousin who had recently married and set up housekeeping. Again, a new feather bed, an array of smells, a different way of frying breakfast eggs and serving milk. He told his story once more, and this cousin mulled it all over and said the very best thing for him to do was to go back where he came from—to Uncle Brake. "No; Uncle Brake and I can't agree; I have quit and shall not go back anymore."

In the morning he was on the road again. He walked eighteen miles, to end up with Uncle Cummins once more, where he had wanted to be all along. He was his uncle's pet, and he knew it. His aunts there fussed over him, too. He was at twelve such a solemn good-looking boy!

Sometimes the Jackson children were together in one house, more often not. For a short while Laura was at Jackson's Mill, but then the young aunts married and left and the conventional wisdom was that a young girl should not be in the care of some boisterous bachelor uncles, especially Uncle Cummins. By then Grandmother Jackson had died and the mill had become totally male-dominated.

One early autumn day Tom's brother Warren, drifting himself between domiciles, got it into his head that all the Jackson children should get together for a reunion, that he and Tom should travel to Uncle Alfred Neale's in Parkersburg where Laura was then staying. Warren could impress his will on Tom, talking a mile a minute, jittery, full of endless plans. He liked to boss Tom around, lead him—and Tom was susceptible to Warren's wiles. Tom would try to please and placate him, but no effort was ever quite enough. No sooner had the children embraced and hugged than Warren wanted to be somewhere else. Always in flight; never still. He said he and Tom should travel down the Ohio River by raft and make their fortunes cutting wood on the river islands and selling it to passing steamboats. Steamboats were around every bend.

On a crisp fall day Tom and Warren set off on a raft down the green river, like Huck and Jim down the muddy Mississippi. They came back in February—windburned and pared to the bone, with one trunk each. Tom gave his to Laura. Tom never once mentioned what happened after the raft floated around the bend and out of sight—nor did the usually gabby Warren, save that they floated past the Ohio and then down the awesome Mississippi for a stretch. Both had coughs and fevers.

Tom trudged back by foot to Jackson's Mill and his Uncle Cummins. From then until he left for West Point he was under the genial care of this remarkable uncle. Warren went back to a small primitive school he had been running in Upshur County, but his ague persisted. If you didn't cough it up and spit it out, you were in trouble. There was no cure; there was no definition for what it was. Warren, the beacon in Tom's eye, died at age nineteen. A lifeless boy in the early nineteenth century South, where nearly all were Protestants, lay in an open coffin. Candles burned, shadows wavering around the red rouged cheeks. All loved ones viewed the body, no excuses, in order to truly mourn. Tom had seen his brother's chestnut-colored curls whip in the wind on the Ohio and Mississippi. A few months later Warren lay propped on a cushion, his eyes closed, his cheeks colored like a clown's. Tom was learning quite a bit about death. His own cough and fever gradually left him, but his other ailment, a mysterious stomach pain, was to plague him for as long as he lived.

Tom Jackson was honest—ludicrously so, almost a caricature of the trait. Perhaps that is why the South has so glorified him, for he lived the myth of Southern Honor. Lincoln was called Honest Abe, but he could be the compleat politician, as wily as they come. In our mythology we see Washington owning up to felling the cherry tree. "I cannot tell a lie, Father. I cut it down." The story was invented by Parson Weems, whose sermonizing was taken to heart and at face value by young Tom. Study, work hard, pay your debts—and always be honorable and truthful. Do what's expected of you—only *more* so.

An incident concerning Jackson's absolute and somewhat ludicrous honesty is handed down from nearly all sources. Tom Jackson liked to fish. He also liked to make money, and soon had an agreement with a gunsmith in Weston to supply the man with all he caught. The grown-up had exclusive rights. It was a contract, a pledge of honor. On a storybook summer's day Jackson hauled in a three-foot pike from the Monongahela water. He strode off barefoot in cutoff homespun, the model of a nineteenth-century boy, the big fish dangling off his shoulder, off to the gunsmith five miles away. By the substantial home of Colonel John Talbott he heard his name called and there stood the substantial Colonel Talbott. "Why, if it's not young Tom Jackson. What do you have over your shoulder there?"

"It's a pike, sir."

"Give you a dollar for it, Tom."

"Can't, sir. This one has already been sold."

"Well, now, I'll give you a dollar and a quarter. No one's going to give you more than that."

"No, sir, I can't do that, Colonel Talbott. I've promised Conrad Kester to sell him all the fish I catch at fifty cents each. He's taken them much smaller. It wouldn't be right to deny him now that a big one has come along."

"Come on, Tom."

"No, sir, Colonel Talbott. I've already sold this fish."

And that was that.

The circus came to Clarksburg. The flaming gaudy banners, sawdust, a brass band, and a big tent—almost too exciting to bear. It brought the Outside, strangeness, wonder. Tom was there. He was there at parties, too, although painfully shy. He never let shyness hold him back from anything. Tom liked the girls, and sat at a gathering all red-faced, totally mute, in some sort of extremis—but trying. It appeared as if it might take a slap to get a word from him. He stared straight ahead. Couples twirled in a hoedown; lanky youths leaned elbows on posts and chatted familiarly with giggling girls. And there Tom sat. Someone might speak to him, and then be surprised by the logically reasoned discourse that followed on any subject. Curiously, this natural-born poker player in time of war, the most secretive of the secretive in battle, had trouble playing a part in peacetime. Being who you were, being unassuming, was part of the frontier. "I have no talent for seeming."

Uncle Cummins looked around one day and saw Tom had grown a few inches and, come to think of it, there was no school-house right then for him to go to. He brought in Professor Robert P. Ray, one of those ready-made frontier teachers who had found he had a knack for instructing the young—or had found he had more of a knack for it than he did for farming or doctoring or running a tavern. An instant classroom was made of one of the outbuildings at Jackson's Mill. Tom wolfed down all that Robert P. Ray had to teach and then traveled on to a more established school at McCann's Run, a few miles away.

There is no record anywhere that says that young Jackson distinguished himself as a student, but he was dogged, unmitigatedly dogged. He solemnly went over and over a problem, solving it not by dazzling insight but by the sweat of his brow. He would not allow himself to lose. Uncle Cummins began worrying about what he might have created. He did not want a bookworm, nor to lose his young mascot. He didn't want young Tom to get too engrossed with book learning. Crops had to be reaped, trees felled, and slaves supervised. Little solemn Tom had a way with black men. He worked well with them. One young slave, not many years older than Tom, showed inclinations toward brilliance. He thirsted to read and write. It was all a mystery that simmered just beyond his grasp. He knew it would make him equal with others; it might even make him superior. "All right" Tom told him, "you keep stoking the fireplace with pine knots so we can see, and I'll teach you to read and write." A bargain. The knots sizzled and Tom dutifully taught the fellow what he knew. The slave kept right on learning under Tom, right on up to writing himself an authentic-looking pass on the "Underground Railroad" and ending up in Canada. Uncle Cummins never saw him again.

The inexorable inroads of civilization bore down on the Western frontier of Virginia. More and more roads were needed, and in 1837 construction on the Parkersburg and Staunton Turnpike began. That summer thirteen-year-old Tom got a job as a surveyor on the ambitious project. The process of making a line from one point to another through all kinds of hindrances appealed to him. There was something cut and dried about it, no arguments or anything elusive. He found he could solve problems of engineering, the compass and the level, and, as he bent over the surveyor's eyepiece, he became transfixed. But it was impossible to become totally enmeshed in any one thing on the frontier. There was no specialization; there was not even one bank in the community to allow someone to be a lone entrepreneur. Everyone helped everyone else, and before a new row of corn was planted several trees had to be taken out of the forest to make room. One man couldn't do it all. There were "apple peelings and corn huskings," social events, and a lot of "house raisings and log rollings." It was a male preserve—and Uncle Cummins reveled in it. He worked hard and sued everyone within fifty miles of the mill, and gloried in racing his horses—in particular a fine mare named Kit.

The racehorse Kit was becoming legendary. Uncle Cummins, florid-faced and eternally fiesty, was there to bet any horse owner that lived that Kit could outrun anything in his stable. He flung down wagers, hoisted Tom in the saddle, and waited confidently for the pack to round the bend—Kit in the lead, little Tom bouncing like a rag doll in the saddle. But then on Crooked Fork, up Freeman's Creek, came word from Simmons Farm that they had some horseflesh that ran like greased lightning. They were so assured that Kit could be taken that they were willing to near bet the farm. Word spread, feeling ran high, and currencies went down on the race all across the county. It became the Big Event, a clear-cut contest that would show without question who owned the best blood. In the end arguments about horses are easy to settle: You just race them.

Uncle Cummins could hardly wait—in fact, he couldn't wait. He commissioned Uncle Robinson and various assistants to take Kit to the Simmons Farm by moonlight and hold a race on the q.t. Which Uncle Robinson delightedly did, without the sleeping, trusting Simmonses—in beds some distance away—finding out. Uncle Robinson took the Simmons horse from the barn and pitted it against Kit, time after time. Kit always won. The next day, betting from the Jackson camp came down heavily. Before the event Uncle Cummins celebrated in advance, taking many toasts. And when the Simmonses made a snide comment about little Tom Jackson's horsemanship, just before little Tom mounted, Uncle Cummins's mood changed from sunny to dark. He took umbrage for Tom, for the slight it cast on family honor, and for horsemanship in general. He cursed the Simmonses out good, and announced that Kit could win with even him, Cummins Jackson, in the saddle. He couldn't be dissuaded. He climbed on, winked

at Tom, and the race began. A six-foot-two 250-pound man with
a load on proved not the best jockey, and Kit lost by a debatable
length or two. Uncle Cummins came galloping up, contesting the
result, already swinging, and a free-for-all ensued, a sea of
swinging fists and tumbling bodies. Feelings between the two
families ran bitter for decades afterward.

In his adolescence, Tom Jackson had several unlikely interests. For instance, although tone-deaf, he developed an interest
in music. He became expert at making a frontier instrument called
the cornstalk fiddle. Tom practiced and practiced, day in, day out,
sawing away while those in residence discreetly found a farm
chore to do that lay a mile away. If someone strained hard, he
might recognize "Napoleon's March" coming from the furious
effort.

At seventeen Tom got his first serious job—constable of his
county. Cummins Jackson helped him gain the political plum,
and he was also aided by Colonel Alexander Scott Withers, who
now taught him in a private school in a far quarter of the courthouse. Colonel Withers was a justice of the peace and an authority on frontier history. His *Chronicles of Border Warfare* was the first
book printed west of the Alleghenies and went through six large
printings. He saw potential in Tom. Cropping up throughout
Jackson's career were people who sensed there was something
special there. Once the colonel came by the mill in his tall silk hat
and tight stovepipe trousers and bought a sack of meal. Tom
offered to deliver it. "No," the colonel said, "we have servants for
that. If you work with your head you don't have to work with
your hands." Advice came readily from these Scotch-Irish: on
how to learn more, on how to keep educating yourself.

"Colonel Withers," Tom told him dryly, "if I had money to
go to William and Mary, then maybe I'd learn enough to work
with my head and not with my hands." Colonel Withers chortled, and kept an eye on Jackson.

In short order, Tom Jackson had to prove himself a man.
Constable Tom Jackson, a teenager, was commissioned to claim
a debt from a tightfisted local resident. The man had taken some
goods from a widow, and refused to pay her. He laughed, taunt-

ing the smooth-cheeked constable. Jackson came politely to him,
time after time. "You ought to pay the widow, mister. It's not
right to cheat somebody."

"Now, you get along, sonny. I'm a man who can work things
out with a lady. You don't want to get involved."

"You're going to pay her."

"Make me." Ha, ha.

Jackson persisted; waited. At Benny Pritchard's blacksmith's
shop the debtor had confidently tied his horse to the hitching
post—when the constable stepped from behind a door, grabbed
the reins, and faced the man. "Look here, God damn your soul,"
the man said, "you let this horse go or I'll make you regret it."

The man climbed back in the saddle and cracked Tom with
a riding crop. He bellowed some more. His face reddened. Tom
wouldn't let go of the reins. He jerked the bridle, horse, and rider
toward a low doorway. The man had to either come to terms with
Tom or have his skull cracked. Tom was ready to run him into
the low doorway; the man saw it in Tom's eyes. He'd never seen
such determination. "Well, if you're going to act that way . . .
Now, young man, don't be hasty. Whoa there, whoa!"

"I'm taking this horse or you're paying your debt."

"O.K. Can't you take a joke, son? I was going to pay the
widow all along. Here's the money!"

At an advanced age Cummins Jackson looked west. Tom had
become Thomas Jonathan Jackson and had long since left the
mill, and his Uncle Cummins got gold fever. It was the spring of
'49, and everyone was catching this fever. *Gold!* Instant riches!
Adventure. You were never too old or too infirm to hear the
clarion call of opportunity in this country. Cummins packed up
some small belongings, left everything else behind, and, with a
party of fellow Virginians, made his way by covered wagon to the
promised land. The Gold Rush was a gigantic magnet, as attractive as the glories of war before blood begins to flow. Whole
valleys of Virginia became deserted.

Cummins couldn't resist. Samuel Langhorne Clemens, in
Missouri, couldn't either. Cummins E. Jackson arrived in the Far
West, caught fever (as Tom's father, brother, and mother had)

and died on December 4, 1849. He never saw gold. Thomas
Jonathan Jackson, by then a veteran of war in Mexico and stationed at Fort Hamilton in New York, was crushed by the news.
Death had taken so many people close to him. It stalked him at
every turn. ["This] goes to my heart. Uncle was father to me," he
wrote his sister.

By the time his uncle died Jackson had left the frontier and
graduated from West Point. He had joined that unusual breed
of Americans who made it to that promontory above the Hudson and, more important, stuck it out. Not all were aristocrats;
in fact, most weren't, then or today. The ranks may include the
son of a general, but there are also the many sons of sergeants.
The Point draws a select crowd to its authoritarian ways, and if
you endure its trials and tribulations, you belong thereafter to a
special society.

A bright young man named Gibson J. Butcher got the original appointment from Congressman Samuel L. Hays in 1842;
Jackson had tried for it but failed because Butcher was thought
the better candidate. Butcher has been described as an "orphan
youth of good character and ambitions." Perfect material for the
Point. Butcher, like many others, liked the illusion of the military
life more than the reality. Once upon the Plain of West Point, he
found he could not stomach such a life—such strict rules and
hard study. For what? He resigned, and Thomas Jonathan Jackson
came as a substitute. Butcher went on to become a prominent
banker. Jackson lit out for Washington in a full suit of homespun,
his worldly belongings in a pair of saddlebags. A young black boy
kept him company part of the way. Jackson was to pick up his
letter of recommendation from Hays, then journey on to the
Point for a further examination.

Congressman Hays welcomed the boy into his home and to
the capital. Young Jackson was enthralled. The Capitol building
was going up, and the unfinished rotunda was latticed with scaf-
folding. Jackson climbed to the top. Through the smokey swamp-
like haze of summer Washington he gazed across the Potomac at
the splendid home on a high bank. Someone told him this was
Arlington House. Far beyond were green hills, no more than an
emerald blur: Manassas.

Jackson borrowed a small amount from the congressman to

see the bright lights of Manhattan on his way up the broad winding Hudson to the Academy. He entered the gates of West Point with a coarse felt hat on his head and his weatherbeaten saddlebags across his shoulders. He was eighteen—tall, angular, and not fully grown; his backwoods origins were stamped all over him. But he had left the frontier forever.

CHAPTER III

The Education of a Soldier

When Tom Jackson crossed the threshold into West Point in June 1842, he made an immediate impression. He looked—*was*—so awkward and ill at ease. Three plebes, lounging against a granite arch, smiled. They were Southerners, of patrician bearing, and had that quality of ease that marks someone sure of his place, in this case West Point. They were Birket Fry, Ambrose Powell Hill, and Dabney Herndon Maury. What an odd fellow this newcomer was. His hat was as wide as an umbrella and his stride double that of most men his size. "That fellow looks as if he's come to stay," Maury said.

Maury, a handsome clear-eyed youth, watched Jackson's lumbering form disappear around a corner. There was just something about Jackson that lingered in his mind, some ineffable nuance that made Maury seek out Jackson soon. He shook his hand, looked him hard and straight in the eye, and welcomed him to West Point. Jackson seemed aloof. His answers to questions were abrupt. He was not aloof, however—he was shy. He almost bled with shyness, and his nerves warred with anxieties without end. He began his four-year stint, and Maury became his best friend.

Years later Jackson claimed that in his whole four years at West Point, he never once spoke to a woman. He liked long solitary walks—his one form of recreation. His first summer, as a newly arrived plebe, he slept under canvas on the Plains. He was up before the sun began steaming the inside of the tent, and at night he lay on damp grass. He became homesick—for the free-and-easy life with Uncle Cummins, for the creek-bank fishing, the easy familiarity of home. He, an orphan, was probably the most homesick of his plebe class. It put him almost in shock—forming ranks, being hazed, introduced to arcane scholarship. He wouldn't admit defeat. He let few, if any, know his troubles. He dug in. The cadet from Weston before him had not made the grade. Jackson was not going to let Weston down, nor his relatives.

In his first year, out of a class of 72, he stood 70th in French, 45th in math, 51st in general merit—and came by 15 demerits for misconduct. To get the job done he set up some rules of his own and stuck by them. He demanded of himself that he would never go on to the next phase of a course until he had mastered the one before. He must master a lesson before going on; consequently, he was nearly always behind. He admitted deficiencies. What God had given him—or not given him—he accepted. He thought he had a poor memory—others, later, would disagree. He forced information into his cranium—banking the coals in his room in Old South Barracks, he stretched out by the dim glow and studied long after taps had sounded. He sweated in the classroom, literally and metaphorically. "Look out, the General's going to flood the place!" He had picked up the nickname "General" from classmates in tribute to Andrew Jackson. Now he stood perplexed at the blackboard, the perspiration running off his high forehead.

He did have a memory, but, in keeping with his other attributes, it was an unusual one. He did not take in knowledge intuitively—it did not swiftly enter his mind, cataloged neatly; but once a fact or notion made it past a certain barrier, into the far recesses, it never left him. Cadet Maury watched him at study and blackboard and noted that Jackson seemed to burn knowledge into his brain. He was a plodder, a drudge, a grind, a fanatic—and in a way West Point put him as much to the test as war later would. "I had to study *very hard* for what I got at West

Point," he said later. To some he seemed to go into a seizure when concentrating.

He kept improving, the tortoise in a field of hares. At the end of his second year he stood 18th in math, 52nd in French, 68th in drawing, 55th in engineering, and 13th in general merit—with 26 demerits. By the end of his final year he stood 5th in ethics (his favorite subject), 12th in engineering, and 11th in artillery, and had pared his demerits down to 7. "If the General could stay here another year, he'd be number one in his class," the story went.

Where everyone seemed cut from the same cloth, Jackson stuck out as different. By one light he was simple; by another, complex. He was rigid, almost a parody of the notion, and yet, in such a stratified society, he proved to be highly democratic. He didn't care from what class or rank his friends came. Nearly every cadet chose his friends from his own class—seldom an upper or lower classmate. Jackson didn't care what class a cadet came from as long as he passed some interior test that Jackson put him through. He knew quite well U. S. Grant, William S. Rosecrans, James Longstreet, A. P. Hill, and, from the class of '45, Barnard E. Bee. He physically towered over George McClellan, who was first in his own class of '46.

Jackson looked like Ichabod Crane in the saddle, and he kept trying to improve his horsemanship at the Point with little success. He had no fear of horses and he had the service behind him of being an overgrown jockey for Uncle Cummins, but riding did not come naturally and riding meant a lot back then. Fellow cadets held back their laughter. Although from one point of view he was comical, from another he was above laughter. Some deep dignity and assuredness about the General kept other students from making all-out fun of him. But he did have some prized quirks. At West Point he began the habit of sitting bolt upright, unbending, in order not to put strain on his alimentary system. He stared at a blank wall for hours while concentrating on some lesson or other. He began making a list of maxims—as a host of Americans have done.

Through life let your principal object be the discharge of duty.

Resolve to perform what you ought; perform without fail
what you resolve.

You may be whatever you resolve to be.

Although hard on himself he could be exceptionally kind
toward others. He nursed sick cadets—with a "womanly zeal,"
according to Dabney. He comforted, stayed beside, was solicitous
to any cadet who had a death in the family. He could always be
counted on to go out of his way to help. Yet he was the sturdiest
of foes when he felt he had been wronged. This quality ran
deeply in him and the people he came from, and the case of the
"exchanged rifle" at West Point is a good example.

A fellow cadet named Tomkins, who had much the same
background as Jackson—at a glance, the same—became Jackson's
most mortal enemy. An orphan, brought up on the frontier, self-
sufficient, Cadet Tomkins, too, suffered the early taunts of classmates. He has been described as handsome, sunny-faced, and
surging with ambition. He suffered the ridicule (like Jackson) and
bore down (like Jackson) to make up for his lack of education. He
showed courage and strong will. He won over most of his classmates—but not Jackson. An intense rivalry, almost sibling in
nature, came between them. Jackson bristled when Tomkins sat
across from him at mess; he would not glance at him in chapel.
It might be thought that Jackson would have been drawn to him,
despite initial rivalry, for Jackson could usually be expected to
lend a hand to someone in misfortune. But Jackson became inflexible. He could not abide the cadet. He saw something there
no one else saw. He saw a defect (for want of a better word) in
character.

"The General's mighty hard on that fellow," the story went.
"He should give him a chance. He's working against great odds
here. He's trying!"

At sunrise one chilly morning Jackson grabbed his musket
for drill and found it dirty and oil-streaked. He had made a ritual
of cleaning the gun every night, an onerous duty, and he knew
someone had exchanged pieces with him. It was wrong; he told
his captain, a senior cadet, about a private mark he had placed on
it. That evening, at inspection, a gun with Jackson's mark was

found in the hands of his enemy. Tomkins claimed no knowledge of how the guns had been exchanged in the racks. It was no more than a mistake and could happen to anyone. It had happened at other times at the Point and no great fuss was made over it. He meant no harm.

It would mean perhaps the end of the youth's career at the Academy if Jackson pursued the matter. One insignificant, trifling action—and then, kicked out, back to the frontier, all his good hard work to better himself for nothing. Surely the General could understand his plight. Don't be so hard on him; give him a second chance. Jackson proved inflexible. No, Tomkins had done it and lied about it. He shouldn't remain. Classmates came to Jackson—upperclassmen too. Then the faculty entered in and put pressure on him. No, Jackson insisted, Tomkins should be court-martialed. "Look at it this way," an older, worldly-wise professor said, taking him aside, "haven't you made a mistake ever?"

"He lied," Tom said.

They put Jackson's insistence down to jealousy, to making rules black and white with no gray, to carrying out a vendetta. Change your mind, Tom. In one of the rare instances in his life (and undoubtedly a lesson to him), he did drop the charge, finding himself alone, aligned against cadets and faculty alike. There was no court-martial; there was a second chance given. In that gray area of guilt or possible innocence the tilt was toward innocence. Tomkins was given the opportunity to continue at the Academy.

Tomkins was sophisticated and well known in the village below West Point. He soon got into real trouble—the charge, disgraceful conduct (of unknown dimensions)—and was put on parole. A few months before graduation (and two years after the "rifle exchange") he was dismissed from the Point. He went to Texas to study law, but found that course too tame and embarked for California. On the way he ingratiated himself with a robber band of Tucson Indians, where his military training came in handy. In time he became chief of the tribe. However, in the murder of a peddler for his wares, he got into a quarrel with tribe members who were less savage than he, and they expelled him from their society—to fade away from the record. By that time

Jackson was known around the world for his ironclad rectitude.

The General left West Point on June 30, 1846, twenty-two years old, breveted a second lieutenant of artillery. Fortunately for the newly minted officers, he and his class had a war to go to—in Mexico. But first he, Dabney Maury, and a few others traveled down the Hudson to New York to celebrate. At the old Brown Hotel in Manhattan they toasted one another and spoke wonderingly of the chance for real honest combat, turning giddy with the prospect. A war! Jackson made his way to Weston to await specific orders and suddenly found himself a hero without firing a shot. A war fever spread over the frontier and here was a West Pointer, one of their own, for them to admire. Hardly had Jackson shaken Uncle Cummins's hand, dropped his bags, than the colonel of the local militia rode up. "Welcome home, boy," he said. "You're just in time for the parade. How'd you like to take command of a company? We need you."

"I'd like to, Colonel, but I haven't drilled under you. I might not be able to follow your commands."

"What do you mean, son? Course you can. You're a West Pointer. Hurry up, parade's about to start. Howdy, Cummins, good day to you!"

The breveted second lieutenant was introduced to his improvised militia company on the parade ground, and the eyes of Weston fell proudly on him. It was a heady moment—a local boy made good. The colonel sang a command, "By the left flank, march!" Down a grassy slope Jackson led his company. "By the right flank, march!"

The colonel got mixed up but was able to stop two companies and start again. He lost sight of Jackson. He screamed, but Jackson couldn't hear. The West Pointer marched his men off the parade ground, onto the main road, kept going, and led them through town and into the countryside. The colonel galloped after him. "My God, Tom," he said, catching up with him finally in the middle of a meadow, "didn't you know enough to stop? Couldn't you tell you weren't supposed to leave the parade ground?"

"Colonel," Jackson said, "I was following orders."

Two days after arriving at Uncle Cummins's, Jackson got his orders for Mexico, to join General Zachary Taylor's army, now pressing toward an exotic city called Monterrey. The trip to the front was typically Jacksonian: odd, but effective. He joined a company of thirty men and forty horses at Fort Hamilton, New York, and they marched four hundred miles to Pittsburgh. There they took a riverboat down the Ohio and Mississippi to New Orleans. Then they piled into a vessel and, with sails unfurled and cracking, rode across the azure Gulf waters, docking at Point Isabel, Zachary Taylor's base camp. It had taken Jackson thirty-six days to reach Mexico.

Wagons rattled down the dirt roads of Point Isabel, soldiers mobbed the thoroughfares, and curses and commands pierced the air. The Mexicans had recently retreated from the hamlet, burning what they could, and the Americans now used it as a gigantic warehouse, with a pervasive scent of recent fires touching everything. Veterans circulated, swaggering and confident, drawing vivid pictures of combat. Lieutenant Jackson pumped them for information.

"What's a battle really like?"

"Well, bullets whiz by your ears so's you can't hear, and the smoke's so durn thick you can't see, you don't know exactly what's happening, but it sure seems worth it when you see those pepper bellies on the run."

Sometimes the speaker had actually been in battle; other times—who knew?—he may have heard the tale or dreamed it up. The days were blisteringly hot, and the soldiers couldn't sit still. Jackson ran across West Pointers, drifters, some with accents he could hardly fathom. He ran into Lieutenant Daniel Harvey Hill, who had graduated from the Point the year Jackson entered. They took an immediate liking to each other, a chance meeting that had a far-reaching impact on both their lives. Hill had seen combat—and now there was a brief respite, an armistice. The two took long walks by the seashore, two young Southerners in their early twenties. What was a battle like? Jackson wanted to know. Did Mexicans make different soldiers from Americans? How long did battles last? When did you know when one had ended? "I want to be in one battle," Jackson said.

He got his wish. General Winfield Scott, the scarred old war-horse, came in to conclude the war, to wrap it up and win it. He decided to move against the capital, Mexico City, and strike

General Antonio López de Santa Anna at his heart. He formed an armada from Lobos Island for a military landing near Veracruz and then for a strike down the National Road, straight for the capital city. It was a bold, imaginative maneuver: a force of fifteen thousand men on assorted craft, making an amphibious assault, setting up a beachhead, and then moving toward the interior. Jackson stood on the deck of a ship, and for as far as he could see there were other ships. His stomach ailment left him; his heart beat tumultuously. He was in the third assault wave and he was a member of the infantry. At first he was nervous as the ships sliced the water. Then as shells crashed and bullets whistled, his nervousness left. He moved his troops out, and suddenly saw a sight he hadn't been told about or hadn't considered. He doubted at that moment if he should be in this strange land, doubted if he really wanted to be a soldier at all. The body he saw lay twisted like a bloated rag doll, flies buzzing near the empty eye sockets. The second body he ran across was simply that—a dead body, a casualty of war. The dead wouldn't affect him anymore in battle. Bullets or cannon never did. He didn't turn from fire, and it was as if the Lord was looking out for him. A cannonball came rolling on a collision course, and stopped five steps in front of him. Santa Anna fled Veracruz after a two-week siege and left the Americans the city. The soldiers fired into the air, took spoils and spirits—and told each other they were the best damn fighters on earth. Jackson was vaguely displeased and uneasy. He thought they should press on, all the way to Mexico City. He didn't think the enemy should get away, now that he was on the run.

Scott, the shrewd tough old walrus, pressed on in his own way. It was a steady, thought-out assault, to simply pound away and pound away, and finally make the enemy surrender. An interesting battle then took place, interesting in its strategy and interesting in its cast of characters. The proud and astute Santa Anna set up a strong position on the approach to Jalapa. Two overgrown hills—called Cerro Gordo and Atalaya—stood on either side of the deserted, ghostly National Road. He put plenty of artillery and plenty of men on them and dared the Yankee to come through. Captain Robert E. Lee of the engineers went on a reconnaissance and returned wearily to say there was an unscalable precipice on one side and impassable ravines on the other. If the troops went down the National Road the overlooking artillery would blow them to smithereens. What had been delirious joy a few days before now turned sour. One after another, men trotted into the bush with diarrhea. The romance of Mexico, and certainly war, had faded. The specter of *el vómito* was with them, too, the yellow fever that could cut them down in a slower, crueler way than artillery. They were miles and miles from home—oh, Lord, had anyone ever been as miserable!

Scott's enormous bulk spread out over a camp chair as he studied maps on his campaign cot. He called for Lieutenant Pierre G. T. Beauregard to give him a fresh report. Beauregard, a dark handsome man, so Spanish in appearance that he might easily fit under Santa Anna's command, had done some scouting and said that the only way—and it was a long shot—was to turn the Mexican left flank. If—*if*—that flank could be turned, then the Americans could command the Mexicans on the right and allow troops to move down the National Road. Only trouble was, that left flank had those deep treacherous ravines that a goat couldn't navigate. This was Santa Anna's home territory—actually, he personally owned it—and he knew it far better than the Americans. Santa Anna was positive no man, especially a *gringo,* could scale it. Captain Lee had labeled it "impassable." General Scott knew there was always a way. He called for Captain Lee and told him to scout the region once more.

Lee saluted, about-faced, marched off, and found a way. It required his untangling brush, crawling on his knees, tiptoeing by a precipice. He not only discovered a path, he found the enemy as well. Suddenly he heard Spanish and saw some Mexican pickets coming toward him. He dove behind a log, and enemy soldiers, unaware, chose that log to sit on and rest. For hours they sat, bellowing and laughing, and Captain Lee, later Commanding General of the Army of Northern Virginia, lay still, hardly breathing, while mosquitoes sucked his blood. At darkness the soldiers stood, shook themselves and left—and Lee, his face and hands in welts, returned to camp down his newly discovered path. He reported immediately to Scott. At sunrise the next day some pioneer troops hacked out a primitive road over the route Lee had found. Then the advance began.

American soldiers got halfway up Atalaya when the Mexicans opened fire. It was hand to hand and vicious, but the Americans, now committed to a flanking maneuver, had to capture the hill or suffer heavy losses—a grand defeat. Reinforcements came, the hill was taken, and the momentum carried the Americans down the hill's other side. By God, they'd take Cerro Gordo, the twin hill! The Mexicans thought otherwise and the two sides battered each other till night fell, neither giving any quarter. At sunrise they began again until the Mexicans at last gave way. Cerro Gordo fell, and with it the defense of the National Road. Scott had won. His troops came down the Road and the enemy fled. Two American field batteries chased after them, bouncing along, and in one of the batteries came Lieutenant Thomas J. Jackson. He wrote to his sister, Laura, that he had come close enough to the enemy "to give them a few shots from the battery."

In Jalapa, which the Americans easily took, Jackson languished. He began garrison duty while others had the good luck, as he saw it, to continue the fight elsewhere. He did have time now for introspection, which he put to good use, and Jalapa provided him with his first taste of the sybaritic. Jalapa, as described back then, was a Garden of Eden. To pass time Jackson studied Spanish, initially with the idea of making the acquaintance of one of the local dark-eyed *señoritas*. But he was shy, the *señoritas* heavily fortified with chaperones, and no romantic attachments followed. He savored the fresh tropical fruits, the stunning vistas of nature, the sense of an old, enduring culture. He visited the dim, musky, quiet church, and his letters to Laura began to include religious notes. God in His infinite wisdom would take care of him. God his Eternal Father would look out for him. If the Lord intended him for garrison duty, so be it; perhaps it was His way of curbing Jackson's excessive ambition. Some youths worry about excessive carnal desire, sloth, aimlessness. Lieutenant Jackson fretted—as he would later at higher rank—about his rampant ambition. He kept it well hidden, as others do lust, throughout his life.

But he struck when he gleaned his main chance, and he did so when he heard there was a vacancy in the field under Captain John B. Magruder. No officer or man was seeking to come under this exacting, difficult commander. Darkly handsome, flamboyant, wildly ambitious, Magruder set most teeth on edge—not

Jackson's. Jackson was attracted to him—in fact, to his type, the prototype being Uncle Cummins. Magruder indeed had aspirations to be a stage actor, and he loved nothing better than an audience. Jackson became one.

He volunteered for Magruder's command, and then had trouble finding him. Riding to the front with a small escort, Jackson ran into a heavily armed squad of Mexicans. Near a pass at La Joya, these soldiers, far outnumbering Jackson's, pounced. Jackson fought back—hand to hand, blade against blade, bullets ricocheting. Forever modest and succinct, he wrote Laura, "I was detached with a few men in the vicinity of LaHoya [*sic*] and succeeded in killing four of the enemy and taking three prisoners together with a beautiful sabre and some other equipment." He pressed on and found Magruder in Puebla. He became second in command, in charge of a section of guns and artillery. He was at the front.

General Scott now had 10,500 men to aim at Mexico City, the plum whose capture would end this war. It was an unpopular war, in any case, debated and lambasted in the States. Scott, himself a Whig, felt it a political if not a moral mistake. But once in, once the artillery cracked, the smoke rose, the flanking began, he gloried in it. Press on to win! Then make political peace and concessions. Jackson and Scott, Lee and Grant, Magruder, Joe Hooker and Sherman crossed the Río Frío Mountains and, from ten thousand feet above sea level, looked down, as Cortés once had, down at the Valley of Mexico, a dreamlike tableau. Lofty, hazy mountains rose above a series of glistening lakes and marshes leading on to the emerald city itself—Mexico City.

From above, it looked impregnable, for to get there an army would have to bridge those lakes and cross a network of causeways along the National Road. Scott and his army took note of the fact that the enemy had fortified each and every causeway. Into the breach once again went Captain Robert E. Lee, to try to discover a way across Pedregal, a forbidding lava field, skirting the enemy. If he could find a foothold, a way to zigzag across, then Santa Anna's flank could be turned. Lee was dogged, like a fly or ferret, turning back this bush and that, crawling, studying. He also must have been concerned that he might be shot. He didn't give up; he found that foothold and that minuscule path.

The inexorable mechanism of advancing toward Mexico City began.

For pioneer troops to widen the path, a diversionary action was necessary. Enemy guns had to be engaged, to keep them from blasting the commando engineers away. Magruder got the order to bluff, to playact as if he had a sizable threatening force so that the Mexicans would shell him and not the pioneers. The part well suited Magruder, and he led his men with much fanfare and dash. His cape twirled and he brandished his saber. When a fellow officer fell, Tom Jackson, his shirt sleeves rolled up, took command of a light battery and moved forward. The Mexicans zeroed in on him, cascading round after round on his position. The shelling lasted three hours and the diversionary tactic worked. American troops advanced while Jackson and his men coolly took the fire. Later Magruder singled out Jackson in a letter of commendation to General Pillow. The letter went through the administration of one Joe Hooker, who would meet Jackson on another field of battle—Chancellorsville.

The battle for Mexico City had not been won, though. Scott's main force still hadn't crossed the forlorn Pedregal. The troops that had were, in effect, cut off that night. Everyone who has ever been in battle says the same thing, over and over: A wild uncertain momentum prevails and individuals, companies, and battalions are unsure as to what is going on. It seems chaos: thunder, screams, fire, smoke. Only later are individual actions noted, moments of bravery and cowardice, genius and stupidity recorded. It's hard to tell who has won—the yardstick of advance and retreat often deceptive. Most action on the battlefield goes unrecorded. Thirst, exhaustion, hunger, and fear prevail, and afterward isolated individual moments are recalled. A few are deemed to have been pivotal to the final outcome—victory or defeat or a draw. Generals most often get the attention of history. On the dark night of August 19, 1847, a captain in the advance party, now cut off, volunteered to recross the Pedregal and inform Scott that they were planning to attack the Mexicans at 3:00 A.M. Scott should mount an assault at that moment, too, to scatter enemy fire and breed confusion. Again, Lee. He traveled through heavy rain, in near pitch-blackness, under the nose of the enemy. His hair black back then and curly at the ends, his manner jumpy, he made his way straight as an arrow to Scott and the attack became coordinated on both fronts.

The Mexicans broke and fled. The Americans chased them, caissons flying, infantry sloughing, to San Antonio and then to an enemy secured behind a high stone fortification—Churubusco. Both sides wearily traded blows. Then, as armies do, they called a truce, not for eventual peace but to fashion better strategy and advantages for when the fighting resumed. Unless the heart has been taken out of an opponent, fighting always resumes. An American peace commissioner, Nicholas Trist, arrived and went through the usual motions while Santa Anna strengthened his fortifications and the Americans regrouped. Tom Jackson received a promotion to permanent first lieutenant and a brevet captaincy for "gallant meritorious conduct." But the one true all-out battle, the one in which he would prove himself fully, had not come. It came.

One side skirmished, then the other, shelling, retreating, inching forward—then a major planned-out engagement. The Mexicans took positions in the castle atop the hill at Chapultepec. It was a fortress, a symbol. It was the site of Mexico's military college, a hill crowned by the palace of Montezuma, and old quarters of Spanish viceroys. Descendants of the English tilted once more against the Spanish legacy.

Scott called for Captain Lee to begin bombarding the south of Chapultepec with heavy artillery. Lee did—for fourteen hours, round after round soaring over the walls and landing smack inside the compound. Scott feinted some troops toward Mexico City, making Santa Anna believe his main force would skirt the bombarded Chapultepec and head directly for the capital. Santa Anna vacillated, debating whether to send reinforcements to Chapultepec or cut off the American troops ostensibly on the way to Mexico City. It was a fatal delay. Pioneer troops began throwing up scaling ladders against the walls of Chapultepec in a scene out of the Middle Ages. Jackson and his battery came up on the left to prevent the Mexicans from now bringing reinforcements or retreating from the castle. From the castle, sharpshooters placed Jackson and his men between their sights and fired away. A one-gun redoubt began targeting him. Jackson realized that the redoubt had to be silenced or no troops could move. He stood in the middle of a road as grape swept down as if in a sudden hailstorm. He pushed a light cannon forward.

"Come on, men! Help me—move!"

None moved except when struck by fire. Men crouched in ditches by the side of the road. They turned inward upon themselves. Booming ear-shattering cannon fire, the pop of muskets, cries of pain, the whinnying of horses, blood and smoke—a seemingly insane moment, the eye of battle.

"Come on," he cried, in his high-pitched voice. "There is no danger at all. See! I am not hit!"

He stood there, shirttail flapping, hair flying, bullets kicking up dust. A cannonball came rolling toward him as if in slow motion. Foolish soldiers sometimes imagined they could safely reach out a hand and touch one. Jackson knew better; one touch and you lost the limb. The cannonball rolled past between his legs. No one volunteered to help him, save a lone sergeant. The two of them pushed a light cannon into firing position.

From a vantage point General Worth observed the mad officer and the flinty sergeant. "Retreat," his order immediately came. "Save your cannon!"

Jackson kept firing, seeming not to understand it was a command. Magruder rode forward and his horse suddenly leaped, lurched, and fell with a bullet through its heart. Magruder came running. "What now, Jackson!"

"Help me get the other gun up here and we'll finish them!"

He and Magruder pushed the other gun up from a ditch and soon two guns began firing—swabbed, loaded, and banged again, time after time. They were at the head of the front. Their being there and diverting attention allowed others to scale the wall and take Chapultepec. The enemy fled, hotly pursued by officers Daniel Harvey Hill and Barnard E. Bee, leading forty men. This impetuous team soon got well beyond the main body of troops and away from support. As they came to their senses and were about to turn around, they saw the lone figure of Jackson down the causeway pushing a gun forward. When he caught up with them, they renewed their assault. Then Magruder, having located a fresh horse, galloped up. "Get back! Are you insane? They'll slaughter you now for good!"

They convinced him it could be done, that this tiny band

could hold off the Mexican cavalry because the causeway was so narrow that it allowed only one horse at a time to charge down it. As enemy horsemen tore forward in single file Jackson, Bee, and Hill—and now Magruder—let off a salvo. The heart went out of the enemy. On September 14, General Winfield Scott and his army entered Mexico City and the war was over.

This army numbered barely 6,000 now, and 200,000 Mexicans crowded the capital city. The soldiers were rowdy, unbathed, often unlettered, and some near mad. They had beaten the Mexican army and now were in the heart of Mexico. A heavy weight had been removed—no enemy to fire on them, no more ear-shattering pitched battles—but some officers recognized a threat in the disproportionate number of victors to vanquished. Extremely fair treatment of the former enemy was therefore established. Soon a euphoric atmosphere of peace descended. Jackson was promoted to brevet major and returned to his shy, diffident manner. His stomachaches returned. At a levee given by Winfield Scott, young Jackson passed uneasily down the receiving line. When he came to Scott, the general suddenly stiffened and put his hands behind his wide girth. He became grave. "I don't know that I shall shake hands with Mr. Jackson." The breveted Major Jackson blushed to the roots of his hair. He tried to speak and seemed paralyzed. Voice booming, General Scott continued, "If you can forgive yourself for the way you slaughtered those poor Mexicans with your guns, I am not sure that I can." Scott's great broad face broke into a smile, and he pumped Jackson's hand.

Among the Mexicans, his former foes, Jackson became a sought-after guest. He had a knack for the Spanish language and became an avid student of it. He read the Bible in Spanish; also Shakespeare and Lord Chesterfield's letters. He even flirted with the idea of becoming a Catholic. His innate courtesy and good manners opened doors for him into the best homes in Mexico City. Fellow officers watched in amazement as the usually stiff Jackson paraded comfortably in one grand home after another while they watched from the sidelines. Few were jealous; they just had trouble believing their eyes. Jackson had superb quarters now, large and comfortable—and most unmilitary. It was as if a secret part of his nature was allowed, in this environment, to emerge. Perhaps in a strange land he did not recognize the Puritan constraints of the frontier mountains.

Jackson indulged in the Spanish custom of taking coffee and cakes in bed in the morning. He developed a lasting taste for fruit—he had a special weakness for lemons. And for a brief shining moment he considered chucking it all—all the ideas of service back on home soil. He thought he might marry a *señorita*. But he never met the right *señorita*. Mexico had added a new dimension to Jackson, but there finally came the time to move on. In July 1848 he left Mexico City for the States. Scott's campaigners were all going home.

If there hadn't been a West Point, there would not have been a Civil War as we know it; there might not have been a Civil War at all. The seeds of its military tactics were sown in Mexico; its generals honed their skills before Chapultepec.

CHAPTER IV

Soldiers Without War

Jackson never quite adjusted to garrison life. He served at Carlisle Barracks, Pennsylvania, sitting on dreary court-martial boards. Then he was transferred to Fort Hamilton, out on Long Island, about ten miles from New York. He dutifully performed his military tasks—got the drilling done, the inspections made, the messes supervised—and then he indulged his love for New York City. The city captivated him even more than Mexico City had. He tramped the streets in open-eyed wonder, the way country boys have been doing since the eighteenth century; he listened to the accents; he blended with the throng. Especially he savored the bookstalls on Fourth Avenue, and he was a determined, discriminating reader. He became well known to the trade. He bought scientific and historical books; he read Melville and would quote him later. He found two of the better publishing houses, Harper's and Appleton's, and paid calls to their offices for catalogs and books. His letter to Laura in 1849 could have been written at any time by any number of enthusiasts from the hinterlands:

"Naturally I recalled to mind, and applied to New York, what the Frenchman asserted of Paris when he said that when a man had seen Paris that he had seen all the world. In New York may be found almost anything which the inclination may desire but peaceful quiet. Everything is in motion, everything alive with animation. In this busy throng none feel the long and tedious hour; even the invalid for the time forgets his infirmities and with wondering admiration contemplates the surrounding scenes."

Garrison duty allowed him ample time to worry over his ailments and seek cures. He investigated doctor after doctor in Manhattan, seeking the perfect one. On periodic leaves he visited the mineral baths in Virginia. He diagnosed himself. A doctor at Fort Hamilton told him to stop concentrating, to let his mind soar and amble, and his digestion would improve. Jackson devised a diet of stale bread, black tea, yolks of eggs ("Whites are hardly worth eating," he said), boiled and roasted meat, and legumes. His stomach pains increased, his eyesight weakened still more—but he knew there must be a cure, if only he kept investigating and denying himself what he really craved—sweets and spices and various treats. Puritan denial—he was never far from it. He spent three hours a day exercising and could be glimpsed strolling briskly, almost at a trot, at Fort Hamilton, swinging his arms furiously, suddenly leaping in the air, throwing himself into contortions. He was never an average officer; never did he fit into the background.

On a visit up the Hudson to West Point he looked up Dabney Maury, now an instructor there. After a happy greeting, they sat and began a lively talk over old times. Maury noticed something startling and strange about his old friend and finally had to bring it up.

"Tom, why are you doing that?"

Jackson, as he talked, had been raising one of his arms straight up in the air. No warning, no explanation, his hand just shot up as if he wanted to be called on in class. While his arm reached stiffly up, he said, "One of my legs is bigger than the other—and so is this arm. I raise my arm so the blood will run back in my body and lighten its load. It's a cure I've discovered. Everything has a cure."

"I see."

He was invited into New York homes and his circle of friends became as extensive as it had been in Mexico City. He flirted again with the idea of leaving the military. Perhaps there was some kind of job for him in New York. Before he could act, though, sudden military orders closed that option. He was ordered to report to the Indian frontier in the new state of Florida. And there one of the most curious incidents in the whole history of Thomas Jonathan Jackson took place.

Allen Tate in his book on Jackson, the first book Tate wrote, skirts it. The Reverend R. L. Dabney in his extensive, loving biography, which goes into the minutest details of Jackson's life—the type of cloth in his wedding jacket—leaves the Florida service alone. It appears a strange passage in the man's life, seemingly an aberration, but on closer scrutiny it fits in with Jackson's character. The incident shows the dark side of the Puritan soul— and why Americans have reason to be uncomfortable at times with the Puritan spirit. The mystery is not why this incident happened but why such incidents did not take place more often in Jackson's life. Although in a way they did, but in the context of battle. The Puritan may be appreciated in war and time of great stress when an unbending will and ferocious sense of right and wrong are prized. In peace this very same trait often appears meanspirited, narrow-minded, and vindictive.

Brevet Major William Henry French commanded the garrison, which included Jackson, at Fort Meade, Florida. French—tall, florid-faced, fleshed out with the result of his taste for good food and amber drink—was flamboyant in the way that Jackson often appreciated in others. French had wit, style, and cut a dashing figure—an Uncle Cummins type, a Captain Magruder. Jackson had served with French in Mexico and they were good friends. French realized that Jackson had a tenacious quality, that he was fearless, that he was a gifted soldier. They resumed their fast friendship in the heart of Florida, in a region of the country that was poised to change from a primitive land into complex modernity. Those on garrison duty did not see the sweep of history; they merely recognized that the Seminoles were still liable to follow their warlike ways and that the widely separated sugar growers, white men all, lived in mortal terror of Indian attack.

It was hard to actually engage the enemy in Florida and thereby garnish military fame; furthermore, routine garrison life began to pall when there was no vanquished enemy with elegant

homes to visit. Officers and gentlemen took to socializing and put
aside much of the sterner side of military life. Major French
brought his lovely wife down to live with him at the fort. She
kept the tea and crumpets moving, eyes sparkling, deferring to
guests, modest in all ways, acting as if it were perfectly normal
to be right in the middle of nowhere, entertaining a group of
soldiers in dress blue. Jackson came to call often, teacup and
saucer on knee, back ninety degrees straight, heart melting at the
sight of a good honest woman and hostess.

Trouble between French and Jackson soon began to develop.
Indians had to be found and dealt with or the camp's *raison d'être*
might be called into question. French directed Jackson to go on
a scouting expedition to Lake Tohopekaliga, forty miles northeast
of Fort Meade, where the Seminoles supposedly camped. With
twelve men, two noncoms, and a guide who couldn't read a map,
Jackson set out and came across not one lake but ten. He meandered ninety miles, not forty, and came back to report, accurately,
that he didn't know what he had found but it didn't include Lake
Tohopekaliga or one Indian. Jackson, however, had flourished on
the expedition; his color rose, his health concerns left. French
simmered. How could a man travel ninety miles and find nothing? What was he going to report to Washington? He went to his
maps and gave Jackson detailed instruction. Find the lake! Jackson set out with new scouts, and this time found the particular
body of water.

He also found rain and mud and knew that his men and
horses would surely sink out of sight in the deep morass if he
stayed around the lake's rim. Besides, there were definitely no
Indians in sight. His health and spirits blossomed, though, and he
scouted elsewhere. In seeming wilderness he stumbled across
sugar plantations whose owners welcomed him grandly. Jackson
at first thought these were ordinary corn farms, like those back
in Virginia, but soon he recognized that here were grand homes,
urbane planters, and that he and his men were most welcome.
Now he was reminded of Mexican days when local gentry had
opened their doors to him. He went from one widely spaced
plantation to another. He still found no Indians.

Back at the fort French stewed. He wanted body counts, an
enemy located. Jackson came back and told him of the fabulous

homes of the sugar planters. A dark feud started from that moment—irrational, past control. It was complicated in that both Jackson and his commanding officer held the same rank, brevet major. French had got his first, and thus outranked him. For his part Jackson felt overworked as his company's commissary and quartermaster officer. He thought French unreasonable to expect, in advance, exact results from his scouting expeditions. The litany rolled on, faults discovered in every aspect of life. They despised each other's clothes, mannerisms, and very scent. French used a pungent pomade on his hair. They stopped speaking except on official business. Each began penning letters of outrage to superior generals, seeking to nail the other. As a result of the strain, Jackson's eyes began to fail him.

Now comes the incident that sets this feud apart from others in Jackson's life; his Calvinism comes forth. Fort commander French had a maid. She was comely, a sparkling magical sight around the fort—skirts flouncing, step lively. The men at the fort had their interest in her enlivened by contraband liquor that was smuggled in. They swapped yarns, they listened—they weren't above spying, peeking in windows. And Jackson, now in confinement at the post for infraction of orders, overheard some of these stories. Around this time he began writing his sister about the abomination of hypocrisy and the duty of a Christian to uphold the strictest of morals. "A hypocrite," he fumed, "a detestable loathsome hypocrite . . ."

In a cold righteous fury Jackson called some enlisted men to his quarters one evening. They saluted, then sat ill at ease while Jackson glowered like a reborn John Calvin across from them. In a courtroom manner, he began direct questioning: "You, of course, are all aware of the servant girl who attends Major French's family," he said.

They eyed one another, a throat or two cleared, and they nodded. One would have to be dead not to be aware of her. But what was up the sleeve of this thin Major Jackson, whose eyes seemed to burn in a fever? What was he trying to pin on them? Was he going to throw them in jail for looking?

"I understand that Major French has been seen frolicking with this woman," Jackson continued. "Who has seen this? An actual example."

"Not me," a grizzled corporal said, afraid. "I wouldn't spread such disgusting rumors."

"Not rumors! Facts, I want facts," Jackson, the prosecutor, the Cotton Mather incarnate, shouted. "I want to know what someone has seen."

A light went on in one soldier's eye. He caught the drift. "Well, Major, I personally saw the major walking with the lovely miss. Just strolling along, pretty as you please. Laughing together, sort of."

"Where were they?" sternly.

"Why, getting near the woods. Looked to me like he was getting ready to take her in the woods."

Everyone guffawed—everyone but the prosecutor. "Any embracing? Any show of physical endearment?" He was getting on with business.

"Sir, I happened to be passing Major French's quarters one night—"

"And peeked in," someone supplied.

"Let the man continue."

"And I saw Major French on a bed with this young woman—but I couldn't see too clearly. I really wasn't looking for to see anything, you see."

"And what did you appear to see?"

"A nekkid foot."

Jackson's eyes searched this man, bore in on him. "Was that foot the foot of a man or of a woman?"

"I ain't too sure, sir. But whatever sex it belonged to, it sure was a pretty one!"

Loud bellows, knee slappings followed, but all quieted with one look at Jackson. The major had the look of a madman.

On returning to their quarters one soldier reported to his sergeant what had transpired with Jackson—the inquisition—and the sergeant immediately let French know. French immediately snapped; he turned purple with rage and lost all reason. His usual cool, witty riposte was not at hand. He screamed, "Put Major Jackson under arrest!"

And so they did, charging him with conduct unbecoming an officer and a gentleman. The steady blue light of Puritan righteousness still burned in Jackson's eyes, but his actual sight dimmed—psychosomatically in all probability. Now that Jackson awaited court-martial he had even more time to brood; certainly remorse or doubt of his actions was never in question. His countercharges against French came hot and heavy, but he couldn't see well enough to put them into writing. And now, one of the most bizarre aspects of the whole affair took place. Jackson called upon Major French to supply a soldier, an amanuensis, to take down his charges against him, French. French assigned such a soldier, and then got down to his own charges of "conspiracy" against Jackson.

The reams of testimony and charges that flowed from Fort Meade in this matter inundated the higher echelons. General Twiggs, who had served in Mexico, tried to wade through the papers and gave up. General Winfield Scott tried his Socratic hand to no avail. A surgeon at Fort Meade paid a call on Jackson and pleaded for him to drop the countercharges—especially the one about Major French's alleged improprieties with the servant girl. "Think of Mrs. French!" the surgeon said. "Think of the pain you're inflicting on that innocent and noble lady!"

Jackson wavered, touched by the memory of the happy evenings in the French home. But kindness never entered his mind when duty called. He stuck to his guns.

The secretary of war, C. M. Conrad, finally took a crack at the case and threw up his hands. He sent the matter back to General Twiggs to do as he pleased. At his wits' end, Twiggs ordered Jackson released from confinement and French transferred to another command. French, so it was thought, was finished in the army. One would have suspected that Jackson was, too, for he resigned his commission almost immediately and departed on May 21, 1851, for Virginia. He was to become a professor at the Virginia Military Institute.

CHAPTER V

"The heart has its reasons . . ."

On March 8, 1861, four days after a tall, joke-telling man from Illinois was inaugurated as president, *The New York Times* ran this headline: VIRGINIA NOT GOING TO SECEDE. The copy that followed pointed out that there were many applications for federal jobs in Virginia, proving Virginia's faith in the Republic. Lower down, however, came this item: "The Court of Henrico County, Va., yesterday decided unanimously that an attorney could not be required to take an oath to support the constitution of the United States, prior to his admission to practice." That meant trouble—as if anyone needed to be reminded. People in the United States were hotly divided over two large issues: states' rights and the institution of slavery.

Like many other men in the nation, Major Thomas J. Jackson kept up with the news, but he had his own life to consider. He was for holding the Union together, for compromise, for the principles of Henry Clay, Abraham Lincoln's hero, but ultimately he was for what he believed the Constitution intended: He believed, as Virginia's Thomas Jefferson had, in states' rights. That was it—reasonableness, solidarity with one's neighbors, keeping a cool head. But often a man does not know what is deepest in his heart until his will is tested. At that time, in Lexington, he called on the Reverend Dr. George Junkin, the president of Washington College and a Presbyterian minister. Duty compelled him to, for Dr. Junkin was the father of Ellie, Jackson's first wife. Dr. Junkin was a strict Unionist—wouldn't entertain the notion of Virginia leaving the Union, hardly the discussion of it. A man of high rectitude, he was someone Jackson had little trouble admiring. He employed Major D. H. Hill, and it was at one of Hill's popular soirées that Jackson had met Elinor "Ellie" Junkin.

Hill was the soldier/comrade who had brought Jackson to Lexington and who had recommended him for a vacant post at V.M.I.—a position for which, nearly all came to agree, the good Jackson was ill equipped. Preposterous figure, many concluded. When Jackson had settled in Lexington in 1851, he had been drawn to the Hill household where the piano was played, polite conversation followed, and young eligible women were frequently in attendance. At age twenty-eight, when most of her female friends had married or assumed the mantle of an old maid, Ellie was still turning down suitors. She has been described as sweet, intelligent, and highly reserved. Her photograph shows a dark-haired no-nonsense woman with strong features. She was extremely close to her then unmarried sister, Margaret, and they were nearly constantly together. For a while it was difficult for Major Jackson to get between them and talk to one separately.

At the evening get-togethers candles glowed and cast silvery shadows on the faces of those in Hill's parlor. A tall jovial man, in the lumber business, might spin tales of a recent trip to New York. Someone had an anecdote about the town character who wore a woman's wig. A certain revivalist was mentioned and several chuckled approvingly over his power to save souls. Sweet cakes went around. Effusive compliments went to the lady who had baked them. Isabella, Hill's sparkling gadfly wife, saw to it that people who should be together got together. She saw to it that Jackson sat by Ellie Junkin. Ellie, who seemed pleased by no suitor, somehow relaxed around Jackson. He sat bolt upright by her and would not allow his spine to touch the back of his chair.

"Is anything the matter, Major Jackson?" sister Margaret asked.

"Why, no," Jackson said, and blushed. He thought it best not to explain that he believed one's internal organs rested on top of each other that way and aided digestion. Such matters were best not discussed with ladies. But he was no fool. He saw that if he wished to speak to one sister he had better include the other. He knew his strategy. He asked simple direct questions and answered in kind. He was living in bachelor quarters at V.M.I. and Hill's parlor proved extremely inviting—the swish of skirts, the carpet underfoot, the lively presence of others.

He kept coming back and back to the Hill home in the early evening—party or not—and often the two Junkin sisters would be there. They would talk of religious matters, of books and music. Margaret (called Maggie by intimates) was the more intellectual of the sisters and seemed, erroneously, the older. But Jackson's eye was on Ellie. For two years he dropped in. Then one night, as Major Hill worked late in his campus office, Jackson burst in. It was not unusual for this man Jackson to appear suddenly out of nowhere. Hill leaned back with one elbow on his desk, and waited for whatever it was that Jackson wrestled with at the moment. Often it was a question as to how to manage the ungodly cadets at V.M.I. Hill smiled faintly as he usually did around Jackson. Jackson could be childlike in his simplicity, and Hill might have felt superior save for Jackson's striking originality. No one else was quite like him. Jackson, in his simple, innocent-seeming way, possessed—or so Hill felt—great originality. He had ideas, some admittedly strange, which no one else had. Jackson now cleared his throat.

"Ellie Junkin has, what I've always considered, a plain face."

"So?" Hill raised an eyebrow. "You've come here to tell me that?"

Jackson nervously paced the floor. "I'm becoming more and more agitated by the sight of her. I don't know what's the matter with me. I look at her and experience a certain giddiness. Could the sight of her face do this to me? I know her face to be plain, but I now think I see great sweetness there, too. How could this be? How could she change so?"

Hill banged his fist on the desk, and snorted. "You are in love. That's what's the matter with you."

Jackson reddened, but carefully considered what Hill had said. "You might be right. I've never been in love before, so I wouldn't know the symptoms, would I?" He straightened and raised his left hand to the ceiling, as if it were a perfectly normal gesture, no more than a shrug. "Something must be done about all this."

He wrote his sister, Laura, to send him a daguerreotype of himself which he had given her. ". . . If you remember, I gave you two, one being taken with a stern countenance, and the other with a smile. It is the smiling one which I want." He did not tell her why he wanted the daguerreotype.

Jackson's courting of Ellie Junkin certainly did nothing to counteract his image of being an eccentric. Nor did his falling in love make him any easier to anticipate. Why a preacher's daughter with a plain face? He was a son of the frontier, a man unused to female society, a West Pointer, a veteran of the Mexican War. He had kept his intentions hidden for those two years. He just popped up at the Junkin home with the least excuse, any excuse, or no excuse. The Junkins were baffled by him, this polite, courtly man who entered their home and then just stood there, blushing.

"Major Jackson—would you like some . . . tea?" Dr. Junkin said, after greeting him at the door.

"No, thank you, sir."

"You are . . . just on your way to the Institute, I suppose?"

"No, I am not."

"Would you care to take a seat, please? I'm not sure where . . ." Dr. Junkin put down the *Lexington Gazette* sadly. It was late afternoon, and he was looking forward to a few moments of private reading.

"I prefer to stand."

Ellie Junkin and her sister Maggie descended the stairs and entered the parlor. They moved in tandem, sharing private jokes and secret signs. The abrupt appearance of Jackson was now taken for granted by them, like a codicil to the day. Ellie's eye lit up at the sight of Jackson. She did not encourage the major, but then she did not bar him from the door. The ritual of Jackson's calling at the Junkin home, standing in embarrassment, and then

departing seemed destined to continue into eternity. Then matters changed. In the spring of 1853 Ellie called a halt; this courtship—if that was what it could be called—left something to be
desired. Enough was enough. Ellie and sister Maggie passed their
time embroidering and composing sonnets, and staying above
ground level, when Jackson's knock sounded. The Reverend Dr.
Junkin did his best to carry on a conversation with Jackson, and
to let the man know that he had been rejected.

Now Jackson really fell in love. Suddenly Ellie had never
been lovelier, holier, more bewitching, desirable, maddening,
than now. He pestered D. H. Hill with various theories on how
he might change his strategy, how he might win her. He turned
some energy loose and got his mind off the matter by correspond-
ing with his sister, advising her on how best to deal with poor
health—a subject dear to his heart. His advice was to call upon
God and to ever keep in mind that life on earth was "an unending
Misery." His tone was somber. He got away from Lexington and
visited Laura and her husband in Beverly in western Virginia.
Jackson talked to Laura about the spiritual worth of Christianity
(while Laura's husband excused himself from the room) and ex-
pressed shock that he found so little religious fervor in this
mountainous region. People were not God-fearing enough anymore. Still restless, he traveled to New York, a city that always
acted as a balm to him, and then on back to Lexington. He had
put on a few pounds, weighed 172, and his face had taken on
a touch of puffiness. Ellie was still on his mind—Ellie with
her sister, together in the upstairs regions, devout, elusive, unat-
tainable.

He plunged into the Lexington social scene, and met two
other sisters. Again, Hill was the conduit. Hill's sisters-in-law
from North Carolina were in town on a long summer's visit.
These were the sisters Morrison—beautiful Eugenia and slightly
older Anna. Their father was a preacher and a college president,
too—the Reverend Dr. Robert Hall Morrison, the first president
of Davidson College in North Carolina. It was bandied in town
that Jackson still had some sort of understanding with Ellie, was
engaged, so these Southern women took a brotherly interest in
him. It was hard to believe, though, that the stiff and proper
major was engaged to Ellie. If so, why weren't the two of them

ever together? The strategic Jackson did not say he was engaged, did not say he wasn't. He acted as if he were indeed an older brother. In the glorious and warm summer of 1853, he would drop by the Hill home and ask if the sisters Morrison had plans for that evening. If not, he would take them on the social rounds. Never was he in a suitor's role. In fact, the sisters liked to tease him, particularly Anna, who had those dark mischievous eyes. Major Jackson was so amusing, so serious and attentive and masculine. His "engagement" seemed like a stage prop, with little reality behind it. In the South this type of "engagement" was not that unusual. Some couples kept one going for thirty years or more, fueled by the drama of it and safe in the knowledge that marriage would never take place.

Once more Jackson cornered Hill, and this time brought up the new set of sisters. Particularly would he mention Anna. "This is purely academic," he said, "but don't you believe Anna is more beautiful than Eugenia? I'll grant Eugenia is prettier in a certain way but Anna's beauty goes deeper." Hill looked at him peculiarly. "This is all academic, as I say."

Stiff and proper with the Morrison girls, making the rounds, the last thing on his mind the elusive Ellie—and one midnight he knocks on Hill's door. "I must come in," he announces, "and see your wife. I must talk to Isabella."

"My God, Jackson, she's in bed. It's twelve at night, man."

"I deeply apologize. But I must see her."

"My wife? Isabella? Now?"

"If you would be so kind."

Isabella, with a robe covering her nightdress, was already halfway down the stairs. She was a born matchmaker, already primed to solve whatever dilemma had struck the good major at this late hour. Jackson took her to a far room and closed the door. He unburdened himself. Isabella must intercede between Jackson and Ellie. The misunderstanding between them had gone on long enough. He was at the end of his tether, and something must be done. The diplomacy, the reasoning, the wisdom of Isabella was what Jackson was counting on. She simply must speak to Ellie and patch things up. When Jackson made his mind up as to what should be done, he acted.

"Why, of course, Major Jackson, I'll speak to Ellie on your behalf. I'll see her first thing tomorrow. We'll clear up whatever misunderstanding there is."

"Not tomorrow. If you will please, tonight."

"Tonight, Major Jackson? Wake up the Reverend Junkin, wake up the two sisters in a fright? Wake up half of Lexington and all the dogs?"

"I see what you mean," Jackson said gravely. "At first light then, please."

"I promise, Major Jackson."

Whatever Isabella did, it was effective and swift. No one in Lexington had an inkling of what was to happen. Jackson certainly kept the secret. He dropped by to see the Morrison sisters from North Carolina, and Anna wrote later in her memoirs, ". . . he spent an hour or more, calling for his favorite songs and seeming genuinely happy. . . ." No hint. The girls flirted and teased, and he managed to blush. There would surely be more balls and parties and teas to go to with Major Jackson—perhaps something to go to that night. He nodded, made his lips move in a smile, and backed out of the door. It was so comforting and convenient to have Major Jackson around. You could depend on him. That afternoon Major Jackson married Ellie Junkin and left immediately for the North on a honeymoon.

Someone else rode in their company. Someone positioned herself in their company and stayed with them through the honeymoon. Ellie's sister Maggie went along with them. She was taking the union pretty badly, her attachment to her sister nearly ironclad—so why not include her? Maggie wrote poetry. For the new bride she wrote:

Forgive these saddened strains, Ellie,
Forgive these eyes so dim!
I must—*must* love whom you have loved
So I will turn to him,
And clasping with a silent-touch
Whose tenderness endears
Your hand and his between my own
I bless them with my tears.

Jackson took the sisters to New York. The visit would allow him to see Dr. Lowry Barney, one of the few physicians who had ever helped him cope with his mysterious stomach ailment. Jackson had run into Barney on a prior trip to New York. Barney had taken one look at Jackson and said, "Buttermilk." He had put the major on a buttermilk diet. It had worked. Jackson, impressed, believing he had at last found his medical savior, had followed the doctor to Barney's hometown of Henderson, New York. At first somewhat disconcerted by having Jackson underfoot, Barney had gradually been taken with the intense young man. Before Jackson left, Barney had said, "Have some fun, young man. Don't be so intense. Get married and relax."

Jackson now introduced Ellie and Maggie to the doctor as proof that he was following doctor's orders. He showed the sisters the sights, the wharves up from the Battery where schooners docked, the fashionable areas in lower Manhattan where carriages swayed on cobblestones and ladies strolled under parasols. The professor was restless. He took them up the Hudson to his old stomping grounds, West Point. He showed them where he had paraded as a cadet, and he renewed contact with officers on the base. As the sisters chatted and drew close together, the professor hunkered down with military history books.

He took the girls to Niagara Falls as a romantic gesture toward Ellie—this was where you went on a honeymoon—and Montreal and Quebec lay close by. Jackson led the party up the St. Lawrence to look over the Plains of Abraham. He was particularly entranced with this battlefield, and the sisters noted how his blue-gray eyes flashed as he walked off the paces where General Wolfe's English troops had faced General Montcalm's French ones. The women had never seen this mood in him before, and they were startled. The sun was setting as he stood by the spot where Wolfe, who had died on the battlefield, had uttered his last words. Jackson swept his arms out and exclaimed, "I die content!" as Wolfe had. He added, "To die as *he* died, who would not die content!"

Back in Lexington the professor discovered that there was a housing shortage. His last dwelling, as a bachelor, had been a small room in the Lexington Hotel. That wouldn't do. There was no suitable private home available for the newlyweds—so Jackson and his bride moved in with the Junkins. Maggie was, of course, living there, and the sisters would not have to be parted after all. It was a regulated, highly polite domain. It might not be everyone's cup of tea, but the young major showed no displeasure. The entire household was devoutly Christian, and therefore there was never a lack of something to talk about. Jackson held religious discussions with Dr. Junkin and with Ellie's brothers, who were destined to be ministers. Hour after hour in the parlor they mulled over theology. The Junkins did not consider Jackson a fanatic, but as one of them. Ellie had married well. Jackson loved the regulated life, loved to know what to expect and to do his duty to the Almighty. He explained that he had the habit of asking the Lord's blessing for each moment in the day, none too insignificant for attention. "I never raise a glass of water to my lips without a moment's asking of God's blessing."

Jackson kept worrying over his sister Laura's faith. He wrote to her in far-off Beverly, inquiring about her devotion to Christ, about her health and that of her family. He asked that Laura and Ellie exchange locks of hair—a peculiar notion in the twentieth century, ordinary in the nineteenth. Yet Ellie was modest and not overly eager to conform to this customary exchange of hair. Jackson had to do the mailing himself: "I send you a lock of Ellie's hair; this she reluctantly parts with because of its color, which she hopes may prove more acceptable to your taste than it has ever been to hers."

Soon after the couple arrived in Lexington Ellie's mother died, and the family rallied around the widower. They were aided in the belief that all pains must be suffered in this world for the greater glory of God—the Puritan creed, in which Jackson, of course, was a firm believer. The Junkins liked to quiz him. What if he were blinded—how would he feel about the love of God toward Him? "Such a misfortune would not make me doubt the love of God." Say he was put on a rack of interminable pain for his whole mortal life—what then? "I would endure it and thank God."

At times the Junkins could not restrain themselves. Jackson's beliefs brought out wonder, argument, and teasing mischief in them. What if he had to accept grudging charity from those upon whom he had no claim; what if he were at the mercy of others

over whom he had no control? Put him on a bed of pain, immobile, sentenced for a lifetime and at the mercy of the eternal
charity of others—what then, Jackson? He considered. "If it was
God's will, *I think I could be there content for a hundred years!*"

Ellie became pregnant. Husband and wife traveled by stage
to visit Jackson's sister. He thought the more bracing air of Beverly would do Ellie good. She was looking peaked, not in the rosy
health of an easy pregnancy but pale and wasted and afflicted by
skin irritations. It was a rocky, bumpy ride. But Jackson was
drawn toward change of scenery. It was during this period that
he tried to leave V.M.I. itself and applied unsuccessfully to teach
at the University of Virginia.

The Arnolds in Beverly were family. Ellie—wan, weak, smiling—did her duty, got acquainted with Laura and these new
relatives. The stay lasted a few weeks, and then the bumpy ride
back to Lexington and the start of the fall semester at V.M.I. The
year, 1854. That year Cadet Thomas Blackburn had been slain by
knife on the steps outside the Presbyterian church by one of
Judge Brockenbrough's law clerks. The *Lexington Gazetter* couldn't
cover the story enough. It had everything: violence, passion, and
people of the best society. The two young men had been rivals
for the hand of Julia Junkin, Ellie's young sister. Julia had been
with the Junkin clan and Jackson inside the church when the
murder took place. Sides were taken in Lexington. Judge Brockenbrough had a falling out with Superintendent Smith of V.M.I.
over it. Day after day the local paper unearthed new facts and
theories about the case.

The edition of October 26 carried a small item in the back:
"Died, suddenly on Sunday the 22nd, at the residence of her
father, Rev. Dr. Junkin, President of Washington College, Mrs.
Eleanor [*sic*] Jackson, wife of Maj. Thos. J. Jackson, Professor in
the Virginia Military Institute."

Jackson wrote letters to loved ones, trying to come to terms
with his grief. Sister-in-law Maggie, sent off to Philadelphia to
soothe her own grief, became alarmed at the tone of the major's
letters. He talked of the sweet joy of joining his late wife in the
hereafter. "Ah, if it only might please God to let me go now!"

Maggie returned to Lexington to be near Jackson, who still

stayed in the Junkin house. She found him more rigorous in his schedule than before. Everything was planned out, to the minute. He rose strictly at the same moment each morning; he observed the dinner hour each evening, to the minute. He let everyone know when meals should be served; he didn't like surprises. He set aside a couple of hours each night to have private chats with Maggie. He would be seated before his high desk, his head bent, absorbed, and then the clock would strike nine. He wheeled around, his expression softening, taking on an air of nonchalance—and Maggie stepped in.

They studied Spanish together. They confided in each other. Maggie, who wanted to be a writer, confided in brother-in-law Thomas how difficult it was to write of family matters—and Jackson did not scoff. She told him the title of a book she had in mind, *Silverwood*. Jackson then confided in her. He wanted to be a writer, too. He had a book in mind, a text on optics. Maggie delicately pointed out that he had previously mentioned that he loathed the subject of optics. One could not become a writer simply out of a sense of duty; one could not command oneself to be a writer. He thought that over. While she was at it, she pointed out that his sense of strict punctuality might be putting a slight damper on the joys of the Junkin dinner hour. Two hours after Maggie entered Jackson's study she left—punctually. Thus the time passed and the memory of Ellie became less sharp.

In the summer of 1856 Jackson went abroad, his only trip to Europe, his Grand Tour. He swung through England, Belgium, France, Germany, Switzerland, Italy, and on back to Paris and London and then sailed for home. He reported late for the fall semester, and friends and the Junkins feared that he might be suffering the torments of the damned because a ship's delay had caused unheard-of tardiness on his part. He came back refreshed and unconcerned. If the good Lord decreed a ship being a few days overdue and his missing the first days of classes, so be it. What he could not will was in the hands of God. If he had intentionally been absent, then he would have suffered and would have expiated the sin. Since he couldn't control the weather and a ship's journey, he had no control over his punctuality. He'd just relaxed and enjoyed himself to the last moment, fretting not a second.

In Europe he had visited museums, reveled in discovering new architecture, thrown off restraints, and had gleefully taken an interest in the sights, smells, and sounds of strange lands. He was not that much interested in battlefields and memorials to soldiers. He paid his respects to Waterloo—well, he couldn't pass that up—but he would much rather stand in front of a Rembrandt or buy a piece of folk art (a handmade doll came to rest on the mantel of his Lexington home and does to this day) than relive someone else's battles. Europe was a course in self-improvement, a postgraduate degree, a time, too, for him to forget his own past. Maybe on the Boulevard Saint-Michel or browsing through the narrow byways of London's Soho he came to a decision about the future. Somewhere in Europe he did, for, back home, he began pursuing Anna Morrison, the preacher's daughter, now down in North Carolina—the merry, dark-eyed young woman he had last seen the day before he had abruptly married Ellie. Virginal Anna and her sister, Eugenia, ensconced in an ivy-covered minister's dwelling—it was a tableau Jackson found irresistible. Some men fall in love with blondes in chorus lines. Jackson fell in love with dark-eyed brunettes who had a sister as closest friend and a father who was a preacher and college president.

He began his campaign with letters, and Anna was surprised at first. Major Jackson, the attentive, somewhat comical but albeit dashing professor from Lexington. He was making overtures, letting—as they said back then—his intentions be known. Then, during Christmas holidays—with no warning—who should she see walking up the front walk, past the latticework, but Major Jackson? He had come to call, although the Morrison clan was a little baffled by his presence. Reverend Morrison was soon taken by young Jackson, for the major was an obviously devout Christian. And he fit in readily as part of the Morrison household. It was a strange visit but a successful one on Jackson's part. Sometime during his stay he and Anna reached an understanding. He went back to Lexington an engaged man.

They married the following summer in Cottage Home, North Carolina. Jackson had become confused about the exact date set and the Morrison family—aware of their future son-in-law's eccentricities—fretted that he might arrive a month late. He arrived a few days early. Clem Fishburne, a Lexington acquaintance, was best man. Thomas L. Cocke was the second groomsman. The ceremony took place in the sweltering parlor of the Morrison home, Dr. Drury Lacy officiating. Anna feared her nerves would crack if her father performed the ceremony.

Jackson wore a uniform from V.M.I. Anna's trousseau came from New York. The newlyweds left for a honeymoon that included stops that Jackson had taken in his first marriage: West Point, New York City, Saratoga, and Niagara Falls. Anna particularly liked Niagara Falls. There was one difference this time. There was no third party; no sister came along. The couple learned much about each other in a very short time. Anna proved to be a good sport, trudging gamely with the major on long exhausting walks. She had a sense of humor. She could laugh with (and at) the professor. And she soon complemented him in another way. She developed health problems. Her primary ailment was a swollen gland in her neck. The search for a cure became a part of their domestic lives.

Returning to Lexington, in time for the new school year, the couple faced a dilemma: where to live. Although the major might easily have slipped back under the Junkin roof, such a move was out of the question. He kept his close friendship with Maggie at first, and she in turn greeted the new bride, Anna, enthusiastically: "You are taking the place that my sister had, and so you should be a sister to me."

But Maggie's time became limited, for she herself, at thirty-eight, had just married—Major John T. L. Preston, a V.M.I. professor and a widower. Jackson had married; she did, too. The new major in her life had, besides seven children, a mind of his own. The children, he deemed, should go under Maggie's care, and he did not quite approve of Maggie's writing and poesy. To him it bordered on public display and he, as a gentleman, should prefer that his new wife refrain. A damper was placed on Maggie's spirited nature, and the record shows she only occasionally saw Jackson and Anna.

The Jacksons stayed first in a Lexington hotel, next in a boardinghouse, and then Jackson settled on the Washington Street residence. It was much too large for the couple, rundown, needing repairs—but it was within the major's budget and housing was short in bustling Lexington. Jackson did many of the repairs himself and filled the house with the plain homey furniture both he and Anna liked. He soon had the house running smoothly.

The major settled into a domestic/professional routine that, left uninterrupted, would have made no mark on history. His eccentricities would perhaps have been passed down to the next generation in town, but there it would undoubtedly have stopped. No "Stonewall" of history, no master strategist, no ruthless disciplinarian of troops in the bloodiest war on this continent. Gone to his grave and remembered, briefly, as a local oddball.

But the mood of the country was rapidly changing lives. Fights broke out in New York saloons over states' rights and Southern principles; Irishmen slugged it out, and New York papers reported on these brawls. New York City leaned toward the Southern cause. In Lexington it was not cut and dried, but the more vociferous, usually students, favored secession. Abraham Lincoln, the Kentuckian who had migrated to Illinois, one of them really, seemed to have sold out to Northern abolitionists and come under their thumbs. It was time to choose sides—you couldn't escape.

In 1859 John Brown made his raid on the federal arsenal at Harpers Ferry. It was hard to tell if he was a harebrained nut or a messiah chosen to free slaves. Maybe both. He sought arms at Harpers Ferry to carry on his cause of liberation, but federal troops under Colonel Robert E. Lee cornered Brown in an engine house where he was holed up with his ragtag band and then he was sentenced to be hanged. Virginia tried to keep everything respectable, to make a dignified show of how law and order should be carried out. Governor Henry A. Wise accepted an offer from V.M.I. that its Corps of Cadets stand guard in Charles Town while the hanging was carried out. Major Thomas J. Jackson handled an artillery detachment. As Brown awaited his final hour the cadets set up bivouac and went through a military routine. By all accounts, Jackson's group was the finest-looking, the sharpest-trained. Their buttons glistened, their chins were raised, and they leaped to commands. Jackson himself had come alive, that poor mad professor who was the butt of jokes and a sadly lacking scholar. His eyes shone.

The year before, in 1858, Anna had given birth to a girl named Mary—a beautiful, seemingly robust child. Three months later the infant died from jaundice. Another death. The Jacksons called for even more support from their Heavenly Father, and sank deeper into poor health. Jackson was losing his hearing, so he said, first in his right ear, then his left. His throat stayed raw, like a wound. He had trouble seeing. Anna equally complained. They held on to one another like passengers in a shipwreck. They told relatives and friends their complaints. They complained to each other. Health problems kept their minds off other concerns, off the past and the future—and possibly they were *in extremis*.

Jackson still confined himself to his diet of plain brown bread, little if any meat, and cold water to drink. Anna tried hydrotherapy. Jackson put cold water compresses on his eyes and gulped down patent medicines. He grew worse. His hearing grew fainter, and his eyesight grew weaker. He dosed himself with chloroform liniment and swallowed a concoction that contained ammonia. He waded through all the local doctors. Then he went to New York, which he had trouble staying away from for long; a doctor rose to the occasion and said, after a thorough examination, that he knew precisely what caused all of Jackson's afflictions: bad tonsils. Part of Jackson's tonsils were removed. He improved slightly or thought he did. Then he worsened and joined Anna in hydrotherapy. He was downing patent medicines, applying compresses, swinging Indian clubs. As the fall semester of 1858 got under way a fellow V.M.I. instructor noted, "Major Jackson has returned not improved in health but on the contrary worsted by his new system of treatment."

Jackson might have killed himself by cures—but the approaching war saved him. His ailments fled as he saw to it that the cadets did their duty in Charles Town. Soldiers camping, artillery pointing, a high command appreciative of his skills— Jackson blossomed. He had a keen eye for drama, the telling detail, and was not unmoved by the momentousness of Brown's hanging. He witnessed it. He described it to Anna:

John Brown was hung to-day at about half-past eleven
A.M. He behaved with unflinching firmness. The arrangements
were well made and well executed under the direction of
Colonel Smith. The gibbet was erected in a large field, south-
east of the town. Brown rode on the head of his coffin from
his prison to the place of execution. The coffin was of black
walnut, enclosed in a box of poplar of the same shape as the
coffin. He was dressed in a black frock-coat, black pantaloons,
black vest, black slouch hat, white socks, and slippers of
predominating red. There was nothing around his neck but
his shirt collar. The open wagon in which he rode was
strongly guarded on all sides. Captain Williams (formerly
assistant professor at the Institute) marched immediately in
front of the wagon. The jailer, high-sheriff, and several others
rode in the same wagon with the prisoner. Brown had his
arms tied behind him, and ascended the scaffold with apparent cheerfulness. After reaching the top of the platform, he
shook hands with several who were standing around him.
The sheriff placed the rope around his neck, then threw a
white cap over his head, and asked him if he wished a signal
when all should be ready. He replied that it made no difference, provided he was not kept waiting too long. In this
condition he stood for about ten minutes on the trapdoor,
which was supported on one side by hinges and on the other
(the south side) by a rope. Colonel Smith then announced to
the sheriff "all ready"—which apparently was not comprehended by him and the colonel had to repeat the order,
when the rope was cut by a single blow, and Brown fell
through about five inches, his knees falling on a level with the
position occupied by his feet before the rope was cut. With
the fall his arms, below the elbows, flew up horizontally, his
hands clinched; and his arms gradually fell, but by spasmodic
motions. There was very little motion of his person for several
moments, and soon the wind blew his lifeless body to and fro.

A high wind flapped the red shirts and gray trousers of the
cadets and whipped the flags of Virginia. Jackson said a private
prayer for Brown's soul; then he marched his crack artillery corps
away.

Later, as war fever took a pause, Jackson took Anna to Brat-
tleboro, Vermont, for the waters. They proved useless, alas, and

so the Jacksons traveled on to a spa in Round Hill, Massachusetts. There a doctor's fine ministration soothed briefly the couple's ills. Someone taking care of Jackson, someone with sure answers, someone in absolute charge—and the mysterious ailments clamored less. There came an irritant, though—sudden and unexpected.

Jackson, up to his neck in bubbling water, eyes shut, receiving the blessings of hydrotherapy, heard a conversation a few feet away: "Damnable ignorant scum ought to stay home where they belong. Nothing but criminals anyhow."

Jackson said nothing—nor did he comment when clerks were abrupt, when his luggage wasn't attended to, when a sly knowing grin spread as he opened his mouth and spoke in his high-pitched Southern mountain accent. He was unfailingly polite, deferential, quiet—moving on his way. He returned to the lectern in Virginia, and kept to his rigid schedule. He frolicked in his home with children of guests. He wrote letters to his sister Laura, showing his usual worry over whether she had sufficient devotion to Christ, with some additional concern that her husband and her son, Tom, were properly Saved. Abraham Lincoln had been elected president of the United States. Jackson had voted for John C. Breckinridge, convinced that his man could better calm the country. Tempers were flaring now and boiling over in otherwise removed, idyllic Lexington—and somehow, someway, a remedy had to be found to damp the firebrands. Jackson wrote his namesake nephew, "People who are anxious to bring on war don't know what they are bargaining for; they don't see all the horrors that must accompany such an event."

Jackson helped form a nonpartisan committee to try to arrest, by a mite, the rush to what Jackson saw as a calamity. Somewhere there was an answer. Tables were pounded, faces flushed, voices roared—but nothing new emerged. Jackson stopped going to the meetings. He became inspired with another idea. What if all across the nation people would bow their heads at an agreed-upon time and pray together for guidance? He brought the matter up with Dr. White, his Presbyterian minister. "Don't you think, Dr. White, that God might listen? Don't you think that if we all beseeched Him He might help us avert so great an evil as war?"

Committees, letters, and now a large-scale beseeching of

Almighty God—Jackson wouldn't rest until he thought he had tried every avenue he could. When a national day for prayer was actually set—January 4, 1861—he relaxed. His nervousness settled a moment. He'd done all he could do. Now it was in the hands of God. Jackson had also had the foresight to lay in a store of the very latest weaponry for his cadets at V.M.I. He had purchased twelve Parrott guns, which had a long range and were much more accurate than the smoothbore guns currently in use at the military school. He read up on the latest advances in heavy artillery. He ordered volumes from the Ordnance Department of the U.S. Army.

Lincoln's election: November 6, 1860. On December 18, South Carolina seceded from the Union, soon taking along Mississippi, Florida, Alabama, Louisiana, and Texas. Virginia waited. It was the pivotal state, bordering Washington, D.C. On April 13 a significant event happened in Lexington. It was a balmy, glorious spring day—the scent of new green grass and flowers in the air, a heady holiday feeling spreading. It was Saturday. Cadets drifted down into the basin of town from the promontory above. They jostled one another, catcalled, some near danced in an excitement they could not explain. A long-building tension was about to snap. A large bulky cadet unfurled a Secession flag— starry and gray—and, with heaves and shoves and whoops from comrades, attached it to a second-story-balcony railing in town. His cap fell and a deep mass of red hair glistened in the sun. "By God, we're for the Old Dominion—or die! We're for freedom!"

"Freedom! *Semper libertas!*"

Sullen townsfolk looked on, shuffling, a few fists drawing up. Using some dang foreign highfalutin' language! Forever these young pink-cheeked know-it-alls had been invading the town— smart alecks, raucous, demanding, *spoiled.* Who were they to tell a man what to do! A new batch came in each year and a graduation class left, but they never changed. Always young, always drunk, always after the girls. Rich, acting superior, not even Virginians, some of them. A burly man, barrel-chested and mean-eyed, a blacksmith, observed the redhead slipping back among his cronies. "Teach 'em they're in the Union!" the blacksmith said. "We were born in the Union, and God damn them to hell, we'll die in the Union!"

Another man, one in a frock coat, took position atop a
wooden box he carried with him. He spoke gently, an understanding smile for the rash and the unlearned. He patiently
explained the origins of the Union, the Revolution of 1776.
Someone near by, galluses holding up tight homespun pants,
began drowning him out: "We'll have us a second revolution!
We'll have us a third or a fourth, too, boys! Until those dadburn
Abolitionists stop trying to tell us what to do! Them niggers
getting all fired up are going to come in our very homes and kill
us. They're telling us a nigger is as good as you are."

"Semper libertas!"

The redheaded cadet and the blacksmith were swinging at
each other and soon rolling in the dust. Others joined, a wild
screaming cloud that covered a block of Main Street—and the cry
went out, "Reinforcements. Go to the hill!"

Three cadets raced away. They came back with a company
of others, many with muskets and ammunition ready. They took
no truck from the nonmilitary *locals.* The odd professor, the one
they loved to ridicule, stepped up from his house on Washington
Street. Something that shone in his deep-set eyes stopped them
before he opened his mouth. He told them, in simple words, that
it would be best if they went back to the Institute with their
muskets and the rest of their comrades. They obeyed, and were
soon herded into Major Preston's commodious Section Room.
Preston spoke to them—of the need to uphold law and order.
They were a privileged few. They must set an example. Their
holiday spirit couldn't be extinguished this easily, though. The
beautiful warming sun. How jolly to raise the Secess flag! One
cried, then another, "Jackson, Jackson, give us Old Jack!"

Jackson shook his head.

Superintendent Smith, pale and exhausted, spoke for a
while, then became tired of talking, tired of thinking. He said,
"Speak to them, Jackson. Tell them what you think."

It was an order. Jackson, in his bounding near-trot leaped to
the rostrum. A fiery light came into his eye. The same light had
stopped their march on the town. It quieted them now. Silence,
a lone cough, then: "Military men make short speeches and as for
myself I am no hand at speaking anyhow. The time for war has
not yet come, but it will come and that soon and when it does

come, my advice is to draw the sword and throw away the scab-
bard."

April 17: Lincoln called for 75,000 volunteers to put down
the insurrection that had started in South Carolina. Virginia
stiffened and said it would not offer volunteers; it was withdrawing from the Union. Secession: The word had entered the lexicon.
The emotion was overpowering: loyalty to forebears, to one's
culture, to those who looked alike and had similar experiences.
Stick with them—right or wrong, stick with them. You were in
it together. Ben Franklin had said, about the earlier Revolution,
not yet one hundred years past, "We must all hang together, or
assuredly we shall all hang separately."

April 18: Dr. George Junkin, president of Washington College, resigned. He could take it no longer—hotheaded youths
who couldn't be restrained, a disregard for learning, insults to
the past. A few days before, a bunch of excited students—past
any control at all—had taken a Secession flag and adorned the
statue of George Washington with it. On campus. Knowing Dr.
Junkin was a strict Unionist, president of the University. This
gesture sorely tried Dr. Junkin. He removed the flag, reproved
the lads, went sadly back to his study and gazed out on the lush
spring foliage. He became restless. He took a path back toward
the statue of the father of the Republic—for reassurance. The
treasonable flag had gone up once again around the figure's
shoulders, like a shawl. It wouldn't be denied; it would cover
everything finally.

Dr. Junkin hastily packed some belongings, took one daughter and niece in tow, and pointed his carriage toward Union soil.
He left books, pictures, family keepsakes; he left daughter Maggie, two sons, and the ashes of daughter Ellie. He couldn't really
leave until he had said good-bye to his favorite, to his ex–son–in-
law Thomas. They shook hands beside the carriage. The horses
snorted and their hooves impatiently raised dust. "Take good care
of yourself, Thomas. You know, of course," he said, holding the
young man's gaze, "that you're welcome to come with me. You
and Anna. You will be free."

"I believe God has chosen that my place should be here."

"As you wish, Thomas, as you wish."

No more leisurely discussion; no more heated debate. Action began. V.M.I. went on a war footing for the Confederacy. Major Jackson had charge of moving the entire student body to Richmond. It was a Sunday, April 21, 1861. Jackson said prayers in the morning at his home. He and Anna dropped to their knees and he read this passage from the Bible: "For we know that if our earthly house of this tabernacle were dissolved we have a building of God, a house not made with hands, eternal in the heavens."

Orders had been hastily posted the night before that the Cadets were to eat at noon and march out at 12:30. A springtime frenzy struck—hoots and hollers and exuberance. Jackson, in a fresh V.M.I. uniform, sat on his campstool in front of the barracks, waiting for the scheduled time to strike. He wouldn't move out a second before. On the stroke of half past twelve he called the troops to attention. Then: "Right face! By file, left march!"

The line of boys marched to stagecoaches, which took them to waiting trains in Staunton. Through rolling honeysuckle-scented countryside they wound their way to Richmond. Along the route people in homespun held out plates of fried chicken and baskets of hot biscuits. It was like a wild holiday. Jackson had known another side to war, the dark side, but he kept his thoughts to himself. He busied himself with small details.

He was never to see Lexington again.

CHAPTER VI

July 21, 1861

The Sunday broke hot and sticky and bright thirty miles from Washington, D.C., on a small, seemingly insignificant speck of geography called Manassas, near a pitiably narrow creek called Bull Run—in Virginia, the latest Confederate state. General Pierre G. T. Beauregard, the instant hero of the relatively painless takeover of the federal arsenal at Fort Sumter a few months before, out in the bay off Charleston, now had charge of dealing with the very serious intentions of General Irvin McDowell and 35,000 blue-clad troops to put an end to the rebellion of the Southern states.

On this stifling midsummer day that began like any number of blistering days in the basin around the swampy U.S. capital, few, other than those who lived in the hamlets, had heard of Fredericksburg, Sharpsburg, and Chancellorsville. Few knew war. Sightseers, congressmen and their wives, vendors—a festive crew—traveled down the Warrenton Turnpike from Washington to have a look-see at war. War was in picture books and grand poems, but one had a chance to witness it now (from a safe distance) as one might see a meteor or a hanging; watch it from a safe secure hill as those of old had watched gladiators from a seat in the Colosseum. These spectators brought their hampers of cold chicken and hard-boiled eggs and cool drinks; some secured a crock of smoky amber liquor. Ladies in flowing crinoline; gents in stovepipe hats and narrow straight pants. They eagerly awaited the sight of McDowell's heroic drill-sharp soldiers putting asunder a bunch of ill-equipped rabble. Watch a war. From a hill. From a grandstand seat. The opportunity didn't come along every day. Right now, at the beginning of it all, the mood was holiday-like.

General Beauregard—Old Borey—wasn't too sure what to expect. He was an eloquent and mellifluous composer of dispatches. He was swarthy and sensual. Back in Charleston he had called home a sand-colored, columned mansion not far from the harbor. Women came in one door and out the back for dalliance. He well appreciated the taste of fine wine and the sight of well-turned calves. He had a sense of drama, of position, of form—and what was later to be called "public relations." He presented a good picture—so striking that in years to come the name "Beauregard" would evoke a certain kind of genteel Southern gentleman, holding a tall sprig-topped drink against the backdrop of Spanish moss. Beauregard was the name that evoked the plantation, darkies in the field, and a chivalrous code of honor. "Suh, Ah'll thank you not to speak that way in the presence of ladies!" Bringing to mind flies, mosquitoes, hospitality, and movements as slow as molasses.

What made Beauregard's dispatches grandiloquent made his military orders confusing. His words got in the way of his intentions. What he wanted done, where he wanted commanders to move, became confusing. Perhaps he himself didn't know what he wanted to do. Bands struck up stirring tunes, the music going like a rush of dope into the weary mind, inspiring action. But to where, to what? Horses pranced, then trotted, the bedecked riders looking this way and that. Artillery was pulled to one spot, and then a courier rushed up with orders to remove it to another. Birds chirped in the trees and insects hummed in the bushes, just as on any other summer day. July 21, 1861. *If* McDowell broke through the Rebel lines, *if* he put their soldiers to panicked and unorganized flight—then his troops could move on Richmond where the illegal government had convened. They could quash this insurrection. It would all be over—locked up, revolt put down, *finis.*

McDowell, too, had strong appetites. He ate enough for three meals at one time, watermelon after watermelon. He was a budding bulimic. As a result he had a chunky figure. But he also had bright eyes, a military demeanor, and a reputation for making quick decisions. He gave off an aura of quiet confidence. Lincoln liked him and had given him a free hand to do what he said he could do: break through the line of the Rebels, whose troops were less numerous than the Federals, and next be seen parading through Richmond. All over—taken care of the way the Whiskey Rebellion had been. He expected that his troops, under Generals Burnside, Sherman, and Porter, would feint an enfilade to their left (the Confederate right) and then strike with full unmitigated fury from the right. They would cross puny Bull Run down from Sudley Church at Sudley Ford and then turn the enemy and break through to glory.

Jackson tugged at Little Sorrel, turning him this way and that. He wore the blue uniform of a V.M.I. professor and a cadet kepi pulled down completely over his high forehead. He didn't look or act like a general—but who is to say how a general is supposed to look or act? Generals go into history books after important battles, where they are given credit for victory or blamed for defeat. There are all kinds. Beauregard changed his mind about where regiments should go and his lieutenants then misinterpreted his desires (or so he said later). Longstreet ordered Jackson to change his troop position five times. And Jackson complied. His men followed him instantly; a wave of his left hand, as he sat on horseback, was enough to start thousands now down a road, up a hill, and into piney woods. He had the undefinable qualities of a *leader,* and men in battle want one. A man who couldn't control fifteen students in a classroom now commanded a brigade with an iron fist.

In the early calm before the fight his lips and hands trembled, his eyes darted with their own special hint of madness. Then came the first volley, a pulsating series of booms and shrieks— shattering the insect-ridden, hot Sunday morning. Off to Jackson's left some gray smoke rose through the trees and billows of dust clouded the horizon. The racket of muskets, the spittle of fire, a strong whiff of powder took the tremble right out of Jackson. He calmed; eyes shone and stared. He looked off to where the first real engagement had begun.

Colonel N. G. Evans, commanding some South Carolinians, was the first to fully take on the Federals. He was the first to say to hell with the hero of Fort Sumter, Old Borey, and follow his nose to where he knew the real action was. He was a high-strung, fidgety man and dubbed "Shanks" by his fellow officers and troops, because his legs were thin as sticks. These military men took nicknames back then, much as sports heroes, adolescents, and mafiosi do today. Nicknames defined and added color. Soldiers needed these names—as gamblers do for each other in moments of high stress. "Lookey there, there goes old Shanks. Son of a bitch is burning up the road. Lookey him go!"

The Federal troops advanced on their right, after feinting to their left. Now they were coming. The dust really whirled and brilliant scarlet streaks flashed through the white vaporlike smoke. The boom-boom-boom of cannon increased. A country boy in an Alabama regiment heard his heart beat in his throat through the increasing noise and confusion. The night before he had wondered what he would do in battle. What would it be like? Crickets had been chirping as he sat around a campfire, a quartet singing a Stephen Foster song softly at another campfire. So this is war now, he thought, as the scream of minié balls sounded over his head and the muskets cracked. The earth shook from the boom of shells, as if an earthquake had started. And he discovered one of the great secrets of war, one that only people who have been there know. You don't determine what you will do or what will happen. It is out of your hands. It was like what happened to your pecker at times: It went about its business no matter how you pleaded and tried to control it. He began to gape and fall back. His trembling legs just started moving him backward. A major with a lush mustache was waving his sword, indicating troops should follow him forward, but this Alabama country boy began moving backward. He couldn't even control his voice. His mouth began to say, "Momma, momma," and he couldn't stop.

He had grown up on a forty-acre farm and had never killed anyone or knew of anyone who wanted to kill him. Now a whole

army, larger than any city he'd ever been in, was tramping his
way with the purpose of killing him. They stamped into a creek
and stamped out, their boots squishing water, their rifles raised.
And they kept coming, their ranks together, their feet moving
forward, one after another. Through the smoke and terrible din.
Momma!

A lanky boy from a Carolina regiment flattened himself
against a tree, became a part of it as its top branches and bark flew
away. He had no say over his actions, either. Might as well have
told him to dance or scream or sing for all it would have mattered.
The tree was where he would remain, hugging it for dear life.
Strange faces passed, caissons rumbled nearby, eventually an
ambulance and, improbably, a sutler's van—and still he stood
flattened there. Then a bugle call, a bombardment, and the other
side came past. He stayed against the tree throughout the whole
battle. At twilight he disengaged himself by degrees, thus becoming a veteran of what became known as the First Manassas down
South—or the First Bull Run, up North. He had been part of its
chaos and inventiveness. He lived to be mustered out from his
short-term enlistment, a veteran who marched in parades into the
twentieth century.

At Manassas Colonel James Ewell Brown "Jeb" Stuart came
dashing up at the head of his cavalry regiment. He was bearded,
wore a plumed hat and brandished a saber. It was hard to miss
him. He sat easy in the saddle, but on the ground stood massive
and somewhat uncomfortable, not as tall as he appeared on
horseback, seeming about as wide as he was high. He was a
momma's boy who had forsworn hard drink and barracks'-style
oaths, but he was a vain man, superconfident, who could wreak
havoc and inspire others to do the same. He saw some Zouaves
running toward him on the field like a band of hysterical pea-
cocks. It was a comforting sight to Stuart because he throve on
theatricality. Here were grown men in glorified bloomers and
turbans in the heart of battle. But they mustn't retreat. These
Alabama Zouaves must show some backbone! "Don't run, boys,
the cavalry's here!"

A bullet sang and Stuart saw a Zouave's hot black eyes fixed
on him and the Zouave was raising his musket. These weren't
Stuart's Zouaves—these dandies were on the other side. The

diversity of uniforms on the battlefield at Manassas was causing confusion. It was not blue against gray in this opening battle; a lot of the Southerners wore blue. Stuart quick-wittedly recognized his own error and began slashing at these oddballs in gaudy costumes. Soon they were scattering in the opposite direction.

The Southern line was breaking, though. It was coming apart. The 13,000 Federals sniffed weakness and plodded forward—like a slugger pounding the weak midsection of a boxer, bam-bam-bam. The Federals kept coming. Shanks Evans held them in check for the crucial first moments. His orderly kept rushing up with a tin cup of whiskey and Evans threw it back. He knew what to do, and he stopped a full-scale rout. He had been the first to give the Federals pause at Manassas, the first to spring into full action. After Manassas he disappears into the mist of the complex war, never at the center of action again. Drink got him, as they say.

So many made a mark in history, then were lost. General Barnard Bee was a nervous, fidgety man, like Evans. He was a West Pointer too. He began moving his men back, waving his saber and entreating them to keep order. Be military! It was, on the face of it, a rung of literal hell. Iron balls and pellets and elongated lead flew, leaving scarlet flashes in smoke and striking flesh with a plopping sound amid unearthly screams and pleas. Who could cope with this? The field became a spectacle of rushing feet, horses shying, sweat, dirt, blood, and swearing. It was near impossible to see through the smoke and dust. The running, the body straining to avoid danger and disaster, the concentration—soon a cotton-mouthed fatigue crept through the ranks.

A fleeing officer came across Jackson, who was aligning his troops on a hill overlooking the pit, where the battle then flared and threatened to spill out and over him. The officer screamed through the racket, "General, the day is going against us!" Jackson faced him and his eyes were almost humorous. "Well, if you think so, sir, you'd better not say anything about it."

Jackson kept to his tasks. He commandeered some artillery from Captain John D. Imboden's battery, which was passing in full retreat. Imboden was happy to stop scampering to he knew not where and put his fate in Jackson's hands. Jackson took what little artillery he could find and placed it in front of his infantry.

The infantry then took cover in a covey of pine trees on the far reaches of the hill. They lay in the shade, raised their muskets, and waited to do whatever Jackson told them to do. Jackson had beaten back some Federal skirmishers to take this high position. Some thought—and said after the battle—that Jackson should have advanced onto the plain where the shooting was, particularly when he had momentum. But Jackson understood *ground;* he had a feel for position. Let the invader come up to him from the plain.

Battlefields are not sports arenas—a designed region, there for the purpose of a refereed engagement. A battlefield is not neatly set up with markers saying what is in and out of bounds. Battlefields come into being when a general decides "Here I'll stand"; when armies stumble over one another; when a marauder seeks out his prey and pounces; by wild chance or divine providence, depending upon viewpoint. An eighty-year-old widow named Judith Henry lived in a small frame house down from where General Jackson decided to take his stand. She lay in bed, a perplexed look on her face. The increasing thud of iron balls filled the air. "Boys, what air we goin' to do?" she cried.

"Ma, we goin' to move you out to the ravine. It's lookin' like it ain't safe here with what they're doin' out there." Her two sons were in advanced years themselves and near invalids too.

"I never heard so much fuss," she said. "Why do they want our place so bad?"

"I don't know, but they're going to tear up the earth if they don't get it pretty soon. Oh, Lord! Have mercy!" A bullet came through the wall.

The elderly brothers carried their wasted mother out the door on the mattress and stumbled to the ravine as lead whined beside them and kicked up dust at their feet. No sooner had they dropped their mother on the mattress in the gully than she spoke: "Boys, take me back. I want to die in my own home."

"Ma, I don't believe we'll be quite able to do her."

Usually it was all the stooped, wobbly brothers could do to navigate a few yards from the house on the best of days. They had just finished stumbling and panting and a few times dropping their mother on the way to the ravine. They had never thought they would make it, but did so because this was Ma and the earth exploding at their feet kept them moving. The firepower of North versus South now concentrated on this small hill in Northeast Virginia that had been the scene of calm bucolic life for as long as the dwellers on it could remember. They knew their neighbor—a freed nigger down the way who scratched out his living and kept to himself, a sullen and wary figure; a good neighbor though. They knew that water tasted best out of a tin cup, that hogs would eat anything but a cucumber, and that Washington, D.C., thirty miles away, was worth only one trip in a lifetime. Northerners were strange, improbable people, capable—as proven now—of anything.

The boys' ma lay at a slant on the mattress. The bed threatened to slide to the far bottom of the fifty-foot ravine. She said again, as the old ticking slipped an inch or two: "Take me back, sons. I want to be home. Oh, God!"

The mattress smelled the way it always had. Its scent reminded them all of the frame home. All their memories were of the home now—who cared about North or South or the Old Dominion? What did states' rights matter or the holy Constitution? Oh, God! "Lift me up, I tell you! I want to go home!"

The elderly brothers had never disobeyed their mother. They had never married lest they offend by making a choice she might not approve. They couldn't lift the mattress now, no matter what. They dragged it, Indian-fashion. Ma's head bounced as the mattress slid over stone and stubble. Lead balls crashed around them. Dirt flew and tree branches broke. The racket increased as they staggered into the very eye of the battle. But there, through a clearing, they saw their home. The old brothers, bent, disoriented, dragged the mattress up the steps and into the house. It was early afternoon but near dark in the house because of the dust and smoke. No one could hear the other's voice. The old brothers lifted the old woman on the mattress onto the bed, where she had uneventfully slept for decades. No sooner had they dropped her and staggered back than a shell tore through the wall, splintering the bed and the woman and sending the brothers flying. Flames sucked through the house, and the war ended that moment for this family.

The Federals were in a fury and seemed invincible. Their infantry stepped forward, after an artillery barrage, over a stone bridge toward Henry House Hill, this slight mound of earth that stood between it and Richmond and the end of these Southern insults. These Rebels dared insult the flag, they dared to taunt the law and human justice. Ignorant trash! Uneducated harebrained louts! Goddamn their asses, now the time had come to make them pay. They had them now!

An officer from a Deep South brigade, his face showing signs of apoplexy, came by Jackson, who sat astride Little Sorrel a short distance back of the hill's crest in a piney grove. What was Jackson doing here? Moving neither forward nor back. He could have been a mirage. All was lost! All their big talk and plans and hatred of these invaders was going for naught. Anything was better than *this.* "General, they are beating us back!"

Jackson kept his eyes forward. Little Sorrel pawed. "Sir," still not looking, "we'll give them the bayonet then."

What? The officer must have misunderstood. He sought to have Jackson repeat, but the crackle of shells and muskets swelled and screams rose, and he dug his spurs into his horse's flanks and made for the down slope of the hill—away from this huge relentless batch in blue. Here the sons of bitches came! Look out! They came, this clamoring steady line of blue, up Henry Hill.

Battle flags slanted into the sun, men pausing to raise muskets and fire, the blue mass dug boots into the soft summer earth up to the crest of the hill. The line began spilling forward, like dark froth over the side of a crock, clumping forward, unchecked, growing in unbridled confidence. Jackson brought his left arm down and the First Brigade opened up from the trees. The earth, the further reaches of hell, seemed now to explode. Cannon and musket clamored in one long grand report, a deafening thunder. The Federal flags slowed, strained forward, lurched, and fell. The Virginians, by God, stood.

General Bee, face now blackened by powder that made him look like a minstrel singer, found his buoy to cling to at last. He could now rouse his disheartened men—stir them before they were lost forever.

"There is Jackson standing like a stone wall! Let us determine to die here, and we will conquer. Rally behind the Virginians!"

* * *

Jackson had been a brigadier general, C.S.A., but a few weeks. The Virginians in the First Brigade had been soldiers only a few weeks longer. Their anger had been smoldering, however, for as long as they could remember. It had come to them as mother's milk.

Nothing carried as much hate and contempt in it as the word *Yankee.* To say the word caused a shiver. The gall of Yankees! Foreigners! The gall to think they were so superior that they had a right to come down here and change the South's very civilization. Virginia had made these United States in the first place. George Washington had been a Virginian—Thomas Jefferson, too. Fueled by hate and camaraderie these country boys of Virginia had learned to drill, had learned rudiments of discipline, and had become capable of shooting and maiming others in a matter of a few short weeks. Those in command came mostly from the colleges, from the gentry and the pulpit—although in a democratic spirit several from First Families entered and left as privates. Jackson's former brother-in-law, Colonel J. T. Preston, commanded a regiment in the First Brigade; the Reverend William Nelson Pendleton, former rector of the Episcopal congregation in Lexington, commanded a battery of eight field guns.

Jackson would keep his medical director, Dr. Hunter McGuire, to the end. McGuire was a pious, self-effacing young man who wasn't prone to killing anyone, by bullet or medicine. John Harman, the quartermaster, was another story. He was in charge of having clothing at hand and wagons to move goods. He was the ultimate housekeeper and travel agent, and his voice, from beginning to end, rang through the valleys and over campfires, down roads and up hollers: "Goddamn sonsabitching whorehopping bastard! Don't move that cannon by that friggin-fuckin horse! That friggin' horse stays fuckin' here!"

Harman brought cursing up to some sort of art form. Men stood transfixed before it. Besides, it was the quartermaster himself letting loose: someone in high authority proving himself human, being like them—only more so, and louder. Real hellfire cussing stole into the Southern camp as effortlessly as morning dew, came as surely as the chuck-a-luck boards for endless bouts of gaming. It was catching, one from another. Until recently these

boy-soldiers had been held in check by womenfolk and preachers. Their land was Calvinistic and evangelical; now, in sweet
liberty, they could explode in the fireworks of blasphemy. What
relief! It was like discovering another country—letting loose,
finding camaraderie. Soldiers since Caesar had been doing it.
Also, it let them yelp about their situation: "Up to my neck in
shit," they said. Years later grizzled veterans in gray made little
of any past talent for swearing and racy anecdote. Forget the
prodigious drinking and gambling. It didn't sit right with the
community. Their kin didn't like to think of Grandpa flinging
oaths around—and they cherished the notion of a gentlemanly
South. But the South nourishes extremes and goes the odd way
(among ordinary folk, a "cock" is the female organ, not the male,
down below the Mason-Dixon).

Great soul-wrenching revivals swept through the gray-clad
armies, too. Souls were saved for Christ. Some men in the heat
of battle might say, "Dadburn that cannon over there!" or,
around a campfire, "This biscuit is doggone tough," but that was
it. They kept the Commandments, save of course the one concerning killing. Not to swear, not to gamble, not to take advantage of sudden willing female flesh—while in the midst of such
raucous anarchy—was a way to test one's fiber, was more a thrill
than a deprivation to some. But cursing would come to stay in the
Southern army.

But the pious remain the pious, and complaints reached Jackson about Quartermaster Harman's salty language. Jackson, however, had seen that wagons moved when Harman directed traffic,
that equipment arrived on time or Harman knew the reason why.
Things got done. Presbyterian Jackson didn't seem all that out-
raged by Harman's salty language. There was even a twinkle in
his eye when Jackson talked to him about his cursing. "Major, it
might be wise not to use such descriptive language as I believe
you've been using."

"I'll try, General."

Harman tried, but never succeeded. "Goddamnfuckin'
bitchin' wheel is put on assbackwards here!" You could find the
quartermaster in this outfit anytime. His voice ricocheted through
the columns, and perhaps his presence stirred memories of Uncle
Cummins at Jackson's Mill.

* * *

Jackson very nearly didn't have any command at all. A short while after arriving in Richmond in April of 1861, his band of V.M.I. cadets in tow, he was assigned to the engineering department. Richmond then bustled with brains and plans. The eccentric professor seemed out of step, not quick enough on the uptake, a little weird. Put him in engineering and forget him. Jackson could not draw a map if his life depended upon it. Engineering and map drawing were his weak points; he could not have been assigned to a worse position. It was a desk job. But he had an ingrained habit of following orders and might have sat out the war there if others hadn't taken up his case. An old companion, Jonathan M. Bennett, just happened to call on Governor Lecher and just happened to say it sure was a waste to lose a West Pointer, a Mexican War vet to the service of quill and ink. The governor mulled it over, and asked, who was that? "Why, Major Jackson from V.M.I. Good man."

The governor then made Jackson a colonel in the Virginia forces and sent word for him to take command of the raw militia encamped then at Harpers Ferry. Put up some defense—whatever soldiers do—and keep the Yankees away. General Lee would go into the fine points. Life was in a high state of flux in the Commonwealth. When Virginia seceded, in fact, the only standing army in the state was a single company of soldiers who hung around monuments and public buildings and tried to affect a military posture. The old militia—a crack outfit in the War of 1812—had fallen into desuetude. When the war cries now rang, the firebrands looked around and found a militia that was more a social club than a fighting machine. The boys had meetings three times a year to play at drilling with no real arms and then off to clink glasses and spin yarns. The militia had become an excuse to get away from women and chores and have a little fun. Now the Yankees were coming!

In Richmond Jackson was strolling near a parade ground, still outfitted in his V.M.I. costume, when a tall, thin boy stopped him. "You an officer, mister?"

"That's correct."

"I thought so by that kind of suit you got on. I must tell you that I don't know what the hell I'm doing. I just been made corporal of the guard, but the man that made me that doesn't know what a corporal of the guard does. Nobody seems to. I just asked somebody with a lot of braid all over him and he didn't know what I should do. He was toting a sword. He said he commanded a division and didn't fool around with stuff like that. He said to look up a junior officer or sergeant. Can you tell me what I should do?"

"Follow me, soldier."

Jackson took him on a full circuit of the sentry posts. He had a quick step and the soldier had to trot to keep up. "Here's how you salute." Then: "Always make a sentry challenge you." And: "Make them come to attention—like this." It was a whirlwind tour, quick, methodical, thorough. It was like a ballet master teaching at the barre. The lanky, flushed-faced country boy had never seen a performance like it. He followed this strange man's quick march with his jaw dropping. Here was someone who knew what he was doing for a change.

"I'm thanking you kindly, mister."

"Say sir to an officer."

"By God, I will, sir!"

"And try not to use the Lord's name in vain. Providence will smile on you more kindly that way. Church services will be held in the field this Sunday. You will be most cordially welcome. Now, salute, soldier!"

The boy felt a strange emotion, something he couldn't quite put into words. It was akin to the stirrings of love.

At his new post at Harpers Ferry, which he had last visited as John Brown swung, Jackson didn't ponder or pontificate. No long-winded memoranda or endless conferring with aides. He and his aide, Preston, Maggie's husband, took rooms in a small hotel near the tracks of the B & O—like two frugal drummers on the way through. Harpers Ferry had just been abandoned by the Federals and a swelling untrained rabble of Virginia volunteers poured in. They had more or less elected their own leaders and officers and operated principally on emotion and rumor. Kill the Yanks! Have a drink! Jackson posted a notice for these Virginians that he was in command now and that their training was about to commence. A bearlike man, a logger from the Shenandoah, took one look at Jackson in his professor's uniform and said that he'd shit pure pork before that man could stop the fun. And what fun! Here was a whole little village—a Virginia village—that Virginians had freed of Yankees. They had captured the arsenals and sent the foreigners flying. These volunteers weren't about to have their frolic ended by some dimwitted authority.

Harpers Ferry was a tongue of land that jutted between the junction of the Potomac and Shenandoah rivers. It had abundant water power and the Federal government had used it to make muskets and rifles, bullets and shells, and the banks of the two streams were lined with factories. The village housed the arsenals. Harpers Ferry was the door to Virginia, to the Shenandoah, and the Chesapeake and Ohio canal passed through it. The great turnpike road from Washington and Baltimore ran through it. The B & O rail line connected it with the coalfields in the West, and Winchester and the Valley below. It was the forward point of this new Confederacy, and priceless.

Jackson saw immediately that soldiers by themselves couldn't hold it. Well and good that the Federal army had abandoned it for the moment, but when those people regrouped and got serious it would be hard to defend: He wouldn't mind attacking it himself. He began looking for the ever protective high ground (as the insecure look for the security of money), and he began to train the 2,100 Virginians and 400 Kentuckians he found himself in charge of. They drank, sang songs, cursed, cried maudlinly, hooted, and treated the Federal armament they had liberated like toys and personal bounty. It was a lynching mob, looking for someone to lynch, lurching this way and that through the village, down back alleys and by river banks, leaderless, dangerous. Everybody wanted a furlough. And now, to top it off, a Mad Professor.

Captain John B. Imboden, a trooper from Staunton, was leaving Harpers Ferry just as Jackson arrived. He was off to Richmond to secure clothing and supplies for this growling beast of a militia which had settled in this lovely river port. He feared for Jackson; he feared for the Cause. What in the world had they done? Had they taken the wraps off civilization and order? And now this fierce-eyed man who suddenly raised his left arm when you spoke to him. This man in a peculiar well-worn uniform was in charge. What would happen next? Secretly he was glad to step into the train bound for Richmond. He was thankful to be off for supplies. Let someone else worry about Harpers Ferry.

He came back a few weeks later and found the beast had been tamed. He rubbed his eyes. Militia officers who had got their commissions through political connections were gone. There was discipline in the ranks. It was an army—with campfires, messes, drilling, passwords, and pickets. The professor turned out to be far more than met the eye. He became even more a man of mystery. Captain Imboden—like others to follow—became a Jackson convert. He urged the militia battery he commanded to sign up for the duration of the war—no matter how long it took, no matter what it cost. He made an emotional appeal. These Virginia farm boys, who had recently been clamoring for furloughs, cried, "For the war! For the war!"

Imboden found Jackson in his little room at the wayside hotel near a railroad bridge. He sat at a small pine table, lost in figuring up troop numbers on a sheet of paper. Imboden proudly handed over the names of troopers who had volunteered for the war's duration—no matter the length, no matter the cost. "Why, thank you, Captain," Jackson said, almost embarrassed by the emotion shown by Imboden. "Thank you—and please thank your men for me."

Imboden wrote of how he remembered Jackson at that special moment at Harpers Ferry in May of 1861:

"The presence of a master mind was visible in the changed condition of the camp. Perfect order reigned everywhere. Instruction in the details of military duties occupied Jackson's whole time. He urged the officers to call upon him for information about even the minutest details of duty. . . . He was a rigid disciplinarian, and yet as gentle and kind as a woman. He was the easiest man in our army to get along with pleasantly so long as one did his duty. . . ."

No matter if others in this new Confederacy thought war was playacting or were unsure what war really was or feared in their hearts killing others—or more appropriately—getting killed themselves. No Hamlet, Jackson knew what he had to do. He acted. Later, others might find Jackson's military plans simple and direct and understandable. Strokes of genius. Back then, in the midst of chaos, he snatched the reins of the beast while others pondered. He forged into the unknown.

And remained honest while military rule pushed civilities aside. On a clear spring morning, a couple of months before First Manassas, Jackson spotted a small horse with a fine brownish-red sheen to its coat—a sort of sorrel hue. Something about its prancing, a vulnerable but determined look, struck Jackson. It was a Yankee horse, part of the booty from a B & O train. He had led in the capture. Now he looked up Quartermaster Harman and asked if the horse had been spoken for.

"Why, no. Funny little animal, isn't he?"

"I want to buy him."

"Buy?"

Jackson insisted on paying for the animal. He wanted to keep the books straight. He planned to give the little horse to Anna—it was like an overgrown pony and had none of the sturdy qualities of a warhorse. But when he saddled and rode him, he decided, well, another horse might be suitable for Mrs. Jackson. He couldn't part with Little Sorrel, as the animal became known. Jackson's legs came far down, not far from the ground, and he bounced on the back of Little Sorrel—but he felt at home. He rode him, not caring how he looked. He rode him on parade, at inspection, into the field reconnoitering. He rode him on long flanking treks, and he rode him into battle. Little Sorrel lasted through Jackson's last ride, lasted to live on display at county fairs long after the war ended—and behind glass today at the V.M.I. Museum in Lexington he seems alive enough to canter the way he did at Manassas.

At Harpers Ferry Jackson ruffled feathers way down in Richmond with his iron will, with doing his job of protecting the harbor town a little too well. He may have been the first Southern officer to foresee that once secession had occurred, once war had begun, you had to think about winning it. You had to think militarily. He had Randolphs, Masons, Harrisons, Hunters, and Carters in his ranks and he taught them to carry slops as well as post guards and raise salutes. With nothing ostensibly threatening on the horizon—just the rumble of war in the distance—Jackson was still put down as madcap at best, and mad at worst.

Old Jack, they called him, and not exactly affectionately. He was such a stickler over little things, poking his nose into the most minute of details—the way an officer's brass buckle shone or limitations on furloughs and visitors to post. These Southerners loved the clamor of war, the romance, the trappings—the fighting they would get around to, the sooner the better, too. They wanted their wives, sweethearts, *mothers* around the garrison; they wanted balls to attend at Harpers Ferry. Jackson, his hard eyes narrowing, wanted Maryland Heights, in the sovereign state of Maryland, across the Potomac, occupied.

He looked to two untested cavalry officers to scout the Heights; in actuality to picket—*occupy*—the high ground that didn't belong to them: Lieutenant Colonel James Ewell Brown Stuart and Captain Turner Ashby. They trotted their horses over that land, primed to give the new Federal army a firefight and their commander, Jackson, an early warning in his base down at Harpers Ferry. Here were two hell-for-leather horsemen who were to set the tone and myth of a particular style of Southern fighting. Who could outdo Jeb Stuart in flamboyance, inventiveness, doggedness, and sheer unmitigated bravado? Turner Ashby.

Captain Ashby was, in looks, a strange sight even among the exotic in the South. He was as swarthy as a black, small, with a curled mustache befitting a Neapolitan. From an old landed Virginia family that had fought in all the country's wars and was always eager to fight more, with an impeccable background and much land wealth, Ashby was a near illiterate. He made up his own rules and regulations, his own learning process, thought up his own turbaned uniform—on the order of a follower of Mohammed—and did what he had to do in his own fashion. He could not—or did not want to—discipline his cavalry corps. They revered him and emulated him by doing as they pleased, too. They were a horde of free-lancers. They were called Ashby's Rangers.

Ashby's peculiar qualities somehow appealed to Jackson, the stern disciplinarian. Once Ashby, a flyspeck of a man, doffed his Oriental uniform, put on plain civilian clothes, and went on a spy mission in the enemy camp of General Patterson above Harpers Ferry. Ashby passed himself off as a veterinarian and went among the Union cavalry on the supposed outlook for ringbone disease and spavin. What he did, though, was gather data on the strength and position of Patterson's troops. Just rode into camp, a tiny figure on horseback, proclaiming himself a horse doctor and went confidently to work. He could have been shot on the spot as a spy. An actor, a showman—fearless. Ashby was Jackson's kind of man. He put him under the titular command of the more renowned Jeb Stuart.

In Richmond the high command fretted about Jackson and what he was up to. Before the bullets started flying and before defense was really at stake, adventurism was held in low esteem. Novelty and daring were highly suspect. Old worries about the professor's sanity now resurfaced. Here was this rather odd Jackson sending strong communications to Richmond: He was writing to Lee down in the capital that he was going to defend Harpers Ferry "with the spirit of Thermopylae." *Thermopylae?* Lee had just doffed his Union blues a few weeks previously. He had just announced his disloyalty to the Union. He wasn't in the mood to be a cowboy. At this early stage he was in no mood for do-or-die thrusts, heroics or bold imaginative leaps into the unknown. That would come later. Right now he was getting adjusted to the idea of war with his old comrades. He didn't want Jackson monkeying around in Maryland, a state that was now wavering about joining the Confederacy. They might hold slaves in Maryland, they might *speak* like Southerners, but they were cheek by jowl with Washington and the North, and anything was possible these days. The fabric of society was coming apart. Maryland could be pushed to turn Yankee.

Jackson kept Ashby and Stuart busy scouting in Maryland while politicians talked. He occupied Maryland Heights, a promontory overlooking Harpers Ferry—*high ground*—with infantry. Just took it. From there he trained his artillery toward the valleys and roads that led into the river port. A problem arose when he could get no food and supplies from Richmond for his troops. He put Harman to the task of relieving the countryside of the necessities—the clothing, grain, and hardware his troops needed. He impressed, he seized. He asked no permission, but got the job done. Lee did not want to seize goods. Never did—from friend or foe, from start to finish. Wanted everyone to be polite, mannerly, and well-behaved—with the notable exception of firing

cannon and musket in tactical military moves. Jackson wanted
nothing gratis for himself, but he favored any means to have his
men fed and ammunition in their hands. Jackson wanted to
fight—from the start.

Lee was forced to rebuke Jackson in the early days. His
communiqué: "I fear you may have been premature in occupying
the Heights of Maryland . . . If not too late, you might withdraw
until the proper time." This was Lee's way of saying, Get the hell
out of Maryland. Jackson of course complied. His own correspondence was pithy and prompt; a main concern was not wanting
mail to travel on Sunday and thus violate the Sabbath. And he
worried about his sister, Laura, in Beverly, beyond the Blue
Ridge, in Northwest Virginia. Southern sympathy was held in
low esteem there, for the South was far from cohesive, one strong
solid block pitted against the Yankees. Northwest Virginia (and
much of the Shenandoah) stoutly opposed secession. These
roughhewn Westerners went to their own drummer—mistrust-
ful, cagey, quixotic, very hard to anticipate or control. They just
got it into their heads around where Jackson came from originally
that they didn't want to be bossed and roped into a Cause. Jackson couldn't convince Laura; she remained a Northern sympathi-
zer to the end. To Lee, Jackson suggested that a force be organized
(hinting that he lead it) and that it travel by stealth into the
Northwest, his native ground, and "at once crush out opposition." From the beginning the mild-mannered professor was a
firebrand.

And from the beginning there was not a minute without a
problem. Three brand-new Confederate officers suddenly
showed up at Harpers Ferry—one a general, Joseph E. Johnston,
whom Jackson recognized from old army days. Joe Johnston was
slight, rather birdlike, and held himself with a stiff military bearing. So many officers of this new Southern army were in their
thirties and forties. Actually, to be in one's forties marked one as
an "old" man. Johnston was in his early fifties. They dubbed him
"Old Joe." Old Joe had patience, and he had experience. He had
"military" stamped all over him, but he was no martinet. He
appeared at the gates of Harpers Ferry and said that he'd come
to take charge. How's that? Jackson had brought order and discipline to the base. He had got things moving, a-bustle—his troops

hadn't prudently waited before setting stakes in Maryland. T. J. Jackson had eyes and saw and knew that Joe Johnston had come to relieve him. Jackson was polite, mannerly as always, and said of course General Johnston was welcome. "By the way"—throwing a little curve of his own—"you do have papers from headquarters authorizing this move?"

Johnston was taken aback. Couldn't Jackson *see* that he, Johnston, wouldn't have come all the way from Richmond if he hadn't been given command? Wasn't he, Johnston, standing right there in front of him? Didn't Jackson recognize him?

Of course, but military rules were military rules. There had to be something in writing. He'd put Johnston up in good quarters, show him the sights, invite him to prayer meeting, but, without papers, Johnston could not take charge. Sorry about that.

Johnston did not fume, hardly ever did—and his patience served him well this time. Much later, against Sherman on the road to Atlanta, his patience would be deemed as dilatory and lackluster and lead to his being removed from command. But by then there had been a reversal in how men's qualities were judged. Johnston faced what he had to face—Jackson this time. He rummaged around in his saddlebags and finally came up with a letter that referred to him as the new commanding officer at Harpers Ferry. At the bottom: "By order of Major-General Lee." Johnston took over.

And showed his prescience by not taking revenge or marking Jackson down as an all-out oddball, but naming him as commander of the most important brigade in his new command at Harpers Ferry—the First Brigade. This brigade had no diverse elements; it was not a potpourri of regions. It was composed almost solely of Virginians, and those of the Shenandoah Valley at that. These were the men Jackson had paid particular attention to when he had been the one thinking up a defense for Harpers Ferry. They understood each other as family members do. They had deep rivalries among their number, but they were also fundamentally stirred by one another's presence. They had come to respect Jackson and be astounded by him too. He was one of their own—yet different.

Jackson's ambition, never under wraps for long, came out in odd ways, in keeping with his character. He fretted that his beloved Anna, the woman in his life, would be disappointed in his losing command of the strategic port city. He wrote that it was his Heavenly Father's wish, this change in command. That let him off the hook. The stern soldier wrote that her "sweet, little sunny face is what I want to see most of all." But he wouldn't permit her to travel from Lexington to visit him in Harpers Ferry. Other gentlemen were bringing their womenfolk in—not Jackson. He persuaded her to move ever farther away, to her father's home in North Carolina. The Lexington home, which he took tremendous pride in, must be closed or rented. War must be waged. No distractions, nothing held in the way.

Anna wrote, fine and good, but tell her about the war. She liked to hear about her sweet pretty face, but she would also like to get some hard news. Jackson penned this: "I have written you a great deal about your *esposo* and how much he loves you. What do you want with military news?"

He let her know what kind of quarters he occupied, and there was no hint of the fierce Cromwell here, more of John Keats: "I have a nice green yard, and if you were only here, how much we could enjoy it together. . . . My chamber is on the second story, and the roses climb even to that height." He did let her know that he was the new commander of a new brigade, the First Brigade. He let her know that he had never felt better physically. He blessed his kind Heavenly Father.

Joe Johnston, thin, sure, methodical, ever the cautious general, decided that Harpers Ferry could not be defended with the forces he had at hand. He withdrew from Maryland Heights the soldiers that bold Jackson had placed there, and then gave orders to evacuate the river town. Back off, get set for the superiorly numbered Yanks. Don't attack Goliath.

Johnston blew up public buildings, the fine railroad bridge across the Potomac, and anything else he felt the enemy might find of use. A tall dashing young man named Henry Kyd Douglas joined up at this time. He was a true pink-cheeked cavalier, someone who had a wry bemused attitude toward this conundrum called a Civil War. He wanted dearly to fight; he also wanted a shot or two of whiskey for breakfast and a congenial set of manners observed by friend and foe alike. His family had a long history in Maryland, but his own heart went out to this new Confederacy. Immediately, his loyalty was put to the test, for he had part in blowing up a bridge of which his father, in Maryland, was part owner. He did his duty, and was liked from the start by Jackson. Wild and somewhat irreverent, he became part of Jackson's close circle—his youngest aide. At this time, Alexander Swift "Sandie" Pendleton joined his parson father's outfit, the Rockbridge Artillery, and became a Jackson protégé.

Jackson had feisty men around him, each one with an itchy trigger finger. One thought coursed through this First Brigade: Fight. Take it to 'em. General Joe Johnston looked at the big picture and feared old General Patterson from Pennsylvania, with 18,000 men to his pitiful 6,500, might attack from the rear, put him in a vise, and knock him out of the war before it really got going. Johnston was thinking and reacting—not necessarily doing. They burned old Harpers Ferry, put the torch to it, and fled for Bunker Hill, which was about twelve miles north of Winchester, hoping to avoid Patterson—to delay, to wait catlike. Jackson moved the First Brigade smartly, rushing up and down his marching columns, waving them on, goading them on. They almost ran—not away from battle but from what they wanted, the possibility of battle. Jackson wanted to find Patterson and those 16,000 invaders of Virginia. He wanted to encounter the enemy, and then invade his territory. Make him know what war was, its cost, and then maybe he would change his mind and seek peace. Johnston didn't want to find the enemy anywhere; he wanted to keep his own peace. At Bunker Hill the troops rested, the officers mulled matters over, and scouts reported that Patterson and those blue-clad people were crossing and recrossing the Potomac. Coming into Virginia and then high-tailing it out. Patterson couldn't make up his mind. So much better to plan strategy, think it up, than to act.

Jackson got a chance to act. He got a loose set of orders to go to Martinsburg, establish a base there in Berkeley County, and destroy what he could of the B & O railroad. Some might not call that war, but Jackson did the best he could. He liberated four locomotives and decided they could be of some use down in Winchester. Small problem, though. Tracks were busted along the circuitous route. Well, Jackson decided, they would be drawn there by teams of horses. And they were, those iron monsters, inch by inch by horses. While the animals strained and lathered, soldiers cursed and heehawed and leaped for safety when the booty leaned. Jackson had other engines pushed into the Opequon River, splashing as if in a gigantic bathtub. His men wrecked rails and lighted bonfires with Union supplies. Destroying goods didn't exactly cheer Jackson up. But he followed orders. And he hoped that the Federals would make just one move, would come to claim their property in Virginia—and fight. But still Patterson kept crossing and recrossing the Potomac at Williamsport, like a traveler unsure of road signs.

Jackson moved his troops four miles north of the town after wrecking the landscape at Martinsburg. Many of the farmers and shopkeepers of Berkeley County, Virginia, weren't as enthralled by these military maneuvers as Jackson wished. His superiors back in Winchester and Richmond might be pleased in time by his spunk, but these civilians were getting a little sullen in the midst of galloping whooping cavaliers and the sight of decimated rails and trains. Some even let it be known that leaving the Union might not be the best idea in the world. Why secede? What would it accomplish except desolation? These folks whom Jackson came to protect were not showing loyalty to their own. That was another depressing aspect of this early moment in the war.

Jackson slept outdoors during this early part of summer, 1861, when troops moved and lines were being drawn up. He got away from civilization, all its subtle rules and overt restrictions. This born-and-bred hypochondriac went to sleep under the stars, flat out on hard damp ground, near dying embers, as horses neighed and soldiers talked and laughed softly. His health problems vanished; he never felt better. He lived mainly on skillet-fried cornbread. It came steaming to him—broken apart by his hands, fed to his face by fingers, warm when it reached his gullet. No tablecloth, menu, or time to mull over diet. If only he could get at those people who were crossing and recrossing the Potomac.

At last Patterson decided to move. He crossed the Potomac at 4:00 A.M., before sunrise, and kept on going. He put over 10,000 men on the road to Martinsburg. Patterson decided, what the hell, he was just going down there a little farther and see what might happen. His soldiers trampled down the road, muskets over shoulders, billowing dust in their wake. They weren't that enthusiastic; they weren't freeing their own land or encountering their own people. And they didn't know what to expect.

Jackson got word from Jeb Stuart of this specter moving south. Stuart and Ashby had been galloping over the countryside, as familiar with the terrain as if it were their own backyard. They were scouts on horseback, and from the ridges, their horses snorting and prancing beneath them, they saw the winding trail of enemy soldiers coming toward Jackson's troops. Jackson was moving in his loping fast stride through his camp at 7:30, his aides trotting behind, giving orders. Here was to be his troops' baptism by fire. He sent a regiment of foot soldiers up to greet Patterson along with some artillery under the Reverend Captain Pendleton. They found the foe coming onto farmland in military formation, in a place called Falling Waters. Jackson's men now had a visible enemy, something tangible. But the enemy wore the blue of the Union, the uniform of the old country, and somehow it felt wrong to aim at these familiar strangers.

The Virginians took the high ground, which happened to be a house and barn. A shot rang—and then a volley of them. A huge blue mass pressed forward, and Jackson recognized—his men did, too—that the enemy's number greatly exceeded their own. Jackson realized he was in the process of being outflanked. On this pastureland, Patterson was about to maneuver a regiment or two around Jackson's right to cut off any retreat. He was about to squeeze him up and swallow him whole. Jackson withdrew, setting himself up for a counterpunch, a quick rearguard action. It happened in a matter of minutes. "Fall back, men, through that orchard!"

The Southerners crisscrossed between the trees, nimble and excited, leaping over the blue-clad bodies of the dead. The killing would continue now; Jackson knew it and they knew it. He waited for Patterson's huge swelling army to make a mistake. It did—and a fatal one. Patterson's army pursued Jackson by the road, in military formation. When a traffic jam developed, Jackson counterattacked. He gave word that the Reverend Captain Pendleton should unload. And that he did. he had named his guns Matthew, Mark, Luke, and John, and he shouted, "Aim, fire low, and may God have mercy on their souls!"

Jackson now withdrew slowly, and left a numerically superior Patterson reeling. Patterson staggered into Martinsburg, but would go no farther. He would be very cautious from then on, and the Union began paying attention to Jackson. Jackson had a talent for the fine art of surprise. His method was simple: Know more than your opponent—make him underrate you, shock him and numb him, and then you can whip him. Give everything you've got and then it's up to the Heavenly Father.

In his first Civil War engagement Jackson reported that of his 380 soldiers, only 12 had been wounded and 13 killed or missing. His cavalry had captured 49 Yankees. General Johnston, always as generous to his officers as he was respectful of enemy strength and ability, recommended that the ex-professor be promoted—and Jeb Stuart, too. On July 4, 1861, Jackson got word that he had been made a brigadier general in this new Confederate army. He was in camp at Darksville, down the road from Martinsburg. He could hear the Federals firing in that town, celebrating the Fourth. His own troops did not. A strange feeling, not celebrating the Fourth.

But there was no time for reflection. Events moved too swiftly. General Johnston was roused from bed in the early morning of July 18 and told that the enemy under McDowell was advancing on Manassas. Beauregard was in a panic and calling for Johnston's help. But Johnston had to consider Patterson, who still stood massed in Martinsburg. He had to elude him, slip away unnoticed. Here, as always, Joe Johnston proved competent in retreat. With Jeb Stuart's cavalry as cover he slipped away—Jackson's First Brigade leading the way toward Manassas.

Jackson didn't tell his men where they were going. He had them break camp and hit the road. He kept them at a brisk pace, and after an hour and a half, as the grumbling increased in the ranks, he called a halt. With no preamble he had the following read: "Our gallant army under General Beauregard is now attacked by overwhelming numbers. The commanding general hopes that his troops will step out like men, and make a forced march to save the country." Wild whoops sounded. Hallelujah! They'd make them scamper now for sure. They sang "The Bonnie Blue Flag" and "Dixie" and left the rest of Johnston's army behind.

As darkness fell they came to the Shenandoah River, which was waist deep. They simply raised their muskets over their heads and slogged right through. Old Jack was beside them, waving them on, and they knew better than to straggle. Then they faced Ashby Gap and a hard climb. They'd just finished marching hard on a hot July day and now, after dark, they must scale some landscape. And they did, arriving at the small town of Paris at two in the morning—the other side of the Blue Ridge. They sank in their tracks, not bothering to eat or remove clothing or set up bedrolls. Dabney later wrote that "an officer came to Jackson, reminded him that there were no sentries posted around his bivouac, while the men were all wrapped in sleep, and asked if some should be aroused and a guard set.

"'No,' replied Jackson. 'Let the poor fellows sleep. I will guard the camp myself.'"

At first light Jackson had the brigade up and on the road again, at an even faster clip than before. "Old Jack's mad. He's going to march us to the ocean, boys!"

He took them six miles to the tiny town of Piedmont, where a curious crowd had gathered, many from the countryside, to get a look at these new soldiers. A line of trains now stood on the tracks of this depot town, all fired up, hissing steam, ready to roll. It was a straight thirty-four miles from Piedmont to Manassas, and the First Brigade became the first of Johnston's troops to board the freight cars for the rendezvous there. The troops were now overwhelmed with flowers, food, backslaps—cheers and happy shrieks rending the air.

It was as if they were off for a holiday in Manassas, and not going to war.

On Henry Hill Brigadier General Barnard Bee rallied his men to stand behind Jackson and stop the Federal advance—and thus went into the history books. Bee was a tall man, handsome, jovial in private, a West Pointer, ambitious, intelligent, solid and brave—and he was shot on the spot and dead in a moment. Throughout the war death would strike randomly in this way, altering the outcome immeasurably. Bee at Gettysburg? Bee at Chancellorsville? We'll never know. Jackson himself never speculated. He quoted Scripture, that "all works together for those who loved the Lord." You went to meet your Maker at His discretion. The Presbyterian said that the Heavenly Father took care of things. One acted to fulfill the Lord's wishes—and the Lord favored Him who loved Him most.

Bee fell, and Stonewall Jackson rode up and down his line, in full view of the enemy, saying, "Steady, men, steady. Reserve your fire, reserve your fire! Wait," he said, "until they come within fifty yards, then fire into them and give them the bayonet." He gave another command, almost as an afterthought, and why he gave it no one knows. The result entered Southern folklore. He said: "When you charge, yell like furies!"

The tip of 18,000 Federals advanced, firm in the sway of their beliefs, certain of their superior firepower, confident in the wisdom of those who had brought them here. Jackson's brigade fired and ran forward, yelling, as one later reported, "like 3,000 foxhunters closing on a quarry."

The shrieking, high-pitched, near-insane yell transcended the exploding arsenals. It rose spookily above the shattering din, and then out of gray wispy smoke, through the streaks of sun, came the Rebels with cold steel attached to their muskets. They struck the center of the Federal line and it reeled. Years and years later, when these hell-for-leather chargers had become elderly, they tried to recall the yell. What had it actually been? They had trouble. With no heart-stopping fight, with old lungs and faint breath, these ancient Rebels yelled as best they could in a kind of squeak; their brethren said, "That's like it, but it's not quite *it.*"

Jackson raised his left hand and took a molten fragment of shrapnel in his middle finger. A red-hot shell fragment caught a piece of his tunic and burned right through it. A few inches over and Jackson would have joined Bee. A stern medical man outside a tented aid station held Jackson's hand palm up, saw blood squirt, and said crisply, "We must take this finger off immediately, sir. Please go in and prepare for surgery."

"Just bandage it."

"Sir, that's against my medical advice."

"Then I'll get another opinion from Doctor McGuire. Bandage it."

He galloped back on Little Sorrel, who had taken a piece of

iron in the thigh himself. The Federals fell back. From the charge of the First Brigade, they began moving back on their heels, first one, then another, breaking into a run for the rear. Slinging aside rifles, dropping flags, flinging past fellow soldiers. They soon became a massed blue mob, leaping into Bull Run, coming out running. The congressmen and Washington elite, their ladies, the sutlers, fancy women, journalists, drifters on the far hills saw their army racing their way. Like a wave. They broke themselves, carriages and victories overturning, picnic baskets trampled on, clothing torn, bottles broken, screams. Unbelievable! Couldn't happen! This was supposed to be the first stop before Richmond. More than one Federal believed it had been a sellout. "They fixed this! The bigwigs have done us in! Betrayal!"

Ninety-day volunteers, the heart of this army, said they had seen enough of war. This was it. No more. "Turn back! Turn back!" the fleeing soldiers yelled to civilians paralyzed by fear. "Leave, leave! We are whipped!"

U.S. officers waved sabers and tried to halt the rout. Confederate Private John Opie noted: ". . . regardless of the threats and expostulations of their officers, they broke ranks, and—many of them divesting themselves of all impedimenta, such as guns, canteens, and cartridge belts—all sought safety in flight." Those who tarried, who tried to make a stand, were swallowed by the long gray line and captured. Congressman Alfred Ely from New York didn't run and was captured. He was caught, shivering behind a tree. By the time he was locked up in a warehouse in Richmond he still hadn't warmed up and was complaining of extreme chill. President Jefferson Davis of the new Confederate States of America sent him two wool blankets. No long before, Jefferson Davis had been a U.S. senator.

A tired, incredulous band made it back to Washington. Some stopped off in grog shops along the turnpike. They drank and talked and swore. Some embellished what they had seen; others couldn't talk but steadily pulled on a bottle. The Southerners— themselves exhausted, unsure of the extent of what they had done—picked over the litter of booty left behind. As night fell they couldn't be organized. Their officers lifted flasks or sat down in their tracks or bathed their faces in the muddy Bull Run and had nothing left in them. They were too tired even to celebrate properly. The pitiful moans and pleas from the bloody, body-strewn field demanded what little attention they had left. Out of 3,000 men Jackson had sent into battle, 111 lay dead and several more whimpered on the ground in pain. Still, Jackson sensed what others only glimpsed and were too exhausted to act upon: McDowell was thoroughly beaten and there was no Federal defense between Manassas and the U.S. capital. He could end the war. The war was over if they acted now. The path opened to Washington. He said to Beauregard, to Johnston, to Stuart, to all who could move—"Let me take my brigade and I'll be in Washington tonight. We'll take the White House. We'll end it all and have no more bloodshed."

Was he crazy, as some said? Hadn't he had enough by now? They said, no. No, sirree. Everybody's too beat. Let me just lie down on this grass and catch a little sleep.

Night fell and day broke. Rumors and reports spread back into the hinterlands, to Richmond and Charleston. The homefolk were so thirsty for news, to know what had happened on that faroff battlefield and who the heroes had been and what had been pivotal. In South Carolina the report came about the brave Palmetto regiment under the gallant Barnard Bee, his lines concerning the Virginian Jackson, and Bee's death. In Richmond Johnston and Beauregard were made heroes. Down in Lexington they awaited word, too. News came in letters from the boys at the front, and large crowds developed around the post office when mail sacks arrived by stage. The good Reverend Doctor White was thus handed a letter from Manassas and saw immediately from the scrawl who its author was. He shouted, holding the letter aloft. "Here, at last, we have the truth! We'll have all the facts now!"

The townsfolk pressed near. The letter was dated the day after the battle, after the South had won its victory. "My dear pastor, in my tent last night, after a fatiguing day's service, I remembered that I had failed to send you my contribution for our colored Sunday School. Enclosed you will find my check for that object, which please acknowledge at your earliest convenience, and oblige yours faithfully, T. J. Jackson."

CHAPTER VII

After the Battle Is Over . . .

So the Southerners had won. But they did not press forward. The wounded cried through the night, and the dead began to emit a sweetish-sour stench. Where the odor had been honeysuckle, it was now that of putrid flesh and decaying limbs. Only Jackson had the heart to press forward. The others sank down, too bushed to move. They were at Manassas, at camp, no enemy to engage—and they soon began to fret. They were young, unformed, and wanted what the young have always wanted: a chance at the other sex, a chance to frolic, and the prospect of avoiding unpleasantness.

The stream that went by their campsite at Manassas Junction began to taste peculiar. They hesitated to jump in and splash about on the hot humid days of late July. A freckle-faced soldier in the 5th Virginia cupped his hands, drew water to his lips, then immediately spat it out. "It's like the dead," he said. "This tastes like those old dead bodies."

They called it Camp Maggot. Typhoid spread, and nearly all had bouts of dysentery. Supplies weren't coming from Richmond as expected, and the bitching increased and swelled. All armies, victor and vanquished alike, want the necessities taken care of.

The belly ached, the bowels rebelled, and the soldiers cursed. Why was nothing happening? Jackson gave them artillery and rifle drills, made them police the area, and kept military order. And he sent Quartermaster Harman to the countryside to find a new campsite. Harman's nose led him straight to a sympathetic farmer named Utterbach a few miles away toward Washington, in Centreville, and he got permission to camp on his ground. The water was clear, unsullied, and there was no more sight of maggots in dead flesh. But with the wind just right a whiff from the battlefield came their way. No matter how hard it rained, no matter the number of dead buried, the scent wouldn't leave.

Fresh tents went up, and the soldiers were paid. The men ate fresh eggs, washed their bodies, and drank hot coffee. And wanted to pack their rucksacks and go home on leave. There was no fighting, was there? What was wrong in taking a few days off? Many had homes no more than a day's walking distance. No, Jackson made clear, no furloughs except for emergencies—and, frankly, no one could come up with an emergency that would satisfy the professor. Anna implored him to take off himself on a little visit to North Carolina, but he wrote, "I ought to not see my *esposita,* as it might make the troops feel that they were badly treated, and that I consult my own pleasure and comfort regardless of theirs."

He turned down a major who had news of a death in the family and another close at hand. His heart went out to the man, but he wrote that "human aid cannot heal the wound. . . . [W]e must think of the living and of those who are to come after us, and see that, with God's blessing, we transmit to them the freedom we have enjoyed. What is life without honor? Degradation is worse than death. It is necessary that you should be at your post immediately. Join me tomorrow morning." And signed it not as his commanding officer but as "your sympathizing friend, T. J. Jackson."

Anna could not be stilled, though. Bright, plucky, with one of those Southern faces that seems ready to jump off the page of an old photograph, she was young and had a sparkle in her eye—fun-loving, teasing, more than a mite mischievous. She let Tom know that sister Sue's husband had come home on leave. All the boys were coming home for visits. No one was fighting and maybe wouldn't again since the Yankees had been thrashed up there in Virginia.

Jackson could not hold out against her altogether. He finally said she could come on a visit. So the preacher's daughter, with those lovely coal-black eyes, boarded a train and made a laborious journey to Manassas Station. The cars bumped and jostled through ravines and up valleys, stopping at hamlets, soldiers and sutlers and determined women boarding and unboarding. Anna's eyes were still bright as the train chugged into the far Virginia station. She stepped down the iron steps, the engine's white steam billowing around her, and there was Thomas, as if he hadn't changed one iota. He was driving an army ambulance, the only conveyance he had at hand. Somehow it suited him and he shook the reins and the horses took to a trot and Jackson drove with élan. His troops cheered the couple. The first stop was church services for the First Brigade. And then Jackson took Anna to her quarters in a spare room the Utterbachs had set up. He himself bunked down in a tent in a farmyard not far away.

It was a moment's pause in the grand onrushing of events. Anna became belle of the ball at Camp Harman—as Camp Maggot had been renamed. She adored the attention. Jackson was in love. She sat at table in the Utterbachs' home and Jackson's staff hovered around her. The energy was electric—jokes and lively talk amid the clatter and clink of china and silverware. Candlelight softened the faces. Anna noticed that the staff was so attentive to Thomas, moving quickly to keep up with his fast stride, leaning close to hear his soft words, these men so different apart but all of one mind together. It could have been Caesar and his tribunes in Gaul.

Anna was tough and wouldn't restrict her visit to the chambers and fields of the Utterbach farm. She insisted that she be permitted to view the first major battlefield of the Civil War. Thomas took her over the land, describing where that regiment had stood and where another had faltered. He pointed out the pivotal spots and landmarks of turning points in the battle. Anna gazed at the Henry house, near the spot where the First Brigade had taken its stand. It was blackened and riddled and cracked from shells and minié balls. Thomas took her by the small stream that meandered through the land: the Bull Run. Anna wrinkled her nose and seemed perplexed for the moment. "What is that odor?" she said. "It's so unusual."

It was faint and came on the heels of a soft breeze. It was the dead, the aftermath that couldn't quite be put away, still calling out.

At night she and Thomas stood outside the Utterbach farmhouse that hadn't been touched by the war. Years later, when Anna was a slight, stooped old woman, living in North Carolina, she could still recall the campfires of the soldiers in the First Brigade on the Utterbach farm. They flickered in the starry night; the young soldiers laughed easily in the evening air, and songs were sung. A whole panorama was set out before her—cheerful, strong, optimistic, almost celebratory. In the morning she boarded a train and began her long drawn-out trip home. She had seen Thomas and she had seen Manassas.

Jackson had innumerable cares. A surprising one came via his old university, V.M.I. The governing body, called by the interesting title of the Board of Visitors, wanted Professor Jackson back to teach. In this moment of tremendous peril, on the brink of a cataclysmic conflict and the country's costliest war, when the fabric of life was on the verge of being torn and shredded, with but Jackson and his peculiar genius guarding the gateway to their homes and beings, this academic governing body brought up the subject of tenure. Not mortal danger, catastrophe, or history's sweep could stay these academics from their appointed rounds. Or perhaps they believed Professor Jackson had sent the Yankees packing and could now return to the lectern. The Institute implied that if Stonewall Jackson did not return, there was the possibility that he might be dropped from the rolls. Nothing certain—just might be, his tenure lifted.

The polite message struck more terror in the heart of the professor than a score of minié balls flying over his head. He knew the sweetness of the academic life, and part of what he was defending was that, for himself. He didn't want to lose his chair in natural and experimental philosophy and the instructorship in artillery tactics. The bravest of policemen, the most fearless firefighter usually quakes at the thought of losing bureaucratic status and all the juicy perks. He wrote the board that he took to the field only from a sense of duty. "At the close of hostilities, I desire to resume the duties of my chair, and accordingly respectfully request that if consistent with the interests of the Institute, that the action of the Board of Visitors may be such as to admit of my return upon the restoration of peace."

He was finally granted leave from V.M.I. for the duration of the war. All of Lexington was becoming aware of the exploits of the professor. He had a new name now, Stonewall. And those country boys he had rounded up from all over the Shenandoah were part of something called the Stonewall Brigade. One of their own, doing such glorious deeds. The *Lexington Gazette* printed his exploits and parlor conversation wasn't complete unless there was some mention of how those Virginia boys beat back those ignorant maniacal savages from the North, all under the cool command of the professor—now their Stonewall. He became the star of the battlefield. Gifts and fan mail poured into his camp.

Jackson kept to his Puritan ways and became more inward. When you triumph, thank the Lord but be prepared for bad times which invariably follow. The Reverend Dr. White couldn't restrain himself any longer down in Lexington and journeyed to Jackson's camp near Manassas. He came for a day and ended up staying four. He found that his ex-deacon was holding evening and morning devotionals for his troops in the field, and that the good man carried in his field equipment a prayer book, prayer table, and a fine brass bell for calling his troops to worship. One prayer he heard by Jackson he said he would never forget as long as he lived. In a near trance Jackson prayed for Dr. White, the citizenry of Lexington, the pastor's family and flock, and prayed that all lost souls would be brought home to worship God. He pleaded that the Holy Spirit would baptize the whole army! What an army we would have then! Dr. White and Jackson talked in the general's tent until midnight.

But now the Yankees, who had smarted from the humiliation at Bull Run, began to pressure Virginia again—this time around from the west, from Romney, a short distance from Winchester. No more congressional delegations in tow, they just gathered a large force and got set to punish these crazed Rebels.

Romney and Winchester led into the heart of the Shenandoah, a breathtaking land, then and today. It rests in fertile splendor between the Allegheny Mountains to the west and the Blue

Ridge to the east. It is but 30 miles wide in most parts and extends 165 miles from Winchester in the north to near Lexington below. One peculiarity: The Valley slopes downward as it moves *north-ward;* hence, its streams flow north and natives say they're going down the Valley when actually traveling north. The Valley seems removed in other ways from usual standards. It is as if nature had simply parted mountains and proclaimed it blessed. It has hot springs to soothe the body's aches and clear limestone water to slake thirst. Its horses and cattle become sleek and fat and its orchards and grain burst with ripeness.

From the beginning the Valley was the breadbasket for who-ever held its terrain. Indians called it "Daughter of the Stars"; early Virginians saw an almost mystical quality in it; the desper-ate Confederacy depended upon it to feed a new nation; and the North saw it as a perfect corridor into the South, whose fields could supply all a vast army might need. Virginians and certain Tennessee supporters from the mountains below felt that this verdant basin, overflowing with grain and livestock and soul-satisfying scenery, was as necessary to preserve and safeguard as life itself. The North wanted it scorched and occupied in order to take the fight out of this fanatical foe. A stake must be driven through its heart. General Philip Sheridan was just the man to do this, and eventually he did with grand brutal authority—but not before General Stonewall Jackson had his say.

After Manassas the First Brigade was called, often as not, the Stonewall. They were veterans, whom no one could pull a trick on—and then General Johnston was named overall commander of the Northern Virginia forces and Jackson chosen to protect of the vital Shenandoah Valley. Johnston had a loose theater of operation; Jackson's terrain was specific and threatened.

Judah Benjamin, secretary of war in the new Confederacy and certainly no fast friend of Jackson's (Jackson had bristled at some of Benjamin's prior orders), favored the professor for this assignment. Benjamin was a Jew, a skilled lawyer from the plan-tation country of New Orleans. His ample girth, as displayed in old tintypes, was all too typical of the time; his graceful, although slightly rococo prose, stood out, too, but was not exceptional. He had gathered high honors—U.S. senator, a high post in the Con-federacy, wealth as a cotton planter, cleverness as a lawyer. Most important, he now held the high unwavering respect of Jefferson Davis. But what really set him apart from others was his uncanny ability to survive, a trait he shared with Jackson. No one could ever count him out. He stayed loyal to the Confederacy until the end, remaining beside President Davis in his hallucinatory, nomadic final days—but when absolute defeat came, Judah Benjamin escaped. He fled to Florida and the West Indies, and sailed across the Atlantic to England. He lived to practice law abroad and to write cogent works on legal subjects. Loyal to his wife, he honored her preference for life in the City of Light and is today buried in Paris.

In 1861 he put the faith of the Confederacy in the professor, the hero of Manassas, and saw to it that Jackson was made a brevet major general. He gave Jackson command of the Shenandoah, but he gave him no men to back him up. The professor would have to rustle up a force from volunteers in the Valley and any militia that might still be around in Winchester.

Now Jackson must say farewell to his brigade, which he thought (erroneously) he was leaving forever. The Stonewall Brigade had orders from Richmond to stand guard at Manassas Junction while its recently elevated general was off to new headquarters in Winchester. On the clear frosty morning of November 4, 1861, the brigade stood in close ranks at attention in a grassy clearing bordered by a red-tinted autumn forest, not far from Bull Run. They said nothing, were uneasy. Torn and soiled battle flags, reminders of the horrible battle of Manassas, caught the slight breeze and whipped about. What now? Nothing was ever done right in this blamed army. They were going to take Old Blue Light away. The only sound came from the birds and the whipping flags. They had come here in hot scorching July and now there was frost on the pumpkin. They had made them Yankees hightail it out of there. They had stuck together, followed this strange man into the jaws of hell, and he had brought them out alive. Now what?

There was noise near the woods, and then Jackson rode before them on Little Sorrel, not unlike a circus performer coming before the stands. He wore a faded tunic, left over from the Mexican War, and the visor of his weather-beaten cadet hat was pulled far down on his forehead so that, as usual, he had to lift his face in order to see in front of him. Little Sorrel gave an imitation of a war-horse in his awkward gait. Jackson sat awkwardly, too, leaning forward into the wind, legs akimbo like Don Quixote. No one could miss his enormous feet in the shortened stirrups, clad in floppy-topped boots that seemed big enough for two men. Old Blue Light wasn't your ordinary commander. Now what?

No sound, except the flags whipping. Jackson took off his cap and looked about with his blue eyes, which were feverish now. "Officers and men of the First Brigade, I am not here to make a speech but simply to say farewell." They had been through Harpers Ferry in quick exhausting marches and over the bloody plains of Manassas together—and now they must part. "I shall look with great anxiety to your future movements, and I trust whenever I shall hear of the First Brigade on the field of battle it will be of still nobler deeds achieved and higher reputation won."

The flags snapped in the breeze some more, and their strange general grew quiet. Was he finished? Little Sorrel shied, and Jackson reined him in. Suddenly, then, Jackson stood in the stirrups, going up and up. His look became even more intense. Whether he thought he saw the future, we do not know—or if he thought the major fighting had been completed. He lifted his left gauntleted hand, like a minister of the Lord, and with the passion that usually stayed buried within, said in his sharp, high-pitched voice, "In the army of the Shenandoah you were the First Brigade, in the army of the Potomac you were the First Brigade; in the second corps of this army you are the First Brigade; you are the First Brigade in the affections of your General; and I hope by your future deeds and bearing you will be handed down to posterity as the First Brigade in our second War of Independence. Farewell!"

He gently settled back in the saddle. He looked pensive and his soldiers wondered if there might be something further. But, no, he gathered the reins slowly and turned Little Sorrel's head to leave. One man whooped, then another. All then broke a barrier and a wild, screaming clamor swelled through the clearing. Jackson uncharacteristically let his emotions go unchecked and began waving his old cap. He galloped away from his troops who were now in a full Rebel yell, the battle cry that Jackson called "The sweetest music I have ever heard." He rode away, to his tent, to the depot to start his journey to his new command, the noise still ringing.

All were mightily moved. It became, though none knew it at the time, the one and only speech Jackson ever made to his troops. It was the lone time he let his iron guard down in full view of his men. The cavalier Kyd Douglas, moved by the emotional leave-taking, retired to his tent and began writing out the speech. "War correspondents" were hardly ever allowed within miles of Jackson's command; there was no one to let the future know exactly what his actual words had been. Jackson prized secrecy in all matters; a reporter showed up one day, lasted twenty-four hours, left. Now Kyd Douglas wrote out the speech for posterity with a Sergeant Towner leaning over his shoulder to help with a word or two. "There," Kyd Douglas said, "we have it!"

The speech changed in the pens of others. Kyd Douglas was there and gave his version. Dabney consulted others and gave his. Anna Jackson wrote in her memoirs what she thought her husband had said. Colonel G.F.R. Henderson, an Englishman, wrote what many consider the definitive life of Jackson, *Stonewall Jackson and the American Civil War*. There are thirty-one differences between the Douglas and Henderson versions of the speech. The dialogues of war may be reflected, like the battles themselves, in individual memory. The Duke of Wellington thought that battles, if not history itself, could never be recalled with total accuracy. He compared the past to a grand ball, where everyone in attendance sees but little moments, and all have different reactions and never the definitive picture.

Jackson got to Winchester, fretted, grew homesick for his old brigade, beseeched Benjamin—and a month after his eloquent farewell, the Stonewall Brigade was back in harness with him as if nothing had happened.

Jackson had reached Winchester in a mad dash, accompanied by Maggie Junkin's husband, Colonel Preston, and an aide, twenty-one-year-old Lieutenant Sandie Pendleton, the son of the pastor. In peace, Jackson married preachers' daughters; in war, he took their sons as aides. Increasingly he relied more and more on

young Pendleton, the kind of Southerner who gives his region a
special enviable character in the eyes of some. From old pictures
he seems to have a distinct English face, the kind one sees in
Holbein's sketches of King Henry VIII's court. It's a bright, handsome, fair face, relieved from being pretty by a slight degree of
the pug in it. He was smart, alive, daring—but appreciated his
traditions. He had entered Washington College at age thirteen
and before he was let out, as a teenager, had instructed some
classes.

The general and his two companions reached Strasburg, the
last rail stop, late on a cold windy night. It was still many more
miles to headquarters at Winchester. The trip had been fatiguing,
nerves were raw, the bouncing and train smoke still impinging
their consciousness. The two aides suggested a few winks, then
an early morning start. Jackson, as always, thought they should
press on. They pressed on, saddling horses, galloping away. Jackson took over the command at Winchester on the morning of
November 4, 1861.

Winchester was the first city of the Valley. It was founded
in 1743 by an Englishman, and British influence is felt to this day:
Streets have names such as Piccadilly, Loudoun, Kent, and Cort.
In the old days it had a whipping post and ducking stool in front
of the courthouse. The stool was, in fact, a broad plank on which
a minor offender was strapped and then dunked into none too
fresh water in a stone-lined pit. In and out went town drunks and
"unruly" females. The stool afforded a practical solution for the
problems of society with the added benefit of a spectator sport.
George Washington spent some ten years of his early career in
Winchester, as a sixteen-year-old surveyor for Lord Halifax and
then as an officer in the Virginia Militia during the French and
Indian Wars. When those Frenchmen in the Ohio Valley began
pressing toward the bounty of the Shenandoah, with help from
the Indians, they assaulted the colonial village of Winchester.
Jackson, in effect, had the assignment Colonel Washington had
had about one hundred years earlier: to protect Virginia's fertile
plain.

The boys and men of the Valley were direct descendants of
those who had fought in the Revolution and had stood with
Washington. Now, once again, outsiders were pressing on toward

their Valley. To most of them, Fort Sumter was way off somewhere, terra incognita. They'd never seen the ocean, most of
them, and a fortification on an ocean's bay was farfetched, mythi-
cal. Forget who started the whole shooting match—it was all
confused, even among the best of minds. These men and boys
knew for a fact that they hadn't started it. Hell, they'd just been
tending the farm. It was the other side who was picking this fight.
God damn it, it was so. For as long as they could remember all
they'd ever wanted was to be left alone. Forget slavery and the
other side saying it was wrong. It was wrong, bad, and, worse,
who had enough money or enough food to go around to own a
slave anyhow? Free them somehow, work things out, but no
matter what anybody did and no matter what anybody thought,
niggers were going to remain around—like the sun, moon, and
stars. They were going to stay right here no matter what an
abolitionist said in Boston. You did the best you could. What
riled a Valley man, really got to his marrow, was an *outsider* trying
to impose his will on him. Talk about gall. And so righteous to
boot. Imagine those abolitionists, safe and sound and full of
chowder or whatever they put in their gullet, making a saint out
of a murderer like John Brown. That did it, that wrapped it up
for a lot of Virginians. Here was a lunatic who had tried to take
over a whole town at the end of a gun—and cause the niggers to
kill folks in their beds. Make him a saint. Robert E. Lee and T.
J. Jackson had seen John Brown, firsthand, at Harpers Ferry.

    And when the Federals placed a foot on Virginia soil they
necessarily had to shoot a few people to get them out of the way
and then real deep-down hatred came—for dead bodies are not
abstractions, nor ideas, nor debates. Dead bodies are mourned by
loved ones. Colonel Turner Ashby, Jackson's "eyes and ears" as
a cavalry scout, had a younger brother, Captain Richard Ashby.
On a forage the younger Ashby got trapped by Federals. As he
tried to escape, he came against a B & O railway abutment and
could go no farther. As he fell and lay beneath his horse's jumping hoofs the enemy encircled him. The Federals drew arms. He
asked to be spared, the report goes. Don't kill me, I give up, I give
up! They killed him. As he lay under his horse, begging for his
life. Turner Ashby rode up, ran the Federal skirmishers off, and
cradled his brother's head. He heard the pained intake of Rich-

ard's last breath, and he was never the same again. With a handful of troopers he went after the skirmishers. They had plunged into a river and were holed up on a midstream island. Ashby plunged in after them and, with bullets whistling, he killed as many as he could and took the rest prisoner. The enemy considered him insane.

He was only comfortable now at the front, wherever that might be. Heroic tales about him abounded. One described him seated outside his tent, wiping off knife and fork to commence a bacon-and-egg breakfast, when fire heated up around him. He sat in the center of a barrage. He continued eating. "Good Lord, Colonel, fall back! All hell's broke loose!"

"No, thanks. I'm too hungry." And he ate; then returned fire and went on the offensive.

He could barely write. He had no military training and knew not an enfilade from grapeshot. But he sat straight on his handsome white horse as if nailed in the saddle. His gaudy invented costumes made him look increasingly like a Turkish pasha. He drew like-minded men to his command, free spirits with no regard for discipline. If there was a fight, they fought. If not, they went home and did chores and hung out. Before the war these young men, stimulated by the novels of Sir Walter Scott, had held medieval jousting contests. Ashby, who couldn't read the novels, loved the idea of tournaments and had entered one as an Indian in loincloth. He rode Indian-style, bareback without saddle or bridle—and won. Now he was fighting and scouting for the odd professor, and he made up his own orders as often as he followed those of others. Jackson understood that this was the way Ashby operated—the only way, in fact—and made allowances.

Nearly all of Jackson's troops were young, hot-blooded, and an inch away from chaos. In garrison there was always trouble, especially with the Stonewall Brigade. Coming from glorious Manassas, champions, the euphoric wash of Jackson's "Farewell" still ringing in their ears, they camped four miles from Winchester. Jackson wanted to instill discipline that would carry over to the battlefield. He wanted reveille, drill, hardtack, and picketing. These boys wanted women. They wanted women with the thirst of parched lips for cool water. They wanted to hear the rustle of crinoline; they wanted songs; they wanted to be treated as what they had been told they were: Heroes of Manassas. What they got was mumps, fever, and diphtheria. The late fall winds ripped their tents and flung aside supports. It was miserably wet, muddy, and forlorn. The militia got to garrison in lovely Winchester. Winchester was made off-limits to the brigade by orders of Old Jack.

Pranks commenced, reminiscent of V.M.I. days. An eighteen-year-old private, in the 5th Virginia, had been in college just the past spring, worrying over the intricacies of geometry, smelling honeysuckle out the window, yearning for blessed relief. He had thought of war as vacation. Maybe he'd meet a girl. Bivouacked outside Winchester, half frozen, stomach growling, watching the twinkling firelight from the town far below, he decided to free-lance. He eavesdropped on a guard post and learned the password. Then he drew an officer's insignia on his shoulders with chalk, and got past the sentry. In Winchester there were girls, girls, girls—and he had outfoxed Old Jack.

Jackson himself was aware of the women now around and near his soldiers. They were like liquor and prized gold, mysterious and bewitching. At night, riding beside an aide, weary from checking sentries, he pulled on his reins. The young aide waited. Soldiers often passed along their deeper thoughts at night among themselves when no shot rang and no quick march was needed. "Tell me, Captain," General Jackson said. "What do you . . . think about the ladies of Winchester?"

The aide began running answers through his head. The general was looking off toward the stars. The aide didn't quite know what to answer. The ladies of Winchester were sure juicy-looking, that he knew. Thomas J. Jackson said, "Well, that's why we're fighting this war, you know."

"How's that, sir?"

"To keep them just the way they are."

His own boys were now the ones penetrating the protecting line around these females. Once in Winchester, after various guises to gain admittance, the youngsters fanned out for the spoils. Guards, Stonewall, God Himself couldn't keep them out.

Winchester homes had permanent meals spread on tables—always there. When a soldier appeared, with no preamble, he ate. Bees were held; there were dances every night.

The troops assaulted Old Jack's strictures against liquor. He ordered it should be taken for medicinal purposes only. You got a drink only after you got a doctor's prescription and that endorsed by both the regimental colonel and the brigade commander. Nothing to it. A man just forged some signatures, made up an illegible prescription, and ordered up in the first tavern he came to. There were several grog shops in lovely old Winchester. This order against imbibing spirits was broken right down the line, from officer to private. The officers of a company of 5th Virginia secured three kegs of rye and had a rip-roaring party. They swigged it down from tin cups, and hoots and broken song made their headquarters tent shake. Soon enlisted men in the company heard the commotion, diagnosed the cause, and decided they'd have some of that stuff too, by gum. They pulled up the back tent pins, rolled out a keg while the officers were bouncing off each other, and filled two tin buckets with the rich amber liquor. Then they drove the tent pins back in and polished off the bucket by their campfire. In the morning a company of 5th Virginia woke not sure where it was. Someone had climbed a tall tree the night before, and there now, from the tallest branch, swung the regimental colors, which only that past summer had led the charge at Manassas.

It was terribly hard corralling this wild unruly pack of country boys. Many were blood-related and didn't want to be ordered around by a third cousin who might have been elected an officer. Company officers were chosen by vote. If someone took a violent dislike to a neighbor who had won the vote to become a captain, this newly minted officer might find himself shot. But these Valley men, young as sin, randy, thirsty, filled with hell-raisers, began to move out under the exotic professor in one of the greatest military campaigns in American history.

CHAPTER VIII

In the Valley
of the Shadow of Death

At nearly every stage of Jackson's career, the projects he undertook offered difficulties that would have paralyzed most mortals. Now he wanted to move against Romney, a sleepy little village west of Winchester, in the hands at present of the Federals. He needed help. He let Secretary of War Benjamin know that he could use the services of some of the new Confederate Army under Brigadier General William W. Loring. Loring had but one arm; he had left the other in Mexico at Chapultepec. He had been at the business of soldiering since he volunteered as a boy down in Florida to fight the Seminoles in the 1830s. At the start of this conflict he had witnessed Robert E. Lee fail miserably in the mountain campaign in the Northwest. Lee had been relieved and was now in Richmond, digging ditches and getting the nickname Granny Lee because he was perceived as being a little too fussy. Loring had his old command in the Northwest, and he proved to be too cautious. Losing an arm can make a man leery of losing the other one. He had seen a lot and didn't want to rush men hither and yon at the capriciousness of that fool Jackson. He let headquarters know that it would take two or three weeks before he could get his troops ready.

But Jackson was impatient. If he couldn't attack Romney at present, then he'd take his collection of Valley boys and stir up some mischief elsewhere. At 4:00 A.M. on a cold December 16 he had his troops roused and, after quick breakfast, had them on the road. He did not tell them where they were going or the purpose. They could have been going to drop off the edge of the earth for all they knew. Still, they marched. A private from New Market saw a peculiar sight. He shook his head and elbowed the soldier beside him. "Is that what I think it is?"

"It's a boat, sure thing. Those are flatboats those men are toting. You think we been transferred to the navy?"

"Far as I know, not."

"You think the general's crazy?"

"Seems so."

The men reached the Chesapeake and Ohio Canal that snaked beside the Potomac along the Maryland line and now realized why they had carried the boats. Here was water. Jackson thought he just might bash some holes in dam number five and thus wreck traffic on the C & O. Yankee coal now came down the canal bound for Washington. Stoves in the Federal capital were burning hotly thanks to this canal and the dams that regulated its depth. The canal had taken twenty-two years to make, had cost a whopping $22 million and had required the labor of six thousand men. Jackson wanted to put it out of business in twenty-four hours. Wreck, tear holes in its heart, let the devils freeze in Washington! Carry the fight to them!

As darkness fell on the seventeenth, Jackson dispatched an unlikely crew to steal down to the water and put a screen of brushes around dam number five—camouflage it. The crew were Irishmen, navvies from the 27th Virginia, from New Market. Most had the pale skin, the hearty manner, the wit of their forebears from the Old Sod. It was best to keep them together, pure and unadulterated. On this bitterly cold night the Irishmen crept down and worked until the first rays of dawn. Then they crawled back up the bank to the protected camp. Why hadn't Jackson simply shelled the dam with artillery and been done with it? The truth was he had no ammunition for bombardment. He had to keep in reserve what little he had for defense in case the

Federals, on the opposite bank of the Potomac, discovered the mischief and opened fire.

Jackson had ordered complete silence in camp, no bonfires, no movement, the stillness of braves on the warpath. And with the stealth of second-story burglars, the Irishmen did their jobs, and a series of miraculous bushes sprouted around the dam. By perverse luck, the Federals didn't spot the phoniness of the bushes but noted some real Rebels on a far hilltop. They had shells to spare, and they opened up a full-throttled hello. Ka-boom, ka-boom, ka-boom! Trees split and shells whined. One private from the Shenandoah, a farm boy, had volunteered a few days before for service in a horse battery, and now—no warning—he was in the pit of hell. Like many of his fellow sufferers he would later look back on the misery and terror and hopelessness with a certain comic spirit. He survived and wrote in his diary, "I laid so close to the ground that it seemed to me I flattened out a little, yearning for a leave of absence."

Make do, keep trying, improvise! Once action has started, keep moving and keep your head. No panic! Jackson called in the artillery he had kept in reserve for just such a moment. The celebrated Rockbridge Artillery had on its roster thirty-five college graduates, seven with master's degrees, and twenty-five theology students. They were committed to a fight to the finish and to Jesus Christ as their Savior. No matter what their spirits said, their visceral reaction was to squirm under the seemingly unlimited hurricane of Federal shells. Men danced from the cover of one pine tree to another, trying to get organized, trying to get to their guns. Jackson stood in the center, barking orders, coaxing gunners to man their pieces. The fire of the enemy rained down. Occasionally even Jackson ducked. Only one man did not: diminutive, feather-hatted Turner Ashby. He strolled about, dirt flying from landing shells, with his arms folded over his chest. As Jackson and Ashby got the guns in place and set to fire, the Federals, believing they had blown whoever it was over there off the map, ceased fire. Jackson decided not to open up. Save shells for later.

That night, numb from the cold and getting no relief from a campfire (none permitted), a fatigue party slithered down to the dam once more. Jackson was already miraculously down there—

the ex-deacon handing out crowbars, axes, and picks. Arms could hardly move, hands could barely grip the handles. Jackson had the ultimate surprise waiting: a keg of whiskey. The Sunday-school teacher who preached temperance was ladling out a cupful for each man. The only way to warm them up. He didn't trust any other soul with the ladle. The fortified men leaped to the job and began swinging their axes and picks like furies.

There were now volunteers in line for the next night—but it was not to be. The Federals opened up again on the Virginians, just to keep their hand in, and torched a mill near the dam. Its blaze meant a wrecking crew would not have the cover of darkness, and so Jackson had to think again. He feinted an attack upriver to draw the Federals out of position. He had the flatboats lifted on high and out in the open for all to see—and then marched a decoy troop off up the riverbank as if getting ready to *invade.* Make them think Stonewall was coming! The Federals bit. They left their positions by dam number five and scurried upriver to blast the supposed invasion out of the water. Immediately the 33rd Virginia and the 27th Virginia rushed volunteers into the water, and pickaxes began flying. They stayed hours in the freezing water and when they sloshed out, the dam leaked and the canal was thrown out of kilter. Jackson had done what he could. So what if the holes were filled the next day? Jackson had acted. He marched his men—near frozen, scared, hungry—back to Winchester.

On the way a classic Jacksonian moment took place. He was trotting on Little Sorrel beside his line of troops when he saw a persimmon tree overflowing with fruit. The old Jackson of strange impulsive tastes came back, and he decided he must have some persimmons—now, no delay. He dismounted and climbed the tree, the Commander of the Valley Army. He ate . . . and he ate. Satisfied, full, he started to swing down, and one size 14 boot became entangled with a branch and then an arm got ensnarled by a limb. He tried to go up a bit, then sideways, down. He became more lost in the tree at every attempt at freedom, and finally was captured by it. The tree claimed him. He called for help, and his aides became convulsed with laughter. His aides held him in high affection and could take certain liberties with him from time to time. Such a sight! They brought some rails from a nearby fence and invented a slide for him to drop down. Jackson was on his way to becoming deified by the army, and this tale, told and retold over campfires, became part of the Stonewall legend.

Back in Winchester, bone-weary, two days before Christmas in this first year of the war, Jackson found that Loring was still fiddle-faddling in the movement of troops. He further learned that the Federals now numbered 10,000 at Romney, with more coming each day. Pretty soon this Romney force might decide to strike Winchester, and then what? Jackson's beloved Stonewall Brigade was getting in the spirit of Christmas and losing its taste for battle. Boys wanted to go home, wrap and unwrap presents, have their mothers feed and hug them and make their beds. They'd been drilling and hating Yankees long enough without a holiday. Lord God, this was Christmas! Wasn't Old Blue Light a nut about Christ? Weren't they going to celebrate His birth?

Jackson kept his thoughts, as usual, to himself, but realized he was in a most dangerous situation. If he didn't soon heat up the enemy in Romney and dislodge him from there, he was as much as giving up the lower Shenandoah. It was a road center and would allow the invader to move down from the north and west. They had the troops, the supplies, the equipment. They must be put to flight before getting set. And still Loring grumbled and moved at a snail's pace toward Winchester. He had trouble controlling his troops, but, all too humanly, put the blame on Jackson. Jackson was somehow causing all his troubles. On the way to join Jackson his men had Christmas eggnog thrust into their hands as they clumped by farmhouses and through mountain villages. His men threw aside tents and blankets and let wagons and horses roll off roads and down mountains. Why not? They believed they were going to Winchester to take up snug winter quarters and they got into a wild holiday mood. Many passed out and were lost for the upcoming campaign, if not forever.

The first brigade to reach Winchester was led by Colonel William B. Taliaferro. Taliaferro had Tidewater written all over him; he was secure in his station. In Tidewater Virginia, some refer to Western Virginia as "out there." Other areas in America have their "out theres." Manhattan has its Hoboken across the Hudson; Johnson City, Tennessee, has its Piney Flats ten miles up the road. Taliaferro had served in Mexico and may have encountered Jackson from Western Virginia there. Taliaferro had gone on to serve in the Virginia legislature and had shown a great aptitude for political maneuvering. He knew how to get ahead; he was very smart; and he was brave. An old photograph shows him with stern eyes, dark bushy hair and side whiskers, hat cocked back insouciantly, sword resting on his lap—a hint of the bully.

On the march to Winchester some of his pointless, highly annoying orders ("Display mess kits before and after eating to the Officer of the Day") caused talk among the men that he might be shot before the enemy got him. A free-spirited Georgian, already sick of the military and discovering the lovely escape route of alcohol, heard one too many irrelevant, senseless commands from Taliaferro and beat him suddenly to the ground. Tidewater haughtiness lost its force somewhere west of Richmond. The Georgian sobered up in the guardhouse after the assault, collected his backwoods wit, and scaled a high fence to escape forever into the countryside, lost to the Cause.

Stonewall Jackson had the same human reaction to Taliaferro that the drunken Georgian farm boy had had. He couldn't stand the sight of him. He hated his guts. He protested the assignment of Taliaferro to his command: "Through God's blessing my command, though small, is efficient, and I respectfully request its efficiency may not be injured by assigning to it inefficient officers." If possible, he cared for Brigadier General Loring even less. The commanding officers that Jackson highly respected and got along with totally could be counted on one hand—make that one finger: General Robert E. Lee.

For admittance to his own staff Jackson was careful and quixotic in selection. He quizzed all applicants closely and felt no shame at delving into their personal habits. He wanted to know, by his own unique standards, if they were intelligent, faithful, and industrious. Most of all, he wanted it ascertained, proved without doubt, that a candidate had the habit of rising early in the morning. He lived by Franklin's "early bird" dictum. And before the Valley Campaign was over, each member of Jackson's young staff (Alfred Jackson, a distant relative; irrepressible Sandie Pendleton; cheerful Kyd Douglas; profane John Harman;

rock-solid Dabney, among others) knew full well why he had been quizzed so thoroughly. Twenty-four hours were hardly enough for what they were required to do in a day. Although Jackson used lightninglike offensive maneuvers (later studied by Rommel and George S. Patton), his overall campaign in the Valley was defensive: to keep the thundering hoofs of a numerically superior, crafty enemy from overrunning the virgin Shenandoah. His enemy was powerful and willful, and not without valor, and Stonewall was ever aware that he was fighting against tremendous odds.

Jackson's men seldom got a glimpse of his other side—the romantic, tender, somewhat daft and comical side—yet it remained irrepressible. Anna Jackson couldn't be kept away from her husband for long. She was proud of his promotion to major general and, according to her memoirs, had the perfect picture in her head of Jackson's headquarters in Winchester. Jackson had written her: "The building is of cottage style and contains six rooms. I have two rooms, one above the other. My lower room, or office, has matting on the floor, a large fine table, six chairs, and a piano. The walls are papered with elegant gilt paper. I don't remember to have ever seen more beautiful papering. . . ."

Anna hopscotched her way to Thomas from North Carolina, traveling through Richmond and then on the final short stretch by wobbly stagecoach from Strasburg. She lost her trunk somewhere en route; she was exhausted, disoriented, and lonely. She heard along the way that Thomas was engaged in some kind of bizarre raid on the C & O Canal. How does one raid a waterway? At midnight the stage clattered to a halt before the Taylor Hotel in Winchester, and little Anna stepped down in the company of a batty old clergyman, her escort, who had lost touch with where he was and with whom. Anna longed for someone, anyone, to meet her. She noticed a group of soldiers nearby—a rather seedy, menacing group in the shadows. One looked familiar and sinister. He was engulfed in a greatcoat and his cap was pulled down over his eyes. There was something about his stance that alarmed her; he was watching her, and he was out for trouble. Where was Thomas? She scurried to the veranda of the hotel and just then the figure in the greatcoat took her in his arms and began kissing her. On the lips. Passionately. It was Thomas.

"Why didn't you meet me? I was waiting. Why didn't you tell me?"

Now the playful Thomas, the one who had once waved a sword over her head in Lexington, jumping on the bed and rolling his eyes—the Thomas his soldiers never met—said, "I wanted to make sure I wasn't going to kiss anybody else's *esposita.*"

He found her lost luggage, guided her ancient escort to port, and took her to the marvelous Moore home, his winter headquarters. He introduced her to the citizens of Winchester and, the next Sunday, took her to church. Throughout he seemed preoccupied with some sort of military decision, making marks on paper, consulting officers around the clock. But Anna learned nothing of what he intended that winter. Certainly she didn't suppose any battles were being planned—not in the mountains at that time of year. Everything was so snug here in Winchester. No one in Jackson's army had any more idea than Anna of his intentions. Loring's army kept marching in, troop by troop, and Jackson became a bugbear on discipline and drill—but where he would lead them no one knew.

On New Year's Day, 1862, of all days, Jackson had his troops fall out for travel amid a barrage of orders. Troops were to draw five days' rations, to keep at the ready one day's cooked ration, and to keep canteens full. New Year's Day! It was agony to leave on a holiday, to leave period. Winchester was where the home fires burned. Life had the prospect of being so pleasant here. No enemy was driving them out—just Old Jack. It was wrenching for Jackson, too. He left Anna at the home of the Reverend Dr. Graham, the Presbyterian minister, who lived two houses down. Then he climbed on Little Sorrel, shot his arm forward, and moved his troops out on the Pughtown road west of Winchester. There had been talk of the enemy building up forces at Romney—were they off to meet the enemy head on there? Just ride in and toss him out? No one in this army had any idea where they were going, no one except Old Jack. He said go; they went.

It was one of those deceptive winter days in the Shenandoah: almost springlike, warm, with a clear blue sky. The balmy air washed over young faces as Jackson's troops briskly strode down a main thoroughfare; Loring's men marched with much less joy on a parallel road. Holiday eggnog was still working its magic on some of them; hormones were still active with the memory of the slim waists of Winchester girls. Townsfolk had waved to them as if they were godlike heroes. The young soldiers, with Old Blue Light off around a bend and out of sight, began jostling and indulging in horseplay.

"Thar's old Rolfe, gitting ahead in that 'ere column. Let's rassle sum bitch to the ground. Come on!" They frolicked—then flung off greatcoats from their sweating bodies. Flung them on regimental baggage wagons or, none around, off to the side of the road when no one was looking. Who needed a big old heavy coat anyhow! This here's springtime! Pick 'em up on the way back when Old Jack's had enough of this fool marching. When hungry they just slowed down and ate their rations. Full—a little more than full—they tossed extra food to the side the way they had the greatcoats.

A rim of clouds began jutting over the horizon and spread slowly against the blue sky. A fat wet snowdrop hit a cheek or two. Then more drops, and finally a haze covered the sky and blotted out the blue completely while a fierce wind whistled through the ranks. Sleet, snow, and then ice. It was a sudden mountain blizzard. Some became hungry; all became cold. Old Jack kept them moving. The baggage wagons, where some had cavalierly tossed their greatcoats, slipped to the side and mired down far to the rear. The men cursed—and those who hadn't served under Old Jack cursed the most. Loring's troops moaned. Why were they marching—and when, God damn it, would they stop?

Historians of a later era grasped Jackson's plan without difficulty. To move on Romney, which lay directly west, he had to secure his right flank. That meant, first and foremost, clearing the Yanks from Bath, on the right, and driving them across the Potomac into Maryland. Simple. Then marching south on Romney and freeing it of Federals with no danger of surprise from the north. Romney would have been cut off. Perhaps if he had explained his plans to his troops it would have made matters worse. They would have known it was impossible. By not revealing ultimate goals, he encouraged them, all too naturally, to think that each day's hard march was the last. Here finally they had made a superhuman effort to reach some goal, Pughtown or Unger's Store or Bath—whew!—and now they could set up quarters for a while. Wait for baggage wagons, greatcoats, and hot biscuits, and get a second wind. But, no, that wasn't what Old Jack had in mind at all.

The first day they covered eight miles and bivouacked in Pughtown. Pughtown was more a wide space in the road than a town, however. Just a few log houses scattered near each other. A sharp wind cut across the road. Jackson asked one of his staff to bring out a bottle that a sensible Winchester citizen had thrust on him as he was departing the town. It was golden whiskey, but Jackson believed it was wine. The weather was certainly freezing now. With no formality Jackson uncorked, tilted the bottle up, and let the gurgles rise. The young men on horseback looked on, unbelieving. Not because Jackson would take a snort—hell, who wouldn't today?—but the quantity, and so swiftly. No reaction at first; as if he didn't know the difference between wine and spirits. He passed the bottle around, and emboldened by the example, the staff polished of the remains in short order. Less than fifty yards down the road, Jackson said the weather must be turning; he was getting warm. It was actually turning colder now at dusk, but he unbuttoned his greatcoat and the buttons on his jacket. He began discussing various and sundry subjects, one of which was the weather's swift habit of change in the mountains. The young men did not realize they were witnessing one of the few times Jackson was ever in his cups.

It was snowing, and the troops fell exhausted to the ground when "Halt!" was sounded. A few got fires started. Those who had blankets wrapped themselves tightly like Indians. The sharp wind, funneling snow, came down from the high hills, through the trees, and lifted sparks and smoke over prostrate bodies. A spark caught a blanket on fire and the soldier beat it out with his numb unfeeling hand.

"I wish the Yankees were in hell!"

"I don't," called his friend. "Old Jack would follow them there, with our brigade out front!"

"He's crazy. You seen them eyes? You can always tell someone who's crazy by his eyes. Them eyes look right through you, crazylike and terrible. I tell you the truth, Bill, I'm more scared of Old Jack than I am of any damn Yankee."

"Maybe he'll get a bullet."

"There ain't none that'll kill him."

"Shit."

Those who had blankets shared them, all huddling together as closely as possible around the few fires. No tents. They were so close they felt each other's heartbeats. Thump, thump, thump.

Jackson and his entire staff fit themselves in a very small room in a small vacant log hut. A fire soon crackled in an open hearth, not giving much warmth, but everyone looked moodily into its glow. Why had God put them in this space at this time? They would never sleep this night and they had run out of things to say—or things they could say in front of Jackson. Someone asked if perhaps there was something to read this night. One or two dreaded that a Bible might appear, but Jackson seemed to take no notice. Sandie Pendleton volunteered a copy he carried of Charles Lamb, and, a good reader, this ex-schoolteacher was soon regaling his audience with Lamb's famous thoughts on roast pig. Some temporarily permitted themselves to be distracted from their misery and uncertainty for a while, Pendleton's melodious voice carrying over the wind whistling outside and the rattling windowpanes. All at once Jackson's voice stopped the reading. "Captain Pendleton, get your horse. I have a message I want you to deliver."

Jackson had been thinking of matters other than the felicities of Charles Lamb. His mind, once locked into military strategy, stayed. He was again the cadet, concentrating on a problem, late at night, before a fire, oblivious to surroundings. Just as naturally, the good aide Pendleton snapped the book shut and was off in the dark of night to deliver a message to a general three or four miles distant. No one continued the essay; all went back to staring at the fire.

They pushed on the next day without supply wagons, heading north, it seemed. Hardly anyone had been fed, few had coats now; it was well below freezing—and Old Jack pushed on. They covered eight miles again this day, and dropped in their tracks at dusk at a spot called Unger's Store, something of an old trapper's station. Reinforcements caught up with Jackson's main body of troops here and he now had about 8,500 very cold soldiers on his hands. The Stonewall Brigade, now under the command of Brigadier General Richard B. Garnett, was holding up best, almost cheerful in spirit. Many had stood with Jackson at Manassas—their Crispian Day. He'd lead them through, wherever it was they were heading.

On the third bitterly cold day the troops discovered part of what Jackson had in mind. Federals occupied the old resort town of Bath, a spot where some remembered "taking the waters" in happier times. Jackson had in mind surprising the enemy and taking him in a pincer movement. Loring's men dawdled, as Jackson saw it. They had traveled but thirty-six miles in three days—not good enough! And on this night before the first attack, with the enemy primed to be taken, Loring bedded his men down four miles from Bath.

In the morning it was as if the near-frozen troops moved in molasses. Jackson goaded the older Loring to get a move on, forget the cold sleet and snow—fight! The exhausted troops moved, but in slow motion. The sight of this starved mass of men in gray, looking like wolves, startled the Federals more than any shells, and after putting up a token skirmish, they hightailed it for Maryland a few miles up the road. Get 'em out of Virginia! Jackson ordered hot pursuit. Make them pay for sullying Virginia. It was not meant to be; bodies wouldn't respond. But Jackson led them, forced them, to the Maryland border. Across the Potomac stood Hancock, Maryland, and Jackson sent word for the town to surrender. Soldiers there felt safe at last and refused. Jackson lobbed artillery on them.

In Bath the ever adventurous and daredevil Henry Kyd Douglas liberated the grand but deserted Berkeley Springs Hotel. He strolled through a banquet hall, imagining the clatter of silver, the clink of glasses in happier years. He entered a spacious ballroom, empty now and musky and somehow telling him as much about the cost of this war as anything ever would. Chilled to the bone, he ripped white lace curtains from the high windows and rolled himself in them. He drew himself into the shape of a mummy, but the more he had covering him, somehow the colder he got. He returned to the banquet hall and his men, and they all huddled together in a great blob against the chill in this once chic, expensive resort.

Taliaferro had given up trying to figure Jackson out. To hell with him! You had to be crazy to follow a crazy man. He began backtracking toward his supply wagons instead of pushing on toward nowhere. He lost ground instead of gaining. But at least his men found their wagons and they ate. Then, by sheer luck, the Stonewall Brigade ran across Taliaferro's supply wagons. They had outdistanced their own long before. General Garnett looked at his troops, white-faced, mumbling and crying for food, and said, "All right, men, prepare a meal."

Jackson, who was charging on Little Sorrel all over the land, came by his old brigade. "What's the meaning of this, General?"

"Why, sir, I've halted to let my men eat. They haven't eaten in two days."

"There is no time for that."

"But it is impossible for the men to march farther without food."

"Get these men moving now. I never found anything impossible with this brigade."

The war dealt tragically with Brigadier General Richard B. Garnett. He went down at Gettysburg, trying to vindicate himself to the ghost of Jackson, succeeding at last in proving his complete bravery. Son of an old Tidewater family, he was West Point, good-looking, smart, and generous. A true gentleman. He was a cousin of Robert Garnett, the first Confederate general killed in the war. He had, as far as one can reach back into the murkiness of time to see, no ostensible fault. Tragic Garnett. He took care of his men, and, through it all, admired the man who felt that he, Garnett, fell somehow short of some unknown standard. Jackson thought he didn't measure up. He wasn't fit to lead the old Stonewall Brigade; maybe no man could in his estimation.

As Garnett resumed military business, one-armed General Loring struck back. Jackson wanted Loring to push his men on so the enemy would be trapped. Pure and simple, there it was. He goaded the man, kept on him. Loring wouldn't be treated that way. God damn, he'd lost an arm in service and had been soldiering since a boy. To hell with this shit. In front of his troops he bellowed at Jackson: "By God, sir, this is the damnedest outrage ever perpetrated in the annals of history, keeping my men out here in the cold without food!"

On January 6, having chased the Yankees across the Potomac, having done all he could do, Jackson started his troops back toward Unger's Store. His right flank now clear of the enemy, he fought the brutal inexorable weather. This march, in fact, has been compared by some to Napoleon's retreat from Moscow. The treacherous mountain road Jackson's army took was glazed now with ice, like a toboggan run—and their horses did not have winter spiked shoes. They slipped, and the wagons, going out of control, rolled backward over them. It became a nightmare. Six inches of snow fell over the ice, and most of the time the men didn't know where the road was anyhow. The temperature dropped to 20 below zero. Here were Southern troops transversing polar terrain. The mountaineers in the Stonewall Brigade had at least experienced winters like this before, albeit with cabin and farmhouse to rest in, fires and featherbeds available.

Taliaferro's and Loring's men—those from Tennessee, Arkansas, and Georgia—thought they had fallen off the face of the earth, led there, furthermore, by a madman. Every sight of this strange scarecrow figure on a runt of horse disgruntled and mystified them. *He* was the one to blame. Damn it, he had even brought on this insane weather somehow. There he rode—could you believe it!—sucking on a lemon. Only someone who had made a pact with the devil would have an endless supply of lemons on this godawful unspeakable road. Jackson was squeezing the tart fruit to his thin lips as he trotted about on his horse—ahead of and beside his troops, making them press forward. No one ever discovered where he got the lemons—from captured enemy supply trains? a gift? through Anna?—but get them he did.

At V.M.I. he had been Tom Fool; to Loring's troops he was Fool Tom Jackson. His back turned, they yelled, "Fool Tom!" and worse. Those who still had spirit "heehawed," a special infuriating mark of derision in the South. The going was too rough to laugh and deride for long, however. At the top of each hill (and there was one after another) a phalanx of men had to put their shoulders against caissons and wagons to impede their rolling back. The march would have called for superhuman effort even under the most favorable conditions. In subzero weather it was nearly impossible. In this crucial, trying moment, Jackson dismounted and put his shoulder behind the wagons alongside his men. Loring's officers jeered and snickered. The mad general had turned into a raw recruit. Jackson didn't hear or pretended not to hear. Men were sliding and slipping all around him—going off the side of the mountain, clawing their way back up. Some would recount long afterward the memory of the sound a body makes when it hits hard ice. "All around it was like the thud of a pile driver, going whomp, whomp, whomp!"

On this Napoleonic march Kyd Douglas lay in a field after a day's brutal effort. It had turned cloudy, with the merest hint of a warm front coming and a possible change in the weather. He slept, and in the middle of the night felt moisture on his face. He drew his blanket over his head and drew his knees to his chest, in a fetal position. At early light he awoke too warm and threw off his blanket. He had been covered by five inches of snow. He looked around and saw an army of prone bodies, "great logs of men," lying in all directions, all covered with snow and "quiet as graves." They resembled the dead—a portent of things to come. Then first one, then another, burst forth—as if rising from the grave. A wag danced and yelled, "Great Jehoshaphat! The Resurrection!"

Horses suffered the most if there was a way to gauge such pain; soldiers who had been raised on farms later said the sight of those struggling animals was the most horrifying aspect of the whole trip. One horse in every team was down, thrashing the earth, at all times. When one rose, another sank. Sometimes all four in a team lay sideways, kicking furiously on the ice. They were in pain. An artilleryman remembered that "from one horse's knees there were icicles of blood which reached nearly to the ground."

Jackson, the kindhearted deacon in Lexington, showed no pity to man or beast. This terrible march, against great odds, was as much a part of war as the stand on the Henry house hill at Manassas. It must be done! No lingering or malingering for any who could draw a breath. In a later war General George S. Patton slapped the face of a white-faced shell-shocked soldier in Sicily and told him he was faking and to get the fuck up and fight. No excuses. None! Jackson considered, without one exception, any who claimed to be weak and weary, who fainted by the wayside, as men lacking in will. If a man's face was white as purest cotton, pulse so weak you had trouble finding it, that man, according to Old Jack, was just a malingerer. No one ever beat William T. Sherman's pithy description of war as hell, and no one ever saw its fuller dimensions than Thomas J. Jackson. If you want to win—and ultimate victory in war is everything, defeat often worse than death—you must never give the enemy pause, relief, or a kind thought. Give him the bayonet. And never let your men forget this. You are far kinder to them in the long run this way.

The army made it back to Unger's Store, and even the fiercest in the Stonewall Brigade thought they'd had enough for a while. The weather had turned even worse, if possible. Men were stealing raw corn from horse buckets and gnawing roots of sassafras plants that they dug up with bleeding hands. Pneumonia and yellow fever spread through the troops, as the snow and sleet fell over them. Many were so frostbitten that hands and feet "peeled like onion skin."

At Unger's Store Loring reported 800 men sick and disabled. Dr. McGuire of Jackson's staff had somehow carted 1,300 very sick Confederates back to Winchester. That city couldn't hold them and the overflow went to neighboring hamlets. With all the misery about hardly anyone bothered to note that but 4 men had been killed and 28 wounded in an operation that had cleared the Yankees from Jackson's right flank. That was a small number for such a large feat.

At Unger's Store Jackson did call a halt but told no one when he might move out. He told no one what he intended militarily. He first roughshod the horses for travel on ice. Then he ordered up huge kettles of boiling water. He had every last man bathe, and the sight and aroma that rose was impressive. Lice scurried in hordes from undergarments while snow hissed falling into the kettles. Pools of slush formed under bare feet as these young soldiers stood naked in the cold and picked small varmints from each other's bodies. The army stood without clothes.

Jackson had about 7,000 effectives now. His latest field report told him there were 18,000 Yankees at Romney. No doubt Jackson would have fought them if there had been a million—attacked from the rear, attacked at night or on Sunday morning, and somehow found an advantage. He fretted at Unger's Store, concentrating on his next move—and then, miraculously, he didn't have to devise a plan at all. The decision was made for him. Wild Turner Ashby came galloping up to headquarters. "General, sir, the enemy has abandoned Romney!" Ashby and his scouts had just ridden through Romney and found campfires still smoldering, tents and precious medical supplies abandoned. Jackson's ferocious reputation was spreading. The Yanks had heard he was on the way and overestimated his strength. His reputation as a fighter won the battle before he had fired one shot.

Jackson put his troops on the road. The sun was shining as it had been when he had left Winchester on New Year's Day. The day now was January 13. Men sang, a little horseplay commenced. Then, as before, the weather changed; now a hard sleet and rain buffeted the army. Loring and company howled. Stoical Garnett and the Stonewall Brigade left them behind and reached the deserted Romney on January 15 after two days' travel. They were learning to follow Jackson. Move quick; don't think; do. By dawdling Loring's men got mired, everyone covered in ice like a Christmas ornament. Loring cursed and waved his one arm. His men cried even louder. Around them everywhere, on the way, they saw the desolation that the Yankees had left—abandoned loot, half-eaten chickens, gored cattle, and rotting meat. Their stomachs turned and some minds went round the bend. Enough, enough! They talked of mutiny, from the top on down. They couldn't see why they were going to Romney anyhow, a filthy godforsaken hole the Yanks couldn't even stomach themselves. When they got there on the sixteenth the stench from rotting garbage, which the Federals had piled in the courthouse of all places, caused some to swoon, to simply pass out. And then, before they had even settled, guess what? Lunatic Jackson was rustling up troops to strike Cumberland twenty miles away, up across the Potomac in Maryland, where the equally crazy Yanks had gone. Too much. Too much, by God!

Taliaferro's eyes blazed now like Jackson's—only from the other side of the question. His outfit was decimated, the men ill, hungry, and cold. His 23rd Virginia Regiment was now smaller in strength than a company. In fact, one of his companies had but fifteen men able even to walk. No more, no more. They wouldn't do it; they couldn't do it. Unless Jackson wanted to go by himself, that was the end of this insane campaign. All right, Jackson said, with what lip-smacking glee we do not know, Loring and Taliaferro would stay put in Romney to guard the road to Winchester and the Shenandoah. Jackson and the Stonewall Brigade were going back to take up quarters in Winchester.

With Jackson back in Winchester and his dark visage absent from Romney, the army under Loring broke into revolt. The occupation of Romney, which had been so hard won, so superhumanly achieved, was now held in contempt by the men in Romney. These men wanted out; they weren't going to tolerate a winter in a pigsty—oh, that stench of rotting meat and the foulness the Federals had left behind! Intolerable, especially when the image crept in of that harebrained professor and his Pet Lambs (as they called the Stonewall Brigade) lolling in the snugness and beauty of colonial Winchester. Wouldn't have it! Loring got together a petition from eleven brigade and regimental officers: "Instead of finding, as expected, a little repose during midwinter, we are ordered to remain at this place. Our position at and near Romney is one of the most disagreeable and unfavorable that could well be imagined."

These officers were not only brave soldiers wanting a deserved respite during the cruel winter months, they were also, and most important, men of politics. They knew their way around Richmond and how to get things done off the battlefield. Colonel Samuel Fulkerson of the 37th Virginia wrote to someone with clout in the capital: "This place is of no importance in a strategical point of view. We have not been in as uncomfortable a place since we entered the service." Since the 37th Virginia was in Taliaferro's brigade, Fulkerson showed his note to his commander with the cocked hat and furious eye. The note was just what Taliaferro had in mind and he added a line or two himself: "The best army I ever saw has been destroyed by bad marches and bad management. It is ridiculous. It will be suicidal to keep this command here."

Loring sent his petition formally through Jackson, and Jackson, just as formally, dispatched it to the War Department in Richmond: "Respectfully forwarded, but disapproved."

The affair didn't stop there. Taliaferro took off for Richmond personally with his own message for none other than Jefferson Davis. He laid out a map before the president; both men leaned over it, hands behind their backs, and contemplated it. In Richmond, where church bells tolled, ladies in crinoline fluttered behind windows, and masses of soldiers of every strip clogged the sidewalk, a bustling command center, Taliaferro took his hands from behind his back and rubbed his finger beneath the spot where Romney stood. It looked so insignificant, so lost up there near the Maryland border. So vulnerable and isolated, too. The Federals could gobble it up like a piece of dog scrap.

President Davis made quick decisions. He was no worry-wart, and he stood behind the men he favored and forged ahead. Shortly after Taliaferro met Jefferson Davis a telegraphed message came to Jackson's headquarters in Winchester. It came from Secretary Benjamin in the War Department: "Our news indicates that movement is being made to cut off General Loring's command. Order him back to Winchester immediately."

In fact, there was no move from the Federals to cut off Loring's command, and Jackson knew it. Jackson had scouts out; he had a direct telegraph line stretched from Romney to Winchester, too. In any case, what was the garrison at Romney for anyhow if not to fight the Yanks and alert Winchester if the Federals began to come down? Jackson opened the communiqué at his headquarters early in the morning of January 31, 1862. He had not had breakfast yet, for he always did some work before his soldiers got stirring. He was domiciled at present, this general of the Valley forces, at the home of Reverend Graham. When he returned from the Romney campaign, he had flung open the door there to find that Anna had made herself a happy part of that home. Young Graham children raced about, family meals were plunked down on time—there were evening devotionals every day. They all wanted Thomas to move in and not take Anna away to live at headquarters in the Moore house. Thomas let himself be persuaded. For weeks he became, in this house, the gregarious fatherly soul he had been among his own set in Lexington. He was the one who lifted the child on his shoulders and trotted up the stairs and down. Anna later wrote, "The memories of that sojourn in our 'war home' are among the most precious and sacred of my whole life. It was there that I was permitted to be the longest time with my husband after he entered the army."

The Reverend Dr. Graham found his new boarder to be the most devout, humble Christian he ever met. For the rest of his life, long after the guns were stilled, when legends were worked over and refined and sometimes enlarged, he protested that there was never anything peculiar about Jackson at all. No idiosyncrasies. "He was just a simple gentleman, such as we meet in large numbers every day upon our streets, and whom we salute without once thinking whether there is anything peculiar about them or not."

At headquarters now, with the early-morning January light breaking through the wavy-paned windows, Jackson wrote Benjamin:

> *Your order requiring me to direct General Loring to return with his command to Winchester immediately has been received and promptly complied with.*
>
> *With such interference in my command I cannot expect to be of much service in the field, and according respectfully request to be ordered to report for duty to the superintendent of the Virginia Military Institute at Lexington, as has been done in the case of other professors. Should this application not be granted, I respectfully request that the President will accept my resignation from the Army.*
>
> *I am, sir, very respectfully, your obedient servant,*
>
> > *T. J. Jackson,*
> > *Major-General, P.A.C.S.*

Still before breakfast, still before the sun had risen much higher, he wrote to his old Lexington neighbor, John Letcher, now governor of the state. He explained what had happened, that an order had come out of the blue from Richmond ". . . without consulting me, and is abandoning to the enemy what has cost much preparation, expense and exposure. . . . I have . . . requested to be ordered back to the Institute . . . [or] to have my resignation accepted. I ask as a special favor that you have me ordered back to the Institute."

Jackson folded his correspondence, sealed the envelopes shut, and sent them on their way. He went down two houses and ate a hearty breakfast—his favorite meal. Quite casually, hardly as if it would cause a ripple of concern or a raised eyebrow, he said that he and Anna would soon depart and take up residence once again in Lexington. *What?* The hero of Manassas, the man they had put their trust in to save the Valley, the first and foremost Confederate—Stonewall Jackson resigning, probably *fired*? Stonewall knew his politics, too. Governor Letcher descended on the hapless Secretary Benjamin and the fireworks began. They weren't going to lose a man of the caliber of Jackson just because of some ineptly commanded troops under Taliaferro and Loring in Romney. Benjamin knew how to make a deal. He didn't want fireworks, and he held off assigning Jackson to V.M.I. He began to see what the grand design in all this might be, who held the strong cards, and acted accordingly. He hadn't been made secretary of war for nothing; he wasn't Jefferson Davis's right-hand man because he lacked political awareness.

Colonel A. R. Boteler, Confederate congressman and a friend of Jackson's from the old days, was immediately enlisted on Jackson's side in Richmond. He led the assault that would soon rescind Jackson's "resignation" and reinstate him with far more power at his command than he had had before. Boteler traveled overland to Winchester and sat up with Jackson through most of one night. He said that in this great war Virginia needed all her sons and Jackson had no right to go home in the middle of a fight, etcetera. Jackson looked at him slyly—the politician now, not the general. Well, yes, seeing as how so many were convinced that staying on was the correct course, he, Jackson, would now reconsider. The next day Jackson wrote to Governor Letcher that his thoughts about the War Department's interference remained as strong as ever but that for the good of the country he had decided to stay on. In other words, he had lined up his political ducks and shown that he wasn't above resigning in the face of humiliation. He wouldn't be humiliated, and he had shown his fury. No one would meddle with his command again.

The Army of the Northwest, under Loring, came back to Winchester with a great deal more esprit than they had had on entering the wretched Romney. They had heard of Jackson's resignation—hallelujah!—but not of its rescission. They planned now to attack with their fists Jackson's Lambs. They sang, they passed tall stories and schemed how they would have revenge.

Loring and Taliaferro rode their horses, heads high, satisfied expectant looks on their faces as they saw the spires of Winchester poke up around the final mountain curve. They returned in what they believed was victory.

Loring returned to find that Jackson had him up on court-martial charges for neglect of duty and with conduct "subversive of good order and military discipline." In Richmond they scurried and quickly found a way to save face. Loring was promoted to major general and transferred posthaste to Georgia before a trial could be scheduled. Then, before many fistfights with Jackson's Lambs took place, Loring's army was hauled away by train for defensive service elsewhere. Loring never saw a brighter moment in the war than the one when he received orders to abandon foul-smelling Romney, no finer day than the one that brought the sight of the spires of Winchester from around the bend. It was all downhill after that. Lieutenant General John C. Pemberton, the defender of Vicksburg, blamed Loring for Vicksburg's fall. Loring led a corps that abandoned Atlanta in 1864; he was second in command of the Army of Tennessee at its humiliation outside Franklin and Nashville. Bad luck right down the line.

Till the end no one ever again tinkered with Jackson's command of the Valley district. It was his. He went back to training and drilling his men and gazing for long minutes out his headquarters' window on the hill. He even relaxed some and let his men roam through Winchester. Some rode sleighs through the streets as if trying to capture the holiday spirit of the past Christmas. Reverend Pendleton put aside his cannons and constructed a chapel. Jackson had around 4,500 men now under his command, and on February 26, 1862, he learned that U.S. General Nathaniel P. Banks, under Lincoln's direct orders, had crossed a pontoon bridge at Harpers Ferry and was coming toward the Valley with 40,000 men to clear this pest Jackson from the war. General McClellan came by train to watch this crossing. The Federals were getting serious now.

Jackson moved in his quick loping stride to pass on commands, to show up for church services, to be with Anna as much as possible. And somewhere, in some secure spot, at the Grahams' or in the Moore house, the Jacksons conceived their child.

CHAPTER IX

Into the Valley

Oh, to resurrect them, to bring them back as they were. We see some of the early photographs or tintypes and the journalists' sketches, and often we fancy we detect a man's character, what made him who he was, what determined his fate in that bloody conflict. For instance, we see the gangly frontiersman, self-made lawyer, one-time rail-splitter (and what capital was made of that!), who was strong enough to hold an ax at long arm's length as long as he pleased. No pictures of that stunt, but well-documented and sketched from memory. He could get off a good 'un, and ease comfortably beside a stove in a backwoods store. He wrote with biblical Shakespearean sweep—sweet, clean, and elegant. The cartoonists liked to depict him as an ape. He wore the wrong gloves—black, not white kid, and that faux pas put young Henry Adams's teeth on edge. Young Walt Whitman adored him. Whitman fulminated against those officers who had "lost" Bull Run, those officers who got into their cups against the rail at Willard's and spun tales of bravery and their men's cowardice; Whitman fulminated—but he loved Old Abe. Honest, plodding, complex, human Old Abe. Scotch-Irish; humble birth; a traveler into America's destiny. Above all, in this war, he was one thing pure and simple—a fighter.

Lincoln had of course not attended West Point as Jefferson Davis had. He didn't know, at first, that a brigade was the main fighting unit of an army. He was a little confused about an enfilade. But he learned after Bull Run—or Manassas. He went to books, as he went to books when he wanted to learn anything. He studied, he devoted himself to learning the intricacies of strategy. Major General George B. McClellan, so daring and decisive at the beginning of the conflict, in the Allegheny campaign, now had a grandiose scheme for taking Richmond and squeezing these renegades into submission. Little Mac had been a classmate of Thomas Jonathan Jackson at West Point. He had entered the Point at fifteen and far outstripped the hayseed Jackson in Academy honors. McClellan always shone, a short man who always seemed in a sweat to prove he was a big fellow. They called him "Young Napoleon." And men under him thought there was no finer soldier. It was decidedly to his credit, the love of the men under him. They revered him. Little Mac, by God, would see 'em through! He had been promoted twice in the Mexican War, and he had represented the United States as an observer in the Crimean War. Nothing was too good for Little Mac; he'd always known success and he didn't intend to lose now in this civil conflict. Poor Irvin McDowell, in effect, got replaced. Washington wanted a winner in the saddle, a real fighter to come to the capital and take charge.

McClellan soon had a spit-and-polish outfit under his command. This volunteer colossus of 150,000 souls put their fate in the hands of Little Mac and seemed determined to beat the Rebs by expert drilling and first-class equipment on display. They'd just outdrill and outspend them goddamn Rebs. Although many had not been serenaded by the minié balls overhead, they had newfound pride, thanks to McClellan. Their splendor would do the Rebs in, they felt, if nothing else did. Here was the Army of the Potomac.

McClellan studied maps, inspected and reinspected his troops, and then, seeming really ready to get down to business, decided on a maneuver that might just be worthy of these fine young men. He was going to take Richmond, but not in a direct march. A common, sensible assault would be to march south from Washington through Manassas Junction and Fredericksburg. Just hit it straight on. Just plow right down fore and aft with these fine gents in dandy uniforms and equipment, brass shining and leather deeply oiled. They even had enough pride to send two-day-old bread back to the cook. None but the best for these troops. But no, McClellan came up with the Peninsula Campaign, one of the most daring ideas in American military history. He was going to sail his 150,000 stalwarts down the Chesapeake to Fort Monroe, which was secure in Federal hands. From there, friends, it was only sixty miles due west to Richmond. He proposed to take the Confederate capital in one fell swoop—by land, sea, and air (he had hot air balloons).

McClellan was a physically brave man—in fact, those Civil War commanders in baggy uniforms and hair in ringlets were generally brave as bulls and daring with their hide. They stood up to cascading showers of lead. The malaise that affected more than one commander was *caution,* the need to be careful, to postpone and deliberate. They didn't have physical fear but the fear of humiliation. This malaise hit the likely and unlikely. It fell, like the rain, on the just and the unjust. Be killed, shot, maimed, and dismembered—anything was better than being outplanned or outflanked or having your face rubbed in the mud. Left alive but beaten like a pup. We can't chart accurately the history of the mind the way we can the history of a battle, but somewhere between McClellan's bravado rampage in Northwestern Virginia—where he threw caution to the wind—and the Peninsula Campaign, the Young Napoleon underwent a sea change. Was it the moment he first looked on the battlefield of Manassas? Did he see something in the ashen face of McDowell that gave him pause? Was the pomp and circumstance of Washington overpowering and the thought of losing his glory there inhibiting? He wanted a Grand Campaign—not a simple pile-driving slambanging dogfight. Others would come up with the dogfight strategy later, near the end in fact, long after Little Mac and his grandiose tactics had been put aside.

Now he had the upper hand. Everyone's faith was in this strutting confident general. He had the trust of all the powerful figures in command in Washington, all save one and the most important: Abraham Lincoln. Lincoln was studying those maps, reading up on what soldiers did in battles—what battles really were and how wars were run. "Well, it all looks very good and well," he said, looking down at a map, looking down in fact on Little Mac, "even brilliant. But, let's consider—if you marched by way of Manassas and Fredericksburg, wouldn't you keep these Rebels away from Washington at the same time?"

McClellan used what he considered great patience in dealing with this new, roughhewn president. He smiled; he shook his fine head; and he pointed to the map himself. It was a given, he thought, that the Confederates—if that's what they were to be called—would mass most of their troops around Richmond since the Army of the Potomac, *his* army, was steaming toward them there. Wouldn't the Confederates put their finest defense up, their greatest number of troops in position, to save their capital, the symbolic source of their legitimacy? "Well, it occurs to me," Lincoln broke in, determined to irritate his little general, "that we must think similarly about our own capital. We must be well assured that Washington is safe before your army sails from here."

Details, simple details, to convince a civilian that his plans were more than adequate to get the job done. McClellan did more of his explaining, pointing here and there, getting the job done smartly. Little Mac on the attack. General Banks would swoop down to capture Winchester in a simple maneuver and then swing over to handle Manassas, in the old one-two, securing along the way the all-important Baltimore & Ohio Railroad line. U.S. Secretary of War Edwin M. Stanton, a roly-poly old-time lawyer and about as hard-nosed an administrator as they came, had huffed and puffed beside Lincoln, wanting assurances about the safety of Washington. Didn't they see, General McClellan went on, there was perfect defense? General Banks would pacify the Shenandoah west of Washington and thus make safe the U.S. capital. Stanton and Lincoln, though, were practical men. They wanted figures, the piper to be paid. How many men would it take to make Washington absolutely secure? Men in the army, in uniform, before the gates? They suggested McClellan and his aides confer on this one. McClellan and aides came up with the figure of 25,000 soldiers occupying Manassas Junction and 30,000 behind the ramparts in Washington itself. No problem.

Lincoln then gave his reluctant approval to the Peninsula Campaign, and kept his eyes open for danger signs. He was going to win this war; he was going to fight. He had many sides to him, all appreciated in later days. In his youth, according to his old law partner, Billy Herndon, he had loved a woman and lost—and lost his mind for a while. He had been a homespun backwoods lawyer. He was kind and simple and the best of us was in him. He also, by God, was going to win this Civil War. He drew every man's measure by a simple yardstick now: Would that man help win the war? No sympathy, no humanitarianism, no sentimentality, nothing—not the Constitution itself—was going to keep Lincoln from winning. He'd take away the writ of habeas corpus, he'd board neutral ships, he'd fire any general—if necessary. He was going to win. So, too, was a general on the other side, the one who had only recently completed the impossible polar-bear Romney campaign. That general counted God on his side while Lincoln was not even sure there was a God.

McClellan could not be toned down. The glory of the moment was too much for him. The March winds of '62 blew across the Tidal Basin, Banks had not placed a foot in Winchester nor Jackson one out, but Little Mac began the pageantry of loading his vast army on ships, preparatory to taking Richmond. Like Ringling Bros. and Barnum and Bailey coming to town. He couldn't help it; the splendor of it all carried him along. A hundred and fifty thousand men, 15,000 horses and mules— 15,000!—1,100 wagons, and all the fandango he could muster. Coils and coils of telegraph wire, piece after piece of heavy black artillery, fat balloons filled with hydrogen soaring aloft. Except for the modern armament, it could have been the armada of Henry V sailing for Agincourt. Those who saw it kept it in their hearts as the grandest military sight ever. It was something from the pages of Caesar—illimitable, efficient, led by a totally confident commander. How the bands played! At the head, Little Mac. "Rely on it," he let Lincoln and Stanton know, "I will carry this thing through handsomely."

As McClellan and his men pushed off into the water, Major General Nathaniel P. Banks began steamrolling his Federal army into the Shenandoah. The strategy, despite grandiose numbers and showboat maneuvers, was simple: While McClellan zeroed in on the plum of Richmond, Banks would mop up resistance in the Valley, guarantee that Washington was secure, and then head down to the Peninsula to join McClellan. Nathaniel Banks began his working life as a bobbin boy in Massachusetts, but rose like yeast from that station, an industrious, frugal lad, a go-getter. After an immediate success in business, he threw himself into politics, campaigning mainly for temperance. He wanted to stop the flow of whiskey, and how it flowed back then—five cents a dipperful from an oak barrel, out in front of the general store, to name but one source. Just ladle it up, boys! Banks served ten terms as a congressman. He became Speaker of the House in the longest contest in history, a 133-ballot marathon over a nine-week period. He had been governor of Massachusetts. And he had, of course, the political capital of having a rags-to-riches story. He had a book written about him by a preacher, the Reverend William Makepeace Thayer: *The Bobbin Boy, or How Nat Got His Learning.* He had everything a soldier of the nineteenth century could want except one thing—military experience.

Banks made no secret of his lack of military knowledge; in fact, he prided himself on this deficiency, while at the same time falling in love with the soldier's life, particularly parades. Because he was gung-ho patriotic, was truculent and had political clout, he had been made an instant major general. That was how high rank was often won at the start of the war—by political maneuver or by the vote of troops; military competence came last and could be determined only in battle. Banks and McClellan both had love of the parade in common, and Banks was more than a match for peacock McClellan in the spiffy-uniform department. There was something of the matinee idol in Banks, a pretty-boy handsomeness, a gallant fair-hairedness. He had a flaw, though: his mustache. In that day of hair worship he grew a bush on his upper lip that couldn't be brought under control by comb or grease. It just fell over Banks's mouth like a mat. No one could see his lips. He stood at the head of his army, yelled at the top of his lungs, and no one saw his lips move. From somewhere behind the foliage the tongue worked, but no one could verify it.

It was as if a ventriloquist was at work. He thought the mous-
tache made him appear manly and military.

When Banks started down, General Joe Johnston at Harpers
Ferry began backing up. The master of retreat went into full-scale
withdrawal. He was a counterpuncher and his aim now was to
retreat ever south and let the Valley army under Stonewall Jackson tie up the Federals and act as a diversionary element. Johnston wasn't even sure, at this stage, if the Valley troops could
even engage the Federal properly. Many short-termers had
checked out of Jackson's little army. It had dwindled down to
barely 3,600 infantry soldiers by mid-March. The frigid Romney
expedition and all the politicking that followed had seemed to
take the heart out of it. Johnston had many doubts—for what
were a few thousand Southerners going to do against Banks's
28,000 that were heading for Winchester. If that wasn't enough,
add the 12,000 troops under U.S. Brigadier General James
Shields.

General Shields was no Banks. There was no pretty boy in
him, little facade. His mustache was close-cropped and stayed
put. In the old photographs he looks like a barroom slugger and
as exotic, in his own way, as the master, Jackson. Shields had once
challenged a young Abraham Lincoln to a duel over a disparaging
newspaper article Lincoln had written about him. Shields showed
up on a Mississippi sandbar ready to shoot it out, but discovered
that Lincoln, who had the pick of weapons, had chosen heavy
unwieldy sabers for combat. A little joke on Lincoln's part. The
duel never took place, and Lincoln in later days, when putting
together a fighting force, chose his old adversary to lead an important army into the Shenandoah. Lincoln had the genius to
throw aside all petty concerns—revenge, pettiness itself, sentimentality, whatever came along (a drunk or the fanatic)—to get
the job done. Shields was a fighter.

Matters looked dark indeed inside Winchester. Banks's army
had pushed down from Harpers Ferry and had pitched tents at
Bunker Hill on March 6. Banks was squatting twelve miles north
of Winchester. The very air in Winchester seemed now to smell
of Yankees. A frightened feeling spread through the town. The
bankers took off. The owner of the old Union Hotel had the "Un"

restored to his sign out front. In a burst of earlier patriotism (and a feeling that the South couldn't lose) he had shortened the name; it had been the one and only "Ion Hotel" for less than a year. Winchester citizens had to have military passes to come and go through the city gates. It was a most distressing time for those who had such faith in Stonewall Jackson to protect them. General Joe Johnston was sixty miles away, ever retreating south, making the enemy pay in blood for every inch it took. Stonewall Jackson was all they had now. What if those Yankees broke through? They'd burn their houses and roast them alive.

Shortly after noon on a brisk March 11, the forces of Banks and Shields tied up and moved like a gigantic fist down on colonial Winchester. There were 40,000 men, many times the number of citizenry in the hamlet. The Yankees carried an array of muskets and gleaming bayonets in the March sun, and their cannons rolled. Officers on horseback rode beside the long winding lines. Banks held important confabs with his aides every mile or so, his limp mustache blowing in and out with his wind. Shields cantered his horse, mean-eyed and taciturn, ready for another Chapultepec, ready to fight.

Horses and buggies raced through Winchester. Homes were boarded up. The road south was clogged with townsfolk beating their own retreat—some heading for relatives, others to whatever farm or field they could find. Babies yelped and old people tottered. Jackson had little less than 4,000 effectives and he pointed them north against the invader, outnumbered ten to one. Suddenly they collided near a fortified hill the Southerners called Fort Alabama. A Confederate officer put a brass spyglass up and saw in the plain a scattered line of skirmishers in blue moving their muskets left and right, looking around, moving forward. Intermingled were the prancing horses of Federal cavalry, claiming ground, riders stopping every so often to stand in the stirrups and look about. The sun was beginning its descent and they planned to bed down in Winchester that night. Massive columns of infantry moved behind cavalry and skirmishers—as far as eye could see to spyglass. The officer on the hill had never seen so many people all bunched together at one time.

Suddenly, out of nowhere, a large white stallion came charging on the field, a small dark man in a plumed hat astride it, a raised saber in his hand. Confusion started among the Federal skirmishers. The blue cavalry reined in, startled. Turner Ashby plowed right into the lead column, whacking necks and upraised arms. Ashby's men followed, all astride fresh quick-footed beasts that tore through the surprised Federals. Hell, give us warning! Not fair! Then, an eerie high-pitched scream rose, and, from over the hills and through the trees came infantry in butternut uniforms, their bayonets catching the now fading light. Troops milled and fought, got confused, regrouped and fought a little more. Federal officers figured they had superior numbers, but this weird band of screech maniacs gave them pause. And that vision of a marauder in a plumed hat on a big white stallion was unearthly enough to give a man a heart attack before he began fighting. As darkness fell the Federals opened up with some cannon—and the battle petered out before real serious down-in-the-pit fighting could develop.

As shadows fell in Winchester, the shutters of the Graham parsonage closed and family members huddled close. Then some familiar steps sounded in the hall. General Jackson. He was a regular dinner guest. He entered, as was customary, with no fanfare, but the sight of him now caused a collective intake of breath. He wore boots, spurs, and a dress sword. A long military cloak flopped. He took his dinner in an ordinary manner, quietly observing family prayers before moving fork to food, not hurrying at all and giving no information about any fighting that might be going on now or would later. He did not comment on his saber and cloak and it might as well have been for a masquerade as for battle. He did ask that a lunch be packed and put in his haversack for the next day—the nearest thing to saying that military action was in the wings.

Under cover of dark his troops dropped back and Jackson held a council of war at headquarters. He knew what had to be done, what possibly might be done, and he realized that probably no one would go along with any of his plans. For once in his career he was going to see what a consensus was like. He would tell them his ideas, and then try for a meeting of minds before pressing forward. After all, he had a very startling plan.

"Gentlemen," he told his young officers, candlelight playing on his gaunt bearded face, "the enemy must be attacked before daybreak. Let the men eat, rest a moment, and then attack. Surprise will be completely on our side. We will rout him!"

Not one young gentleman spoke. They shifted in chairs, looked at their hands. Faraway sporadic musket fire sounded. Garnett, the aristocrat, spoke. West Point through and through, he knew his duty. He must be the one to tell the general the truth. "The army has fallen back south of Winchester, General. We have abandoned Winchester and our army is now in camp about five miles away."

"Winchester can't be abandoned. We're in Winchester, aren't we?"

"We're in Winchester, but the army is now five miles south."

"Why? Why are our men so far south?"

"They have gone to tie up with supply wagons."

"Then we'll untie them, sir, and march them north to battle. If we strike now, in the dark, we shall win."

"General, it would be an eight-mile march now in complete darkness. They could not possibly engage the enemy before first light."

"Then they get no rest. They get no food. They will cover that ground before daybreak if they double time."

"They fought today, General. It is . . . physically impossible."

"If it were physically possible, what would you advise, General Garnett?"

"That we not do it, sir. We're outnumbered ten to one. Surprise will carry us only so far, sir."

Thomas J. Jackson, from Clarksburg on the Western frontier, looked at the clean-cut features, the handsome unlined face of R. B. Garnett from the Tidewater, from Richmond. He didn't speak for a while. He finally asked what the others thought. Fight or retreat? "General," they all said, one way or another, "we've already retreated."

At midnight Jackson evacuated headquarters and rode south to meet up with the bulk of the troops. He rode beside young Dr. Hunter McGuire, not speaking, gripping the reins of Little Sorrel. At the top of the first hill they halted, as if by mutual consent, and looked back. Winchester lay below, a few pinpricks of light showing from homes, from candles and kerosene lamps. McGuire turned to look at his commander and saw what he took to be an unholy expression of pure ambition. In a dark angry mood, Jackson said, "That is the last council of war I will ever hold!" He indeed had held his last one. All the tricks, all the superhuman effort would now be triggered from one mind—his.

All now had folded their tents and pulled out of Winchester save the free lance, Colonel Turner Ashby. The Yanks were finally there and so was Ashby. He had been the first to attack them north of the city and now he was the last to leave. He sat deep in the saddle, holding the reins tight with his forearm a straight line out from his body, like a fox hunter primed for quarry. God damn these Yanks! The black plume still jutted from his brown felt hat, and a long fat saber hung at his waist. Around that waist was a scarlet sash. He watched the lead cavalry troops of Yankees enter, and then, on the broad Main Street he wheeled his stallion and made his way out slowly, as if inspecting his fields and taking a leisurely ride. Suddenly two Federal riders appeared on the road, unsure what or who or what specter this was coming toward them. Ashby whipped the stallion into a gallop and charged. He shot the first man through the heart and took the second by the throat. He carried the gagging struggling man to the nearest Rebel outpost and left him gasping and throwing up on the ground. Now, it could officially be said, Winchester had been evacuated.

Banks did not pursue them. Banks was an ardent politician, an eloquent speaker, a passionate abolitionist, a short man in a well-cut blue uniform—but he did not know what moved men to battle and how one army prevailed over another. It was a mystery. He held Winchester now; men in blue stretched out around him as far he could see; the locals had a wary stricken look in their eyes. He was just going to set up headquarters here in Winchester and drill and parade a little. Only thing to do.

Jackson had time then to plot down in camp at Mount Jackson, some forty-six miles south. He scoured the mountains and valleys for volunteers. He needed men, anyone able to pick up musket or stone. One man came forward, stepped out of nowhere, who was most essential in the Valley Campaign. Jedediah Hotchkiss, thirty-four, was an ex-New Yorker who had fallen in love with Shenandoah on a summer's hiking trip in golden antebellum days. He had pulled up stakes and settled happily in the Valley as other visitors have done, before and since. He was a schoolmaster—like Jackson—and a successful and natural one— unlike Jackson.

A handsome, dark-eyed man, who, in photographs, has a somewhat brooding look, Hotchkiss loathed the institution of slavery and had argued heatedly against secession until it came. But the pull of the South and Southerners in peril drew him along and he joined the Confederate ranks. He was an amateur map maker, a devoted hobbyist of the art, and he had first served in Lee's disastrous campaign in Northwest Virginia. It was a personal disaster for him, for he came down with typhoid almost immediately after taking up station and had to return to the Valley, an invalid. But when he heard that this peculiar General Jackson needed men to save the Valley, Hotchkiss sought the commander out. Some nervous keen-eyed youths stood guard before the flaps of Jackson's tent. Hotchkiss talked his way past them, and stood face to face with a tired unsmiling Jackson. He gave his credentials, mentioning along the way that he made maps in his spare time and that he had served briefly under a General Lee. Jackson put his hands on the campaign table before him, put his eyes squarely on this pale sickly man and rattled off a command: "I want you to make me a map of the Valley from Harpers Ferry to Lexington, showing all points of defense and offense between those points. Mr. Pendleton will supply you with whatever outfit you need. Good morning, sir!"

Thus entered cartographer Jedediah Hotchkiss into the Valley Campaign. Jackson soon had knowledge of every turn, hill, dip, stream, and ford that stood between him and his enemy. He had knowledge. And so he could move in the dead of night, on a moment's notice, and be certain of where he was going and how to get there. He found little-used paths over the mountains. He could then strike, whereas Banks and others to follow would have to feel their way along, subject to confusion and inaction. But a few days before Hotchkiss miraculously appeared, Jackson fought his first major battle in the Valley—Kernstown. He relied not on maps or lessons learned at West Point but on instinct.

The Federals had advanced south of Winchester, seemingly pressing on. But then on Friday, March 21, came a dispatch from the ever-watchful Turner Ashby. These Yanks were pulling out now, heading north. To Jackson, reading and rereading the message, it meant one thing. McClellan was taking most of Banks's army out of the Valley to use in a pincer movement on Richmond. Taking men out! They must not fear Jackson's poor forces at all! It was a grave moment, one all the Confederate military brass feared, that Banks *would* leave the Valley. He must *not* be permitted to join McClellan! Jackson's ultimate goal was to keep Banks in check; he had direct orders to that effect from General Johnston. Jackson told his men to break camp and march at first light, carrying three days of cooked rations. Jackson just put them on the road—the new recruits, the old vets from Manassas and Romney—and said, "Press on, press on!"

Some men made it, others not. Stragglers dropped by the wayside, like so much litter off the highway. Those who marched covered over twenty miles by foot. As Old Blue Light—mad as a hatter, more than one thought—kept saying, "Press on, press on!" They began thinking of themselves as foot cavalry. That Saturday night Jackson bivouacked in Strasburg, not far from Winchester, keeping his own council. He called for Ashby, and the colonel rode up on his big white charger, full of news and truculence. The Federals were undoubtedly pulling out of Winchester for Harpers Ferry. He'd been skirmishing with their rear guard all day. They were vulnerable—but they had a large force, maybe 30,000. Jackson calculated he had, at best, 3,000. Ten to one. And tomorrow was Sunday, the Lord's Day. Normally this good Christian wouldn't read or mail a letter on the Sabbath. Now he must decide whether to kill men on this day. Of course he decided to fight and he told his staff to prepare to move out at the crack of dawn.

On the other side General Shields, a tough old bird, had experienced that day what fighting men are subject to if they keep on fighting: a wound. He had been directing action against Ashby's wild impetuous cavalry charges south of Winchester and had received some lead. He was carried from the field to Winchester, where he had kept his wits about him. Prone in bed, face contorted with pain, he directed that a brigade be moved north, giving those goddamned Rebels the notion that his army was retreating—having thus suckered the enemy, he wanted a heavy force, kept hidden in reserve, to spring south in attack. Knock them off guard. Lure these pesky people to fight against heavy odds. He'd beat their goddamned asses! He took a little brandy and went to sleep.

The battle of Kernstown took place on a cold raw day. General Richard B. Garnett's Stonewall Brigade reached that speck on the map, four miles south of Winchester, at two in the afternoon of this Sunday. Here the enemy was about to make what Jackson considered a rearguard stand. They were bobbing about, these bluecoats, in a wheat field. They were protected by the cannon of two batteries on a knob called Pritchard's Hill. In a flash Jackson saw what he must do—move swiftly left, avoiding potential fire from the cannon, and encircle these people before they escaped or dug in so well that they couldn't be dislodged. Ashby was given the task of keeping the cannon busy on the right while the main body of Jackson's troops, led by the Stonewall Brigade, took off on an end run.

It was terrain these Southerners knew well: green pastures interrupted by waist-high gray stone walls, neat apple orchards, and clear wheat fields. Heretofore it had been a peaceful, idyllic scene where cows grazed and a horse might occasionally trot. Now these boys in butternut and gray began desperately trying to get around the Federals from the left and cut them off. Ashby held to his part of the bargain, peppering the other side of the Federal line, the right, keeping the guns on Pritchard's Hill busy. For the moment it was like a choreographed dance, the principals taking their turns, the corps de ballet rushing busily around in support. Artillery from Federal and Confederate began to sing. Jackson, astride Little Sorrel, gained a hill and saw a Confederate cannon lob a screaming shell into a barn filled with blue-coated sharpshooters—the whole shebang going up in splinters. He reined his horse, clapped his hands, and said, "Good, good!"

The fighting was heating up. Colonel Samuel Fulkerson, leading a Virginia brigade, had been a malcontent in Loring's corner on the Romney expedition. He had bitched and delayed and bellowed that Old Blue Light* couldn't command a shit-

---

*This nickname, referring to the strictest of Presbyterians, was applied to Jackson for obvious reasons.

house. Now he was prodding his men to race through woods and down gullies to fulfill Jackson's commands. Somewhere along the way he had been converted, he had reassessed his opinion. It was as if he must prove to himself, if not to Jackson, that his earlier incarnation hadn't been the accurate one. He was a fighter; he would go through any hardship or danger to prove it. Character changes happened not only under Jackson but throughout the armies of both sides. Character change was the focal point of *The Red Badge of Courage.* It was in keeping with the American idea of being able to change oneself, of not being forced to remain static. Swallow your pride if need be; bite the bullet. Circumstances couldn't keep you down; social class couldn't mire you; disability and hardship couldn't do you in. This willingness to change—in some cases the absolute *need* to change—was in the very bones of Americans. Their progenitors had come to America to tame a wilderness, to carve out totally new lives. This need for change, to reinvent oneself, became an integral part of those who followed—long after the frontier had been tamed.

Fulkerson took up a position behind a stone fence and was soon joined by Garnett and the Stonewall Brigade, all crouching down, poking muskets over stones and through cracks, and firing away. Here came a line of blue and then the steady wham wham wham of Confederate muskets. From Jackson, "Press on, press on!" The boys in gray borrowed ammunition from one another. Clots of blue staggered and fell, and still that awful line kept moving toward the stone fence. This was serious. Cannon from the Federal side increased; from the Confederates it diminished. The battle plan began to unravel in seconds, right before Jackson's eyes. Victory was falling from his grasp. His men were running out of ammunition!

Jackson spurred Little Sorrel and caught up with a trooper from the 21st Virginia. It looked suspiciously as if the boy was advancing the wrong way. "Where are you going?" Jackson said.

"I ain't got a bullet left, sir." He ducked his head as shells raised dirt around him. "I got to find some!"

"Bullets!" Jackson said, drawing out the word. "You go back and give them the bayonet. We're going the other way. We're going forward!"

Jackson rode forward himself. He found something radically

wrong. An aide galloped up, raising a hasty salute. "General, my compliments. There are ten thousand Federals coming at us. They've tricked us. This is no rear guard."

"Say nothing about it," Jackson said. "We are in for it."

Then, to his horror, he found that his beloved brigade, under Garnett, had *retreated*. Why had these men fallen back—before 10 men, 10,000, or 10 million? Who had given such an order? He spied at last Garnett and nearby a small drummer boy. "Halt these men, General. Halt and rally!"

He dismounted, grabbed the drummer boy, and led him to a tiny knoll. "Beat a rally, boy!"

The fellow went at it, the drumbeat rolling over the fire, the crash of arms, and the splintering of wood. Retreating soldiers paid no attention—to boy or general. A borderline panic had set in, that reaction that comes with the sight of fellow humans stampeding, making an escape while we have been rooted to one spot. Why me, when others are hauling ass? Out of the way! Jackson learned that Garnett was falling back to cover the retreat of Fulkerson. Call it what you would, it was all one big retreat and none of it, as far as Jackson knew, had been ordered by him. If he couldn't stop his men from abandoning the field, at least he was going to make sure none of the wounded were left on it. "It may take too long to remove these men," Dr. McGuire told him. "We may lose every one of us if we stick around."

"This army stays here until the last wounded man is removed," Jackson said, looking full into McGuire's eyes. "Before I leave them to the enemy I will lose many more men."

But the Federals suddenly, fortunately, ran out of steam. Their hearts went out of the battle, and Jackson collected his wounded and the rest of his army and headed south. One way to look at it was that he had been suckered. Shields had pretended a massed army was a rear guard and Jackson had fallen for the bait. But Jackson's character had remained the same. Retreat? What's that? As always he had been willing to fight. He wouldn't back down. The problem was that his preferred method of fighting—striking quickly against an outnumbered isolated segment of a larger army had not been possible. He was the one surprised. Now he warmed himself before a fence-rail fire near Newtown that night, four miles south of the battle. A young beardless soldier saw his chance for glory, for his opportunity to speak to the chief. "The Yankees don't seem willing to quit Winchester, General."

"Winchester is a very pleasant place to stay in, sir."

The soldier was almost giddy with excitement, with being able to badger a general who was warming himself like a common soldier before a fire. As he was warming himself.

"General, it was reported that we was retreating. But I reckon they was retreating after us."

Jackson kept looking into the embers. He suddenly cut the young soldier off from further discussion. He said sharply, "I think I may say I am satisfied, sir!" And the youth knew enough not to say one more word.

His army had suffered 718 casualties against 590 for the Federals. He had been beaten from the field, the first and only time a Union force would do that to Stonewall Jackson. He had to curl up this night, not in a bed in Winchester, as he had expected, but beside a rail fence. He had fought on the Sabbath. He had seen the breakdown of discipline.

Back at Mount Jackson he took command of the Stonewall Brigade from Dick Garnett. He didn't stop there: He put Garnett under arrest for ordering retreat when no command for that had come from higher up. No matter that the brigade had run out of ammunition. They had bayonets, even stones to throw. No, he sealed Garnett's fate: Garnett would be court-martialed, shamed, ensuring that he would one day die in a foolish charge at Gettysburg, proving his bravery.

Actually, the Battle of Kernstown turned out to be a victory in reverse for Jackson's army. The Union knew by the ferocity of Kernstown that they had a fighter on their hands in Thomas Jonathan Jackson and that they had better keep Banks in the Valley and not ship him down to Richmond to help out McClellan. Jackson's Valley Campaign properly dates from the Battle of Kernstown.

CHAPTER X

The Men Around Him

In April 1862 the conflict had still not jelled; there was still no clear sense of what the final outcome would be. The Confederate Congress passed the first conscription law in American history. The Congress of the United States passed a bill calling for the gradual abolition of slavery in the District of Columbia. In the Western Theater the great Confederate General Albert Sidney Johnston went down at Shiloh, bleeding to death in some woods near a peach orchard while his surgeon was away tending wounded Union officers. Grant, at the end, held firm. On the wide muddy Mississippi, a Union naval fleet under David G. Farragut, from Tennessee, fought like a demon and took New Orleans, Baton Rouge, and Natchez into Federal hands. "Conquer or be conquered," he had told his officers, and he prevailed. In Washington Lincoln longed for a Farragut to take to the field. In the most important theater of the war there remained indecision and a menacing ominous stalemate. In the Peninsula before Richmond Little Mac listened to the advice of one man: private detective Allan Pinkerton, a civilian, who told him the Confederate forces under Joe Johnston contained close to 120,000 men (actually there was less than half that number). In Washington Lincoln scratched his head, as Little Mac cried for more men. More, always more. Lincoln went himself down to the Peninsula to check on Little Mac.

Everyone seemed to need more men—even Jackson, in the Shenandoah. How could he strike at the awesome blue line before him, or defend himself, if he didn't have more soldiers? But Richmond was now preoccupied with its own defense (the Confederate capital!), and more or less wished Jackson well and let it go at that. (In the general chain of command Jackson got guidance from General Johnston and direct gentlemanly orders from General Lee.) Jackson insistently kept to his request—more and better officers, any troops who could be spared. Anyone at all. So guess who came his way, via General Johnston's direction? Taliaferro, the bad penny. Came trotting up on his steed, cap cocked to the side, an air of disgruntlement; same as always. Inside he had changed. He no longer had the desire to fight Old Jack. Like a bucking bronco, he had been broken. Somewhere, somehow, after the Romney campaign he had been tamed. Like others before and later, he now wanted to prove his mettle to this strange brooding obsessive ex-deacon. Jackson of course took him back. He was ordered to. West Point code. Taliaferro had been assigned back to him—so be it: Taliaferro would be there until court-martial, death, crippling wound, or reassignment. Jackson let the brass back in Richmond know what he felt about Taliaferro, but he kept his mouth shut around his own camp. He didn't spread rumors or bad-mouth a man behind his back. Taliaferro went about his business, trying to redeem himself in Jackson's eyes. He became a fearless officer who obeyed commands—a man pleasing daddy, a prodigal son coming home.

Nothing could—or ever would—tame Turner Ashby. He was sui generis, so popular now, so much more a living legend than Jackson himself, that country boys far and wide came to enlist and ride under his banner. Forget Old Jack—where's Ashby? The whole Confederacy would have enlisted under him if allowed. And why not? Here was his idea of how a man should fight: The commander, the one at the top, rode out in front of his men and fought the enemy, just rode out and put the saber to him. There was no need (or time) for drilling, for pickets, for strategy sessions and maps. Hell, he knew the country like the back of his hand.

Besides, he couldn't read a map. He gave no furloughs because that involved paperwork and record keeping. Anyhow, after a day's battle a cavalier simply went back to his farm or wherever and waited to go to the next battle. Ashby just wanted to fight; he didn't need or want any of the extraneous stuff.

Ashby scouted for Jackson. He got so close to the Federals that if one of them sneezed, he said, "Bless you." Near Columbia Furnace on the upper reaches of Stony Creek, the Federals ran over one of Ashby's companies one morning. Ashby hadn't put out pickets and his men were sleeping late and the Federals simply rode over them and, both sides surprised, took the Rebels prisoner. Fifty men, their horses, baggage, and equipment went to the Federals. Ashby got orders to retire to Rude's Hill and—most important—demolish a lone access bridge close to it. Jackson's Valley army was holed up on Rude's Hill and he didn't want the Federals rushing over them as was done to Ashby's company that had slept late.

For a few weeks in April, following the Battle of Kernstown, Jackson had made himself at home on Rude's Hill. The name of this locale came from the fact that a minister named Rude and his family owned the land. Pastor Rude invited Jackson and his staff to occupy rooms in his home and Jackson made nervous use of the opportunity. He bent over maps that Jed Hotchkiss put before him; he gazed out the window for changes in the weather; he drilled and inspected his troops. He said little, gathering his strength, getting ready. He was now in the position of the enemy he had faced in the mountains of Mexico. He was in the position of Santa Cruz at Chapultepec.

Unlike during battles on foreign terrain, domestic cares and woes drifted in and out of Jackson's army as they fought, then regrouped. They were not in a land where foreign tongues prevailed and native food scorched the tongue. They were in their own backyard, some only a few miles from home. John Harman, the leather-tough, spittle-flying quartermaster, lost two of his children, who lived not far away, to scarlet fever. His fellow officers mourned. The children of Reverend Rude scampered through the house where Jackson and his staff planned matters and bedded down. The name "Hotchkiss" came tumbling out of out their lips as "Mr. Lipkiss." Jackson was a favorite of the children, seemingly ever ready to play and invent games and listen to their delights. Jackson's staff got only the barest instructions from him—and those to the point. As the enemy hovered near and frenzied Ashby rode to rejoin him, Jackson ordered his troops to fall back to New Market.

Here came Ashby! He was riding his big white stallion, a magnificent beast, galloping toward his own lines. He was so close to the onrushing Federals that from a distance he seemed to be leading them. He was only a few strides in front, spurring the stallion from side to side, leaning down into the wind like a jockey. A bridge suddenly loomed around a turn. Too bad he wasn't farther in front or he could torch the bridge and leave the Federals behind. But the Federals were practically in his saddle, and the clomp of their horses' hooves sounded on the bridge's wooden boards immediately after bearded Ashby flew across. The Confederates had drawn their line a short distance away and now leveled round after round on the surprised Federals. Ashby called, "Boys, pick your man like a squirrel in a tree, and FIRE!" There were an awful lot of men in blue—and they just kept coming.

A melee developed, a wild-swinging, bullet-flying free-for-all. Ashby's white stallion reared and four Yanks charged him. He swung his saber like a sheik—side to side, up and down, hitting heads, shoulders, chests. Specks of blood hit faces like rain. If those Yanks got to him he himself would undoubtedly be dismembered in short order. They had the stallion by the mane, and then a dismounted Rebel came crashing out of the swirling dust and smoke to strike one Yank to the ground. Horses stomped on him. A captain and a private twirled around and chased the others off.

Ashby struck with his saber and then struck some more as he gave the spur to his horse and broke through the melee. Just as he broke free a stray bullet ripped through his boot, nicked his calf, and sank itself in the stallion's chest. It made a deadly soft plunking sound, something like a plunked watermelon, as sabers rattled in scabbards around him. Ashby rode his dying mount toward a Confederate battery on Rude's Hill. He gently rode the horse the last few yards it took. As he dismounted, covered in blood and sweat, the white stallion fell to its knees, then rolled to its side. Ashby looked briefly in the horse's eyes, and pulled the trigger of his heavy service revolver. The horse's head jerked up and fell, no stirring. Not a moment to lose. Ashby called for a mount just as big as the white one. A black beast pranced up, rearing back, head twisting. No one in this army of expert horsemen could ride him; he hadn't been broken. But he looked great and he was fed and kept around just for his magnificence. Ashby climbed on and gentled him, trotting him around, then took him at a gallop back into the action. As the sun dropped behind the western ridge, the Yanks called it quits. Jackson, thanks to Ashby's scouting and a little artillery, had made it away with but negligible loss.

Jackson quick-marched his men to New Market and took up quarters himself in the friendly home of a family named Lincoln. It was a guest home—and, war or peace, offered lodging for the weary traveler. The family was related to President Lincoln. However, these Lincolns were Confederates, and were curious about Jackson's name. "You aren't related, sir, are you, to the Jackson who used to stop here?" Old Mrs. Lincoln asked.

"Are you referring, Madam, to Old Hickory?"

"I am. Yes, sir. He became president, I believe."

"I am a great admirer of Old Hickory," Jackson said, highly pleased, forgetting the question. "He was a Democrat like me, you know."

If men couldn't be spared from Richmond (or from Tennessee or Alabama or wherever), then to swell his meager force and defend the Valley Jackson had to bring in what other armies remained near. Brigadier General Edward Johnson commanded around three thousand weather-beaten veterans on top of the Allegheny Mountains west of Staunton. Johnson was just as weather-beaten and grizzled as his men. He had the nickname now of "Allegheny" Johnson because apparently no Federal force alive could budge him from the Alleghenies. He and his men just dug themselves into the hillside and blasted away all threatening armies who tried to pass. Like moonshiners warding off the revenuers. General R. H. Milroy, U.S.A., was currently trying to break through from the west and join up with Banks. No such luck.

Allegheny Johnson rode over to meet with Jackson, and the two spent long hours, heads close, quietly speaking, the conversation broken now and then by Allegheny Johnson's squirting a thin thread of tobacco juice in the dust. Johnson was like a ward boss with a number of votes he could deliver to the right man at the right time. He was judging whether Jackson was the man who might swing this election, might win. He didn't want to throw his three thousand men into a losing harebrained scheme. He spat some more juice, wiped the back of his hand across his whiskered lips, and rode back to his Allegheny mountaintop.

Banks, competent or not, a real general or not, mustache drooping, had a lot of men, animals, and guns—and he kept pressing on. He hadn't cornered Jackson yet, but he thought he could.

Jackson kept moving. He marched his men over mountains and through vales and they had absolutely no idea why they marched or where they were going from one day to the next. On the road to Harrisonburg one late afternoon, as a heavy cold rain fell, Jackson called for young Kyd Douglas. They saluted and then immediately Jackson reached under his rubber rain cape and brought out a piece of paper. "Here, I want you to take this to General Ewell. He's over on the other side of the Blue Ridge. Around where the Culpeper Court House stands. It is," he continued, staring hard at Douglas, rivulets of water running down his cheeks, "a pretty important message. I need to have this dispatch given to him by daylight tomorrow. I want him to unite with us at Swift Run Gap as soon as possible."

Douglas understood that Jackson meant for him to leave immediately, travel through the night and through a rainstorm and find Ewell in early morning. "General, I will start at once if I can get a horse." Douglas had already ridden twenty-five miles that day and his horse could hardly make another mile. He didn't know if he himself could. But Jackson had called, and Douglas thought he was being put to some kind of test, weighed in the balance right there. His adrenaline began pumping.

A friend provided a horse and Douglas charged off, hearing in the background a parting salute from Jackson: "Good night. . . . A successful and pleasant ride!" Was the man being sarcastic? Douglas was too young to know for sure. First, he had to go in the right direction. He rounded the base of the Massanutten Mountain, which eerily rose to the near heavens in the rainy night, and rode on toward the Blue Ridge. He stopped at farmhouses and asked directions. He beat upon doors and saw the pale glow of a kerosene lamp appear and someone cautiously coming forward. Douglas knew priorities—he got a bottle of whiskey "for an emergency." Then back on his steed and up the black mountain. The road was narrow and twisting. He heard water rush under him and tumble in torrents so far down that he felt he was traveling on a perilous edge. Actually he didn't know for sure where he was traveling. He could not see in front of him and had to depend upon his horse's instinct. He reached over to feel her neck and ear, but could not see them. The night was getting blacker and blacker.

Suddenly he reached the crest, the summit of Swift Run Gap, about halfway there. At this gap, it was commonly believed, the white man got his first view of the Valley of the Shenandoah. But Douglas could hardly appreciate the view. Miraculously, he heard hoofbeats coming in the opposite direction. A bedraggled, nearly asleep courier was on his way to deliver a message to Stonewall Jackson from General Ewell. They shared information, Douglas got more precise directions, and the drowsy courier got a long pull at Douglas's whiskey flask. Throughout the war Douglas was the cavalier—to friend and foe—and he impetuously gave the flask to the man to keep. The whiskey, by all accounts, was extremely vile. Then he plunged down the mountain after General Ewell. So far he had traveled thirty-seven miles.

More adventures followed. He woke a farmer, who at first declined to give up a horse to Douglas and then relented when he found Douglas served on the staff of Stonewall Jackson. "I have a boy, maybe your age, with Stonewall Jackson." He gave Douglas a beast as big as a dromedary, one used to pulling the plow, not covering roads by bridle. The beast sank so far in the mud at times that Douglas had the feeling he was moving by gunboat. It was another time, another way of life. Horses moved you places, carried your goods, made life and—if you didn't have one—made life hard. The dromedary horse made it to a livery station in one of the small hamlets along the road and Douglas swapped it for a light gray horse. He clattered through the streets of slumbering towns, in and out in minutes. No road signs; he had no compass. It was a society geared to the use of horses: The scent of them and their droppings all around, businesses everywhere to facilitate their use, an understanding among the people of how they were used and why. No explanations needed. You wanted to go someplace; you needed a horse. The little gray horse made a few miles, then keeled over, dead.

Douglas took off the saddle and waited in the dark, in the heavy rain, by the side of the road. A small dark boy soon passed, on the way to fetch a doctor for "ole missus." "Good Lordy, what's that?" he said, stumbling over Douglas. Douglas gave him a dollar to run to the nearest tavern/inn and pass the message that he needed a horse. Douglas ended up this time with a large white horse, one suitable for a Turner Ashby. He spurred on for nine miles and then changed to a tall gaunt roan for the last eleven miles to Culpeper Court House. Night still fell—the rain, too. As a glimmer of light broke, the rain turning to a heavy mist, he came near the courthouse and ran into General Richard "Dick" Taylor, son of former President of the United States Zachary Taylor and brother-in-law of Confederate President Jefferson Davis. Taylor had been schooled at Harvard and Yale, had traveled widely, and was an omnivorous reader. Before the war he had operated a grand plantation in Louisiana. He was not West Point, but he had read about important campaigns and studied military leaders. He had the confidence that came from being landed gentry, not to mention being the only son of a president. He just happened to be fighting against the U.S.A. at the moment, and he had roused his men for early reveille to march in a direction away from Jackson. "Better hold your men, General," Douglas told him. "I have a message from General Jackson to General Ewell. It may change your plans."

Douglas got yet another horse and was off once more. Ewell's camp was six miles distant, at Brandy Station. Douglas arrived just as Major General Richard Stoddert Ewell was rising. "Old Baldy," as his troops called him, had no hair atop his head. He had a lisp and was prone to expletives of a very salty nature. He was a good cook but had a bad stomach—like Jackson. A West Pointer, he had resigned his captain's commission from the U.S.

1st Dragoons to join the Cause in his native Virginia. He was a fighter—like Jackson and Lincoln—and as eccentric as both of them put together. When his troops had once complained about the shortage of beef, Ewell had exploded. "Cattle's everywhere! I'll bring in some goddamn beef myself!" He had ridden off and returned triumphantly with a lone aged bull. "But, General," an officer reminded him, "we have eight thousand men." Ewell was willing to admit mistakes: "Ah, yes, I was thinking I still commanded fifty dragoons, I guess."

Douglas rushed up to him and thrust the wet, crumpled dispatch on him. Ewell started to read, frowning, pulling his shirt on with his free hand, when he saw Douglas totter. Jackson's aide had ridden over a hundred miles in less than twenty hours. Ewell supported him and let him lie for a moment on his own cot. "God damn it, coffee for this gentleman! Let's have some brandy, too. And breakfast! Have you had breakfast, son? No? Make that a big breakfast!"

Douglas was eventually put up in a hotel and slept for twenty-four hours straight. Then he retraced his route, securing horses by the same hit-or-miss method, and got back to Jackson at ten o'clock at night. It had rained almost continuously since he left. He woke Jackson, who turned over in bed, and listened to Douglas's crisp summary. "Very good," Jackson said. "You got there in time. Good night." And rolled back over and was immediately asleep.

Major General Ewell rode into Swift Run Gap thirsting for combat, ready to fight. This high-strung, popeyed man could hardly restrain himself. Ewell had eight thousand fighting men in tow and had just burst onto a campsite that Stonewall Jackson and his men had recently abandoned. Embers still glowed in campfires and grass lay flat and beaten down from recent camp life. The scene reminded the old Indian fighter Ewell of an empty tribal village when the braves had just taken to the warpath. Jackson had ordered him here, and no Jackson was in sight. What kind of strategy was this? His instructions from Jackson had been most meager: Stay put, and keep an eye out for the Yankee Banks. Assail him if the opportunity arises and if there aren't too many risks. Otherwise, keep cool. What kind of orders were these?

Another lingering problem was that Ewell, although of high rank, a major general, wasn't too sure whom he was taking orders from. Lee sent them; Johnston did; and now this odd man Jackson was getting into the act. Most peculiar to have force-marched his men to a designated spot, then to be left stranded—troops to feed, strategy to plan, a war to wage. Colonel James A. Walker of the 13th Virginia happened to call at headquarters here at Swift Run Gap. Walker had been the cadet at V.M.I. who had once challenged Jackson to a duel; he had matured and mellowed somewhat, and having commanded troops in combat, he was more aware than before of the travails of those in authority. But he certainly hadn't forgotten his old professor. General Ewell was fuming and asked, in his high-pitched shriek, what Walker's considered opinion was of the man.

"I don't know, General. We used to call him Fool Tom Jackson at V.M.I., but I do not suppose that he is really crazy."

"I tell you, sir," Ewell stormed, "he is as crazy as a March hare. He has gone away, I don't know where, and left me here with instructions to stay until he returns. But Banks's whole army is advancing on me, and I have not the most remote idea where to communicate with General Jackson. I tell you, sir, he is crazy, and I will just march my division away from here. I do not mean to have it cut to pieces at the behest of a crazy man." This fragile-looking man then began pacing around in circles.

Walker galloped away to join his brigade commander, General Arnold Elzey. That man, too, was fuming. He pounced on his subordinate. "I tell you, sir," he bellowed, "General Ewell is crazy, and I have a serious notion of marching my brigade back to Gordonsville!"

Just then a lanky, hollow-cheeked private, a conscript, broke in. Just ambled up and threw his face and a piece of paper an inch from General Elzey. "I want you to sign this here paper, mister. I want a discharge and I want to go home!"

"You what!" Elzey went out of control. He went for his pistols as the conscript ran with a swiftness no one would have suspected. A wild long-legged scramble. Elzey went after him, firing. He returned, out of breath and a little subdued. He had missed his mark. "Colonel Walker," he said, "I want you to know that is the sort of man we're getting in the army now. That's who you're dealing with at the Thirteenth Regiment. Imagine that rascal talking to me that way, me a brigadier general. If I only could have gotten hold of my pistols sooner!"

Walker, a firebrand at V.M.I., now chuckled. Everyone in this army might be a little touched in the head. He said, "Well, sir, I was up to see General Ewell just now, and he said that General Jackson was crazy; I come down to see you, and you say that General Ewell is crazy; I don't doubt that man who just ran from you will report it all over camp that General Elzey is crazy, too."

Elzey broke into a loud laugh. He saw what Walker was driving at. General Ewell, though, had no occasion to laugh yet or change his opinion about Jackson. Jackson kept sending him concise contradictory messages from across the countryside where he was moving his army, seemingly pell-mell.

Jackson bewildered all, staff as well as troops. Now you see him; now you don't. No one anywhere—friend or foe, at Ewell's camp or down in Richmond, with Frémont or on the run with Banks—could be sure on any given day what Jackson's battle intentions were, even where he was. On May 3, 1862, Jackson took his Valley army eastward up into Brown's Gap of the Blue Ridge—right smack out of the Valley it was supposed to be protecting. For the nonce he just abandoned the Shenandoah. Ring around the rosie. Some spirited farm girls, observing from beside the road, yelled, "Why you leaving us, soldier boys? Scared the Yankees might get you?"

"We're just marching!"

"Where?"

"God only knows!"

They trudged out of the Valley. Then at a junction called Mechum River Station they came across a long line of train cars, behemoth engines hissing steam, ready to roll. Jackson put the sick and barefoot into baggage cars, the healthy he made to stand up in freight cars. A lot could be fitted in if they stood. All aboard, a shrill whistle echoing through the mountains and the Valley army, now traveling by rail, returned to the Valley it had just abandoned. The trains chugged back over mountains and ended up in Staunton. The town was having its own nervous break-down, the citizens convinced that they had been virtually handed over to the Yankees. Allegheny Johnson was off to the west. When last heard from, Jackson had pulled up stakes from Swift Run Gap and probably had said good-bye to the Shenandoah itself. Refugees were scattered over the roads outside of town. Fear everywhere, a feeling of loss and abandonment. And then, without one rumor heralding it, here came Jackson's boys—by train! Everyone, troops and townspeople, broke into a wild spontaneous celebration. War wasn't so bad after all. Plenty of girls around here, and liquor, too.

That was noon. Jackson came on horseback shortly before dark and immediately sealed off the town and stopped the revelry. People had to have a pass to leave the town gates. He didn't want his plans or whereabouts known anywhere. Everyone could tell he was itching to fight, but what bunch of Yankees out there—and there were plenty—no one knew. He sent word through the district that he needed volunteers. They came, Superintendent Smith furnishing two hundred cadets from V.M.I. These boys paraded down Staunton's main drag in natty gray uniforms, brass shining, hair trimmed. Reviewing these smart-looking cadets from his old university the professor took stock of his own appearance. He got a haircut and he took off the old U.S. Army blue uniform he had been campaigning in. He bathed and put on the gray uniform of a major general of the Confederate Army.

He didn't lessen his iron will, however, and its force spilled over into his army. They pulled a giant locomotive from a bog where it had tipped over. Through sheer will they pulled it out. Engineers and infantry dragged B & O Locomotive 199 from deep mud and uprighted it on the rails. And rolled it into Staunton. They wouldn't give up. Give them a problem, an obstacle—anything—and they would overcome it.

Jackson was going to attack Frémont's army, but only he, Jackson, knew it. "Pathfinder" Frémont was another one of those swashbuckling grandstanders Jackson loved to take on. Son of a French father, American mother—illegitimate and born in Georgia—Frémont's life constituted a colorful slice of early nineteenth-century history. He ran for president against Buchanan; he helped wrest California from Mexico, had the good fortune to have gold discovered on his land, served as a U.S. senator, was an explorer, a *pathfinder* indeed in the west. A politico but no warlord. He'd rather pathfind than fight.

Jackson kept his intentions secret even from his staff. He rode south toward Lexington while his army marched west toward the Alleghenies. His staff had to catch up with him to find out what was next on the agenda. He led them on a side road to join the main body of troops in the Allegheny foothills. The Rebels then began to climb the tiered ridges above them with the doggedness they had used to wrest Locomotive 199 from the bog.

Troopers who had been "Loring's men" in Romney now sweated up the slopes, Taliaferro among them. They trusted their crazy general—or perhaps they had become crazy themselves. They were infused with Jackson's ardor. They wanted to fight, and they smelled the enemy.

Jackson gained the high ground. It was called Sitlington Hill. And there he joined forces with Allegheny Johnson who had come on the scene. Down below lay a mountain crossroad called McDowell, where, like sitting ducks, Frémont's men camped. They were commanded by General Milroy. Artillery from this high ground could blast them right off the face of the earth. Jackson realized this and longed for artillery. But even Jackson had his limitations. He might condition and will men to scale high slopes but not with heavy artillery on their backs. Some things were impossible, even for Jackson.

Rebel skirmishers began the fight with a startled but game Milroy. Jackson, in an uncharacteristic move, now delegated authority of command to the old war-horse Johnson. The Alleghenies were his territory, so Jackson fell to the rear. He figured that his presence might inhibit Johnson, keep him from using his full talents. Johnson knew this territory, every stone, and Jackson didn't want to distract him. Johnson certainly got enough to occupy himself. The firefight heated up, shifting from skirmishers to heavy barrages. The Federals were at first alarmed by the sight of these wild clamoring Rebels; then they took stock, and gave them back shot for shot, measure for measure. The Federals were outnumbered, but they had stationary positions and had their supply and ammunition wagons close by. They slowly but surely began to make the Southerners pay for their audacity. The Federals rolled the back wheels of gun carriages into holes in

Brigadier General Turner Ashby made the Federals believe that several men led Ashby's rangers—for how else explain his many feats? His last words: "Charge, men! For God's sake, charge!"

Private Edwin Francis Jennison
2nd Louisiana Cavalry
Killed at Malvern Hill, age eighteen

At First Manassas the Henry House was where the Union charge ended and the Confederate advance began.

General Joseph Hooker believed in the trappings of rank. Much was expected of him, but he never overcame the Federal defeat at Chancellorsville

Major John Pelham, the daredevil cannoneer from Alabama. A West Pointer, he fell, mortally wounded, in the battle of Kellysville, March 17, 1863.

Boy soldier, C.S.A.

For these young men of Ewell's corps, the war ends on this
dusty road.

Stonewall Jackson—two weeks before his mortal wound at Chancellorsville. His last picture

Lieutenant Thomas J. Jackson, the young soldier around the time of the Mexican War

Jackson in February 1862, rested and ready for war. In five months he would send Banks reeling down the Shenandoah, tie up three armies in pursuit of him, and defeat two of them.

The Union sends a German-led division against Jackson.
Brigadier General Louis Blenker stands imposingly with
hand on belt near center. At his left is Prince Felix Salm-
Salm, a Prussian officer. At his right, General Stakel, who
led the Federal left against Jackson and Ewell at Cross Keys.
The German division fared no better than any other against
Jackson.

Private William S. Askew
Company A
1st Georgia Infantry, C.S.A.

The general and his staff. Like his soldiers, his staff first feared Jackson, then learned to adore him. He demanded a lot—a forty-mile ride, for instance, after a day's fighting and marching. Off duty he was easygoing and affable. At war he could not share his command. He took no confidants as to his military designs.

Private Walter Miles Parker
1st Florida Cavalry, C.S.A.

A U.S. soldier from Ohio

General Richard S. Ewell, called "Old Baldy" by his men.
He first thought Jackson insane, then became one of his
greatest admirers.

Jackson's Valley troops strike Federal lines of communication in Virginia in 1862.

The aftermath of the unholy fighting at Dunkard Church (SHARPSBURG)

order to raise the trajectory of their cannons, and thus they began hammering those raucous visitors on the high hills. All at once they rushed the Confederate center, just ramming and banging right into it. Who said these Yankees couldn't fight?

The Confederates began to run out of ammunition, for they could carry only so much up a mountain. The 31st Virginia had commenced to lose ground on a vital hillock, when Taliaferro and his men came charging up, muskets blazing, to save the day. In action Taliaferro kept saying, I was wrong, I was wrong in frigid Romney. The center of the Confederate line had spilled over the mountain in its initial enthusiasm, down to lower ground, practically on top of the Federals—and now the Federals began walloping them in earnest. The 12th Georgia held the center, and in the fading light this bobbing, weaving silhouette of an outfit made an excellent target. "Get back, get back, boys," an officer called.

"Shit, no, we ain't running!"

A colonel personally dragged one man after another back to behind the lines only to find the man running forward when the colonel's back turned. It was the opposite of a rout. It was unprecedented. Their fever to fight could not be quelled. Boys of the 44th Virginia also declined to go into reverse drive. "Goddamn Yankees, come and git us!"

The blackness of night was fast descending and outfits had trouble distinguishing friend or foe. Some straying Federals stumbled across a line of Confederates in the dim light and set off a surprise volley. Everyone was confused, Yank and Rebel. Lines became entangled and they all mixed and mingled. General Johnson tried to straighten his men out and went down, his ankle shattered. Once again, Taliaferro to the rescue. Hat cocked, eyes mad, he took charge, ready to hold all night and fight all next day.

The litter bearing Johnson passed Jackson on the far side of the mountain. Johnson's foot was flopping over the side, his ankle oozing blood, his face white with shock. Jackson leaned close and got a sketchy account of the nightmare in process on the mountaintop, of the maelstrom above. He sent word to Taliaferro to hold on, Stonewall Jackson was on the way. The First Brigade, now under Brigadier General Charles S. Winder, was dispatched immediately to lead the way. Winder was West Point, thirty-three, the picture of a model soldier of the time: He had a curling beard, a high intelligent forehead, and wore flawless uniforms. No matter the time of day or night, he looked as if ready to step out on parade. But he was no parade general; certainly no Banks. He was a veteran Indian fighter and had soldiered in Mexico.

When Winder replaced the cashiered but popular Garnett, the men of the old Stonewall Brigade hissed as he reviewed their ranks. He pretended not to notice, kept a stone face, and stayed in the saddle as if above it all. Immediately afterward, though, he acted. He told a colonel of the men that any soldier who caused such a disturbance again, i.e., hissed or hooted in ranks, would find himself at play in the stockade or in chains. Stricter rules followed. Any soldier who overstayed a furlough would be considered a deserter and subject to being shot. He set limits. The brigade, which had considered itself special and had prided itself on being removed from ordinary rule, got rudely shocked. Fine, Old Jack was strict and took no nonsense—but, look, he was a sloppy dresser, like a private, and he hunkered down by the campfire with his men after a battle. Winder would not have lasted except for one quality. Winder, with his broad shoulders, fashion-plate attire, and clipped, impatient speech, was one brave man. He stood right in the midst of battle with his men. He led the way. Jackson's man.

The brigade found more confusion than expected on the mountaintop. It began to fight whomever it could find to fight, whomever it could see to fight, but by 9:00 P.M. the light failed. The crack of musketry dwindled away. Men were left roaming through the battle area, seeking comrades, seeking their units. "Hey, anybody know where the Tenth Virginia's at? I can't find my outfit. They retreat or what?"

"Help me, oh Lord God Jesus, help me," the shattered and struck moaned in the darkness.

Jackson put the Stonewall Brigade and the V.M.I. cadets to work collecting the dead and wounded. The cadets had a right to feel disoriented. A few days before they had been in Gothic academic buildings in Lexington; now they stood on a dark mountain, searching for the dead and wounded; thus, war. They did their duty, as if it were a perfectly normal occurrence in life. Down below Yankee bonfires blazed in the tiny village of McDowell. That meant that Milroy was burning supplies and fleeing north. Jackson had stopped him. By quick forced marches, by surprise, by tenacity, by a willingness to fight in light or dark, most important, by a willingness to be hurt (the Confederates suffered more killed and wounded than the Federals), the Rebels had forced these Northerners to flee and didn't have to undergo a retreat themselves. They had won. It was a very important Southern victory now that so much was going against the Confederacy in this spring of '62—defeats on every hand and Richmond under imminent attack. Jackson had given his people hope and a strategy for holding on and not knuckling under.

He wired one sentence to Richmond: "God blessed our arms with victory at McDowell yesterday."

But he did not rest. What good was victory if you didn't press your advantage? After Milroy! Go get those Yankees before they tied up again with Frémont! But wanting was not the same thing as getting. Nothing went right in the pursuit. Supply wagons couldn't keep up with the infantry. And just when the Rebel troops were gaining on Milroy, the wily enemy set fire to the forests along the road. Jackson's troops coughed and waved arms in front of themselves, trying to see. Federal snipers picked them off around every turn. It was worse than fighting in pitch-blackness. Furthermore, this smoky battle was being fought on Sunday. Jackson might be forced to fight on the Lord's day if absolutely necessary, but not if there was no military advantage. Milroy was nearing Frémont's camp; the Yankees had escaped— so Jackson turned back.

He sent a letter of commendation to his troops, congratulating them on the McDowell victory and announcing that "Divine Services" would be held for all in the field. He stood himself, out in the open, until the last hymn had been sung, as a light misty rain turned into a downpour. A captain recorded that Jackson "stood with his head uncovered, his arms crossed on his chest, and his form bowed. As he stood thus I thought it, and have always thought it since, a sublime exhibition of his noble religious character."

Prayer, as well as the bullet, was part of Jackson's campaign. Soldiers reported that he often went off by himself into the woods for private prayer. His men suspected that he also prayed silently as he walked around camp, for he was once heard to say that he could find nothing in the Scriptures that forbade one to pray with his eyes open.

Private John Opie observed Jackson praying this way on more than one battlefield: "General Jackson would often sit upon his horse, in the hottest fire, oblivious to the existence of danger, his eyes lifted towards the heavens. I often wondered what he asked for in his petitions. It was certainly not Scriptural to pray for the annihilation of his enemies, yet, under the circumstances, he must have desired it."

His Christian duties satisfied, the former deacon put his troops on a return march to the Shenandoah Valley. He refined his technique of troop movement to get the maximum distance covered with least trouble; he cut essentials; he drew from all he had learned—on the frontier, in Mexico, in these early Civil War battles. There would be no dawdling. There would be absolute discipline. He was going to make superhuman marches an every-day occurrence. He issued a new marching order and had it read to the troops: Men would march as though on drill and at route step, getting a ten-minute break every hour. Roll calls would be had at beginning and end of each day's march; a dawdler, one who strayed, could expect the worst. Jackson meant business. He was going to turn his infantry into "foot cavalry," men who could pop up anywhere in the Valley after a day's march or two. He was out for blood.

The quick marches had their costs. A private in the 31st Virginia noted in his diary that he wore right through his shoes, right down to the skin of his feet. Not having shoes was no excuse for Stonewall; he marched at route step as did several other bare-foot soldiers now. His feet bled but toughened. He was limping eighteen miles a day, shoeless. Rain fell, torrents, bucketfuls, for five days straight. Clothes and blankets stayed soaked, food mil-dewed, fires couldn't be started, swollen creeks were treacherous to cross, dirty yellow springs all that was there to drink. Misery. And still they marched as if on drill. They were more afraid of Jackson than of fatigue, rain, hunger, and pain. Here they were, these few thousand Southern boys, trudging barefoot and near-barefoot, in ankle-deep mud, off to fight they knew not where, for an ideal they weren't too certain about, led by a fierce-eyed man on a small sorrel horse.

Some broke and thought they couldn't take it—or shouldn't. A fragment of the 27th Virginia just threw down their muskets when they neared McDowell on the return march from chasing Milroy. Just said, To hell with it. They had signed up for a twelve-month enlistment and it had expired. There was something about being "drafted" back into the army, some sort of order, but to hell with it. They had volunteered for a year. A year had passed. God damn it, they had paid their dues, they had served their time. They wanted out. This liberating mood affected a wide swath. "Free! Free at last, O Lord!"

Their colonel, Colonel Grigsby, appealed to them. Appealed to their patriotism, to their sense of brotherhood and pointed to others who were making sacrifices. He appealed to them as men. They weren't listening. Grigsby, defeated by their stares, by the sight of their bare feet and filthy clothing, sought advice from his commander. He sent a courier immediately to Jackson to ask what he should do.

Stonewall didn't hesitate a moment to tell him. "What is this but mutiny?" he roared. "Why does Colonel Grigsby refer to me to know what to do with a mutiny. He should shoot them where they stand."

Jackson spelled out the fine points. The mutineers should be paraded before their regiment, charges should be read, and then they should be offered one last chance to resume duty. Those who refused should be shot on the spot. Grigsby complied. On the field an officer barked out the charges into the rainy air, the men of the 27th considered their options for the barest of seconds, and then turned and rejoined their companies. No further talk of mutiny came.

As the 27th Virginia returned sulkily to the endless trek, the V.M.I. cadets received orders to report back to Lexington and resume studies. Some were shoeless or using twine to hold leather scraps around their red swollen feet. Now—back to academy, as if the McDowell battle had been part of a student-assistant program. Back to the promontory overlooking Lexington, back to books and lectures and compulsory chapel. They didn't want to return. They wanted to stay with Jackson and fight. But the Old

Professor bowed to the Board of Visitors and the cadets left the
ranks. V.M.I. cadets would return for other emergencies, consis-
tently courageous.

Meanwhile, Ewell fretted in camp at Swift Run Gap, waiting
for Jackson. His men drilled, stayed on edge, and listened to their
regimental bands play spirited tunes such as "Listen to the Mocking Bird." His officers were special. Brigadier General Isaac Trimble, who commanded a brigade of boys from the Deep South, was
a ramrod-straight snow-haired man of sixty. West Point class of
1822, a Baltimore railroad executive just prior to the war, he
knew how to fight like a son of a bitch. His first act after the start
of the war was to commandeer a train from Baltimore and burn
as many bridges north as he could in order to delay Federal troops
in reaching Washington. He just goddamn got things done—told
divisions which men to elect as officers and court-martialed anyone who didn't buckle under to his brand of discipline. There was
General Elzey, with pop eyes like Ewell, who had fought in nearly
every battle in Mexico. Add to the illustrious list Colonel Bradley
Johnson of the 1st Maryland. A Princeton graduate, former
Maryland state's attorney, an eloquent orator and skilled lawyer.

Then there was Brigadier General Dick Taylor, the former
president's son. Taylor had charge of a gaggle of cutthroat New
Orleans dock workers, French-speaking Acadians, and aristocratic plantation owners from Northern Louisiana. These officers
and men weren't simple revolutionists with a burning ideology,
gathered together in the mountains to overthrow an all-powerful
central government. In fact, they seemed to be what they claimed
to be—people of a real country, with their own laws and customs
and bondings, who were trying to stand off an invading force
from another country, i.e., the U.S.A.

A distinct segment of this motley crew at Swift Run Gap was
a group called the "Louisiana Tigers," led by Major Roberdeau
Chatham Wheat. The redoubtable Wheat was six feet four and
carried over 240 pounds, most of which was muscle. He had
fallen under the spell of combat in Mexico and after peace there
had continued on as a soldier of fortune in Cuba, Nicaragua, and
with Garibaldi in Italy. Even someone with the proportions and
truculence of Wheat had trouble, though, reining in the Louisiana
Tigers. They were a battalion of Dirty Dozens—wharf-rat crimi-

nals, back-alley murderers, the dregs of Southern society. Some-how they had gathered together under one banner. In peace their fate would have been the gallows or life behind bars. In war now they were respected and feared by one and all, indiscriminately, by their own side as well as the other. On the battlefield they fleeced the dead bodies of both armies, nothing held sacred. Nothing save death stopped them from their appointed tasks and they were the living definition of the mad warrior: At First Manassas, when they ran out of ammunition, they threw aside muskets and charged with bare knuckles and knives. It was hard to tell if they were drunk or sober or sane. Only the toughest iron fist kept them reasonably in line. When two of Wheat's men broke into a guardhouse to free some fellow Tigers and were momentarily subdued, General Dick Taylor knew his duty. He had them shot within minutes and double-checked to make sure they were dead before he turned his back.

Thus this band of fighters who twiddled their thumbs at Swift Gap Run in Old Virginia, waiting for the professor from Lexington. What no one knew, but a few vaguely suspected, was that the fate of the whole new country, this Confederacy, de-pended now on what Stonewall Jackson could pull off. The weight of the country was on his shoulders. If he didn't somehow keep the quartet of Banks, Milroy, Frémont, and Shields occupied in these parts and prevent them from joining McClellan's drive on Rich-mond, then the South was finished. The Visigoths would follow.

Ewell didn't know what to do with his large trigger-happy army plunked down in Swift Gap Run. Stonewall kept dispatches flying, but they in essence told him nothing—except to stay put and harass Banks if that Northern general roused himself and made a move his way. Ewell learned that Jackson was in Brown's Gap, then Staunton, next McDowell in the Alleghenies. Jackson was marching hither and yon—but he never told Ewell *why*. Then General Lee, in his gracious way, let Ewell know that it might be feasible to leave Swift Run Gap and head south toward Freder-icksburg in central Virginia; Federals were swarming there, and their next stop would be Richmond. In other words, split from the Shenandoah. But Jackson had told him to stay put. What a pickle! No wonder he couldn't digest anything. What did this mad man Jackson have in mind?

CHAPTER XI

They Ate Oysters
and Drank Champagne

Richard Stoddert Ewell was not a man for inaction. If anyone thought this, he had another think coming. He called for his horse, saddled up, and then rode off at dusk on Saturday, May 17, to find out personally, at first hand, what the score was. A sleepless night, nodding over the saddle, his horse trotting over a mountain road in the moonlight, Old Baldy kept on. At dawn, on the eighteenth, he entered Jackson's camp at Mount Solon, just down from Harrisonburg. Every second now counted. Richmond under imminent attack, the enemy scattered dangerously through the Old Dominion, bad news from all war fronts—everything looked bleak. A plan, some action, must be devised. And quickly. And what did Ewell find? Jackson's troops were spread out across the camp field, sprucing up, getting ready for—church! It was Sunday morning.

A skeptic who had been given no reason to regret his lack of belief, Ewell cursed, considered bolting, and then pressed on once more. Jackson greeted him in his usual crisp way, gave him no time to fume, and led him to a deserted mill where they could confer in privacy. Anyhow, church wasn't for an hour or two. The two West Pointers, both old veterans, went over the string of defeats the South had recently suffered—from Shiloh to the abandonment of Norfolk, with McClellan now reported thirty miles from Richmond and over 100,000 men strong. Things indeed appeared dark. The two campaigners took out maps, spread them out in the quiet mill, and pinpointed exactly where they knew the Yankee armies to be. Marked the spots with a stubby pencil. Shields, good old battle-scared Shields, was on his way to Fredericksburg to join McDowell and then to move inexorably toward Richmond. They made a mark on the map. Here was Banks up near Strasburg. Another mark. They knew that Frémont was biding his time west at Franklin. Mark it down. They knew far more about the Yankees than the Yankees knew about them. It was no fun being attacked on your native soil, but there were advantages. You knew the land better and you could count on home-grown spies; also, Jackson's maniacal secrecy in troop movements was now paying off, all those blistering marches over hill and dale and no one knowing why.

Jackson marked where the Confederate armies were in the Valley. They were near each other and totaled around 20,000, ready to fight. There it was marked down, by stubby pencil. "General," Jackson said gravely, "do you see what I see?"

"I see," Ewell said, his popeyes widening.

The Federal armies had spread themselves thin; the Rebels had positioned themselves closely together, all done in Jacksonian secrecy. Banks was isolated and could be dealt with harshly.

There was a problem, though, and they both realized it at the same time. Actually, was there ever a moment when there wasn't a problem? When you could just see your way clear to do something in this war, to settle things once and for all? General Johnston, down in Richmond, had issued orders for Ewell and Jackson to chase Shields if he broke from Banks and headed east of the Blue Ridge toward Fredericksburg and Richmond. At least, they were pretty sure that this was what Johnston wanted. So many vague and contradictory commands came from Richmond that much was left to interpretation. But . . . but if Jackson and Ewell did what they believed Johnston intended them to do—go after Shields—then they couldn't smash Banks.

Jackson didn't mull over the dilemma long. He was as ambitious as any man alive, a trait he unsuccessfully tried to curb by prayer. He took the risk. He disobeyed what he knew to be Johnston's orders in order to reap a golden opportunity. He acted. He did not debate or worry the problem. Ewell would move out of Swift Run Gap and get set to strike Banks. Jackson would move his own troops down the Valley and tie up with Ewell. They would combine, and strike. But it must be done swiftly—at once.

Son of a bitch! Ewell threw his hands on his knees and chortled. Action. God damn—action at last! A fight! He was so pleased that he attended church with Jackson that sunny Sunday morning. They weren't in such a hurry that church would be forgotten. Old Baldy stood right up there with Old Blue Light, opened his thin lips, and piped out "In the Sweet Bye and Bye."

Then the bantam Ewell flung himself on his horse and galloped back to his troops.

Jackson had his men up at 2:00 A.M. the next morning, well before dawn. Breakfast fires glowed across the campground, and then equipment snapped and clanked, and by 3:00 A.M. men, horses, and wagons were on the road. Off to clobber hapless Banks! The line of troops snaked down the road in the still-shining moonlight, a slight crispness in the air, perfect for marching. No one told them, though, where they were off to. In the strong morning sun, at the village of Bridgewater, they came to a swirling river that offered no bridge, no means of crossing over. Here was an itchy army, pressing to attack, facing water. Rivers had been stopping armies since the Babylonians—but Stonewall always found a way. Wagons from the village, from owners only too willing to supply them for the Cause, were positioned side by side in the river—just pushed in and sunk. Then planks were laid across them, and there was an immediate bridge. Troops, horses, and equipment crossed and hurried on in a continual rumble. Secret messages between Jackson and Ewell flew—strategy, troop concentration, who should be where, when.

At New Market Jackson's force tied up with Taylor's Louisiana Brigade, the first outfit from Ewell's banner to do so. Jackson's men were taking one of their ten-minute breaks. Shoes had been doffed and feet were being rubbed and released from bondage. These Valley troops lay on their backs, knees bent, blades of grass in several mouths, shirts unbuttoned. Suddenly, stirring band music, parade tunes. From around the bend came pelican-bedecked banners raised high. Taylor's troops marched in view in fresh gray uniforms with snappy white gaiters. What was this? The sun flamed the polished bayonets as the men smartly cut onto the campground. "Order arms!" and hundreds of rifles left shoulders and butted onto the ground at the same time. Stonewall's troops gaped and spat out the grass blades. They were used to tramping twenty miles a day. That regime didn't allow for the niceties of parade drill and a spit-and-polish life. These new men, all 3,000 of them, seemed to belong to another army, if not another species.

General Taylor rode off to find the famous Stonewall Jackson of whom he had heard so much. He expected to be ushered into a command headquarters; instead, a mounted officer pointed to a figure perched on a fence overlooking the road, someone sucking a lemon. The officer said *that* was Jackson. Taylor dismounted and approached, saluting and declaring his name and rank. Jackson wore cavalry boots that covered feet of a gigantic size, a mangy cap drawn low over his eyes; he was dark-bearded and weary-eyed. In a low and gentle voice Jackson asked how many miles Taylor's men had traveled that day.

"Six and twenty," Taylor said proudly.

"You seem to have no stragglers."

"Never allow straggling."

"You must teach my people," Jackson said, ending the confab. "They straggle badly."

When the rest of Ewell's troops joined up at New Market, Jackson counted heads. He had 16,000 effectives, the very first time in the war that he had command of an army that could do full battle. He wouldn't have to improvise or call on superhuman effort—he had the horses. And also another problem. Ewell had received a further specific order from General Johnston. Ewell was to march immediately for Richmond. Nothing could be more clear. Was Jackson to release him to do so? Jackson could—and probably should if he was going to respect orders from a commanding general. But with Ewell gone, he would not have the horses to take on Banks. Sure, he could put on a stage show and improvise some action, but he could never hope to crush the enemy. Now, with Ewell's fine troops at the ready, he had Banks right under the hammer. Stonewall Jackson was too ambitious to act like an ordinary officer and man. He found a way. He telegraphed—not Johnston but his old friend General Lee: "I am of the opinion that an attempt should be made to defeat Banks, but under instructions just received from General Johnston, I do not feel at liberty to make an attack. Please answer by telegraph at once. T. J. Jackson, Major General."

The telegram might be considered insubordination. His return of Johnston's order to Ewell, in effect disregarding it, might well be considered mutiny. What Jackson intended to do, covering his tracks as best he could, was attack Banks. He was simply going to do it. General Lee did not reply to Jackson's telegram, letting matters work themselves out. Tight control was impossible now. You worked things out, let them slide, corrected mistakes as they came up. You didn't fix something that was working. Jackson had his men up the next day before dawn. He rode down the lines of Louisiana regiments, inspecting their formations and weapons. He gave marching orders, boiled down to one word: *North!* The Rebels moved out in the breaking dawn and as they came to Cross Street in New Market, Jackson, in the lead of thousands, brought his gauntleted hand down to the right. *East!*

Now, what the hell? The Louisiana men had come from that direction. The snaking line of men tramped toward the Massanutten Gap, moving east. The sun heated up, and a fog of dust from shuffling feet clouded vision. Dirt caked around mouths. Shoes filled with pebbles and clots of earth. Sweat flies buzzed. They were marching—where? They began climbing through Massanutten Gap, resting ten minutes every hour, no more, no less. Lord, only last month Jackson's original troops had left Swift Run Gap, and now they had covered well over two hundred miles. They had defeated mud, mountains, and even burning forests. They'd had only four days of rest. Some were so weary they didn't know where they were. Late Wednesday, May 21, they wound down the Massanutten Mountain and set up camp near Luray. General Taylor, who had been riding beside Jackson, kept a puzzled look on his face. He was as confused as his men. They had marched in superhuman effort to join Jackson at New Market. Now, Sweet Jesus, they were about twenty miles from where they had started. Count now Taylor among a select crowd: He thought General Jackson might be insane. To keep his humor, of which he had an ample source, he thought, No, the old man wasn't insane, he was just an ardent lover of nature who wanted to show these visitors from the Pelican State the beauties of the Valley in the springtime. That was how he put it in his memoirs after the war was over.

Ashby as well as some remnants from Johnson's Allegheny army joined up with Jackson. Jackson's strength rose to 17,000 men and fifty big guns. They kept marching, and Ashby reported to Jackson that he had been engaging Banks's skirmishers outside Strasberg, keeping them pinned down, keeping Banks's scouts— if such there were—from foraging out and discovering Stonewall's thousands. On May 22 Jackson's army bivouacked near Front Royal, a scant twenty miles from where Banks was holed up at Strasburg. They were told to clean their weapons, to trim down their baggage to the minimum. The veterans knew what this meant: Battle the next day. But where? With whom? Old Jack would show them.

If the Rebels were unsure of the coming battle's dimensions, Banks's army in Strasburg was dwelling in a fool's paradise. Rumor upon rumor came their way, glorified scuttlebutt and dead reckoning, and all more or less said Johnny Reb was coming. But they paid no heed. Their general, Parade Ground Banks, could be sighted transporting himself around in a fine carriage. Strasburg streets were well-lit at night and oh so busy. It was a festival, not a war city. Sutlers' wagons were well stocked with the finest cheeses and meats, and by paying a little extra a man could purchase oysters and lobsters—in the hills of Virginia! In *wartime!*—and wash it down with champagne. Bands played, and there was raucous laughter down every street. Under canvas a traveling minstrel show performed grandly and the large blue-jacketed audience howled.

"Mr. Interlocutor, how come dis heah town of Strasburg look so fine?"

"Mr. Bones, it cuz it part of the U.S.A. now!"

Banks, star-crossed Banks, learned from his illustrious intelligence service that Jackson had been pinpointed, no doubt about it, eight miles west of Harrisonburg, and Ewell was for sure at

Swift Run Gap—16,000 men altogether. He was informed nearly accurately about the number of men, but way off about where they were. He telegraphed Secretary Stanton in Washington for reinforcements, but then all the generals were calling for more troops—McClellan, McDowell, you name them. His telegram might have been more urgent if he had known where Jackson and Ewell actually were: less than ten miles away now, on May 22.

In any case Secretary Stanton had other things on his mind besides reinforcing Banks. McClellan's great push up the Peninsula to take Richmond had started. The pincer movement from McDowell's army pushing down from Fredericksburg was about to commence. President Lincoln and several Cabinet members were already packing their bags to go review McDowell's grand army—40,000 stalwarts and more than one hundred big guns— and send them on their way. Richmond was going to be taken, you could bet on it. Already the Federal government was making plans for a parade through the Southern capital, which would put a symbolic end to this insurrection. Confidence ran so high in Washington that army recruiting offices were now boarded up. The Confederate Congress had evacuated Richmond and President Davis had packed his family off to North Carolina—a very ominous note. Richmond's *Daily Dispatch* cried, "The enemy are at the gates. Who will take the lead and act, act, act?"

It was indeed black, the Confederate sky, on May 22, 1862. In the capital coffee now went for $1.50 a pound, if you could find it, and boots cost $30 a pair. The Army of the Potomac had lumbered to within eight miles and occupied Cold Harbor. Their observation balloons swayed in the breeze, high up, and the men in the baskets beneath looked out on the church spires of Richmond a slight distance away.

Then Jackson struck. First, with the paladin, Ashby. Ashby and his wild cavalry slashed communications between Strasburg and Front Royal. Like an Indian brave Ashby dismounted and zigzagged forward to reconnoiter Buckton Station, the outpost that lay between the two towns. He found a formidable sand-bagged redoubt with the enemy dug in for the duration. He came back to his troopers and told them they were going to take it. They formed a rough line—and then charged like furies, yelling their heads off, and firing on the run as they soared over fences and ditches. Some went down, bullets through their hearts. The startled Yanks couldn't believe at first that anyone idiot enough to mount a cavalry charge could take a redoubt such as theirs. No cannon had been fired; no infantry was in evidence. They placed their muzzle-loaders through holes in the redoubt and banged away. A captain had his horse shot from under him, rolled free, and used his saber to hack his way inside the fort. A handful of his men followed and they took on the enemy from room to room. Five minutes later the captain came out, his arm held high, a Yankee banner wrapped around it.

The remaining Federals fought their way to a bridge and set up defense while Ashby torched the train depot, slashed telegraph lines, and gathered his riders to round up those at the bridge. "Let's get all of 'em, boys," he cried. "Let's get every one of the Yankee sons a bitches!"

They charged, Ashby in front. But the Federals, who were well supplied with ammunition, were not so accommodating. A steady rain of lead came from the bridge and Ashby's troops faltered; Ashby's black horse had its ear torn off by a stray bullet, but Ashby soothed the beast with sweet talk, kept it trotting, and regrouped his force. They charged hell-bent once more, were flung back—then said, let them live. Win some, lose some. They left the band of Yankees firing for all they were worth, and raced on to cause more destruction at Front Royal. They began to isolate and seal off that mountain hamlet, and begin the process of sending the Yankees there to purgatory.

May 23 broke clear and hot in the Valley, one of those bright blistering days that make heat waves shimmer in the distance. Snow and ice at Romney, now heat and dust and a windless day at Front Royal—circumstances over which Jackson had no control made no difference. Weather, time of day or night, or terrain made no difference to Jackson. Attack! Jackson led his foot cavalry in the stifling heat, nearly double-timing them, toward Front Royal. Four miles from the town he suddenly veered right, seemingly off to scale the Blue Ridge, and not to lay siege to Front Royal. It was too much, too goddamn much. He had Marylanders in his ranks, men as divided as the state itself about the war. Half had served the time they had enlisted for, and now, by God, wanted out. They were not being let out, and so were now being

guarded by the other Marylanders. Half the Maryland Confederate line was being guarded by the other half—and the whole
shebang was marching to attack Front Royal which was garri-
soned ironically by another group of blue-coated Marylanders
under the Union flag. A typical Jackson situation.

Jackson's men took a path that rose five hundred feet straight
up the Blue Ridge, and soldiers began dropping—vomiting and
gagging to the side, trying to escape the sun. As entire columns
started to stagger and begin to fall, mercifully they came to
Gooney Manor Road which ran left and straight toward Front
Royal as a sort of back-door approach. Jackson, with General
Dick Taylor beside him, kept the men moving. High pine now
shaded them, and gentle brooks offered cool limestone water. It
was quiet, and thousands of feet crunched steadily on the leafy
forest floor. Jackson rode at the front, then trotted to the rear to
make stragglers rise. Not a minute to lose!

All at once Front Royal poked up around a bend in the
woods. Federal skirmishers, lounging near some fences, suddenly
saw a whole Rebel army descending on them. They opened fire.
The Rebels hardly slowed, and puffs of acrid white gun smoke
rose. Then, like a vision, a woman all in white ran from the
outskirts of town toward the Southerners. She waved her white
bonnet like a flag of surrender, and cavalier Kyd Douglas recognized at once lovely seventeen-year-old Belle Boyd. He remembered her fondly from days of grand balls and a gracious social
circuit. She was out of breath and had to gulp to get her words
out. A small hill separated her from the firing line. Belle Boyd was
a Confederate loyalist in an occupied Southern town: She was a
full-fledged spy. "I knew it must be General Jackson when I heard
the first gun. Tell him quick that the Yankee force is very small—
one regiment of Maryland infantry, several pieces of artillery and
several companies of cavalry. Tell him I know, for I went through
the camps and got it out of an officer. Tell him to charge right
down and he will catch them all. I must hurry back."

Jackson already knew the size of the Federal army but didn't
mind having facts confirmed. The battle for Front Royal began at
two in the afternoon, May 23. The 1st Maryland, C.S.A., pushed
the pickets of the 1st Maryland, U.S.A., under Colonel John R.
Kenley, back into the village. Jumping into the fray, unable to be

restrained, came the Louisiana Tigers under the large presence of
Rob Wheat. They came on the run, swearing, shouting, and
shooting. Kenly's Marylanders reeled before superior numbers,
but had their pride pricked by discovering familiar accents, by
finding landsmen among the attackers. Brother against brother.
God damn if they were going to be rooted out by those from their
own state! Kenly, a tough, gallant fighter, got his men out of town
where they would certainly have been slaughtered, and up on a
hill. He was able to roll his two big guns up there and soon began
unloading hot lead balls onto the Rebels. Somehow in the mad
rush the Southerners had neglected artillery and they couldn't
answer the Federal cannon in kind. Louisiana Tigers and Marylanders began moving up the hill, crouched over and determined.

At the same time Jackson was trying to plug up the South
Fork bridge, an escape route to Winchester, but Kenly saw the
threat and began racing ahead of the Rebels. Jackson watched the
long blue line beating a full retreat, getting out of his reach,
escaping! "Oh, what an opportunity for artillery! Oh, that my
guns were here!"

Jackson called for every rifle and every available brigade to
chase this fleeing army. His prime stricture of war was now at
test: When your enemy is down and nearly out, don't let him get
away. Annihilate him or he will come back to fight you another
day. Colonel Thomas Flournoy was soon dashing with his cavalry
over the burning Pike Bridge farther down the road, 250 strong,
Jackson somewhere in their midst. "God damn, sombitch, git yore
ass out of the way!" Some young soldier was screaming at Jackson's back, blocked from moving forward. "My God, man," one
of Jackson's young aides said, "this is General Jackson!"

"Three cheers for Old Jack!" the man yelled, recovering
himself.

Jackson didn't seem to hear. He wanted those Yankees
crushed—totally, without pity, mercilessly. Nothing else mattered. Near the small hamlet of Cedarville the Yankees could flee
no farther. Exhausted, harassed, they decided they would make
their stand. They formed a line of battle. Jackson personally gave
the order to attack. A bugle sounded and 250 gray riders charged
with wild abandon, yelping at the top of their lungs. *Yaaaooweee!*
They charged right into the enemy's center, outnumbered, as rifle

fire cut some of their horsemen down but did not slow their charge. The Union center broke—and torn asunder, the blues scattered pell-mell, leaderless, panic-stricken. They took cover in an orchard, the first cover handy. Jackson waved for another charge—no mercy!—and it came swiftly. Now it was a wild rout, everyone for himself. The 1st Maryland, C.S.A., rounded them up, captured their guns and flags, shot rounds into the air and whooped it up.

It was a day when nearly everything went perfectly. The Federals had 904 casualties, including a desperately wounded Kenly. He was literally shot to pieces. The Rebels took 600 prisoners and captured a whole wagon train. Their own casualties numbered but 50. Most important, Banks was being isolated in Strasburg, his supply lines from Winchester just about severed. A trap had been sprung on Banks. He was in peril.

And when he got word of the Front Royal debacle, he couldn't quite grasp it. He was like a man who has received a haymaker, becomes groggy, and doesn't know what hit him or where to turn. His instinct—proved wrong—was to hold fast. "By God, sir," he shouted to the courier, who had just ridden up with the bad news from Front Royal, "I shall not retreat!"

Physical bravery was once again not the issue. If Banks could have faced Jackson, man to man, saber against saber, he would not have flinched to do so. Possibly after a full-dress parade, the exchange of cards—but nonetheless he would have done so. No, the concern that lay heavily now on Banks's poor shoulders was political. What were his *superiors* to think of him? Was the bobbin boy living up to expectations? Would the Northern politicos oust him from command and deem him incompetent?

Banks laid down a steady stream of telegrams to Washington, trying to show his energy and awareness of the situation. What came across in his contradictory wires was utter confusion. It became apparent that Banks didn't know what the hell was going on—and now Washington began to panic. Jackson sat before a campfire the whole night after his Front Royal victory, gazing into the flames. Dick Taylor thought he might be praying. What he was doing was conceiving strategy, for early the next morning Ashby and Poague's battery were rushed to cut off

Banks at Middletown should Banks choose to retreat toward Winchester. Think of every contingency, every alternative, the smallest detail. Smoke the enemy out, cut him off, kill him!

Banks himself was worrying through the night, not able to sleep, mystified as to the action he should take. At three o'clock in the morning, the darkest moment of the soul, he decided to take action. He would send his sick and unfit to Winchester. Leave only the hearty ones in Strasburg to fight! But by mid-morning, as a gray pall spread over his troops, as an ominous stillness filled the air, Banks made his final commitment. He would abandon Strasburg altogether and head for Winchester, bag and baggage and guns. Safer there. No one could touch him in Winchester and he wouldn't be further embarrassed and made to feel worthless and incompetent. Jackson's men caught him on the Valley Pike, this May 24, swooping down from the hills like wild Celts of yore, slashing into the rear third of Banks's columns. A contagious wave of fear spread through the Federal troops. Why can't they leave us alone! Discipline vanished. Veterans who might have stayed to fight were crushed under the mad scramble to exit . . . but where? Wagons collided. Horses stampeded. Give him credit, Banks stood tall, riding through the firestorm in shock, up one column, down another, explaining in a singsong that they must press on to Winchester. Then he lost control and the real retreat began; Banks abandoned wagon after wagon of supplies, all those delightful cheeses and tins of fois gras. The ground was littered for a good six miles. The vision of such plunder stopped Ashby's troops dead in their tracks, the way no bullets or shells ever could. The scarecrow cavalry leaped from horses and began gobbling up their finds. It was Treasure Island: fruits they'd never tasted before, tins they never knew existed, hairbrushes, mustache curlers, fine wool clothing—the vision was dreamlike. Whew! Banks made it into Winchester just as night fell. He deserved a good soak, a chance to get his bearings, but his troubles had only begun.

His army had been mauled on the road, and Jackson didn't want to give him a moment's peace. The Confederate general was appalled at the alacrity with which Ashby's men went for the spoils. He wanted pursuit and let Ashby know it. He gathered what infantry units he could find along the road and led them himself. His aides were fast at work, too. Kyd Douglas gathered a hundred Louisiana Tigers behind a fence to stop any Yankees he could find. He didn't have to wait long. Some Yankee cavalry came cantering up, blindly keeping to the road and for the eventual haven of Winchester. Douglas gave the sign to fire just as the lead cavalryman rode up, and the Tigers didn't waste one shell. Union cavalrymen began falling in a tangled pile. They rode into each other, the wounded and the well, and soon a nightmare tableau evolved, a "shrieking, struggling mass of men and horses, crushed, wounded and dying," as one observer noted.

The Tigers did not have weak stomachs and leaped into the mass for whatever loot they could come up with. Their general, Dick Taylor, came riding up to find them diving in and out of wagons like rabbits in a warren. He was one of the few—perhaps the only one—who could distract them. He had a deserved reputation for sternness, and had fought in several wars. The Tigers snapped to attention and looked, in Taylor's words, "as solemn and virtuous as deacons at a funeral." Ashby's men couldn't be disciplined at this point. There weren't enough Taylors or Jacksons around. Ashby's troops were near home, too. Several roped two or three horses and took off. They found whiskey barrels and struck holes and let the liquid splash in their mouths. One who drank as much as he could hold had piled booty behind his saddle, then in front and across. He couldn't resist a fine saddle and finally tossed it on top of the rest. He himself cradled an armful of wine flasks and mounted. His horse wobbled and collapsed, and he lay passed out beside it.

For the hungry, the bone-weary, the sight of such refreshments proved too inviting. Even Jackson broke for the briefest moment—he reached into an overturned wagon and brought out a lone cracker, his only food since breakfast. Jackson kept the men moving. One determined man kept a whole army pressing forward.

A dark night descended and still Jackson pressed on. His thoughts were on the high ground around Winchester. He must take the heights before Banks came to his senses and fortified them. He remembered Pritchard's Hill at Kernstown, when the enemy had the high ground and punished the Rebels dearly because of it. Long after the war, when veterans met to trade anecdotes, the night of May 24 to 25 was recounted as one lulu of a night. It was as if the moon hadn't come out, as if a battle hadn't been fought that day. Jackson wanted Winchester, and the army must move. At 3:00 A.M., after being on the road since daybreak the day before, Colonel Fulkerson of the 37th Virginia caught up with Old Jack. Winchester or no, his men had had it. His army was sleeping as it stumbled along. They were incoherent with fatigue. "My men cannot fight unless they have some sleep."

Jackson didn't seem to need any sleep himself. He also didn't seem to need any protection from Federal bullets, for rearguard ambushers sent volleys into the Southerners at every turn. The whizz of bullets seemed part of the night breeze. Men dropped, just collapsed in their tracks from exhaustion or from a stray bullet. Jackson moved as if protected in some spiritual way, and it struck Dick Taylor that those near Jackson became invincible too. "Colonel," Jackson said to Fulkerson of the 37th Virginia, "I yield to no man in my sympathy for the gallant men under my command, but I am obliged to sweat them tonight, that I may save their blood tomorrow." He had to take those hills—but he knew limits. "Your men may have two hours' rest."

Jackson stood sentry over the army for the next two hours. Then he roused the men and put them on the road again. It was 4:00 A.M., before first light. And nearing Winchester Jackson spotted a vague blue line of skirmishers on the hills skirting the colonial town. He reconnoitered personally and observed the enemy on a strategic ridge. He called for the Stonewall Brigade. He said only five words to General Winder: "You must occupy that hill." Winder saluted and rode off, and very soon his men were moving to take the objective. The two-hour nap had been just sufficient.

Jackson had sent another of his messages to Ewell: "Attack at daylight." He sent along one of Hotchkiss's maps to show Ewell exactly how to do it—strike the Federal left. At 5:00 A.M. Ewell moved out—into a dense Valley fog. There was no visibility, and suddenly murderous fire came from the Federals. One Confederate regiment seemed to disappear completely, blown to shreds. On the Federal right Jackson pushed off with complete determination and in heavy numbers, shoving the Federals back yard by yard. Old Jack rode up to Colonel John Neff of the 33rd Virginia and asked, "What are your orders, sir?"

"To support that battery," the colonel said, pointing to two guns just going into position.

"You are to hold this hill, sir. I expect the enemy to try to bring artillery to this hill, but they must not do it! Do you understand me, sir? They must not do it! Keep a good lookout, and your men well in hand; and if they attempt to come, charge them with the bayonet, and seize their guns. Clamp them, sir, on the spot!"

It was 6:00 A.M., and the battle could be turning sour for the Rebels. The aroused Federals outnumbered the Southerners and they hadn't been marching for two days. But neither had they been inspired by the likes of Jackson. Jackson galloped around, seeking out Taylor. Kyd Douglas claimed to know Taylor's position and led Jackson past veteran Valley troops. Jackson had given strict orders not to make noise, so these men took off their hats and waved silently. No more were they the Romney troops who had jeered Old Jack. Now he was the master general, someone superhuman and mystical. He'd get 'em through. Old Jack would get 'em to Winchester with as few casualties as possible. They'd win! Jackson caught up with Taylor, who rode at the front of his troops.

"General," said Jackson, "can your brigade charge a battery?"

"It can try."

"Very good; it must do it then. Move it forward."

Taylor was to take yet another hill, one that held Federal guns. He rode at the head of his troops to the far end of the Confederate battle line and then began his charge. As he spurred his horse he noticed that Jackson was still with him. The general of them all—right up on the firing line! "Don't you think it might be wise to retire behind the lines?" Taylor asked. Jackson couldn't hear—or didn't care. He stayed beside Taylor as fire began to pour down, and gaps opened up in the ranks, and blood spurted. Taylor's men began to falter, to drop to the ground, to seek merciful cover somewhere. Taylor swore and waved his sword.

"What the goddamn hell you dodging for? If there is any more of it, you men will be halted under this fire for an hour!" The men resumed their pace up the hill. Suddenly Taylor noticed a hand on his shoulder. Jackson had an amused expression on his face. "I am afraid you are a wicked fellow," Jackson said gently, and rode off to the highest ground he could find to better observe the heated fight.

He saw Winder's Stonewall Brigade moving down the hill, on the attack. Ewell was breaking through the lifting fog and making the Federals abandon ground. The momentum of the battle hovered, nothing really giving, everything in a delicate balance. And then the fabric began to tear. The Federals began to fall back. At first only by slow degrees, then increasingly, then at full heat. Jackson had done it. By taking abuse and shrugging it off, by not faltering, by going past fatigue, by forcing his men to endure beyond fatigue, he had seized the day. He rode up to Taylor once again. "Order forward the whole line, the battle's won."

Then Jackson took off his grimy cap, waved it wildly above his head, and yelled, "Now let's holler!" And they all did—that Rebel yell that never failed to send terror through the enemy's heart.

Banks had not had a moment's peace. He hadn't been properly able to rest, to collect his thoughts. You shut and bolted the front door, here came Jackson through the window. You did what you had to do during the working day, and the man attacked you in the dark at night. It was too much to bear. Now Winchester! His army was falling back through the streets like crazed rabble, not like the disciplined troops who had looked so smart on parade. Where were those happy-go-lucky men who had the best to eat, whose supplies were always the first priority, and who should show respect for good treatment and, yes, for country? His troops raced through town, no one in charge. The delirious townspeople began taking potshots at them, too. Not only Jackson but the citizenry was firing on him. These panic-stricken men who came through the streets kept saying, "Oh, Lord, you don't know what it's like. They're coming! If we dont' get out of here, we're lost. Lost!"

Banks grabbed a boy from the 3rd Wisconsin, grabbed him by the collar and held on. "Stop, in the name of all you cherish, stop! Don't you love your country?"

"You goddamn tootin' and I'm going to get back to it just as fast as I can!"

Some of the Federals made up their own rules as they scattered through town. They threw up barricades at street intersections, shoving up furniture from homes, overturning wagons, anything to impede these furies bearing down on them. The townspeople were as wild now as anyone. Dreadful, despicable Yankees. Come into our homes and defile our landscape. Barbarians! If they had guns, they fired them. They threw kitchen knives and heavy kettles from windows. They unloaded boiling water on blue-jackets below. Southern troops came up with Parrott guns, got civilians to take cover, and then blasted the barricades away. A knot of Federals hung out around the courthouse square, just ambled there and milled around, waiting . . . for what? The 5th Virginia, composed of local Winchester boys, then came sprinting down the street and sent them flying. There was the steady pop of gunfire, like an exaggerated Fourth of July, smoke, hoofbeats, splintering wood, cries, yelps, and chaos.

The blue-jackets spilled out on the road north from Winchester and kept going—fast. Now was the time, the setting for a sweep from the gray cavalry. With such a maneuver the whole of Banks's force could be taken and rounded up. A whole Federal army, from top to bottom, would be corralled. The question now was, where's Ashby? Jackson looked around and could find no Ashby. Come to think of it, he hadn't seen Ashby since daybreak. "Never was there such a chance for cavalry," Jackson cried. "Oh, that my cavalry was in place!"

You did then with what you had at hand. Jackson ordered horses unhitched from guns and used as a makeshift cavalry. The dray horses broke into lumbering trots and covered a mile or two, then began slumping, keeling over. So did the infantry—these boys and men who had marched a hundred miles during the previous week and had been at hard combat for the past thirty hours. The horses didn't know what had hit them. The last thing they knew, they had been pulling plows and wagons in the quiet Shenandoah fields. Soldiers and beasts dropped and couldn't rise.

The amazing thing was not that they crumpled now, but that they had driven themselves so far and against such odds.

And still Jackson fought and pressed his enemy. He sent Sandie Pendleton to locate the Maryland cavalry under General George Stewart and get them cracking. The Yankees were getting away! The militarily proper Stewart was three miles east of Winchester, resting his men and letting his mounts roam in a clover field. It was a nice day, and Stewart's men and animals deserved a break. "Ride," Pendleton yelled at him. "Ride toward Martinsburg, and cut off the Yanks!"

No, General Stewart avowed, he couldn't quite do that. He was under the command of General Ewell—technically, following the book—and he wasn't moving till Ewell gave the word. Pendleton got back in the saddle and galloped away to Ewell. "Goddamn the goddamn chain of command! Doesn't the man know to *ride* now! Here's the order! Shit!" Stewart was moving his sabers out as soon as Pendleton galloped back, but two precious hours were lost. As they rode to engage Banks, Ashby came out of the hills and added a few more troopers.

Ashby had been free-lancing once more, circling to the right of Ewell's line and trying, on his own, to catch Yankees. If the mass of Yankees had been there, he would have carried the day as hero. As it was, he became the focus for some high-level anger—namely, Jackson's. But Ashby remained in Jackson's affections as well as in his commander's consciousness as someone impossible to discipline and force into a common mold. Jackson had tried to discipline Ashby—Lord, he had tried. Back in April, Lee had inquired why only one colonel and one major—*two* officers—composed the entire officer corps in Ashby's regiment. Ashby hadn't bothered about making people officers or not—you rode, you killed Yankees, that was about the size of it. He wasn't a great one for drilling either. He believed that when someone came up and said he wanted to fight Yankees, he should be put to that task. Who needed training? He figured he was leading some kind of legion and let it go at that. Jackson took Lee's inquiry about the lack of officers into consideration, and tried to outflank Ashby. He broke Ashby's cavalry into two regiments and sent them off to Winder's and Taliaferro's brigades for disciplining. Get them to shape up; let them have a little basic training. Afterward Ashby could apply for the troops he needed.

The ploy fell apart immediately. Ashby sent in his resignation, and his troopers made arrangements to return to the farm. If they couldn't ride the way they wanted, shoot the Yanks any way they felt like it, have old Ashby beside them in the saddle—then, to hell with it. Let someone else fight the war. Winder became alarmed, sensing that perhaps two implacable forces had met. He arranged a personal meeting between the two, and Jackson and Ashby sat down to a powwow under canvas on an April evening, a lantern glowing on a camp desk between them. Far into the night they talked. They exited with a solution. The next day a general order went out that "detailed" all the cavalry units *back* to Ashby while keeping them "technically" on the rosters of Winder and Taliaferro's brigades. It was facesaving semantics. The troops went back under Ashby's command. Major Harman chortled. "General Jackson has just plumb backed down." This was during the period when Quartermaster Harman was circulating the theory that they were in great danger from "our cracked-brained Genl." Jackson, though, knew what he was doing. He knew that he must keep Ashby in the saddle. He couldn't afford to lose him, for there was no one like Ashby.

Now Ashby joined in chasing what could be found of Banks's retreating army until Banks had the presence of mind to set up some artillery on the outskirts of Martinsburg and halt the winded Rebels momentarily. Meanwhile Banks's dispirited, broken army, what was left of it, crossed the Potomac and got safely off Virginia soil by nightfall. It happened on May 25, another Sabbath.

The Confederates poured into Winchester in high holiday mood. Everywhere they turned there was booty. Everywhere they looked there was Federal calamity. Banks had been tossed out of the Shenandoah completely with the unbelievable loss of 3,500 men, 3,000 of whom became prisoners. (Jackson's troops suffered 400 killed and wounded.) Lying around were nearly 9,000 small arms, two big cannons, warehouses brimming with medicine and supplies; here were fat cattle and sheep, untold amounts of food and delicacies. Harman, who had the sharp eye of a tradesman, figured the booty came to half a million dollars—

a solid sum in that day. They christened Banks "Commissary Banks" and toasted him with the champagne they came by through his stores. They doffed their filthy, lice-ridden home-spun gray and donned the fresh, smart blue uniforms of the Yankees. (Jackson later had to issue orders that any man found in Federal blue would be considered the enemy and dealt with accordingly. It was the only way to get the new clothes off these men.) What joy now!

Jackson received the wildest applause of all as he rode Little Sorrel into Winchester. He waved his sun-and-sweat-soiled cap, dismounted in his oversized boots, and then strode immediately for Reverend Graham's house. He frolicked with the children, swung them over his head, was then induced to take Sunday dinner with the family. He wanted to thank his Heavenly Father for the great victory, while Reverend Graham kept quizzing him on what brilliant strategic strokes he might have used to so completely rout the invader Banks. Jackson's mind seemed elsewhere—on a family meal, cheerful table talk, romping with the children, being his shy social self.

Lincoln, in Washington, was not taken in by Banks's barrage of cables, many of which were sent to soothe the chief executive. He understood completely that Banks was a disaster and that Jackson, left unchecked, just might gallop into Washington. He ordered McDowell to leave Fredericksburg, not for the expected strike at Richmond but to attack Jackson to the north, from the rear. A command went out to Frémont to move across the Alleghenies and strike Jackson from the west. It looked as if Jackson could be brought to his knees, be annihilated himself, if swift action were taken now by knowledgeable troops. The price, however, was that McClellan would not get the number of men he had expected.

But Jackson was already thinking of attacking farther north, of driving the war closer to the heart of the Union. First he would let his men rest for a day and attend church services, which had been delayed by the fighting. Right now, on this Sabbath, they were having a glorious celebration.

CHAPTER XII

A Hero Is Made

Thomas Jonathan Jackson had become a hero in the Confederacy. Except for the Shenandoah Valley, the war was going pretty badly for the South. The U.S. flag now flew over City Hall in New Orleans. The Confederates had sunk the ironclad Virginia rather than have her fall into Federal hands. Everywhere bad news and bleak prospects—except where Stonewall Jackson commanded. Jackson now gave people hope and the image of someone who could win. What had once made Jackson seem foolish now seemed endearing: the well-worn cap, the oversized boots, his habit of sucking on lemons—in fact, the mystery of how he came by the lemons was as enchanting as the sheer mystery of the man himself. He was not quite like anyone else, although he embodied many of the characteristics of others from his region. He was suspicious, self-reliant, dogged, spiritual, and highly practical by turns, humble and then arrogant when he felt he was in the right. He was a workhorse and, finally, he was imaginative. He was recognized now when he rode by on Little Sorrel; he was stared at in church and pointed out as he rested by the campfire or sat on a fence.

But people seeing Jackson for the first time still couldn't

accept it. This man a hero? Confederate officer and novelist John
E. Cooke wrote:

> The outward appearance of the famous leader was not impos-
> ing. He wore an old sun-embrowned coat, now almost out at
> the elbows. The remainder of the General's costume was as
> much discolored as the coat. He wore cavalry boots reaching
> to the knee, and his head was surmounted by an old cap, more
> faded than all; the sun had turned it quite yellow indeed, and
> it tilted forward so far over the wearer's forehead that he was
> compelled to raise his chin in the air in order to look under
> the rim.
>
> His horse was not a "fiery steed," pawing and ready to
> dart forward . . . but . . . a horse of astonishing equanimity,
> who seemed to give himself no concern on any subject, and
> calmly moved about, like his master, careless of cannonball or
> bullet in the hottest moments of battle.

His own men, who had once cursed and railed against him
as if he were some Simon Legree, now swung their hats and yelled
when he appeared. Of course, they did not become perfect soldiers or even better soldiers—but their attitude toward Old Jack
became different. They realized that though they sweated and
were driven near mad by him, he saved their blood. They were
not massacred. Naturally, they disregarded his expected orders
not to roam through Winchester and to stay holed up in bivouac
outside the hamlet. They wanted girls, they wanted booze. Only
a cannon fired directly in their midst could have kept them from
the abundance of Federal supplies around them. How those Yankees had treated themselves! These Southern country boys now
dug into oranges, oysters, lobsters, and fresh coffee with cream
and sugar. And there was the harder stuff. Two deep-chested
young bloods from the Maryland line liberated a dozen bottles
of champagne. They had never tasted champagne before.

"Lookey here at this stuff flow. You ever seen such as this
in your life?" one said. "Tastes like a phosphate."

"Think we oughter turn it in?"

"You crazy? You want them officers to drink it up for you?"

"How we goin' to hide it—or tote it?"

"Tote, shit! We goin' to drink it."

And they did, all twelve bottles. The next day Old Jack had them moving out for Harpers Ferry early. They survived the war, and years later, at every reunion, the first thing they recounted was the night they had champagne and moved out before daylight in a trance, near dead. Such were the memories of the war. But that was later.

Winder's Stonewall Brigade marched toward Charles Town and Harpers Ferry—men and boys who knew war as tramping in the dust, sloughing in mud and pelting rain, lying facedown on the ground to rest for ten minutes every hour, and then firing, running, and having limbs blown off in sudden violent collisions. A courier caught up with Winder a mile from Charles Town and told him the Yankees were entrenched south and west of the town. Be careful, plan to lay siege possibly. Winder just kept plowing along, didn't even stop for a confab and strategy session. Keep moving! The brigade just pushed the Yankees back, pushed them right out of the town and up on Bolivar Heights.

General Joe Johnston down in Richmond was cheering the Valley army on. He had retreated into a tight knot in the capital and enjoyed keen fantasies of Jackson beating the Yankees back to Washington and into Maryland. Jackson had the same idea— but was cautious, alert. He was there. He took the 2nd Virginia to join forces with his old brigade under Winder and set up headquarters in Charles Town. The ladies of the town came to call, and Jackson received them courteously. "How do you do, ladies? So very nice to see you, and have the opportunity of visiting your lovely town. I apologize for the occasion which has made it necessary. So very glad to see you."

In Washington Lincoln had not been asleep. He was as offensive-minded as Jackson and certainly as much of a fighter. He had called on McDowell and Shields to attack this miserable annoying Valley army from the east, coming over the Blue Ridge and taking Front Royal. He called on John C. Frémont to strike over the Alleghenies and take Harrisonburg. He pored over his Shenandoah maps, Secretary Stanton beside him, both marking where armies stood and how they might be used. Lincoln saw his more than adequate Federal armies used as an anvil. Shields and Frémont would close the bottom of the sack, leaving Jackson no exit, and then McDowell and Bank, in superior numbers, would chase and eventually annihilate him. Simplicity itself. Take Harrisonburg, General Frémont; take Front Royal, General Shields; and the anvil will ring. After that, in Lincoln's way of looking at it, it was "a question of legs." Every athlete knows the term—"legs." Can they carry you? Can you still be standing when others drop? Have you got a little more in you than the other man?

On May 30 Jackson rode off to the front, a short distance north of Charles Town, and watched an artillery duel and some hot skirmishing. Then a light rain began to fall, getting heavier. Jackson took cover under a large spreading tree. It was not in his nature to waste time, and when he didn't have anything else to do, he slept. Usually he had more important things to do. He stretched out, the rain pelting the ground around him, and was asleep in an instant. When he opened his eyes, he saw that Colonel A. R. Boteler was busily sketching him—putting down his form and substance, just drawing away. "Let me see what you have there," said Jackson.

He went over it without praise or comment. "My hardest tasks at West Point were the drawing lessons, and I never could do anything in that line to satisfy myself, or indeed, any one else." But enough pleasant chitchat; Jackson didn't have the time anymore. Boteler was here, the man was a proven trusted ally— Jackson had a job for him. "I need you to go to Richmond," he said. "I must have reinforcements." He explained what scouts and spies and his own intuition told him: A pincer movement was being formed by the Federals to trap him, to squeeze shut his escape route and wipe him from the face of the earth. But if . . . if he could get his strength up to 40,000 men he would transfer his campaign north of the Potomac to the banks of the Susquehanna, in the heart of Pennsylvania. He would realize the dream of fighting this bloody, unholy war on Northern soil.

"When should I go?" Boteler asked.

"I'd like you, if you please, to go as soon as you can."

In other words, immediately. There was never time for reflection, gathering forces, waiting for the right moment, pussyfooting around. Standard Operating Procedure was "do it now," never ask why. Boteler threw a leg over his horse and was off for Charles Town, where a train would carry him to Winchester. Before the train left, Jackson was there beside him for the trip.

Jackson had begun moving his troops "up" the Valley right away, meaning to the south, moving backward. Everyone—all the foot cavalry, the supply wagons, the mounted under Ashby, began falling back. The right name for the movement was retreat. But Jackson never apologized, never explained. You could say it was movement in the opposite direction.

"General," a young cavalry officer asked, riding up to Old Jack, "are the troops going back?"

"Don't you see them going?"

"Are they all going?" the officer said, persisting. Was he mad? Had the heat got him?

Jackson turned to a nearby colonel. Never explain, never apologize. "Colonel, arrest this man as a spy."

The young lieutenant might have been shot save for Turner Ashby coming up, being informed of the situation, and arguing the young officer's case. "He doesn't have much sense." It wasn't much, but enough to save the lieutenant's hide.

For speed Jackson boarded the train at Charles Town and took the seat beside a rather startled Boteler. He further surprised the newly appointed messenger to Richmond by falling immediately asleep. He just rested his head against the seat in front and passed out.

The rain increased, slashing against the train windows and streaking down in little rivulets. Boteler kept his hands busy by focusing and unfocusing a pair of field glasses. Rumor had it that the Yankees were on the march everywhere; Lincoln had had enough of Stonewall and was going to throw the whole might of the Federal army against him.

Boteler thought he saw a lone figure galloping on a storm-swept field outside his window. It could have been hallucinatory, and he brought his glasses down, rubbed his eyes, and put the apparatus up again. It was a lone rider, in a Confederate uniform, and he was waving wildly. Boteler woke his friend Jackson. "General, I believe that rider out there has something to say to you."

Jackson took little time to come awake, and called for the train to halt. He opened the window, and the rider saluted and handed a message in to his general. Jackson scanned it, tore it up, told the conductor to proceed, resumed his prior position, and fell to sleep again. In Winchester the word spread about the message stuck through the train window. Shields—fierce, profane Shields—had taken Front Royal. Colonel Z. T. Conner of the 12th Georgia had been in charge of the Confederate garrison there and had—the only word—panicked at the sight of Federals. He had lost his nerve—happened, happened to the best of them. He had marched his regiment to Winchester and abandoned all the booty the Confederates had recently come by, courtesy of Banks. All those brogans, tents, fresh-smelling saddles, *supplies*— gone. Not only was Front Royal lost but the Pathfinder Frémont had crossed the Alleghenies and was heading for Strasburg.

The pincer was hours away from locking shut. They were closing in on Tom Jackson. Not the hunter now but the hunted. But first, business. He called for Colonel Conner to come to a room he had taken in a Winchester hotel.

"Colonel, how many men did you have killed?"

"None."

"How many wounded?"

"None, sir."

"Do you call that much of a fight?" Tom Jackson said, and then ordered Conner arrested.

That night Jackson called for Boteler to come to his room. The rain still fell outside his window, shaking the panes and coming in waves. It was dark and gloomy. And when Jackson strode to the window occasionally, hands behind his back, peering out, he saw column after column of his troops laboring down the street—retreating. Boteler, a worldly man and a compleat son of Virginia, had the presence of mind to order two hot whiskey toddies delivered to the room the moment he received his summons. "General, I believe the occasion calls for a little nip."

"No, no, you must excuse me; I never drink intoxicating liquors."

Old Boteler shook his head, looked gravely downward, as if about to prescribe some distasteful medicine, and said, "As you know, I am not a drinking man. But there comes a time when a stimulant is a necessity, a medical prescription. I would never take a drink myself and certainly I would not offer a slug to you if this was not such an occasion. You must break your rule and join me in toddy tonight."

Jackson considered the offer. The sound of lashing rain and the tamping feet of lines of soldiers came from outside. The Confederacy was in deep peril. Jackson took a glass and sipped, face expressionless. He took a few more sips. "Do you know why I habitually abstain from intoxicating drinks?"

"No, I don't believe I am quite aware of the reason."

"Why, sir, because I like the taste of it. I like the effect. I like it a lot—too much, you might say. When I discovered this, I made up my mind to do without it."

Jackson cut short his drinking, signed some formal requests for additional troops for Boteler to take to Richmond, and kept working. He could find time to sleep in the afternoon, sitting up in a railroad car, when no work was at hand, but here in his hotel room, in the middle of the night, things to do, he continued going at a fast pace. At three o'clock on the morning of May 31 he was knocking on the door of Jed Hotchkiss, his map maker. He wanted Hotchkiss to go immediately to Charles Town and bring "up" the Stonewall Brigade under Winder. Get it out of there. There was not going to be any invasion of the north in the near future. The important news of the moment was that his Valley army was in danger of being trapped by Lincoln. Lincoln was exhorting his generals afield that they must drive on Jackson with all available speed. The object of this concern, Jackson, rattled off orders, kept moving, and appeared for all the world in fine spirits. He just kept doing what he had to do.

Jackson rounded up all the captured Federals, some 2,300 in number, and included them in the tramping feet leaving Winchester. The Winchester locals looked sadly on the departing Confederate soldiers. Only six days before there had been a wild celebration, a liberation, and Jackson had ridden Little Sorrel down Main Street to wild hurrahs. Now they waved farewell to the general. He was in the saddle and leading his troops away. Was this war? They were becoming a little confused. Didn't anyone win and that was the end of it? Winchester would change hands eighty-two times before the conflict was over, but none of the townspeople could have anticipated it. Jackson marched his men at a rapid pace for an hour and then let them rest ten minutes—as always, nothing changed. Columns were closed and stragglers were roughly handled. Any moment they expected a wave of blue-clad figures to appear from around a bend or to stream down a hillside. They expected artillery to begin peppering the road. The rain kept falling. They kept marching.

Young John Worsham was marching with the 21st Virginia, and like so many others, he just kept putting one foot in front of the other. That was all he knew how to do. But here were all these Yankee prisoners around him. It had fallen to the 21st Virginia through default to guard these pesky Yankees. No one else wanted them. They surrounded young Worsham, and one lanky, nervous-acting Northerner got beside him and said, "You're carrying a fine gun there, boy. Looks right like the one I lost when you folks took me prisoner."

"It's not your gun. This here's my gun. I know my own gun, don't I?"

"Well, whoever's gun it is or was it's goin to be my gun when we get retook. And we are going to be retook. Everybody knows that. Your generals, everybody. And when we are, I'm goin' have that gun and I'm goin' to use it on you."

"No, you're not! Now you git!"

Frémont, who had crossed the Alleghenies, now had the more difficult task of striking Jackson and closing the pincers. He immediately overestimated Jackson's strength, and began thinking up reasons for delay. He wired Washington that his scouts estimated enemy strength at 60,000 men. Lincoln fumed. Old Abe wanted to fight. If he had been a general there was no doubt he would have found Jackson and fought. Lincoln wired back that Jackson probably had 15,000. "Where is your force? It ought this minute to be near Strasburg."

Then Frémont began complaining of the hardships his troops had undergone. They had suffered in crossing the mountains; many of his men were shoeless and in a wretched condition. In war, as well as peace, there can be excuses. Lincoln simply wanted results. He wanted Frémont at Strasburg, but Frémont was not there and Jackson was inexorably moving out of the net. Once again Banks was no help. Banks claimed his command was too shaken by recent events to get moving in a hurry. He would not move until June 10, long after Jackson had, so to speak, escaped. Shields had shot his bolt apparently in taking Front Royal. He had captured a plum and wanted to rest on his laurels. He as waiting for reinforcements under General E.O.C. Ord to join him before he advanced. Everyone had excuses for not attacking Jackson.

Up the Valley road came Jackson, who kept twisting his head around to make sure his infantry was keeping to a quick step. Supply wagon after supply wagon listed from side to side down the rutted road in the rainstorm. In an offensive, a chance to strike the enemy, Jackson stripped down his bag and baggage. In retreat he wouldn't abandon a shovel. The enemy must be punished on all levels, and nothing given him gratis.

As Jackson neared Strasburg he found no Frémont. There was no sign of Shields. He ordered Ewell to bring his troops forward and then swing west and give it to Frémont. He was going to open the pincers wide and pass through. Ewell was delighted. "God damn, sum bitch, let me at 'em!" He had his men up and out at dawn, his skirmishers soon finding some lackadaisical Frémont soldiers to engage. They drove them back, and Ewell was soon joined by Dick Taylor and his Louisiana Brigade. "I am completely puzzled," Ewell announced. "I have driven these people back and I have no fight. What's wrong?"

"Perhaps I could send my brigade against their right and see what happens."

"Do so," said Ewell. "That may stir the sons a bitches up. I'm sick of this fiddle-fartin' around."

Taylor moved his troops at the flank in quick order and Frémont's troops scattered. They backed up and fled. Taylor sighed. "Sheep would give more resistance than that." And he knew, Ewell knew, and soon Stonewall Jackson would know, that Frémont, as a general of troops, represented little menace. As soon as Winder and the Stonewall Brigade caught up with this main body of troops, they were all on the way of escaping Lincoln's trap.

On June 1, in late afternoon, the lead skirmishers of Winder's brigade were sighted by Ashby's cavalry coming down the road from Winchester. It was a bone-weary group of men, soldiers who had marched as much as thirty miles a day,

but they had made it. They had made it to the safety of the
main body. Jackson thanked God, as was his custom, writing
his darling Anna, "The [Yankees] endeavored to get in my rear
by moving on both flanks of my gallant army, but our God has
been my guide and saved me from their grasp." He now had his
troops marching on to New Market—into still another downpour. Lashing rain, deep, deep mud, and wagons that had to be
pushed from the mire at every step. He wanted the wagons well
in front and the cavalry guarding his rear. Exhausted men began
to drop. Jackson cornered a harried, out-of-control colonel. "Sir,
why do you not get your brigade together, keep it together, and
move on?"

"It's impossible, General; I can't do it!"

Jackson's eyes blazed. "Don't say it's impossible! Turn your
command over to the next officer. If he can't do it, I'll find someone who can, if I have to take him from the ranks."

The Federal cavalry did annoy the army, breaking through
occasionally in the rear and then being repulsed. Jackson was
burning bridges behind him, making Frémont throw down pontoon bridges if he wanted to pursue him. But Jackson didn't fear
Frémont as much as he tolerated and patronized him. His only
concern was that Shield and Frémont would join together before
he got out of the perimeter. After a melee with the Federal cavalry, Colonel J. M. Patton reported to Jackson. Jackson listened
quietly to the details. Patton ended by saying that he regretted
seeing the bluecoats shot down, raked down from their mounts
and slain.

Jackson said, "Colonel, why do you say that you saw those
Federal soldiers fall with regret?"

Patton was taken back. After all, weren't they all civilized
men—Northerner and Southerner alike? "Well, sir, these men
showed a bit more courage than I'm used to seeing, and I guess
I just like to witness brave men. I was just hoping their lives
might be spared."

"No, sir," Jackson said, "shoot them all; I do not wish them
to be brave."

At night, the rain turning to drizzle, Jackson warmed himself
by a campfire with Dick Taylor. The fire crackled and the smoke
curled and shadows played around their exhausted faces. They

were staring somberly at the flames when a large black man came up with a steaming tin mug of coffee for Taylor. He said nothing, extending the mug. This was Tom Strother, Taylor's body servant, never far from his side, in battle and at rest. As was customary back then, he did not speak until spoken to. Without a word Jackson rose and grasped the black man's hand tightly, shaking it. They both nodded, and Jackson sat back down.

Taylor asked the commander why he had just done this. Jackson told him that a couple of days before he had come upon Strother in an exposed position during a particularly nasty firefight and told him to run for safety. Tom Strother had thanked him, but had said that, if it was all the same, he'd just stay there and wait for General Taylor as he'd been directed to do. Jackson appreciated this kind of physical courage and liked to acknowledge it when he found it. Taylor noted in his memoirs that there appeared to be an unstated understanding between his servant and Jackson—that they often looked at each other with a mute sympathy as they sat by a campfire.

By June 6, 1862, Jackson had moved his van to Port Republic and the heights between North River and the Massanuttens. He had escaped entrapment—narrowly, but he had escaped. It was a day of mixed blessings, this sixth of June 1862. He received clippings from Richmond papers that acclaimed him the South's first true general and full hero. They expected him to lead his battalions eventually through Maryland and into Pennsylvania—which actually was Jackson's plan. Jackson received copies of Northern papers that lamented their losses and blamed Jackson for them. No one ever doubted that Jackson thirsted for military distinction, but he liked to have God given the glory for all military victories. Of course the papers did not include the Lord in their accounts of military officers. Jackson stopped reading the papers after the sixth—or no one saw him reading them after that. He got word from Richmond on that date that he was to get no reinforcements, that the request that Colonel Boteler carried to President Davis had been turned down. More bad news: General Joe Johnston had been severely wounded in the defense of Richmond. By his own hand, though, President Davis congratulated Jackson on his brilliant campaign in the Valley. Jackson wired back that if he was needed in Richmond he would come. But June 6, 1862, was not over. Another event overshadowed all others.

Frémont's cavalry kept annoying the rear guard of Jackson's army. Any fear of the Pathfinder might had long since passed, but Turner Ashby, for one, realized that there might be frisky elements under Frémont who could still give the Valley army trouble—as he himself was able, on his own, to bring grief to the Federals. For instance, there was an Englishman in a cavalry regiment who had a personal vendetta against Ashby himself.

Sir Percy Wyndham was one of those unusual, unlikely characters who pop up from time to time in this extraordinary war. He had soldiered beside Major Wheat with Garibaldi in Italy and was a skillful warrior. He was a true soldier of fortune and a man with a sense of humor and fun. He had made a boast that he was going to capture the flamboyant Ashby and make him eat crow. Everyone on the other side worth his salt wanted to put the quietus to Ashby—but none had.

Ashby had been promoted to brigadier general on May 23 on orders from Richmond. Jackson had actually opposed the promotion and didn't even congratulate the man. Now, on a muddy June 6, Jackson's cavalry in the rear was attacked by . . . Sir Percy Wyndham of Britain, lately of New Jersey. Ashby was astride his horse a moment after the first shot rang. "Mount and charge!" As usual, Ashby met a challenge with aggression, a charge with a countercharge. He galloped straight into the Federal line, leading the way. After a brief fight, the Federals began to weaken and sixty-four were taken prisoner. Among them the leader of the 1st New Jersey: Sir Percy Wyndham. Ashby courteously accepted his surrender, passed on a witty line or two, took a few, and sent Sir Percy behind the Confederate line. He would continue keeping his eyes open for any stray blue cavalry that might have escaped.

Wyndham himself nonchalantly moved toward the Confederate officers' quarters, calling greetings to former foes here and there. Those who witnessed his arrival described him as a "stalwart" man. He had huge moustaches, cavalry boots adorned with the spurs of a caballero and a slouched hat and plume. Major Rob Wheat of the Louisiana Tigers sprang from his horse at the sight of the man.

"Percy, old boy!"

"Why, Rob. You rascal!"

They embraced, and brought each other up to date. Kyd Douglas thought it might be diverting if this strange member of the English aristocracy got to meet the old man. He was brought before Jackson, who immediately offered him a chair and began a quiet chat. At nine o'clock, as full darkness fell, an officer appeared and asked if he might have a word with the general. Outside he gave Jackson the worst news that had come to him in the entire war. Ashby lay dead.

After Sir Percy Wyndham had retired behind Confederate lines, Ashby still thirsted for a fight. He got it. Some Union cavalry came trotting forward, a few hundred and some men astride snorting, head-swiveling beasts. He thought out a plan, a spur-of-the-moment inspiration. He borrowed two infantry regiments from Ewell and led them toward a dark wooded area, which he considered deserted. He planned to have some cavalry lure the Federals to a road beside these woods, at which point the infantry—and Ashby—would spring.

The plan was brilliantly conceived save for one point: Some Federal sharpshooters had infiltrated the woods and were now in secure positions—behind trees, obscured by foliage. Rifles were steadily, quietly being raised. Just as Ashby came near the woods, savoring the expectation of surprising the Yanks, someone remarked, "Look at Ashby. See how happy he is."

The crack battalion of Federal sharpshooters, some Pennsylvania Bucktails, put the Confederates in their sights and squeezed the triggers. The 58th Virginia began to bolt. Ashby's horse reared, whinnied, charged one way, then another. Ashby was a series of streaks, into the woods one moment, racing out the next—imploring men to stand and fight, firing his heavy revolver when he could. Suddenly his mount weaved, stumbled, and went down. Ashby was on his feet immediately, charging, still imploring: "Charge, men, for God's sake, charge!" The 58th Virginia wheeled around and followed. The 1st Maryland came next, all behind this strange, enraged, swarthy-featured man with an oversized revolver in his hand, a plume in his hat. A private took a bullet in the mouth; a stoop-shouldered youth felt the plunk of lead go into his chest and he sat down. The man beside him took a bullet in the head that toppled him over. A color sergeant turned around with a bullet in his stomach. A corporal caught the banner and was cut down before he could raise it. The pop, pop, pop from the sharpshooters shook branches and kicked up the dirt. Cries and whoops filled the air. The flag kept changing hands as first one, then another took it. But the advance continued— even as a musket ball found Ashby and entered his chest, and he sank to the ground, dying.

The Pennsylvania sharpshooters dropped back and then began, slowly but inevitably, to fall subject to a rout. They had been flushed from the woods, and they were in disarray. Southern cavalry now began beating back the Federals who were on horseback, sending what remained of the attackers scampering toward Harrisonburg. The frenzy that Ashby had created couldn't be stopped although he lay lifeless. The very best of Frémont's cavalry and infantry had been beaten.

The troopers raised Ashby's body up and carried it to the rear in disbelief. Not Ashby. Who could ever lead them now? A deep gloom spread through his camp, as the word went out. In a farmhouse he was propped up in a chair and his photograph taken in the laborious process of the time. The finished tintype was then colored, his cheeks made red, his bushy beard and hair black, his uniform gray. Then his eyes were painted open, as if he might still be breathing. It was a remembrance to send back to his home.

The formalities of grief went on, but little time was available to savor the impact of death. Jackson viewed the body in a room in Port Republic, and then began the plan of confronting Frémont and Shields. He was going to fight not one but two battles simultaneously. He meant to slam-bang Shields and then polish off the Pathfinder Frémont. He sent out battle orders to Ewell and Winder of the Stonewall Brigade, and late at night flung himself onto his bed without even removing his boots and sword. An hour before daybreak, Colonel John D. Imboden, searching for another officer, burst into Jackson's room. He found him as he had fallen—facedown, in full battle gear, out like a light. "Oh, I'm so sorry, General."

"That's perfectly all right. Time to get up."

Jackson was on the field before first light. Ewell had charge of keeping Frémont occupied near Cross Keys while Jackson took command of those forces at nearby Port Republic, the spot to which Shields was now advancing. Simply put, they would both fight the Federals and keep them from joining up—divide and conquer, keep 'em guessing. Although Frémont had superior forces, Jackson continued to hold him in low esteem. Frémont, like Banks, hated losing more than he savored winning. He became cautious; he became aware of history's judgment, of how the headlines back in Washington might read. His heart might have been stout, but it was also troubled. He didn't dare take the bold step, the necessary risk. Jackson had his number.

And the days were now so crowded with action, with possibilities, that it became difficult to make detailed plans—to sit down and fret. The day before, June 8, was an example. It had been a Sunday. Jackson had not been able to observe the Sabbath since May 18 and he longed to. He hoped that this one day Shields would not advance and Frémont would adhere to his usual dilatory, ineffectual tactics. He had the Reverend Major Dabney primed to preach. At 8:00 A.M. he and his staff were biding their time on the front porch of headquarters, the home of a Dr. Kemper. The Sabbath had a bright, special sparkle; in the old days (only a couple of years before) Jackson would have been suiting up for services in Lexington. He would have been securing his pocket watch, putting a final comb to his hair, giving a last swipe to the shine on his shoes. Now Reverend Dabney lay on his army cot going over his sermon while Jackson paced the front porch, looking nervously off into the distance.

He heard galloping hoofbeats and then saw a rider come up, howling as drew in the reins, "Yankees coming! Yankees coming, General!"

At the same instant, as punctuation, a shell exploded over the center of town. Then pandemonium. Jackson had not positioned his troops with his usual fanatical care. Jackson was tired; his very bones ached with tiredness; each day could be a millennium; he was just looking forward to praying, singing a few hymns, remembering the Almighty. "Yankees coming!"

"Where's my artillery?"

"Don't know!"

"Then get!"

Jackson and several of his staff made a beeline for the high ground to get a counterattack going. Shields had broken through his lines, and his rear was defenseless. Jackson and some others spurred across the North River bridge through a spray of rifle fire while Federal cavalry rode up Main Street to discover Confederate wagons piled high with supplies on the road leading south to Staunton. In the process they captured Jackson's chief of artillery, Colonel Stapleton Crutchfield. The poor man was mortified, and it was a unique moment in the war. Jackson had been surprised—and on the Sabbath.

Jackson made for a bluff overlooking the town, sending commands to Taliaferro and Winder and Taylor, getting set for a counterthrust. Down below, at the Kemper house, a mere captain was all that stood between the Federals and Jackson's wagon trains. Captain Samuel J. C. Moore came on the scene from the south with twelve men. He was seeking orders and ended up with the whole command on his shoulders. His tiny band positioned themselves behind a panel fence, and waited. The Federals came down Main Street, their heads swiveling, alert, rifles ready. They believed, right up to the last moment, that they were going to take the prize. When they were less than two hundred feet away, Moore and his Rebels rose as one and squeezed off a round into their faces. The Federals fell back, regrouped—and got terribly angry. They came charging in a fury, but by this time a six-gun battery had been wheeled into position at the Kemper house. The Federals had got to within half pistol range when the gun let loose. It blasted the fence away but its fire sailed over the Yankees' heads. They fell back again in shock—and now the Reverend Major Dabney was among the Rebels at the Kemper house, having commandeered a couple of guns. Half dressed, bathed in sweat, he yelled furiously and directed shells into the heart of his enemy. Scarcely an hour before he had been lying prone, preparing his Presbyterian sermon. Such was this period, such was this war. The Federals coming down Main Street were stopped, and Colonel Crutchfield was liberated and got his saber and his dignity back.

On the bluff above Port Republic Jackson spied an outfit in blue wheeling some artillery at the far end of the North River bridge. Some of Poague's Rockbridge Artillery had arrived to aid him and he ordered them immediately to shell the blue-clad gang. "No, General, sir, we can't do that! Those men are Confederates!"

"How can that be? Those men are dressed like Yankees."

"I visited them last night," Poague said. "They had on blue uniforms. Those are our men down there, General, sure as God made little green apples. Let's not kill our own men."

Jackson spurred Little Sorrel down toward them. He rose in his stirrups, and called out: "You men bring that gun up here!"

They looked sullenly at him, saying nothing.

"Bring that gun up here, I say!"

Instead, the gunners began screwing their piece so that it faced uphill, right at Jackson. A shell took the ground away in front of him. He wheeled Little Sorrel around and trotted back to his artillery.

"Let 'em have it!" His artillery began blazing away as he sought out infantry to help. He ran into Fulkerson's 37th Virginia running toward the noise of battle. "Down there they are," he said. "Charge right through, Colonel!"

The 37th Virginia did so while Jackson waved his cap above his head, as he did at the start of many charges. The Confederates tore through the village, sending the Federals racing across the river and northward in the direction from which they had come. All the while Poague's artillery shelled and punished them. Then the air became still. Acrid smoke floated down the town's streets and lay beneath the hills. Horses began snorting and couriers raced between commands. Here and there came the crack of musket fire and a heavy gun's report. It was past the hour of worship on this Sabbath now.

Such pummeling, helter-skelter events—the near capture of Jackson, the capture and release of Crutchfield, the Reverend Major Dabney flinging himself from sermon preparation to the unloading of heavy shells—all of this might have made talk and recollection for a generation. But through the stillness of this sunny day Jackson heard the sound of battle now coming from nearby Cross Keys. Ewell must be mixing it up with Frémont. Jackson put Little Sorrel to the gallop and went through picket lines and found Old Baldy, who held a beatific smile on his face. Jackson knew immediately that the fighting had been hot and Ewell was winning. Actually sixty-year-old Issac Trimble, the erstwhile lawyer from Baltimore, had been the hero this day. When Frémont had opened up with artillery and had started a tentative advance, Trimble and his troops met him head on and flung him back. Not satisfied, still bloodthirsty, Trimble drove the Federals back a good mile, and would have kept going until death save for Ewell calling a halt due to fear of overextending the troops. Trimble even wanted to keep fighting that night, make an unheard-of night foray against the pussyfooting Pathfinder, but Ewell said no. "Just take it easy there, Trimble," Ewell had said, in his high-pitched voice. "You've done enough for one day."

Seeing that all was under control, that afternoon Jackson went back to Port Republic to prepare for the morrow's battle. He was near crazed from strain and kept looking at the ground and acting in a peculiar way. He said to Dabney, "Major, wouldn't it be a blessed thing if God would give us a glorious victory today?" A lieutenant who overheard him thought he spoke like a child— like a child hoping to receive a present. In fact, he had. Cross Keys was a victory—and more was to follow the next day.

But at first all he had wanted on this Sunday, June 8, as he lingered in early morning on the Kemper house porch, sucking a lemon, was to hear Reverend Dabney preach and himself to pray. On Monday the ninth, a regular workday, he had his battles. Up before sunrise, down to business. Ewell was to keep Frémont occupied while Jackson went after Shields. He sent the Stonewall Brigade under soldierly General Winder through some ripening wheat toward the Union lines. Winder meant to take them, and kept coming while the Federals zeroed in and began scything down wheat and men with heavy ammunition. Jackson, with only a hour or two of sleep the night before, didn't ponder. He called for Trimble and he called for Dick Taylor to abandon the battle with Frémont and come to Winder's aid. Jackson rode Little Sorrel slightly ahead of Winder's thin line, a few lengths from Union skirmishers who were now moving themselves through the wheat to get at these infernal Rebels, these crazed ignorant crackers who couldn't read or write or speak intelligible English and who kept yelling like banshees. Something—Someone?— must be protecting Jackson, for there he rode with shells exploding all around, calm, deliberate, and confident.

Winder was outnumbered in the wheat and now under heavy fire. He was exposed. He attacked. The startled enemy drew back in shock, overly cautious before these maniacs. Winder reached a fence beyond the wheat and took a position. The Federals began matter-of-factly lobbing shells onto his troops. Prudently, from a distance, they rained round after round on them. Some Rebels broke from the line and began falling back as officers raised sabers and yelled at them to re-form. Then Ewell appeared on the scene. He gave the Federals something new to worry about, but not for long. They simply changed positions, left Winder alone, and began slamming Ewell and his Second Brigade into some deep woods on the right of the Confederate line. Jackson was all over the scene, and it seemed absolute bedlam. No rational, detached observer could look at it and think there was some grand design or plan working here, some orchestration from a supreme commander.

Then Dick Taylor arrived and, at heavy cost, stormed and took the heavy guns that had been causing havoc. All right, get mixed up in this and you'll have to pay, the Yankees said. They dropped Ewell and Winder and methodically pressed into Taylor's small army. Like a move in chess, Winder was now free to advance once more. He was Jackson's man, and he charged. So did Ewell. The Federals suddenly found themselves having to contend with three sides. It was too much, particularly when Taliaferro's brigade rode into the fight with wild inhuman shrieks. The Federals just pulled back—no rout, just a steady orderly withdrawal. It was not Manassas, but they did keep going. The battle was over and it was not quite 11:00 A.M.

Jackson rode up to the skeptic Ewell, touched his arm gently, and said, "General, he who does not see the hand of God in this is blind, sir, blind!"

Everyone was tired, thirsty, winded woefully, and gasping for breath. Jackson told them they must pursue the Yankees now that they were on the run. Old Jack led them himself until they came to dense woods that could easily hide dreaded sharpshooters. He turned his infantry back, but led his cavalry after the Federals for another four miles. He had paid for the victory— eight hundred down, the most he had ever lost in Valley combat—but he had broken the back of the Federals. He captured over a thousand of their troops, and rounded up a great deal of booty. On June 10 his Valley army was perched high on a Shenandoah mountain, safe from all attack. He controlled as far as the eye could see. Frémont, Shields, and Banks had given the best they were capable of, and they had lost. Given their characters, they had given their best. Stonewall wanted it more—from his mysterious streak of ambition, from his very genes, from an ingredient in him that no one else had.

John Imboden, who served closely with him, explained it this way: "Jackson's military operations were always unexpected and mysterious. In my personal intercourse with him he often said there were two things never to be lost sight of by a military commander: 'Always mystify, mislead, and surprise the enemy, if possible; and when you strike and overcome him, never let up in the pursuit so long as your men have strength to follow; for an army routed, if hotly pursued, becomes panic-stricken, and can then be destroyed by half their number.

" 'The other rule is, never fight against heavy odds, if by any possible maneuvering you can hurl your own force on only a part—and that the weakest part—of your enemy and crush it. Such tactics will win every time, and a small army may thus destroy a large one in detail; and repeated victory will make it invincible.' "

Jackson made it sound simple—but it wasn't. There was a dark side to the picture, as there generally was with Jackson. There was that moment in the battle at Cross Keys when a young Federal officer on a white horse rode in front of his attacking column. Such a sight—so brave, so daring, the picture of a hero! The Confederates were mesmerized. Let him live, let the brave officer live to surrender. Take his sword, treat him like a Tidewater gentleman. "Kill him," Jackson said, and they did. "This is no ordinary war," he explained to Ewell, as if Ewell the unholy needed to be told. "The brave and gallant Federal officers are the very kind that must be killed. Shoot the brave officers and the cowards will run away and take the men with them."

Ewell had come around in his thinking. On first encountering Jackson he had considered him insane—as some others had, too. The man was bonkers. "I never saw one of Jackson's couriers approach without expecting an order to assault the North Pole."

Then, after the battle of Port Republic and Cross Keys, Ewell admitted his mistake. "I take it all back and will never prejudge another man," he told a fellow officer. "Old Jackson is no fool. He knows how to keep his own counsel, and does curious things, but he has a method in his madness."

Jackson knew how to win. You try to do anything and everything when the stakes are high, when the enemy is on your land and is in a position to subjugate you. You hang on. With 16,000 men he defeated an invading army of around 60,000. And he gave those in his army sights and experiences they would never forget, those who lived through it. Some of those sights and experiences they would just as soon have missed. There went Ed Moore of the Rockbridge Artillery up the steep mountain after the victory at Port Republic. He followed behind a caisson that carried a headless body. It shook and swayed as the caisson groaned up the incline. Some thoughtful soul had pinned a handkerchief over the spot where the neck had been severed, and practical Moore used its whiteness to lead him in growing misty darkness. A man saw so much. He saw the headless, intestines creeping out, a bloody stump for a leg. He heard choruses of moans and pleas. Oh, please, please, please, just a little drab of water—oh, God, please. My guts is on fire! A man could get so scared it seemed his heart was going to go out his ears. These Valley men often just went away themselves—back to their farms if they came near. They didn't like Jackson's insistence on drilling and all that Tomfoolery. They didn't like to have to say passwords and be kept out of hospitable towns where the girls were.

Later, as veterans, those who survived, they cherished his memory—because they never met anyone who equaled him, because he had a mystical specialness they hadn't realized at the time. But while they fought and served under him they liked one thing above all: He knew how to win.

CHAPTER XIII

Beyond Endurance

Now Jackson was poised in Brown's Gap, having licked all the Federal armies who had faced him one way or another. He kept planning, kept fretting. Possibly, with some added troop strength furnished by Richmond, he could move rapidly up the eastern side of the Blue Ridge and get behind the now and forever groggy Banks. Get in behind Banks, who was groping around in the air with his hands out, and seal him off. Cut off his path of retreat and butcher him. Collar him and take every last Federal prisoner. Then, Jackson envisioned, he could cross over into Maryland and Pennsylvania and give the Union a taste of its own medicine. Why not?

Because McClellan was encircling Richmond and moving, albeit glacierlike, but moving to take it. The Confederacy couldn't continue as such with its new capital taken, with blue-jacketed ruffians smoking long cigars and walking her streets. Mustn't even entertain the thought. Jackson mulled over the situation; so did Lee; and a few days passed in June 1862. Jackson took his men down from the mountains. He spread them in camps along rolling green meadows and soft gentle streams. Sixteen thousand men and boys was no small number, and each and every one of them needed a bath—badly. They cleaned up, scrawled messages home, and visited the countryside. This was a land of caves, deep subterranean miracles that had attracted hordes of visitors before the war. Jackson pitched his own headquarters now by the famous Weyer's Cave.

The caves were not that popular with the troops. The boys wanted girls, they wanted to roughhouse and play pranks on each other, they wanted to gossip about future battle plans and spin yarns about past glories—but few wanted to crawl into those cool eerily-still vaults beneath ground. Two freckle-faced Georgians, chums since birth, got inside one cave, aided in their progress by a pine torch. They gazed in wonder at the vaulted ceiling, the long dark tunnel that disappeared past the torch's parameter. Their ears still rang from the musketry and cannon fire of a few days before—the overpowering scent of burned powder and seared and decaying flesh. So quiet here, so cool and removed. One boy couldn't restrain himself: He yodeled behind the ear of his companion. "YaaaHeee!"

"Don't never do that! You like to skeer me to death!"

"Let's git out of hyer anyways. I don't like this kind of place."

"You got me to go! You plumb talked me into it!"

"Din't neither. You wanted to, same as me."

"Don't now. This is the dadburndest thing I ever seen. You know what it reminds me of?"

"What?"

"Reminds me of death. Reminds me of going off away from everything. Reminds me of a dadburn tomb."

The caves remained unpopular with the troops, but would return to the favor of tourists after the war. Jackson got reinforcements from Richmond, but no one knew for sure where the army would now be used. Hit Banks? Take Washington? Fly to Richmond? Where? Certainly Jackson was not going to broadcast the news. Lee decided that Jackson and his force should come to scatter McClellan away from Richmond. He put it in his diplomatic way by saying Jackson should come—if he concurred in Lee's views. Lee wrote, "To be efficacious, the movement must be secret. Be careful to guard from friends and foes your purpose and your intention of personally leaving the valley [and coming to Richmond]. The country is full of spies, and our plans are immediately carried to the enemy."

It was hardly necessary to warn Jackson to be on the quiet, secretive side. A veil of secrecy and deception covered Jackson from his first day in this war. Periodically, his staff and men rebelled. Harman, the hard-swearing quartermaster, could take it no longer. He never knew where to send a wagon train, and what's more, he could never reduce his wagon train. Jackson wanted everything. He wanted to win the war and not tell anybody about it. Harman sent in once again his resignation. "Goddamn sonsabitchin goddamn fool! Fry me in axle grease if I stay one more friggin' day in this man's outfit!" Once again he was prevailed upon to call his resignation back, reconsider, and continue as quartermaster.

Jackson didn't miss an opportunity to work the magic of deception. When Frémont's emissaries came over, under a flag of truce, to discuss burial arrangements for both sides, they heard Confederates whispering about large reinforcements, about massive movements down the Valley. They proudly reported these asides to Frémont, who thereupon hurried his retreat. Jackson treated his own generals curtly, telling them nothing of his plans. He carried the frontiersman's caution and need for secrecy to the end of his days. No one save Lee—his commander and the one person in uniform he thoroughly trusted—learned at any one moment what Old Jack planned to do. And even Lee was sometimes left in the dark.

General Winder of the Stonewall Brigade came to Jackson after the end of the mighty Valley battles and asked for leave to go take care of some business in Richmond. Winder was only a West Pointer, a gentleman, the bravest of the brave, and Jackson turned him down for leave as if he were a buck private. An officer, Jackson thought, stayed at his post no matter what. He wasn't taking leave, was he? Winder turned in his resignation, but Dick Taylor interceded and somehow a satisfactory arrangement was worked out—in effect, Jackson getting his way. And it was while Taylor pleaded Winder's cause to Jackson that he got what seemed to him an insight into Stonewall's heart. "Observing him closely, I caught a glimpse of the man's inner nature. It was but a glimpse. The curtain closed, and he was absorbed in prayer. Yet in that moment I saw an ambition boundless as Cromwell's, and as merciless," Taylor wrote in his book *Destruction and Reconstruction*. He believed that Jackson fought this ambition, loathed it, perhaps feared it, but could not escape it. It was part of his flesh. Taylor wondered if that was why Jackson prayed so much.

On June 17 Jackson's staff understood that Stonewall had come to some sort of decision about where to go and how to get there. At midnight he ordered that camp tents be struck and that the troops move out. They marched toward Waynesboro, resting at first at the base of Rockfish Gap. At night campfires winked for miles along the Blue Ridge as Jackson's army rested and took stock and waited for the next command. All were dependent upon one man.

He watched them march in hot sun, sitting astride Little Sorrel with the Reverend Major Dabney, his chief of staff, beside him. A cheer went up for Old Jack, and then hoots were directed toward poor Major Dabney. Dabney, who wore a Prince Albert coat and beaver hat, sat on his horse holding a large umbrella to ward off the sun. If there was one man who could cut a more comical figure in the army than Jackson, it was his chief of staff. "Come out from under that umbrelli! We sees you under there!"

Jackson rode off, and Dabney—brave, but no horseman— tried to keep up. His horse took him through brambles and under low-slung tree limbs and he lost his beaver hat, tore his Prince Albert coat, and had to fling his umbrella away. It was not easy staying up with Jackson. But the one person Jackson trusted with the troops' destination was Dabney. And Dabney had trouble keeping the secret. Ewell didn't know where they were headed— and Dabney couldn't tell him. "I'm the second-ranking officer in this army and I don't know!" Ewell piped in his squeaky voice, but Dabney couldn't tell him. Jackson had taken the train south, and directed that the troops follow him. Rumor had it that they were heading for Fredericksburg, where they would unite with other Confederates and then move on Washington. No, someone said, it must be Richmond they were going to. Then why, another asked, have all these reinforcements come from Richmond just to go back? Doesn't make sense. The troops moved by train, wagon, and foot. The heat was stifling and dust swirled around them. They all ended up in the small town of Fredericks Hall, Jackson there ahead of them. But he didn't remain long.

At one in the morning, June 23, he saddled up with a few companions, who were instructed to call him "Colonel," and then took off for Lee's headquarters at High Meadows, some fifty-two miles away. They galloped like pony express riders, passed by unsuspecting Confederate sentries, and reached Lee some four-teen hours later in midafternoon of the next day. It was to be a most important meeting of Confederate generals, who would decide how best to disabuse Little Mac of the idea that he could seize Richmond. James Longstreet, "Old Pete," had a broad im-passive face, deep-set Scotch-Irish eyes, and the ability to hold his temper. He was not impulsive, but a slugger, a dependable war-horse—Lee's war-horse.

Then there was A. P. Hill—called "Powell" by intimates—a nervous high-strung man who seemed to carry the look of per-petual melancholy, as if suffering a grievous wrong and sadness. And yet he was flamboyant in a certain way, as if to offset his downbeat nature. He liked to spur into battle in a red shirt, giving Yankee sharpshooters a perfect target. He was West Point through and through, a classmate of Jackson's. In fact, Powell Hill had been one of the three plebes who had first greeted the green-horn Jackson as he crossed West Point's threshold with saddle-bags over his shoulders. Hill went on to serve in the peacetime U.S. army and to fall passionately in love with one Ellen Marcy, a colonel's daughter. The courtship and aftermath had a curious twist and an indirect effect on the war. Colonel Marcy saw to it that Powell Hill's suit was rejected—too little money, dim pros-pects, and, what's more, a Southerner. Ellen Marcy married, to her colonel father's great pleasure, dapper George McClellan, a railroad president at age thirty-three and at present commander of the Army of the Potomac. To rub salt in Powell Hill's wound, Colonel Marcy became McClellan's chief of staff. Hill himself was now happily married to a Kentucky beauty, redheaded as he and so devoted to him that she sometimes had to be yanked from the battle line while at his heels. Now he especially savored donning his red hunting shirt at the prospect of fighting Little Mac, the husband of a girl he had once loved, and the man who had almost became his father-in-law.

Included in Lee's powwow at High Meadows was another Hill, the dour D.H. (called "Harvey" by those close), Jackson's brother-in-law.

When Jackson appeared all eyes fixed on him. He was the general who now generated the most talk, who was the center of most speculation. How had this trained artilleryman, who had been a godawful professor, cleansed the Valley of Yankees? There was nothing spectacular about him. He was caked in dust and his uniform was soiled and stained. He looked ready to bury. Then there were his gargantuan boots. They looked as if they might accommodate a whole company of feet. Jackson had ridden without food, and he took a glass of milk before entering the conference. Lee got down to business immediately. He looked like a success, with the manner and face of a Tidewater gentleman, someone accustomed to authority. He was handsome, and his eyes were what distinguished him most—gentle, steady, kindly eyes.

The plan, as Lee explained it, was to get McClellan out of the trenches around Richmond. If he remained, he might soon level the town with siege artillery if he didn't capture it first. What was needed was an en echelon from the cavalry of Jeb Stuart on the left and Jackson dislodging Yankees from their entrenchments so the rest of Lee's forces could cut them down. Like many of Lee's plans, it was complicated but brilliant—taking a leap of imagination and depending for success on good timing. Everything should move like clockwork to make it a success. Details about roads and bridges, enemy and Confederate positions, were mulled over and some problems solved. Longstreet, the steady, direct soldier—he had once been paymaster in the Federal army—turned to Jackson who seemed half asleep.

"General, you have a lot of distance to overcome, and more than likely quite a few obstacles. But your move is the key to the campaign. Without your presence we cannot hope for success. We must coordinate, time it just right. When will you have your troops in place?" Jackson answered bluntly. "Tomorrow, and ready for battle the next day, sir."

Longstreet knew the terrain around Richmond, knew the roads and byways. He also, somewhere in his secret heart, had a disdain for most people. Previously he had called Jackson's Valley army "second-raters." Now he said, "Please give yourself more time, General. It may be more difficult than you think."

"Very well. Another day."

Almost immediately Jackson was back in the saddle and off again. He covered many miles before he reached the head of his army—the rest of it sprawling for fifteen miles behind, fifteen long winding miles. It was raining, and Jackson saw first that discipline had broken down. Dabney, who was in charge, had unfortunately fallen victim to the plague of the Confederate army—rampant dysentery. He lay abed when he wasn't riveted to the toilet. The men who had fought Shields and Frémont like crazed warriors had now developed a strange lassitude. Jackson knew he should close his columns immediately and get the troops together, but he was running out of steam. The lassitude, a debilitating, awesome weariness, captured him now. He removed his wet, muddy gear, put it before the fire to dry, and then sank on his bed. Strangely, he picked up a novel and began to read as if the war had suddenly gone away and he was needing to unwind before sleep.

The next day he had the men on the road, but curiously, he didn't seem to care whether they hurried or not. Usually he ranged up and down columns, shouting the familiar "Press on, men, press on!" Now he stared straight ahead and he didn't spur his horse. He let the head of his army rest while lagging troops caught up. It was as if Stonewall didn't know where he was or that an all-important battle was about to take place and he was an essential ingredient. His weary, overloaded mind was taking leave, going on furlough.

A courier rode up with a message from Richmond. It was a detailed battle order from Lee with the usual attention to exact timing and placement of men. Jackson read it with hollow eyes. The man who had stood his ground on Henry Hill before the whole might of the Union, the man who had led green troops through the frigid Romney campaign and who had stuck it out at Kernstown and prevailed at Cross Keys, was now in a trance. He was on automatic pilot, his mind, as the Victorians put it, having "left him." He kept looking at the message: "Maj Gen Jackson to be in position on Wednesday night on the Hanover Ct. Ho. road, or near that road, about half way between Half Sink Bridge, and Hanover Ct. Ho. He will communicate to Maj Gen A. P. Hill, through Brig Gen Branch at Half Sink Bridge his position. Gen Jackson will commence his movement precisely at 3 o'clock Thursday morning, and the moment he moves, send messengers to Gen Branch in duplicate, to inform Gen Branch, who will immediately move himself . . ."

On and on it went, like directions to a complicated Tinker Toy one must steady oneself before and concentrate about in order to assemble. Jackson shook his head and tried. Unbeknownst to him, too, a deserter from his army had run into Union scouts near Hanover Court House and had been captured. At first he said he was from a Federal outfit, just another Billy Yank who was escaping the Rebs. By time-honored means they impressed upon him the need for telling the truth. A gun to one's head does wonders at such moments. He then, in detail, described Jackson's army as containing fifteen brigades, all of whom were moving to attack McClellan's rear outside Richmond. All of Old Jack's care at secrecy, all the pains he had taken, went down the drain.

Jackson was late, according to Lee's timetable, but he was coming. On Wednesday, June 25, he managed to shake off some degree of stupor. He just willed it off. The broiling Virginia day roasted his men and animals, but he became again the old Jackson who kept them moving. Streams were rough, flooded, and Jackson had to rebuild bridges along the way to get his troops through. At dark that night his veteran pacers had covered twenty miles—five short of the timetable. Jackson woke up to distress, to begin nervously pacing and goading one and all. He cornered the always correct General Winder and told him to have the Stonewall Brigade fed and ready to march at early dawn.

"Impossible," Winder said crisply. "My baggage train is too far behind and I can't move these men without supplies. It's beyond endurance."

Jackson's eyes flashed. In a snarl he enunciated each of his words precisely: "General Winder, it must be done."

Jackson's troops moved out on June 26 at 8:00 A.M. Not perfect, but better. The fierce fighters were up against terrain and climate and an enemy they couldn't shoot. Jed Hotchkiss had been left behind to continue a survey of the Shenandoah. He was sorely missed now. Although Jackson had local guides, he grew cautious without Hotchkiss to recommend shortcuts. This was not the Valley. It was flat dank land—what a mountaineer loathes. A vague, sickly aroma came from the swamp around them. The rain that fell occasionally was not refreshing but more like humid, oppressive steam. Jackson prayed. Ewell barged into Jackson's quarters one night for a saber he had left behind to find Jackson kneeling on the floor in fervent, deeply felt prayer. Old Baldy bowed out, chuckling, superior, still a nonbeliever.

At 5:00 P.M. Jackson reached Hundley's Corner—well behind schedule. He should have been there sooner and perhaps he should have sent Lee a progress report. But then Lee had made no effort to find out what was holding Old Jack up—no scout or courier came to Jackson from Lee to find out his position. And so battles are fought. Ewell had joined Jackson at Hundley's Corner, but the divisions of A. P. Hill and D. H. Hill were incommunicado. Where were they? Jackson heard some heavy firing and artillery dueling to the south, but didn't know what this meant. In former times he might have raced to find out—and take part—but not now. Lee had said Hundley's Corner and Hundley's Corner was where Jackson would hole up for the moment. His troops were happy anyhow to make camp now in the growing twilight; they were happy to banter, to take off packs and shoes and get some grub inside their bellies. Everyone wanted to blot out the sound of the increasingly savage boom boom boom coming from the south. Whose was it?

Actually, it was the forces of the two Hills attacking the Federals along Beaver Dam Creek. A. P. and D. H. Hill made an impulsive thrust against the Yankees and paid dearly for it. They were thrown back and lost 1,400 men—just thrown back in a bloody pile. It turned out that if Jackson had been where he was *supposed* to be, then the enemy would have been flanked and victory ensured. Jackson was brooding, unwilling to move, didn't know where to move.

When the troops arose on June 27, there was a new vigor, a renewal. The old-timer Trimble wanted to fight; he was disappointed they had not responded to the sound of the fusillade the night before. He was champing at the bit. Singular Major Rober-deau Cheatham Wheat of the formidable Louisiana Tigers rose and boomed, "Boys, now for the day's rations." He was a swash-buckler, a gun-for-hire to the nearest bidder, but he was also a preacher's son. He took his family Bible and roared out the lesson for the day: "Fear not your enemies, though they be ten thousand strong!"

Jackson led his troops out now, sucking a lemon, pointing his lead column straight south toward Walnut Grove Church. He could hear the sound of battle in the distance. As he neared the church he spied A. P. Hill, and he rode up to him. What was happening? The nervous, fidgety Hill explained that he was forc-ing the Yankees, who were now retreating, toward Gaines's Mill. He hoped to stand them up there and fight them to the finish. Just as he concluded his briefing, a jingle of harnesses and spurs came their way. Here came Lee and his immaculately dressed staff to find out what was going on. Hill touched his cap, rode off to the sound of the firing, and left Lee and Jackson to confer.

The two generals put their heads together while their respec-tive staffs sized each other up—Jackson's threadbare and mangy, Lee's well rested and alert. Well, forget the delay and what had taken place; never apologize, never explain. Lee now wanted his most prized lieutenant, Jackson, to put the heat on McClellan at a spot called Cold Harbor. A swift move here would turn the enemy out of a strong north-south line. Jackson would have the aid of his brother-in-law, D. H. Hill. When the Federals tried to turn, Old Pete Longstreet and A. P. Hill would hold fast on the other side of them and drive them into Jackson's line of fire. The two generals made marks on the ground, quarterbacks designing improvised plays in sandlot football.

Jackson was determined now. His former self had returned—as mysteriously as it had left him. He desired most now to please his Heavenly Father; next, and not far behind, came Robert E. Lee. On the road Jackson corralled a local boy to show him the way to Cold Harbor. Well and good to fight, but he had to find the place. "Well, sir," the boy drawled, "I reckon I could lead you, sir. Got nothing else to do."

On the way Jackson heard thundering, deafening cannon fire. "Where is that coming from?"

"Well, sir, I reckon that must be old Gaines's Mill."

"Does this road lead there?"

"You're right as rain there, sir. This 'un goes through Gaines's Mill right into Cold Harbor."

"This one? You mean there are two roads?"

"You said it just right there, sir. There are two roads. I'm taking you by the widest one. Thought you'd like to have that 'un."

"I do not. I do not wish to go to Gaines's Mill. I wish to go to Cold Harbor and to leave Gaines's Mill alone."

"Then dadblamit you should let a feller know. We should have done took the left-handed road back there a piece. If you'd told me directly what air you wanted, I could have showed you much better. You done lost some time, mister."

Jackson reversed his column to take the left-hand road. D. H. Hill had ridden on the left-hand road to begin with for some reason and for his prescience got fired upon by some of Jackson's troops now taking to this road. They thought his troops were Yankees. No one knew what would happen where they were going—or actually where they were. But there were rumors, traditional army rumors. "We're going to surprise Little Mac in his camp." "The shit you say. Old Jack's going to swing us around and take us back to the Valley. You think all this blame marching is for Little Mac?" "I don't know what it's for."

Jackson found D. H. Hill at Cold Harbor. Did he know anything about what was going on? No, nothing. They could hear the din of battle coming from Gaines's Mill and both decided it must be Longstreet and A. P. Hill who were driving the Yankees their way, toward Cold Harbor. Jackson then staked out men along a strip of woods facing the direction of Gaines's Mill. Let 'em come. Jackson would level them. Then he listened some more. The battle sounds were shifting, and he understood immediately now what was happening. Unhappily, he understood. Both he and Lee had been wrong. Major General Fitz-John Porter, who commanded McClellan's forces here, was not in a north-south line but in a vast convex east-west line. They could never outflank him in their present positions. Yet a fearsome battle raged.

Porter was a handsome man with a full well-trimmed bush

of beard and thin hair smoothly combed above. He was steady. Not a hair out of place. Everything slicked down. The Rebs were the frantic ones. A. P. Hill's men were past exhaustion. Winder was galloping around trying to figure out where to throw the Stonewall Brigade. Old Pete Longstreet, never one to panic or show excitement, though, calmly got in place to advance. The only chance now was to concentrate on Porter's entire line, let him have it, and hope you broke his back. Otherwise, if he lasted until dark, he could slip over the Chickahominy, burn his bridges, and join the rest of Little Mac's crew at his base. All of Lee's careful, imaginative planning would go for naught. He wouldn't have surprised Little Mac. Fitz-John Porter would have surprised him.

Down the road Jackson galloped to confer with Lee. He sucked a lemon furiously. They conferred about how best to correct the mistake, how best to use the scant daylight hours they had left. At parting Lee said, "That fire is very heavy. Do you think your men can stand it?"

"They can stand almost anything. They can stand that."

Lee watched Jackson's back as the general galloped off, back to the battle. Jackson's uniform was particularly grimy and his horse lathered in sweat. Lee waited and the air returned almost to normal, the occasional crack of musketry sounding, artillery now and then as if by reflex. Lee's Traveller pawed the ground and bent down to gnaw a clump of grass. Then he heard it. A loud, swelling, high, shrill cry—like the herald of death, the Rebel yell. His boys were attacking.

Old Isaac Trimble, his black-plumed dandy's hat perched at a jaunty angle, a gent near retirement age, raged up and down his line, "Charge, you men, *charge*!" Winder was out in front of the Stonewall Brigade, saber raised. Now there was no doubt about the condition of Stonewall Jackson either. Over the cascading battle din came his high-pitched cry: "Let's decide this affair right now! Sweep the field with the bayonet!"

The Rebels, lethargic and whipped down only an hour before, were now sprinting across fields, rifles outstretched, bayonets attached. Stonewall was in the thick of them, waving them on, crying, "Forward, forward, men!" Rob Wheat of the Louisiana Tigers caught up with him. "General, we're in a hot fight. Please do not unnecessarily expose yourself. What'll happen to us if you get killed and we're left here in these swamps!"

Wheat rode off to take his Tigers against the very center of Porter's line, a white-hot caldron, and there he fell. His last words, looking up, a soldier cradling his head, was to ask if Jackson was all right. Thousands fell; a few made their way into history books, others became memories of families who passed these memories down from generation to generation. But once they had breathed, once they had charged. The Federal line broke, and the Yanks ran. They ran toward the river and then many got caught. As night descended the Confederates took in an army of prisoners and many guns and much ammunition. Word went to Richmond about the victory, and the capital went wild. Hours later some reconsideration took place. Among the dead, maimed, and missing had been 8,000 Confederates.

In the morning Jackson's scouts found that an important bridge, the Grapevine Bridge, had been wrecked by the Federals. That meant that a number of Porter's men and Porter himself had crossed the Chickahominy and rejoined Little Mac. But, what the hell, Jackson's men deserved a respite, most figured. They roamed over the battlefield of the day before, looking for buddies, relatives, and what they could uncover as booty or souvenirs. They slept, dropping where they stood, and roused themselves to eat and pen letters home describing the horrendous battle of the day before.

Lee kept his mind on McClellan and directed that the Grapevine Bridge be fixed—pursuit might be necessary. Jackson's men, like most soldiers at any era, did not relish repair work when no fighting was imminent. An old bridge, what did it matter? What was the hurry? Early on the twenty-ninth came word that McClellan had been spotted concentrating his army south of the Chickahominy, an obvious move toward the James River and the protection of Federal gunboats. Little Mac was a worrywart; he never seemed to have enough guns to protect himself. It became imperative then that Jackson see to it that the bridge was repaired so his army might push south and east and catch McClellan.

Lee came up immediately with a brilliant plan. He would use all of his commanders to encircle Little Mac, wrapping his troops around in a baglike way so that the only way the diminutive

Napoleon could escape would be east, down the very road he had taken coming up the Peninsula like a Caesar. He might reach the James and he might not be completely whipped, but his troops would be faced with the hard fact of a retreat. No doubt about it. They would go down the same bloody road they had come up. O.K., fix the Grapevine Bridge and get cracking.

The Reverend Major Dabney was put in charge of repairing the bridge and his men went at it at the speed of a tortoise. It was Sunday and Dabney's mind might have been elsewhere. He could not seem to keep his men from shilly-shallying. It would take a year this way. Jackson fumed. He called in Captain C. R. Mason, who commanded a group of Negroes and told him to relieve Dabney and get the job done. This band flew into their task— boards laid, nails hammered. A courier arrived from "Prince John" Magruder, from across the river, asking what Jackson's intentions were. Jackson sent word that he should be on the other side in two hours. But in two hours the boards were still being laid, the hammers singing. In a fury he rode across the partially fixed bridge himself and inspected what lay on the other side. He rode south into uncharted territory, and now, more than ever, missed map maker Hotchkiss. When Jackson viewed landscape in battle, he immediately understood it; understood where artillery should be placed on the high ground and paths the infantry must take. In travel, though, he became confused without a guide, without some aid to get him across uncharted ground. Now he heard firing toward the south. Odd. Lee had ordered him to move east to meet the Yankees, not south. The firing must come from Magruder who might now be in trouble. It was around three in the afternoon and, bridge fixed, he might get his men into the fray before dark once again.

Then another courier reached him, this one galloping furiously. It was a message from Lee saying that Jackson should hold to his present position because the Federals might try to recross the Chickahominy, might try to break through and race across the very bridge Jackson was now having trouble fixing. Jackson scrawled an endorsement and started back to his troops. Then *another* messenger caught him, this one from Magruder's command. Where was Jackson? Could they count on his aid in this quickly developing fight to the south? He was desperately needed. Once again Jackson scrawled a message. He could not come—he had "other important duty to perform."

Jackson now quit worrying about repairs to the bridge and taking it easy. He dropped now the way his soldiers had. The night before he had lain beside Jeb Stuart on the battlefield, going over events and making plans and losing precious time for sleep. He dropped now and fell immediately asleep. But about one in the morning he felt pellets of rain; he roused himself and took cover by a wagon, but he was awake now and had had his fill of sleep. He saddled up and took off to find Magruder. Magruder and his predicament had been on his mind, on his conscience. He woke Dabney before he left and told him to start the troops across the bridge at earliest dawn. McClellan wasn't coming. The Yanks had changed their minds. He was going to help Prince John, a fellow officer from the Mexican War. Prince John was nearly out of control when Jackson rode up in the night. He must have reinforcements! Must! The enemy was everywhere, no one was safe. Jackson reassured him and said his troops should arrive to help around daylight.

At daylight Lee himself arrived before Jackson's troops got there. He was delighted to find Old Jack. The two went over plans and strategy once more, and when Jackson's lead column came in sight, after crossing Grapevine Bridge, Jackson immediately led them to where Magruder had fought the day before, thinking he might have a battle on his hands. He found instead that Magruder had won the day before without realizing it. The Yanks had turned tail and abandoned equipment all over the landscape. A complete hospital had been left, and there were 2,500 sick and wounded Federals lying there, waiting to be cared for. Jackson took in an amazing number of blankets and whole mounds of small arms. He detailed two regiments to pick up the booty and round up stray prisoners.

He wrote Anna. He was thinking of home. "You must give fifty dollars for church purposes, and more should you be disposed. . . . I would like very much to see my darling, but hope that God will enable me to remain at the post of duty until, in His own good time, He blesses us with independence. This going home has injured the army immensely."

Jackson marched his men forward now for the bridge across

White Oak Swamp, after more Yankees. He found them. His chief of artillery, Stapleton Crutchfield, was already there, looking for a good place for his heavy guns. Federal artillery was poised high at the southern end of the bog, and Jackson feared that any movement from him would bring on a devastating shelling. But he had been a professor of artillery tactics at V.M.I., and he had his own idea about how to counter those big Federal guns that were out in the open. Crutchfield had wanted to place his own guns on high ground and have it out with the Yanks. Jackson said no, mass all the Confederate guns, all twenty-eight of them, but load them under cover. The main thing was to keep them hidden. It was a new use for artillery—mass firepower, a blitzkrieg. When the twenty-eight guns, all hidden, were loaded and aimed, Jackson lowered his raised arm and they all went off simultaneously. The Federals didn't know what hit them. It was as if the entire earth had exploded. Some Federal infantry ran to the rear, but others stayed. Jackson sent a reconnaissance across the swamp to see what damage he had done, and they were met by a host of sharpshooters. It was hard fighting in a swamp—impossible now. The Yankees were too deeply entrenched for Jackson's taste. What did he do? He lay down right where he was and went to sleep.

When he woke he walked over and sat on a tree trunk. He stared at the ground, too weary and confused to raise his head. But off in the distance, toward a place in history called Frayser's Farm, came the sound of a raging fight. This was Longstreet, now in the battle of his life. He could sorely use Jackson's troops now. All Jackson had to do was cross the swamp and head for him. Once again, Jackson couldn't focus. Over the next few days an actual battle went on in Jackson's head, emotions surfacing that couldn't be straightened out, for the punishment of continuous warfare was taking its toll. He could not drive himself indefinitely, nor work military miracles constantly. His body and spirit rebeled, seemed to say, Enough. His fundamental nature might have been warring against itself, and later psychologists might have called him shell-shocked (though probably not to his face). A peculiar lassitude descended upon him—the origins of which remain, in the final analysis, a mystery.

One of his new brigadiers, Wade Hampton from South Car-

olina, reported excitedly that he'd found a way to cross the
swamp—just behind the enemy's right flank. Jackson seemed to
snap to. He appeared like the old Jackson. His questions came in
rapid fire. Could Hampton build a bridge at that spot? "Yes, sir,
I can do it." "Will it support artillery?" "No, sir, but infantry can
cross. We can get them across to join the fight. What do you say,
sir?" "Build it," Jackson barked.

Hampton fell to with his men working furiously and returned happily to Jackson to report the span completed. Infantry
could cross. Jackson showed no emotion, as if General Hampton
might have passed on a comment regarding the weather. He
showed no emotion, no real sense that he had heard. Hampton
repeated his report—and still no reaction. A long silence followed, and then without a word Stonewall Jackson stood and
walked away.

Longstreet continued fighting a short distance away at Frayser's Farm with all his might. He was so close that all Jackson
would have had to do eventually was turn his artillery that way
and let loose on the Yanks. But Jackson did nothing. He was too
tired, possibly too befuddled even to realize that fighting was
going on. His mind again had left him. At supper his staff looked
on in amazement as Old Jack's head fell forward with a biscuit
in his mouth. Could he be dead? They shook him and he came
to briefly to say, "Let us to bed, gentlemen. Let us rise with dawn,
and see if tomorrow we cannot do something!"

Little did he know that across the swamp, leading one of the
Federal brigades, was one William H. French, who had caused
him all the grief in garrison duty down in Florida. Old French was
firing away at the Rebs and having a good time at it. The Federals
were going to escape. Longstreet and A. P. Hill couldn't whip
them at Frayser's Farm—and so a golden opportunity was missed.

The next day, after a full night's sleep, Jackson became himself again. He was quick and decisive, and got his men across the
river. The enemy had fled! At Willis Church the Confederate
generals, including Lee, met to discuss grand strategy for the final
time in what was later to be called the Seven Days' battle. The
Federals must be a short distance away, and the informed guess
was that they must be up on Malvern Hill. D. H. Hill, who
seemingly had no fear of man or beast or terrain, said, "If General

McClellan is there in strength, we had better let him alone."

Longstreet had a mean side to him. He said, "Don't get scared, now that we have got him whipped."

But this enemy was far from being whipped.

Malvern Hill was a scant three miles from where these generals bent their heads together. When the Southern troops marched to within sight of it, they viewed a rather serene tableau. The hill was puny, but that was unfortunately (for them) deceiving. McClellan had a bluff crowned with heavy guns. But not all of Malvern Hill could be investigated. Jackson called for his guns. He indeed had to do it personally because Stapleton Crutchfield had taken that day to go on sick call. Jackson knew his artillery. Yet even he, in his refreshed state, had great trouble shoving his guns into position. Batteries lagged behind. Dabney flew around trying to help with the artillery but did no real good. Jackson fired some volleys and the Federals then unleashed an unholy barrage from above. Lee looked on in horror as Jackson took personal control of a battery. Here was his best and most favored general now down in the pit firing rounds. Lee sent one of his staff off immediately. "General, General Lee presents his compliments and directs that you return to his side at once." Jackson obeyed.

Despite all the generals on the scene, the battle of Malvern Hill became improvised and quixotic. It developed into a landscape of total carnage. Lee thought he saw an opening on the left and sent word for Longstreet and A. P. Hill to exploit it. But before they could find a way to flank the Federals on that side, word came that the Yanks might be withdrawing and the right flank offered the best opportunity for attack. Magruder didn't get the message and, thinking he was obeying current orders, launched an attack on McClellan's strong left side. He was joined by Huger's lead brigade, and as these troops charged across a wheat field, the Federal crescent of guns above began to wildly buck and jump, sending screaming balls and lashes of fire their way. Through this cannon fire D. H. Hill heard the Rebel yell and thought it must be a general advance. Hill, as religious and as much a Presbyterian as his brother-in-law Jackson, was a firm believer in predestination. Earlier Hill had been sitting in a camp chair, in an exposed position, while Federal fire fell around him. Get back, some of his officers urged. "Don't worry about me,"

Hill had said calmly. "I am not going to be killed until my time comes." Immediately a shell landed beside him, the concussion lifting him straight up in the air and rolling him down an incline. He got up, brushed himself off, and resumed his seat.

Now, hearing the infantry yell through the cannon fire, Hill took it as a signal for a general advance. He then led his men into one of the bloodiest chapters of the war—and one that had no hand-to-hand combat. Southern men tried to climb the puny slope of Malvern Hill while Northern shells fell on them. Five thousand lay dead and wounded. Some still wanted to fight, old Isaac Trimble among them. Jackson caught him setting out for battle in the dark. "What are you going to do, General Trimble?"

"I," said the graybeard, "am going to charge those batteries, sir."

"I guess you had better not try it. General D. H. Hill has just tried it with his whole division and been repulsed; I guess you had better not try it, sir."

Then it began to rain and storm. Soldiers groped up the hill, trying to locate fallen comrades. They slipped on ground wet from rain and blood. Their torches lit the faces of the dead and fell into the shining eyes of the wounded. It was, in the words of Kyd Douglas, "a dark, hopeless, starless night; surely it was a gruesome picture of war in its most horrid shape."

There was no more firing, and Stonewall Jackson lay down to sleep. Three hours later he was wakened by Ewell and D. H. Hill, who excitedly reported that they thought McClellan was getting set to launch a dawn attack. What were they to do? Jackson replied in a flat dry tone: "Oh, no, McClellan will clear out in the morning." He knew his McClellan.

CHAPTER XIV
A Born Again Jackson

On a rain-swept morning the Confederate high command gathered to consider the present situation, which boiled down to one overriding question: Where was Little Mac? Could the Confederates get to him and strangle him? At the Poindexter farmhouse Lee arrived. He appeared tall in the saddle, certainly rode ramrod straight. When he alighted, though, he appeared only slightly above average height. He was, in fact, a little under six feet. He was distinguished by large powerful hands and small feet. And there was something about him, some mystery. This mystery caused men to take off their hats when he came near. They showed respect, one and all. And in his letters, in his commands and dealings with comrades-at-arms he was most considerate and gentle. At the farmhouse on July 2 Longstreet was in attendance. Old Pete kept a lot of opinions to himself, but outwardly he was blunt. It was not spoken about openly but there was tension between him and Jackson. Jackson might be a little too nervous and high-strung for the taste of the brusque Longstreet. He had the recent experience of fighting his heart out at Frayser's Farm and Stonewall Jackson had not come to his aid. He made a point of leaving the farmhouse to check on his men from time to time so he wouldn't have to be around Stonewall Jackson.

Then out of the rain came two lanky riders, soaked to the skin: the president, Jefferson Davis, and his brother, Colonel Joseph Davis. Ever the considerate man, Lee noticed the moroseness of Jackson now and remembered the disagreement between Davis and Jackson over the Romney campaign. "Why, Mr. President, have you not met General Jackson? This is our Stonewall Jackson." Davis bowed; Jackson saluted.

Davis and Lee pored over a map, running their fingers over various routes Little Mac might have taken. They did not ask Stonewall Jackson's opinion. They talked about the horrific weather now and how muddy and near impassable the roads were. They came to the conclusion that no pursuit should be made that day. No matter what road the Federals had taken, they weren't going after them this day. Jackson would have. He never let rain or mud or time of day or night stay him. If a Yankee could trudge through mud and mire so could any patriotic Confederate, trying to save his country. The meeting broke up, and Jackson went back to his troops. Longstreet went to his.

On July 3 Jeb Stuart, who was becoming increasingly important in Jackson's military machinery, reported that Little Mac had taken refuge under protection of gunboats at Harrison's Landing some eight miles from Malvern Hill. Little Mac had trudged in the mire for eight miles, hardly a marathon. Now Jackson's temper began to flare. His disposition wasn't sweetened either when Longstreet was selected to lead his columns first toward Harrison's Landing, an unspoken way of showing who had come out better at the Seven Days. He laced into a private who had the misfortune of answering incoherently when Jackson asked about the condition of certain roads. The youth had been selected as a guide and had crumbled under the explosive commands of Jackson. He told his staff to be up and ready at dawn, July 4, ready to move out. "We must burn no more daylight."

Jim Lewis, a short, dark, fussy man, was Jackson's totally devoted body servant. He was at Jackson's side, practically attached to him—even as bullets flew. He took great pride in his position, too, and had a survivor's instinct. Long after the cannons finally ceased, after quiet descended and there was peace, Jim Lewis loyally carried on his association with Jackson, bedecked with Confederate medals and becoming a star attraction at Southern fairs. The one man who rose before Jackson, he was now up well before dawn on July 4. He had a large, sumptuous breakfast laid out, for no matter what hour Jackson arose—three, two A.M., five in the morning—Lewis had the gift of having just prepared breakfast for him. Another man who had arisen early this morning was poor Reverend Dabney. He had the gift of being caught in delicate moments with his hero, Jackson. Now Jackson exploded. "Major, why is my staff never punctual?" Poor Dabney tried to appear tall. "I am on time," he said. As if that mattered. Jackson wheeled on devoted Jim Lewis: "Jim, put that food back in the chest, lock it, have the chest in the wagon, and that wagon moving in two minutes. Do you hear?"

At the best of times Jackson was no gourmand. He could skip a meal and not think twice. Poor Dabney had seen this marvelous breakfast, a most favored meal, had whiffed a bouquet from the scalding hot coffee. He yearned to dig in. It had been jerked from him. Nothing to do now but climb in the saddle and be off to find Little Mac.

When Jackson and his men reached Harrison's Landing, Longstreet was already in place. Old Pete favored attacking the stronghold immediately. Jackson looked up and saw a great array of cannon barrels pointing down his way from Evelington Heights. Little Mac had put himself once again onto a kind of Gibraltar. No, Jackson thought it best to leave Little Mac alone here. No more Malvern Hill. Jackson had a great deal of experience at this point; he could remember the hill at Chapultepec in Mexico, too. Why didn't they call in General Lee and get *his* opinion. Lee arrived, took one look at the fortress, and agreed with Jackson. They weren't going to lose Southern blood here. And so the campaign against Little Mac ended.

Jackson and his men then caught up on rest. They washed the Chickahominy mud from themselves and settled down in camp about three miles from the capital of Richmond. The citizens of Richmond had stars in their eyes regarding Jackson. They found his camp, they brought gifts: exotic foods he could never digest with the stomach God had given him; weird-looking straw hats; and poems of uncertain literary merit. They wanted to be near someone with his divine reputation. He wasn't an ex-professor and Presbyterian deacon; he was the one general who could save Virginia. Jackson had had a good press. He had to slip in the back at the Presbyterian church in Richmond to hear a sermon, and duck out at the end in order to avoid star treatment. Some inner voice in Jackson warned him against getting carried away by his treatment as a folk hero. He might be trapped, encircled, and whipped. He never missed an opportunity to credit his Heavenly Father with any success he might have had on the battlefield. Reverend Ewing, with whom he had stayed on the way to Richmond, said, "He did not pray to men, but to God. . . . He seemed to feel more than any man I ever knew the danger of robbing God of the glory due for our success."

On the practical side, though, Jackson fretted in Richmond. After catching up on his sleep and getting the swampland vapors out of his system, he wanted to fight. He looked up his old friend, the politician Boteler. "Do you know," he said, in an excitable tone, "that we are losing valuable time here in Richmond?"

"How so?"

"Why, by repeating the blunder we made after the battle of Manassas, by allowing the enemy leisure to recover from his defeat and ourselves to suffer by inaction."

He told Boteler what he wanted to do: Invade Union territory. He yearned to lead troops into Maryland and take the fight to the enemy. He didn't believe in standing still and taking punishment. Boteler had a question: "Why don't you speak to General Lee on the subject?"

"I already have."

"What does he say?"

"Nothing."

"Is he slow in making up his mind?"

"Slow! By no means. With the responsibilities now resting on him, he is perfectly right in withholding a hasty expression of his opinions and purposes." Jackson considered his words and said, "I have so much confidence in General Lee that I am willing to follow him blindfolded. But he cannot give me a definite answer now because of influences here in Richmond. I want you to see President Davis and urge the importance of prompt action."

Jackson remained canny politically; he knew when to trot Boteler out. But it did not work this time. Davis listened and then turned the plan down. The military picture had abruptly changed in Virginia. Lincoln had once again reshuffled the deck and introduced a new general to command Federal troops in Virginia. He was a major general and his name was John Pope, and finally the folks in Virginia had someone they could really hate. Even Lee hated John Pope. Lee seldom got into personal vendettas, but he made an exception with Pope. He could hardly pronounce the man's name, his anger against him was so great. Major General John Pope, U.S.A., came fresh from victories in the West, and he was bursting with enthusiasm to rub the South's nose in the mud. Lincoln's kind of man. He was a man of action, not a reviewer of parades like McClellan. He had some pithy pronouncements to make: He was used to seeing the *backs* of his enemy. They retreated from him, not the other way around. In a message to his troops he said, "I hear constantly of 'taking strong positions and holding them,' of 'lines of retreat,' and of 'bases of supplies.' Let us discard such ideas. The strongest position a soldier should desire to occupy is one from which he can most easily advance against the enemy."

Sounded a little like Jackson.

But Pope added a note of brutality to his general orders to his troops. He went further than either side had gone before. He announced that his troops would live off the countryside. Vouchers would be given to owners of confiscated supplies, and these could be redeemed at the end of the war *if* the owner proved to have been loyal to the U.S.A. Sabotage would be dealt with as the Gestapo later would do in World War II. If any U.S. soldier was fired upon from a house, that house would be razed immediately to the ground and all inhabitants "sent off." Any persons detected in such outrages (in effect, any and all suspects) would be shot "without awaiting civil process." In other words, he intended to terrorize Virginia.

John Pope had a round pampered face. His cheeks and upper lip were cleanly shaven and his black beard hung from his chin like a child's sand shovel. When he talked, which was often, his beard flapped rapidly up and down. These Confederate West Pointers didn't mind fighting this man at all.

Davis wanted Stonewall Jackson to take on Pope and his newly formed army, which was called, without consulting its people, the Army of Virginia. Although Lee had been disappointed in Jackson's performance at Seven Days, he knew Jackson's qualities and he approved the selection of Stonewall. Jackson might halt the invasion by Pope from the north; then he could return with his men to Richmond and guarantee its safety.

Jackson moved out from Richmond with his staff in mid-July and one familiar face was missing. The Reverend Major Dabney had had enough; the lowlands had given him acute lumbago and he returned home to recuperate. In his place Sandie Pendleton was promoted to adjutant general. Jackson led his staff at a fast gallop down Mechanicsville Pike, in the first leg toward Pope, and found after a while that it was choked with army wagons. Wanting speed more than anything, Jackson went against one of his own orders, and began riding through a large oat field. His soldiers had been ordered to stay off civilian land unless invited. Suddenly a short fat farmer raced from among the oats and grabbed Jackson's bridle. "Goddam to hell, what you mean riding over my oats? It's against orders!"

Highly embarrassed, Jackson looked around for help and could find none. His staff, on occasion, liked to tease him. "Dammit, man, don't you know it's against orders? I intend to have you arrested! What's your name anyhow?"

"My name is Jackson," he said, blushing.

"Jackson, eh? Jackson! Well, sir, Jackson, I intend to report you and all your gang. You commissaries think you can ride through oats as if it was the highway. Yes, sir, I'm going to report you to old Stonewall myself, that's what I'll do."

"They call me that name sometimes" came a small voice.

"What name?"

"Stonewall."

"You don't mean to say you are Stonewall Jackson, do you?"

"Yes, sir, I am."

As his staff began laughing and Jackson turned a deeper red, the man's tone changed. He waved a big bandanna over his head, and yelled, "Hurrah for Stonewall Jackson! By God, General, please do me the honor to ride all over my old oats!"

Jackson and staff trotted off quickly through the field and back on the highway. Matters were looking up.

Jackson established headquarters at Gordonsville on July 19 and began planning his move against Pope. Citizenry flocked to see him, to touch him, to get near his aura. As was his custom, he accepted the hospitality of a clergyman; he pitched his headquarters tent on the front yard of a parsonage belonging to the Reverend D. B. Ewing, with whom he had stayed on his way to Richmond. He delighted in taking part in their family life while his war councils went on. He was particularly taken with one little Ewing daughter, who enjoyed playing games with him. He promised her a brass button from his uniform the moment his coat wore out—and he did indeed keep that promise. His tent flap opened on the soothing vista of the Blue Ridge in the distance, and, like all mountain men, he became invigorated with the constant sight of hills and valleys around him. He relished the sharp air at night, and the panoply of sights and smells that went along with mountains.

In a mellow mood, he solved various administrative and disciplinary problems. General Winder had gone overboard as a disciplinarian, and Jackson had to correct the man's overzealousness—a strange role for him. Straggling was a constant and eternal problem with the troops, and Winder, the commander of the Stonewall Brigade, resorted to "bucking" any unlucky trooper caught doing it. This form of punishment involved tying a man's hands together, slipping them over his bent knees, and then running a pole beneath the man's knees and over his arms. He couldn't move from his bent-over position and he must stay that way for a day. Some said it was inhuman torture. But there was more. Winder practiced "gagging" and also tied miscreants up by their thumbs. A delegation of officers visited Jackson's tent and asked that these inhumane practices be stopped. Jackson listened sympathetically, and agreed, yes, Winder might have gone a little far. He ordered the commander of the Stonewall Brigade to cease such extremes.

A few weeks later, in a pause between unholy battles, Old Jack cracked down on four deserters and left no possible doubt about the extreme lengths he would go to to keep his machine intact. Early in the afternoon his division was assembled in a three-sided formation, the Stonewall Brigade facing the open end. The condemned were led blindfolded into the center under heavy guard and then placed in a kneeling position beside an open grave. Twelve sharpshooters stood at attention twenty paces away, half with loaded muskets, half with blanks. A lieutenant read the sentences, then shouted, "Ready, aim, fire!" And the rifles exploded, sending the deserters toppling back into the pits. Next, under Stonewall's orders, the regiments marched past the graves, every man getting a sight of what could happen to those who left their posts and didn't measure up.

He was delighted to welcome Jed Hotchkiss back on duty, so he could rely confidently on someone to point out shortcuts and byways off the beaten track. He got a replacement for Turner Ashby and was immediately disappointed in him. As was often the case with Jackson, he took an instant liking to someone or he did not, and it could not always be anticipated which way he would go. Beverley H. Robertson was West Point, class of 1849. He had a bald pate, stern eyes, and mustachios you could hang from. He was in love with discipline—but despite it all Jackson just didn't like the man. He didn't trust him somehow.

Lee sent A. P. Hill and his renowned Light Division to serve under Jackson in the anticipated attack on Pope. That was another matter to contend with. Lee, the gentle diplomat, realized that these two strong personalities might grate on one another, and advised Jackson to consult his division commanders as to his movements (meaning tell Hill what was going on) and therefore avoid a lot of trouble. Lee could have saved his breath—or rather saved a dispatch. There was a murky subterranean part of Jackson that simply distrusted the outside. It was in his genes. Powell Hill didn't stand a chance against him.

And then there was the leftover matter about the court-martial of General Garnett, whom Jackson had charged with neglect of duty in retreating at Kernstown without orders. A board was convened in Gordonsville, and Jackson gave stinging testimony against the Tidewater aristocrat. Garnett fought back, and fought back hard. He cross-examined Jackson and wasn't gentle. He testified, in his own behalf, that Jackson had never told him his military plans and that if anything had happened to Jackson, he, Garnett, would have had to take charge with no more knowledge than the lowest private. Garnett hotly denied the charges. "General Jackson is not content with arresting me and depriving me of my command but is determined that I should not be restored to active duty. Such covert attacks are inconsistent with honor and justice, and should arouse grave doubts as to the motives and truthfulness of these allegations."

Jackson did not in the least mind the counterattack from his erstwhile subordinate. He seemed to relish it and all the legalities that followed. It was his dark side, the side that held a nasty streak. He gloried in court-martials and had a sharp mind for legalistic argument. Court-martials had passed the time in Florida. He had been involved with the complicated one with his superior French, and had enjoyed the contest. He never shied away from a fight. And, after all, he was the son of a barrister. If things had been otherwise, he probably would have made an excellent attorney—albeit an eccentric one.

Garnett's court-martial was adjourned precipitously when scouts burst in to say that Pope had occupied Culpeper. In the process he had also split his forces. He was cut in two—a big error on his part. Now was the time to strangle him, make him rue the day he ever set a boot in Virginia and started razing houses and shooting civilians.

Jackson sent out the order to saddle up. Charles Winder, who lay in bed stricken with some undefined illness, rose. He rose with a fever and trembling hands, put on his uniform and spurs, and climbed on his horse. Pale and unsteady, he sat in the saddle and was ready to lead the Stonewall Brigade.

The infantry, Jackson's "foot cavalry," took to little-used country roads that Hotchkiss had discovered and which were not patrolled by Yankees. No one really knew how Jackson was going to attack Pope—not even Lee had a clear idea of his plan. It was at this moment that Lee took a really big imaginative leap and turned the judgment for Jackson's battles over to Jackson himself. Lee gave his most trusted lieutenant the latitude he knew he thrived on. "Make up your mind what is best to be done under all the circumstances which surround us, and let me hear the result at which you arrive."

Although Lee was the son of Tidewater aristocracy and Jackson had been raised on the Western frontier, they had been similarly molded in several vital ways. They had had absent fathers and they adored their mothers. Light Horse Harry Lee, a Revolutionary War hero and spendthrift, couldn't stay put and had died when young Robert was eleven. The responsibility of the household had fallen on his shoulders. He had cared for his mother when she became an invalid, in the end carrying her in his arms for carriage rides and ministering to her with the gentleness of a nurse—this, when he was a schoolboy. When he had left for West Point, his mother had said, "How can I live without Robert? He is both son and daughter to me." Jackson had shown a similar gentleness when he had taken care of certain sick cadets at the Point. In this war the two began a unique working relationship based on what seemed to outsiders as mental telepathy. Lee would give a loose order and Jackson would devise a plan, in his own way, of carrying it out. Jackson operated best when given the least amount of specific instruction.

Alas, A. P. Hill was not part of this mental-telepathy circuit—and when Jackson changed his mind during the march and told Ewell to get off a main road and travel by a side road, he did not tell Powell Hill. The unfortunate Hill had direct orders to follow behind Ewell on the main road, and so he waited with his swift Light Division for Ewell's troops to pass. And waited. And waited. Then in the distance he saw troops marching forward, and he got his men ready. The new troops came into sight and Hill saw that these were Jackson's own division. He let Jackson's division past and then their supply wagons. Then he began marching at last, but after a mile got bogged down in a traffic snarl. That was where Jackson found him—making him look (and possibly feel) like a nincompoop. Jackson gave him a withering look and ordered his troops halted. Hill had covered but three miles that day. Hardly a blitzkrieg.

Jackson's troops were moving so slowly that surely Federal cavalry, which was skirmishing with Robertson, would warn Pope that Jackson was coming. Further, his slow march might allow time for the rest of Pope's troops to reach Culpeper; then Pope would be at full strength. A disaster! He wanted to fight, not dawdle. Then, when he was about eight miles from Culpeper, he got some stirring news from General Ewell. Yankee cavalry was getting stronger and some Federal cannons had begun shelling his troops. This meant they were now facing an army that desired a fight.

Looking around, Jackson saw that the most valuable piece of land in view was Cedar Mountain—actually more a hill than a mountain. It must be seized. Ewell was to install his batteries there and his infantry below. Winder was to take a position on the left in support of Jubal Early so that the two might turn the right flank of whatever Federal force was out there. That Federal army happened to be commanded by Jackson's old adversary Nathaniel P. Banks of Massachusetts, the ex-bobbin boy. As Jackson himself observed, "Banks is always ready to fight, and generally always gets whipped." Not a bad man to face.

Jackson went into battle quickly—some might say too quickly. He brought up infantry and began answering the Federals with cannon of his own. Banks then began pressing Ewell in the center and probing Early's right and front. He started gaining ground until A. P. Hill's men roared on the field and beat the Federals back for the moment. It was slowly but surely turning into a hot fight. But there was one thing that had gone unchecked . . . some woods on the left. Winder and his Stonewall Brigade were over that way, but his conclusion was an attack would most likely come through a field to the right near Early and had formed his line at a right angle to Early's front. It was the perfect alignment—*if* the attack came through the field. But it courted disaster if the ex-bobbin boy should try a turning movement, should perhaps pop out of those quiet-seeming woods to the left. Jackson's plan assumed that all of the enemy was *east* of the Culpeper road. The woods were west.

It took some minutes to get infantry aligned, a vital but rather routine task, and Jackson used the dead time in his rather unorthodox but customary manner: He went to a nearby farmhouse, lay on the front porch, and took a snooze. Following the chief, Ewell laid his tired old bones under a shade tree and fell asleep at once. War had such odd moments. Jackson had kept the secret of his overall strategy to himself.

Trouble began when the artillery duel heated to a crescendo. Winder, the good soldier, stood with his staff in a cluster of his batteries. Due to his high fever he had taken off his tunic and wore but his gray shirt. His face now was the color of that shirt, but he kept his binoculars to his eyes, calling out range corrections to his gunners. God damn, we're going to fight! A captain near him received shrapnel directly to the head and fell. His brother, a lieutenant, who made it a rule always to stay by his sibling, took charge of the Parrott gun his brother had commanded. Now the Confederate fire began to find range, and Winder smiled in his feverish delirium. A shell then eviscerated another man near him, but Winder hardly turned. He continued to direct fire because his battery was finding the range and the Yankees were getting their due. Winder, tall, wavy-haired, handsome and feverish-eyed, yelled a change of distance to a gunner. In the din the boy could not hear him. Winder turned, cupped his hands around his mouth, leaned, and began to repeat when a shell passed through his left arm and side, taking his ribs off on that side of his chest. He went straight back, lay full length, and began quivering spasmodically.

One of his staff leaned over him. "General, do you know me?"

"Oh, yes." And then the general began to talk to his wife and children in Maryland. He spoke lovingly and quietly to them, like a gentle man rocking on a porch, at peace. He was carried to the rear and died just at sunset.

Jackson's plan to outflank his enemy on the left had now backfired; his troops were the ones being outflanked. A melee of blue-coated men came tearing out of the woods and their wild clatter of musketry filled the air. Jackson came bolt upright on the porch, hopped on Little Sorrel, and galloped toward the Stonewall Brigade and the bluecoats overrunning them. It was a picture of carnage and chaos. The air was thick with smoke and dust; a deafening roar and clatter sounded. Through it all ran riderless horses, crazed, some struck, trampling the wounded and dazed. Jackson ran into a moil of gray-clad fugitives who were moving backward in shock and horror. The battle teetered on the edge of becoming a great military disaster—but it changed direction because of the will of one man. Jackson drew his sword—something he had never done in battle before—raised it above his head and called above the havoc: "Rally, brave men, and press forward! Your general will lead you; Jackson will lead you! Follow me!"

It was as startling a sight as the bluecoats had seen, coming from the woods. Confederates stopped in their tracks, gaped for a moment to make sure the sight was real, and then began to rally. First one, then another began to yell like Jackson, and the tide of retreat turned into an assault. The blues then began to fall back, and Taliaferro, the man who had been Jackson's nemesis in the Romney episode, caught up with him and said, "General, please, for your safety and the good of our army. Retire from the range of these bullets." "Good, good," Jackson said, in his characteristic way and fell back to watch.

Now that Banks was in flight Jackson didn't want to let up. He ordered his brigades to pursue. Even as dusk fell, he ordered his men to keep after Banks and punish him. A. P. Hill's men took the lead, coming to some heavy woods. He shelled them and then began taking in hundreds upon hundreds of shell-shocked prisoners. At last Jackson could press no farther. Banks formed a line and a scout reported that heavy Yankee reinforcements were coming forward. Jackson's troops fell where they were. When the call went out to "stack arms," they just fell on the ground and closed their eyes. Jackson rode back toward the battlefield and knocked on various farmhouse doors. The dwellers warmly received him but said their rooms were filled with the wounded; there was no place for the general to sleep. He finally selected a grassy spot, dismounted, and sank to the ground like his soldiers. "Do you want anything to eat, General?" one of his staff asked.

"No, I want *rest,* nothing but *rest!*"

Jackson rose the next day to find a battlefield littered with arms and the accoutrements of armies—also, a piteous array of moaning, badly wounded men. Jackson put his surgeons and burial details to work but he would not allow himself to indulge in grief. He must act at once and check out the whereabouts of Banks and Pope. Where was the enemy and what was his strength? The cavalry scout, Robertson, who may have been demoralized by Jackson's carping and eternal faultfinding, furnished no fresh, startling intelligence. Old Ashby would now have been in Banks's coat pocket, Jackson fancied, getting information. That was the duty of the cavalry! So therefore Old Jack turned to someone he had an inexplicable weakness for, and confidence in: Jeb Stuart.

Jingling and jangling, Stuart came riding into camp the next day and boomed his greetings to one and all. He was like dancing, sparkling water and just as hard to catch and hold. He was off the next day to scout the enemy's position, and he didn't disappoint. But the news he brought back wasn't good. Banks had been heavily reinforced as feared, and even Jackson knew that an attack on him now would be foolhardy. When enemy horsemen appeared carrying a flag of truce, Jackson welcomed them. They wished to succor their wounded and bury their dead, and Jackson, with a poker face, raised not one objection or condition. While this truce was in effect, Jackson secretly got his supply wagons on the road back to Gordonsville. His troops pulled out in the dark, leaving campfires burning.

On August 13 Longstreet arrived with his troops in Gordonsville. It was a mixed blessing. Jackson could use the troops but had to endure the slight affronts from Old Pete. Longstreet's men joked openly about what a cruel crackpot Jackson was—obvious sentiments from their chief. Old Pete let it be known that Jackson might be a very skillful man against such men as Shields, Banks, and Frémont, but when pitted against the best of the Federal commanders he would not appear so well.

These Confederates squabbled and showed jealously and dislike at times—even court-martialed each other—but it took the likes of a John Pope to draw them together, to show what their real hatred could be like. The peripatetic General Lee arrived in camp now with a new plan to deal with Pope—his word was to "suppress" Pope. Speed and secrecy were needed; just up Jackson's alley. Lee had word that McClellan had been ordered to join Pope in a strike at the Confederates in Virginia's North. Therefore, while Little Mac was hitting the road, the Confederate Army of Northern Virginia would unleash its might. That meant T. J. Jackson with the additional troops he had just received plus troops commanded by Lee himself. Could Jackson move immediately?

Jackson had haversacks on his men's shoulders almost at once, three days' rations cooked, and marching orders given. John Pope's army had camped hardly twenty miles away, had plunked itself down on a sliver of earth between the Rappahannock and

Rapidan rivers. It numbered around 70,000 men. Pope had entered this Shangri-la via a bridge at the Rappahannock Station;
it was in fact a cul-de-sac with the bridge his only exit. Stuart was
to burn the bridge and Lee and Jackson were to coordinate an
assault. Simple. But snafus developed—delays, foul-ups in logis-
tics, bad staff work. Stuart got behind in schedule and Lee could
not get in position.

Jackson squirmed. He was camped beside the Rapidan and on
the other side lay Pope in all his innocence and delusion. What a
time to strike! At night Jackson couldn't sleep and called for Sandie
Pendleton, Blackford, and a few other troopers and said, Saddle
up. He led them into total blackness on the night of August 19.
Their clothing caught on brambles, the faces were torn by
branches, and they had no idea what was up. Captain Blackford
came to the conclusion that this jaunt was another one of those
freakish urges that sometimes seized the old man and which made
people think he was deranged. Blackford fell asleep in the saddle,
and when his head struck some foliage he came awake with a start
to say, "Sandie, where is the old fool taking us?"

"How's that?"

He turned in horror and saw that Jackson rode beside him.
Jackson took them to the top of Clark's Mountain, where, in the
fresh morning light, they looked down on the spectacular sight
of miles of Union tents. Here were the Yankees in camp, here was
Pope. Jackson studied the position of troops for half an hour and
then the men rode back to camp. He licked his chops. If only
General Lee were in position—and Stuart ready! Lee did cross the
Rapidan the following day, but the Confederates' luck had run
out. Pope had smelled danger somehow and had moved his
troops somewhere north. Lee calmly determined that the troops
should follow him and try for another opportunity of attack.
Don't cry over spilt milk. He designated Jackson commander of
the left wing of his new army and Longstreet of the right.

Jackson wanted to get started pronto—and issued orders to
move out at "moonrise." He himself turned out at 3:00 A.M. Jim
Lewis was there with breakfast. Sandie Pendleton was rubbing
his eyes; Blackford was in a trance. But all were moving, ready
to roll. All except A. P. Hill, who was supposed to be in the lead
position on the march. His men still lay about and he himself

wasn't fully ready. Hill simply wasn't an early riser. It might have been easier for him to fight all night than awake early in the morning. Jackson fumed. If he missed the chance at Pope, look out! Hill would join Garnett at the dock.

As Jackson approached Beverly Ford on August 22 he found Pope once again. His troops were spread out on the opposite bank of the Rappahannock like a large armed camp meeting. Jackson called up his guns and sent an array of shells their way. The Yankees answered in kind. Then Jackson rode down the bank of the river, looking for a crossing to get to Pope, just checking. At Warrenton Springs he found a broken bridge. It might be fixable, and no enemy appeared in sight on the opposite bank guarding it. It looked promising. Some of Lawton's Georgians made it across to check, and Jubal Early's brigade managed to cross on an ancient dam about a mile downstream. So there was Lawton's regiment and Early's brigade on the riverbank close by Pope. It rained, a lashing torrential downpour which raised the river and made a recrossing impossible. Jackson became alarmed as night fell. He had sent his men across to possible entrapment and massacre. But here was where he took Pope's measure. Although Pope's cavalry skirmished with Early's troops, Pope did not strike with his might. He let a golden opportunity pass. The next afternoon a makeshift bridge had been built, the river fell somewhat, and Early and the Georgians escaped back to the Confederate side.

Pope did have other things on his mind. Jeb Stuart had crossed the Waterloo Bridge well upstream and circled the rear of Pope's position. The same violent storm that caught Early struck him and his troopers. He called it the darkest night he'd ever seen, but a fantastic bit of luck fell his way. He captured an orderly in Pope's outfit, who said he knew where the private quarters of General Pope were and, what's more, would lead Stuart and his riders there. The appeal of such a moment made Stuart almost delirious. Stuart's men surrounded Pope's brightly lighted camp, and then the fantastic Stuart had his bugler sound the charge. His horsemen then descended like Arabians off the desert, swinging sabers and firing revolvers. The bluecoats thought the whole of Lee's army had come and began a footrace into the countryside. There had been no defensive plan for such an emergency. They could run, though. Lightning would illuminate a whole road clogged with racers; then the next would show it deserted.

Stuart bagged more than two hundred prisoners, some of them staff officers, and many blooded horses. By sheer luck the eminent Pope happened to be away from his tent and missed his visitor. But Stuart walked into his personal tent and took it apart like a second-story burglar. Stuart's troopers carted off Pope's personal baggage, a payroll chest stuffed with $350,000, and a dispatch book containing headquarters copies of all messages sent or received during that past week. Fitz Lee, General Lee's nephew, was part of the raiding party and he came away with Pope's dress uniform. He wore it around for a while, the cockaded hat and blue dress coat of a Federal major general. The coat and hat were later sent to Richmond and put on display.

Jackson and Lee appreciated the joke, but they were after larger game: They wanted to "suppress" Pope more emphatically. Lee came up with a plan. It would pose the most danger to Jackson. Since Pope's army was now, from reinforcements, larger than both Longstreet's and Jackson's combined, some diversionary tactics were in order. Lee proposed that Jackson slip away, and using the screen of the Bull Run Mountains, get in behind Pope's supply train. He would then attack and cause the jumpy Pope to fear that his supply base was threatened if not the security of Washington. Pope would retreat, drawn away from his reinforcements on the lower Rappahannock, trying to protect his goods. Then Longstreet and Jackson would join their wings somewhere in the vicinity of Manassas and do as much damage to Pope as possible. The plan was certainly imaginative, but it went against a cardinal military rule: Never divide your forces when facing a larger army. Yet Lee had no choice. When could General Jackson leave? At earliest dawn, of course.

So Jackson moved out again. He didn't even allow his troops to carry knapsacks. If they got hungry they could pull green corn from the fields along the way. Jackson ordered Taliaferro's men to step on the heels of Hill's should they lag one bit. He wrote Anna, "I have only time to tell you how much I love my little pet dove."

Neither his men nor any of his officers had the least idea where they were going—only that they would get in one hell of fight when they got there.

CHAPTER XV

The Return to Manassas

It was cool the morning of August 25, perfect marching weather. How those men and boys hooted and jostled each other! Off to tame the Yankees and they were Jackson's troops entirely—23,000 of them now. They cut off main roads, through fields, over country streams, past farmhouses off the beaten track. Toward evening a tall Virginia farmer was bringing his cattle in when a column of troops suddenly and near silently crested the hill of his pasture and came his way. What was this? They came . . . and they kept coming, mile after mile of them.

"Hey, where you boys going?"

"How the hell should we know? Ask Old Jack."

It continued as a brisk march, no slowing down, just the ten-minute break every hour. No one could sniff a Yankee anywhere. Near twilight they came toward the mountain village of Salem, well to the right of Pope's main army and behind the Federal flank. The beauty of the mountain setting touched Jackson in the fading light. He filled his lungs with that special crisp mountain air, dismounted, and climbed to the top of a giant rock around a bend in the road. The Blue Ridge took on a purple hue in the distance and on the other side lay the important Bull Run

Mountains. The troops spotted Jackson up above them and began cheering—a spontaneous, deeply felt cheer, a yell of love. To march twenty-five miles in one day at route step and then to break forth in a cheer for the man who ordered it—it must be love. Jackson sent word for them not to cheer. Who knew where Yankee scouts might lurk? They then raised their tattered hats and he waved back to them.

Up the next day at earliest dawn, they came to Thoroughfare Gap in the Bull Run Mountains, leading to Pope's main artery of supplies, the Orange and Alexandria Railroad. Troops began shifting muskets; battery officers began to prepare to station their guns. Surely there would be some hot fighting at Thoroughfare. But no enemy, and the Rebels passed through the Gap unchecked, almost trotting, huge billowing dust clouds above them. The cavalry was a few miles in front, scouting and detecting no enemy. The men were exhausted now, their feet moving without their willing it. Down below they saw the rolling green countryside around the place called Manassas. They kept moving.

At sunset they neared Bristoe on the Orange & Alexandria line. Hot firing came suddenly from Ewell's division in the lead. Finally, action. Ewell had captured two trains but learned that one other had just passed through toward Washington and another had stopped short and was heading back toward Pope's position. Now the cat was out of the bag. The Federals would know in hours where Jackson was, if not what he was up to. These Rebels wanted to bed down now that twilight had come. Think about all the problems tomorrow. But, no, Jackson wanted to push on to Manassas Junction, Pope's supply depot. He was so close.

Old Isaac Trimble got his brigade under way at midnight, and in the heart of darkness—three o'clock—the Stonewall Brigade moved out. Colonel William Smith Hanger Baylor now commanded the Stonewall Brigade. He was Old Virginia, from a nonmilitary background, a brilliant student in his youth (entered Washington College at sixteen), the son of a judge, a lawyer by profession himself, and one of the bravest men the South ever fielded. He was truculent and daring to the end. The head of a militia unit, he had been on his honeymoon in New York when John Brown raided Harpers Ferry in 1859. He had the misfortune to be stricken with typhoid fever on his honeymoon and got the news on his sickbed that his unit had been called up to repel Brown. In his delirium he thought he was already *there* and, a bear of a man with long flowing hair, had to be wrestled to the ground by his doctor and wife to keep him from making a charge. Feverish or no, his first instinct as a soldier was always to charge. It cost him his life almost immediately after being named commander of the Stonewall Brigade.

The lead columns of Jackson's tattered band entered Manassas Junction just as the sun rose on August 27. It became Christmas in the heat. All around these country boys lay acres of supplies. Who could have dreamt it? In warehouses, sheds, railroad cars, and simply piled up in the open air was everything a body might long for when hot, thirsty, ill-dressed, and hungry. Here was 50,000 pounds of bacon. *Fifty thousand pounds!* Not to mention 1,000 barrels of corned beef, 2,000 barrels of salt pork, and 2,000 barrels of flour—but those were just openers. They found tailored, spiffy uniforms, thick-soled brogans, campaign hats to ward off the sun and rain, and fancy goods more appropriate at Delmonico's in New York than at a country station in Virginia.

Lieutenant John Chamberlayne wrote, " 'Twas a curious sight to see our ragged and famished men helping themselves to every imaginable article of luxury or necessity, whether of clothing, food, or what not. For my part, I got a toothbrush, a box of candles, a quantity of lobster salad, a barrel of coffee, and other things.

"Our men had brought no wagons, so we could carry little away of the riches before us. But the men could eat for one meal at least. To see a starving man eating lobster salad and drinking Rhine wine, barefooted and in tatters, was curious."

As troops filed in they fell on these wondrous supplies. They hadn't properly eaten in three days and many were without shoes or a decent shirt. What a feast! At eleven o'clock, though, word came that the Yankees had stirred themselves and were advancing to attack. Jackson went to meet them—a New Jersey brigade under General George W. Taylor. Confederate batteries opened up on it across an opening and blue-clad figures broke for the woods and trails in confusion. Confederate shells rained down on them at will and even Stonewall had misgivings about the slaughter. He took a white handkerchief, waved it wildly above his head, and rode out to shout, "Surrender before you are all exterminated!" There was a pause and then a rifle volley whizzed by Jackson's head. He galloped back to his lines and said, "Give it to 'em, boys!" Many Federals lived to escape, some were even allowed to escape, but 300 were captured and 135 casualties inflicted. It was plain that more would soon follow, that Pope was on the way.

Farther out Ewell let the enemy have it in sharp fighting—crisp, well-aimed, and punishing. He rushed a Pope regiment, fell back, rushed again, all in an orderly, careful manner. As he crossed Broad Run, he destroyed a bridge and kept the enemy on the other side near Bristoe Station. But news of the enemy advance reached Jackson, and he realized it was time to head for better ground. What to do with the plunder, all the stores, all the beautiful ammunition? Jackson had created his diversionary action, the Federals had grabbed the bait, and now they were on their way en masse. There was no time to save the loot. Jackson took one look at his scarecrow troops, and looked the other way when they grabbed what they could carry. One barefoot man speared a lobster from a bottled jar with his bayonet, chewed it up, and washed it down with Rhine wine. Men stuffed cigars, beer, lemons, and oranges in their pockets. And then off. As the last squads moved out, torches were flung into the bounty that was left. High flames leaped into the darkening sky as the troops wound their way north. Then shells and musket balls exploded, like a giant Fourth of July display—the heavens shook and Manassas Junction disappeared in a large fiery bowl. It was as if they were leaving a still-raging battle.

Jackson took them to a low ridge north of the Warrenton-Alexandria Pike, a mile west of where, on a hot July day in 1861, it had all begun—Henry House Hill. The general may have been subliminally drawn to the spot to fight, and surely what was left of the Henrys must have wondered why the whole Civil War had to be fought in their front yard. Why, Lord, select us and blow us to smithereens? There had been liquor at Manassas Junction, and the good Taliaferro had had the good luck to liberate some of Pope's fine cognac. Due to the rush of spirits—or because

Jackson's ingrained secrecy left many in the dark about the proper placement—his divisions became widely dispersed. Ewell's force, which was trying to join Jackson, now had begun going around in circles because Ewell's guide thought he was somewhere else. Ewell ended up camping well south of Jackson's main body on Bull Run.

And John Pope was getting feisty in the extreme. His scouts now knew approximately where Jackson was, and Pope realized Jackson was outnumbered. Ah, ha! Jackson thought that by going through Thoroughfare Gap he would outflank him and surprise his rear. The fact was, Pope determined, he now had Jackson! Jackson was outnumbered and caught in a trap! Pope arrived at Bristoe in person at night and got the impression that the Rebels had been thrashed there and sent on their way, retreating. They were just an angry, riotous mob—looting and tearing up rails—and needing to be mightily disciplined. These Rebels were coming closer to his grasp—and what was a depot of supplies, all this whiskey and boots, compared to crushing Jackson.

To the Federals, Jackson's *reputation* of invincibility was maddening. A government official from Washington had been on his way to Pope when his journey had been interrupted. Jackson's troops had wrecked his train, taken him prisoner, and broken his leg in the process. As he had lain in agony on a stretcher he saw a figure by a campfire a short distance away. A surgeon said proudly that this was Stonewall, Old Jack. The official asked to be carried nearer so he might have a look. It was a once in a lifetime chance. He was carried, and as he got nearer he saw an improbable figure in a grimy uniform, enormous mud-caked boots, and a tiny filthy cap drawn low over his forehead, almost covering his eyes. The man was hunkered down over the fire like a lowly private. The official looked in wonder, then disbelief, finally in disenchantment. He moaned, for all near and far to hear: "O my God! Lay me down again!" Word of his reaction somehow spread and the Rebels picked up on his cry. From then on, on long forced marches with no rations, extra picket duty, and needless drilling, the cry went out: "O my God! Lay me down again!"

This war and its images were confusing. It was a tableau of chaos and exhaustion. Afterward, people saw the magic. While it was going on—who could tell? A band of gaunt riders heralded an advance, and they rode into a village or across the countryside like wolves. Then came skirmishers, advancing across fields and through woods, their muskets swinging, their eyes wide. Behind them followed the foot cavalry—long-winding, route-stepping youths, many barefoot, muskets at sling arms. Officers rode back and forth, up and down columns, their swords clinking and their mounts in a lather. The artillery, supply wagons, ambulances, sutlers, a band, a spy perhaps, sometimes a fancy lady got included in the irresistible procession that moved in a halo of dust and curses. And inside one man's cranium was the master plan that everyone accepted as justifying their being driven to a point beyond exhaustion. Jackson had pressed beyond his army at one point and had stationed himself on a cabin porch to wait for his columns to close up. He used the time to ease himself down in a split-bottom chair, tilt it back, and catch a few winks. A staff officer awakened him to say a brigade commander had failed to put a picket at the last crossroad, as ordered, and the next brigade had taken the wrong road. Jackson had snapped opened his eyes, two slits of blue-gray shone, and he said, "Put him under arrest and prefer charges!" Then he shut his eyes and went back to sleep for the few precious seconds he had left before he had to hit the trail.

Now, on the morning of August 28, Jackson was ensconced on his hill and Pope was coming to get him. Pope's message to his generals left no doubt: "Assault him vigorously at daylight." He knew in his bones that he had the damnable crazed Stonewall cornered. From his intelligence service he knew that Jackson had at most fourteen brigades. He therefore flanked him with thirty-four crack brigades, seventeen on one side and seventeen on the other. Thus, a vise. Somewhere in there was the man. He'd get him. "I see no possibility of escape," he added to his confident and terse message.

But Jackson was waiting for just this. On the hill.

At noon an isolated Federal force, the lead outfit, approached Bull Run headed for the Stone Bridge. Jackson's men watched, all as quiet as possible, their low whispers no louder than the hum of bees. The boys in blue had no idea, as the sun beat down, birds flew through the air, and clouds drifted overhead, that the Southerners watched and cocked their muskets. A kind Providence caused the commander to order a turn just before the bridge, going another way, and thus missing the assault. The sun lowered as Jackson's troops stretched out and idly, quietly chatted. Band members cleaned their instruments and polished the metal. Then as evening mess call was nearing, a tightly formed outfit in dark blue rounded the corner and headed, as the others had, for the Stone Bridge. This group *marched,* as if they were untried and fresh.

But now the light was fading, broad evening shadows beginning to fall. Taliaferro and Ewell's troops were in position slightly north and could take part in an ambush. But that fading light—could the Rebels do the job before dark came? Could an attack be risked? Jackson came out of the woods himself to find out. Trotted down the hillside on Little Sorrel and sat on Little Sorrel as upright as if posing for a statue. He rode within easy range of the Federal skirmishers who were out there protecting the advancing foot soldiers. Occasionally lone Rebel horsemen had skirted close to these Federals, nothing unusual there, except this one perhaps seemed a little more threadbare than most. Hardly worth a round—so they went on marching. Jackson suddenly pulled up reins and spurred Little Sorrel back up the hill and into the trees. He touched his kepi, saluted, and said, "Bring up your men, gentlemen." In a calm, soft voice.

His staff knew what he meant and the order went out: Attack! Down from the hill and out of the woods they came, shattering the soft evening air with that piercing unearthly Rebel yell. Ancient Isaac Trimble was in their midst, screaming in his broken voice, "Forward, guide center, march!" Three batteries swung their muzzles around and leveled them on the blues. The Stonewall Brigade dashed forward, its battle flag gleaming blood red in the sun's last light. This sudden spectacular apparition should, by all rights, have sent the blues into wild panic. Such an attack at the First Manassas might have kept them running well past Washington. Not this time, boys, not this time.

The Rebels ran up against John Gibbon's Iron Brigade, composed of one Indiana and three Wisconsin regiments. It was actually this brigade's first engagement, but the war had seeped into their bones and they were ready to fight. Gibbon himself was from North Carolina and three of his brothers were on the Confederate side. The Iron Brigade wheeled and stood, and soon were joined by Abner Doubleday's brigade. No one had told these Northern troops that they were supposed to lose and fall back; no one told them they were now engaged against fighters with the highest reputation on either side—Stonewall Jackson's troops. They held. They stood in parade formation, fired back, and couldn't be moved. Moreover, they wore outlandish black felt hats. Gibbon had issued these nonregulation chapeaus and another name for his outfit was the Black Hat Brigade. Ever after the Southerners shuddered when they saw troops wearing black hats. A picket would scream when he spied one: "Oh, son of a bitch God almighty here come them black hatted fellers! Look out!"

The Iron Brigade stood firm and Stonewall couldn't budge them. Gibbon wouldn't back off, and the losses began to pile up incredibly. It wasn't the strategy of Pope that was winning here (or at least fighting to a draw)—it was the sheer unparalleled valor of the Iron Brigade. The two armies fought, often feet apart, slugging, firing, whamming with whatever they had, as the sun sank and the light went out. The carnage piled up past human reckoning. Taliaferro later said, "It was one of the most terrific conflicts that can be conceived of."

Brave Taliaferro went down, but not until the fighting ceased completely. He had worked his way up in Jackson's affections until he now commanded the Stonewall division—and he took not one but three wounds in the battle. Bleeding and white from exhaustion and near mad from the effort, he yelled commands until the last shot and then was carried from the field. The wily Ewell, hardly as big as a sparrow, went down. He had gone forward, unable to stay in the command in the rear, and had joined the 21st Georgia just before a charge. As he duck-walked up, getting in the midst of a squad, a Georgia boy said, "Hey, boys, look! Here's General Ewell with us!" Everyone cheered, drawing the attention of the Federals. Thus alerted, they let off a volley. A minié ball shattered Ewell's knee and he fell back and lay there until it was all over. He was then gathered up and taken to the rear, where a surgeon sawed off his limb.

The figures were staggering, higher than any other casualty list Jackson had suffered. The Stonewall Brigade now numbered but around 425 men, having taken 635 into the twilight battle. At First Manassas it had numbered around 3,000. The 21st Georgia, among whom Ewell was with when he went down, had only 69 out of 242 unhurt. Jackson had seemed, once the bullets started whizzing, to have a relapse into the lethargy of the Seven Days. He just watched, mesmerized by the scene. He did not grab battle flags and rally the troops. He did not send crisp commands down and try new maneuvers. He relied on the sheer might of Confederates to overpower Federals—an unlikely attitude for him. But when it was all over and the dead and wounded had been rounded up, he had got what he was looking for: Pope's undivided attention. Pope would now come with his full might— and when he did, Longstreet and Lee would be on the scene and, among them, they would destroy him. Pope would believe he had Jackson cornered, but what he would eventually find was that he had walked into a trap.

The men got what sleep they could that night, falling where the fighting ended, and the next morning they formed a battle line three thousand yards long. A. P. Hill held the left. General William E. Starke, who was not a professional soldier, had been elevated to command Taliaferro's division on the right. His men had taken the brunt of the fighting the day before and brought muskets to their shoulders in a daze. Around 10:00 A.M. the main body of Pope's force came down the Warrenton Pike and its batteries opened up on Jackson's right. Shells passed back and forth, both sides unloaded on each other. Where was Longstreet? If the Federals charged, the plan would go asunder. Jackson by himself was vastly outnumbered. Then that unmistakable harbinger appeared on the horizon—a slowly rising dust cloud. The cry went down the line. "Longstreet's come!" Jackson's right was now covered.

The Federals went for Jackson's left. They attacked A. P. Hill by sending wave after wave at him. There was a dense growth of brush around this front, and they cut a path through it and charged. Hill beat them back. Decked out in his red fighting shirt, he rode among the ranks, keeping his men in line. Finally, during a pause, as the smoke rose and the noise died down, there appeared a gap in Hill's ranks. Immediately these determined Federals charged for it. If they split Hill in two, then they could tear

Jackson's army apart and it wouldn't matter if he had Longstreet and Lee and the whole Confederate army. Pope would demolish this wing and get to his rear where all the supply wagons were. He would defeat Stonewall.

Hill's line gave—then closed up again. Once again men were fighting toe to toe. They were just one big ball of fury. The Rebels clubbed them, hit them with large stones, cursed them, yelled, used the bayonet and their fists. Next they'd have to use their teeth. Kyd Douglas rode up into the maelstrom to ask what the situation was. "My compliments to General Jackson," Hill told him. "But please convey to the general that I believe I cannot hold out much longer. I cannot beat back a further thrust. I am probably going to fail."

Douglas reported back to Jackson. "General Hill sends his compliments, sir, and reports that he will probably fail."

The staff observed Jackson. All realized the army was destroyed if this happened. Jackson said calmly and evenly, "Go back to General Hill. Tell him if they attack him again he must beat them." Better yet, Jackson would accompany Douglas and both would bolster Hill. As they galloped off, they saw a figure in a red shirt racing toward them: Hill! He alighted and sputtered out the desperate situation. He drew on the ground the position of the armies and how he was being walloped. Jackson said nothing; he looked off toward the thundering roar of battle, then said so quietly Hill had to strain to hear: "General, your men have done nobly; if you are attacked again you will beat the enemy back."

Just then the foliage around them began to be ripped apart, and Hill remounted and charged where the firing came from. "They're already coming!" he yelled back.

"I'll expect you to beat them," Jackson called.

Hill held his line by the skin of his teeth. As it teetered he called for whatever reserves might be available. Early and Forno came forward, but seemed to make not one bit of difference. Was there no end to this Federal assault? How could they be so angry and determined? These bluecoats weren't supposed to be such good fighters. First one bluecoat pressed with all his might, couldn't go forward, and then fell back. And more fell back until the Rebel yell came down Jackson's way, a sign that the tide of battle had turned. The Confederates were now chasing the Federals.

A staff officer now galloped up to Jackson. "Sir! General Hill presents his compliments and says the attack of the enemy was repulsed."

Jackson smiled—almost laughed, but not quite. "Tell him I knew he would do it."

That was August 29 and the veterans of that day who lived into ripe old age all said it was the longest day they had ever seen. "The sun went down *so* slowly." Isaac Trimble lay wounded, old Isaac Trimble who seemed indestructible. Hill had lost over 1,500 killed and wounded. Among the dead was young Will Preston, son of Jackson's brother-in-law, Colonel John Preston. Jim Lewis, Jackson's black servant, rolled on the ground when he heard of Will's death—he had helped raise the boy. And Will had been one of the first in Jackson's Sunday-school class back in Lexington. Jackson almost broke himself when he heard the news—gripping Dr. McGuire's shoulder until the doctor winced. "Why did you leave the boy!" Then Jackson walked in the woods alone to compose himself.

He came back to hear Dr. McGuire's statistics, the number of dead and wounded. He sat at a campfire with McGuire and some staff officers as they slowly brought scalding coffee to their lips and tried to rest before it would begin all over again tomorrow. There was no doubt that it would continue and no doubt that others would join the number of dead and mutilated. At times like this, staring into the fire, sinking in complete exhaustion, it was hard to remember why and how the war had started. But it was here, and they would continue, no matter what, to fight. Others always seemed to appear to replace those who were knocked out of action.

That evening Captain Hugh White, a ministerial student before the war, held worship in the tent of Colonel William S. H. Baylor, who commanded the Stonewall Brigade. Colonel Baylor prayed fervently.

The next morning, August 30, dawned hot and sticky. A sort of breathless quiet spread over the land as the butterflies and birds returned and the sun bore down. Jackson and his staff observed from a hill the enemy marching and getting positioned as if to attack Jackson's right flank. He saw some Federal guns facing Starke's line on the right and in a crisp way he ordered the Rockbridge Artillery to open up on them. Smartly the Rockbridge crew fired a few rounds and the Yankees withdrew. Quiet returned.

And 4:00 P.M. arrived, the sun again sinking, and Jackson began thinking the bluecoats had had enough. Just then a wild clatter broke forth as if from the center of hell. It came on all fronts. The blues seemed to spring from the earth like some instant evil pestilence. Just seemed to spring instantaneously out of the very ground. Not just against Jackson's right. They were everywhere, and they were devastating. Much worse than the day before, and the Rebels had barely contained that. Had Jackson trapped Pope—or was it now the other way around?

Once more the troops ran against each other hand to hand, flinging whatever punishment they could. Jackson trotted around on his horse, looking to exploit whatever advantage he could find. John Pope smoked a cigar and looked on confidently. He had drawn up a brilliant battle plan, had paid scrupulous attention to detail, and now expected everything to go off perfectly. The Federals hurled themselves against the Stonewall Brigade which could now muster only a thin line. As the men fell back on a second assault, the Stonewall color-bearer dropped. Colonel Baylor, the brand-new commander, raised the flag and shouted, "Boys, follow me!" They did, cheering and shouting. And then a thunder of gunfire erupted and Baylor was lifted high in the air by minié balls; he was dead before he hit the ground. Captain Hugh White, who the night before had earnestly prayed with Colonel Baylor for the Lord's aid, rushed over and picked up the colors: The colors should never fall; their symbolism was all-important as battle seesawed. White had taken but three steps when bullets ripped him apart and he fell back into someone's arms. The colors passed down the line. Colonel Andrew Jackson Grigsby was the ranking officer now in the brigade and he took charge.

A courier rode to Jackson and gave him the news. The commander of the Stonewall Brigade had gone down; they were falling back; all looked lost. Jackson had trouble hearing. He asked the courier to repeat and then said, "Go back, son, and give my compliments to Colonel Grigsby. Tell the Stonewall Brigade to maintain her reputation."

Once more the two sides were clubbing each other—a fight to the death. Worse, far worse than the day before. Stonewall now called for help from Longstreet, who was across from him on the opposite hill. Longstreet saw he couldn't get there in time. Instead of sending infantry, he turned his batteries toward the Yankees, aiming in a risky way over the Rebels' heads. He was sending fire straight across Jackson's front and into the Yankee left flank. Longstreet lowered his hand and shells left muzzles in a blazing orange glow, the cannons bucking. The Federals took the fire directly. The assault stopped and the blue-clads started retreating, at first slowly, then in a rout. Longstreet's men began running to catch them, but Jackson's troops were already out front.

An awesome slaughter followed. The gray-clads acted as if possessed by demons, screaming, firing, chasing the Federals toward the Stone Bridge on Bull Run. Lee looked on now, his plan going exactly as he had hoped. He had suckered John Pope into a piecemeal battle where Pope could never quite mass his force against him. It had been Jackson and Lee against the invader. The Rebels chased Pope's defeated men all the way toward the Henry house, stopping only because of pitch-black darkness. They had chased John Pope into the Bull Run river and completely torn his force apart.

John Pope was soon reassigned to duty in Minnesota, to fight the Sioux. He never saw action again in the Civil War. And Jackson got set to take the war into enemy territory.

CHAPTER XVI

Into Another Sphere

In the aftermath of battle there are two courses: Go forward or go back. Lee ordered Jackson to chase the Yankees after the victory of Second Manassas. So once again Jackson's bruised and battered troops took to the road, the foot cavalry route-stepping, the caissons bouncing, and the skirmishers out front. They ran head on into a Federal force on September 1, in a heavy blinding rain. After the fury of Manassas the Southerners would just as soon have taken prisoners or maybe chased the Yankees a little more in a dreamlike trance. But the Federals were tired of being humiliated. At Chantilly they turned and began swinging with all their might.

It was an odd battle in several ways. The rain came down in torrents. On the Confederate side Colonel William Smith, ex-governor of Virginia, had an abiding contempt for West Pointers (they seemed to be everywhere and directing everything). In retaliation against what he considered their military strictness, he wore not a kepi or martial braid into battle but a tall beaver hat. He also calmly raised a large blue cotton umbrella to shield himself from the downpour, as he directed companies and changed positions. Another ranking officer, who undoubtedly would just as soon have missed this fight, sent a message to Jackson: "My compliments to General Jackson and my request to be permitted to take my command out of the line because all my ammunition is wet." As Jackson shifted under his heavy slicker, he answered: "My compliments to the Colonel. Tell him the enemy's ammunition is just as wet as his!"

The Federals almost carried the rainy day and chased off the more numerous foe—but in the end it was not meant to be. Their two commanders went down and that was too much finally—the heart went out of them again. General I. I. Stevens was shot dead in his tracks, and that fine figure of a military man, Major General Philip Kearny, was so active on the field that he rode past Rebel skirmishers right into and among Confederate soldiers. He looked gallant up there on his large white mount. They shot him as he tried to gallop off, not really relishing the task. The general was laid out on the porch of a cabin not far from the battle and troops who were interested passed by to have a look the next day. A. P. Hill had known him well in the old army and had been quite fond of him. "Poor Kearny," he said, looking down. "He deserved a better death than that!"

After Chantilly, Lee took a pause and considered his options. He could not stay in place because this part of the country was stripped of food. Soldiers did more than fight. They had to eat— and thousands of soldiers a day with hungry bellies was quite a problem to solve. He could now fall back to the Shenandoah or—in a more imaginative leap—invade the North. Lee weighed all considerations and then made plans to cross over into Maryland.

Although Maryland was under the Union flag, it was Southern in many cultural ways and had many Confederate sympathizers. In one way these Rebels would be coming as liberators as much as invaders. They were all worn out, gaunt, hungry, wounded—like scarecrows. Their dead on the battlefields were so lean that they decomposed much less rapidly than the Federal dead. With no outward identifying mark, you could always tell a dead Rebel from the Yankee corpse. The gray-clad looked half starved.

Naturally Jackson was happy to push on for the Potomac. His main complaint was straggling in his army. His men would simply not move out at the appointed time and often dawdled on the road. Wouldn't have it! He blamed his commanders. And at the moment his disposition wasn't at its sweetest. Little Sorrel had become shell-shocked perhaps and had been missing for several days. Jackson mounted an unfamiliar cream-colored clay-bank, and felt uncomfortable in the saddle.

On September 4 they moved out and Jackson soon became upset at his men's lack of celerity. Where was Hill? When a job was to be done there was no time for sentiment. Hill might have saved the day at Manassas, but that day had passed. There was not going to be rest until the final day—when the war was over. Hill had his own rhythm and was not at the rear of his columns, making sure they were closed. He rode in the lead and stragglers abounded in the back. Also, as Jackson now noted, Hill did not call for the ten-minute breaks on the hour. Hill was simply not following orders, and it would not do. Jackson ordered Hill's leading brigade to halt for a rest. Hill rode back in the kind of fury he usually reserved for the battlefield. He was a high-strung, jittery man, a redhead, and he yelled, "Who ordered my men halted!"

"Why, General Jackson, sir."

Powell Hill rode up to Stonewall Jackson. The hero of Second Manassas, which was not even a week old, removed his saber and handed it to Jackson. "If you intend, sir, to give orders to my men, then perhaps you should command them."

"Consider yourself under arrest for neglect of duty," Jackson said, turning without another word. Hill rode in the rear from then on, relieved of duty.

Later in the morning the troops came to the Potomac, the boundary between North and South. The Virginians plunged their horses into the water, lifting aloft the flag of Virginia. On the bank the musicians limbered up their battered instruments and then broke into "Maryland, My Maryland." The mood in the ranks was that they had reached the promised land, the other side. No longer were they going to be punished on their own ground. They were now going to impress their will. It was a holiday mood, a celebration. Stonewall Jackson plunged the clay-bank into the river, and halfway across he doffed his soiled kepi and the men cheered—feeling this was a momentous occasion.

Some Federal pickets on the Maryland side let off a round or two, but soon they were chased away and the long procession of Southerners rode and tramped onto enemy soil. Lee had given strict orders for no pillaging; nothing must be taken from the countryside. But there seemed to be no problem in that direction. The people on the Maryland side began showering gifts on the Confederates. In the afternoon Jackson was presented with a new mount, and he was too embarrassed to refuse. He treated the horse extremely gingerly that day. The next morning he climbed on more confidently, applied the spurs—and the horse promptly threw him. For a while after that the conquering hero had to move through the countryside in an ambulance.

But the gifts didn't stop, nor the enthusiasm of the crowds. Jeb Stuart in his plumed hat had a field day with the ladies. Several young women actually embraced Jackson before he could make a break, his face flaming. On Sunday evening, able to move around now, he asked young Kyd Douglas, who was a Maryland native, if he would care to attend church services in Frederick, a few miles outside of camp. Of course, such a question from his commander had to be answered in the affirmative. Jackson had passes written out to get them through the picket lines, although Douglas assured him that all knew who he was. It made no difference. It was written: "Pass Maj. Genl. T. J. Jackson and two staff officers and attendants to Frederick to church, to return tonight. Signed, Major Genl Jackson." Rules were rules.

Jackson asked Douglas to recommend the seat of worship and the young adjutant took his chief to the Reformed Church, since no Presbyterian church was available. A Reverend Dr. Zacharias preached that night and made note to the congregation that a famous Confederate general was in the congregation, Stonewall Jackson. But, brave man, he did not temper his sermon and he was a straight-out Unionist. He prayed fervently for Abraham Lincoln. The minister might have taken less pride in his bravery if he had known that Jackson, as was his custom, had slept through the sermon.

Henry Kyd Douglas reported: "As usual he fell asleep, but this time more soundly than was his wont. His head sunk upon his breast, his cap dropped from his hands to the floor; the prayers of the congregation did not disturb him, and only the choir and the deep-toned organ awakened him."

Now in Maryland and changing the direction of the war—what? Although the word went out, posters tacked on walls, calling for volunteers to the Confederate cause, not very many Maryland men felt the necessary stirring of Southern patriotism. Lee got few volunteers, and that was very discouraging. The old problem of feeding his men was not being easily solved here in Maryland, either. It took a lot of supplies to feed 53,000 mouths. Lee's quartermasters combed the countryside diligently, but there was only so much to eat out there. Lee decided that the answer might be to go to Pennsylvania. Once there a supply line could be run down through the Shenandoah to Richmond. They would have food, they would have supplies. One problem: The Yankees now held the strategic Harpers Ferry, gateway to the Shenandoah. He called for Jackson.

Jackson stood in Lee's tent, looking grave. The question was posed: Could he sneak off, not letting those people out there know, capture Harpers Ferry, and then rejoin Lee's army in Maryland? It was of course rhetorical. Jackson would move at once. He and Lee went over details. Generals McLaws and Walker would aid Jackson, helping to rim the heights around Harpers Ferry with artillery, but essentially this would be a Jackson operation. And both men now knew how best to work. Lee stated what was needed, offering a general plan with a loose framework, and Jackson in a semi-independent way would think up fast, daring actions—often in split-second inspirations on the battlefield—to pull them off.

General Longstreet was heard clearing his throat outside the tent flaps, and Lee courteously invited him in. He asked Old Pete's opinion of having Jackson leave to remove the Federal troops from Harpers Ferry and then return to the Army of Northern Virginia. Old Pete was a war-horse, not a racehorse. Besides, behind those narrow eyes and tight lips was his secret opinion of Jackson. He was like Jackson's sibling around Lee, the father; he was jealous as hell. He offered some thoughts, none too cheery or practical. One was to take the whole army and liberate Harpers Ferry. Lee thanked him for his counsel, and the meeting broke up.

Longstreet went back to his staff to bad-mouth Jackson. Jackson went off to his troops to prepare to march. Lee sat down and drew up Special Order 191, which assigned the routes his various lieutenants would take to cover Jackson and then the timetable for regrouping.

A written copy of Special Order 191 later almost destroyed the Army of Northern Virginia—in a manner Lee and Jackson would never have expected.

Jackson was now back in the saddle, his equestrian bruises having healed, and he was rousing his staff to move out at 3:00 A.M. Some still nodded on horses as the vanguard, Jackson himself in the lead, entered Frederick at sunup.

The reasonable expectation was that the town would be asleep, but the streets were mobbed as Jackson's army rode through—curious, glaring, wondering what these strange half-starved Southerners were up to. Contrary to legend and Whittier's poem, the ninety-six-year-old Barbara Fritchie neither glimpsed nor scolded the general. Jackson made a point of loudly asking for a map of Chambersburg, Pennsylvania, and otherwise alerting any spies present that he was going in ten different directions, none the correct one. Not many were doffing hats, for this part of the country wasn't too friendly. They were close to enemy lines.

Now that a fight was looming at Harpers Ferry, A. P. Hill requested that he be given back his command and Jackson was more than willing. Wait till the battle smoke cleared and then the court-martial and rancor could pick up where they left off. Jackson immediately ordered Hill to move straight on Martinsburg, which was west of Harpers Ferry, while Lawton's and Starke's divisions should race to cut off the Yankees if they should try to escape. Jackson was improvising as he went along. He crossed the Potomac at Williamsport and not Sharpsburg as he had first planned. Stay after the Yankees; catch them where you could!

Hill found that the Yankees had already left Martinsburg, had got wind of Jackson, and had themselves raced to Harpers Ferry to add to the defenders. Which left Martinsburg, a Virginia city, to welcome Stonewall's troops without the aid of Yankees. The town went wild as the barefoot scarecrows in gray entered. In one town Jackson had been greeted with mute grudging silence; now, in Martinsburg, there had never been a greater hero than Jackson. He rode through town, waving his kepi as he had upon entering Winchester. But the accolades and attention didn't end with the street celebration. As he sat at a desk in a newly established headquarters, in a private home, the cheering and fanfare continued outside. He fastened the shutters and bolted the doors and still it went on. So completely had these Southerners, in need of a hero, deified Jackson that some pulled hair from his horse's mane, not realizing it was not the legendary Little Sorrel, who was still missing in action. Before they were through the poor horse had had its tail cut off. Not a very presentable animal then to take into battle. The shutters finally broke under pressure as Jackson penned dispatches, and then he found noses pressing against the window—and that did it. He could withdraw no farther. It was principally young women outside now, forcing the windows up and then tossing in roses.

Jackson admitted the ladies, who immediately swarmed over him, asking for his autograph, each trying to be the one nearest. One very small girl reached and grabbed a brass button from his coat. Could she please have it? He gave way and snipped it off. Others demanded equal treatment and soon half his buttons were gone. Here was Stonewall Jackson, who only a few days before had been in the midst of heavy firing, sudden death all around, and now he was surrounded by young women in the middle of a parlor in Martinsburg. He came to his senses when one asked for a lock of his hair. Blushing, highly courteous, he ushered them out and went back to planning for more war.

He got another taste of battle the next day when he had his columns on the way to Harpers Ferry and the Yankees. At around 11:00 A.M. he spotted blue-clad figures on Bolivar Heights; he was two miles away. According to Lee's plans, Walker and McLaws should now have taken positions on Loudoun and Maryland heights, respectively. Jackson skimmed those high promontories with his field glasses, but caught no sign of life. He did hear a clatter of firing, but wasn't sure where it came from. They should be there! He then put into operation a new semaphore signal system which was dear to his heart. He had great hopes for sending swift sure messages by it, not having to rely entirely on couriers. Jackson liked the modern touch. His semaphore operatives kept wigwagging with their flags, but got no response. Finally in midafternoon he sent a courier over, who reported that the generals were now taking positions on the two heights and their artillery was going into place. Jackson moved in and took Bolivar Heights.

Jackson had now pinned the Federals down below from three sides. He had his artillery in place and his foot soldiers ready to cut off escape. When he had commanded the Confederate garrison at Harpers Ferry, in the position the Federals were now in, he had known the place was indefensible, at least in theory. Now he was aiming to prove it in fact. He had received, though, a disturbing message from Lee, which said Little Mac was on the warpath once more and had attacked South Mountain, nearly cutting him off. Unless Jackson took Harpers Ferry immediately and then joined him to ward off McClellan, he might be terribly beaten or forced to flee into the heart of Virginia. The Confederacy depended upon Jackson.

On the fifteenth a deep morning mist covered Harpers Ferry. Then slowly it began to lift, revealing the long muzzles of artillery pointing down on the town. Jackson gave a signal or two from the semaphore and suddenly one rim of a hill sent down a rain of shells, then another. The terrible racket lasted an hour, with arsenals exploding down below, horses stampeding, homes blown asunder. They just blasted and blasted and blasted. Then there was a pause and A. P. Hill's Light Division began moving forward, bayonets out. There were heavy works in front of them, high barriers and any number of muskets pointed their way. The Light Division made ready to suffer a lot of casualties, when suddenly a white flag popped up. Just popped up, waving from side to side. The Federals had had enough. Jackson had won the day with nothing but artillery.

Even the Federal troops who lined the streets of Harpers Ferry cheered as he rode in, and one was heard to say, "Boys, he's not much for looks, but if we'd had him we wouldn't have been caught in this trap." These Northerners were moved by the fame of Jackson, the myths, and they saluted him as he came from Bolivar Heights and into the small river-depot village. Jackson took 11,000 prisoners, 12,000 arms, 70 pieces of artillery, and warehouses filled with shoes, clothes, and other supplies. General

Julius White, in an immaculate blue uniform, complete with braid and brass, rode a prancing, gleaming black horse to the ceremony of surrender. He handed over his sword to a man in a sweat-begrimed uniform, who sat uncomfortably in the saddle. A Northern newspaperman later wrote that Jackson wore a hat that looked so disreputable that a Northern beggar would refuse to wear it. Actually it was Jackson's new hat. He had retired the old kepi three days before.

Confederate officer J.F.J. Caldwell wrote:

> Jackson was the great theme of conversation [among the Federal prisoners]. The Federals seemed never weary of extolling his genius and inquiring for particulars of his history. They were extremely anxious to see him, and made many of us promise to show him to them if he should pass among us that day.
>
> He came up from the riverside late in the afternoon. The intelligence spread like electricity. Almost the whole mass of prisoners broke over us, rushed to the road, threw up their hats, cheered, roared, bellowed, as even Jackson's own troops had scarcely ever done. We, of course, joined in with them. The general gave a stiff acknowledgment of the compliment . . . drove spurs into his horse, and went clattering down the hill, away from the noise.

Jackson left all the details of the surrender to A. P. Hill, and went back to his troops. He gave orders for them to cook two days' rations and be ready to move out that night. During the packing up some unexpected visitors arrived—two brothers of Ellie Junkin, Jackson's first wife. George Junkin had chosen the Southern cause, been captured in battle, and had just escaped from a Federal prison. His brother, the Reverend David X. Junkin, held fierce loyalty, like his father, toward the Union. The minister was now actually in enemy territory, behind the lines, but he wanted to see his erstwhile brother-in-law. Jackson was delighted. He rode for some moments alone with the two brothers on a private stretch of road. They all embraced, tears flowed, and then Reverend Junkin entreated dear brother Thomas to forgo his godless ways in support of the rebellion and return to righteousness. He was of course talking to the wrong man.

Thomas listened, quietly made counterarguments, and then they all reminisced about the long evenings at the Junkin home when things had been much different. Reverend Junkin said his old father often thought of Thomas, now one of the South's most famous generals, and wished to see him once again. They all embraced once more—and Jackson rode off, never to see them again.

Jackson had his men up and at 'em by one in the morning, and marched them off in the moonlight. A few hours after the sun came up he reported to a much relieved General Robert E. Lee at Sharpsburg. Lee was usually the most sanguine of men, certainly stoical, and in his own way as much a fatalist as Presbyterian Jackson. Now he was highly agitated. Little Mac, who could always be counted on to stay put, to have a deep aversion to quick attack, had moved on Lee with ungodly speed to cut him off at South Mountain and to rip him to shreds. What had got into Little Mac? Lee discovered that McClellan had come by the famous Special Order No. 191 in a most peculiar and outlandish way. He hadn't had to pay a spy, hadn't made a raid and captured information—a Federal soldier had noticed a package lying in the middle of the road. It had dropped from the back pocket of a Confederate officer. It was Special Order 191 wrapped around a pack of fine cigars. Little Mac was notified, and, emboldened, became a different sort of man for a brief period.

When Jackson arrived Lee relaxed a fraction. Now he could make a stand here in Maryland and not have to worry about being chased back into Virginia like a whipped dog. Yet, even with Stonewall there, the picture was not rosy. Lee was now able to spread out an army of around 25,000 along the meandering Antietam Creek a few miles east of Sharpsburg. He was going to take his stand against 60,000, maybe 80,000 troops under McClellan. But he did hold certain advantages. A rolling countryside lay outside Sharpsburg, land well suited for defense. A fortified ridge overlooked Antietam Creek, a decided advantage. Little Mac was going to have to cross that creek. On the minus side in all this was the fact that the Potomac lay a mere four miles to his west. If McClellan got across the Antietam in large numbers, then he could drive Lee into the Potomac. Jackson was there now to see it didn't happen.

Jackson's men, who couldn't remember when they'd had a full night's sleep, now went into battle position on the left wing at around 11:00 A.M. near a small Dunkard Church. It had just been picked out by fate, like the Henry House Hill, for a page in history. Those who took positions near that church, and lived to tell it, never forgot its shape or the shells it took. These Rebels on the left wing were begrimed, past exhaustion, and hungry as hell. Their food for the moment was green corn plucked beside the road and eaten raw. In the last three and a half days they had covered over sixty miles. Dust swirled around them. Now the durn Yankees—fresh as daisies, smarting from past humiliations, endowed with a plethora of gunpower—were coming.

As the sun sank this first day of Jackson's arrival shells began to fall on the Rebels. Artillery opened up, confident and well-aimed. Union skirmishers pressed against General John Hood's men, who were dug in next to Jackson. A lively racket of musket fire erupted over the steady artillery bombardment and then dwindled off to nothing when dark fell. Just a little welcome, Rebs! As the crickets chirped and bullfrogs croaked, Jackson found just the tree he was looking for. One with a protruding root he could use as a pillow. He lay down and fell immediately asleep. Suddenly he was awakened by Hood, who had a request. Could Jackson please relieve Hood's force, take over his position in the line for a while? Hood's men were woefully tired and near starved. They needed some rest desperately and the chance to cook up some rations. Jackson agreed to send his men in as temporary replacements and asked only one thing in return. Hood must agree to send his men back into action if called. Agreed.

At three in the morning all hell broke loose. Long-range Federal artillery, well back of the Antietam, sent screaming shells into Rebel positions—ka-boom, ka-boom, ka-boom! And then as dim light spread over the horizon, through the blue haze of powder smoke, Fighting Joe Hooker's men came forward, crouching low, firing on the run. Rebel brigades went down, scythed like so much wheat. A pounding from the faraway artillery, then bent-over Yanks stalking up on foot—these bluecoats were going to kill everyone! Send for Hood! Hood popped up, swinging his suspenders over his shoulders, calling for his bugler. *Charge!* In the face of an onslaught he called for his men to go forward, not back.

In nearby Shepherdstown the citizenry awoke to the growing sound of this battle: sudden roars, a steady hum, then shrieks. They heard whistling shells, explosions, and then the thrilling roll of muskets; and, borne by wind, human cries. . . . Jackson rode down his line, noting that Hood's men formed a thin gray line and were moving through a cornfield that was turning red with blood. General Starke fell. Colonel Grigsby, who was used to leading a division, now commanded no more than a corporal's guard. Old Jube Early had flung himself into combat, gathering scattered troops the best he could, remnants of other commands. From what he could determine, only a few Confederates now stood between wave after wave of bluecoats at several points.

The unlikely Dunkard Church became the eye of the storm. Hood's men now formed a line there with Early's force holding a position on the left and dependable D. H. Hill coming in on the right. Into this box the Federals advanced in a steady stream—and so began to be cut down by a tremendous crossfire. Jackson was in effect guiding the overall battle here and he sent Pendleton to Hood: Could he hold? "Tell General Jackson, unless I get reinforcements I must be forced back, but I am going on while I can!" Jackson sent whom and what he could find—McLaws, Grigsby, and Leroy Stafford, anyone and everyone who could fire and move. Hood steadied his front and then miraculously pushed the Federals back, a hard foot at a time. In a terrible din and clatter, a huge billow of smoke covering the field, he pressed the Federals back from the Dunkard Church.

Now McClellan, with his huge numbers, sent his full attack toward D. H. Hill on the right. Let's see if Harvey can take it! Little Mac's men kept coming and they kept being shot down. Body after body was added to the pile of corpses and this memorable stretch of earth became known then and ever after as "Bloody Lane." In the Federal charge came jolly Major General William Henry French, Jackson's old adversary in Florida. French didn't encounter his old nemesis. They came close, but never met on the battlefield. Hill's men seemed to all but disappear under bluecoats, held on by the skin of their teeth, and then threw the Yankees back once again.

While the battle seesawed, Jackson sat on his horse by an

apple tree and munched on an apple while he considered options. As he chewed, branches cracked and bullets whizzed by, and he relaxed by throwing a leg over the pommel of his saddle. Then he tossed the apple aside and returned to the fray.

Dr. Hunter McGuire accompanied Jackson on a battlefield tour of the old Stonewall division. He wrote: "They had been reduced to a very small body of men and were commanded by Col. [A.J.] Grigsby. While talking to Grigsby, I saw off at a distance in a field men lying down, and supposed it was a line of battle.

"I asked Colonel Grigsby why he did not move that line of battle back to make it conform to his own, when he said, 'Those men . . . are all dead. . . . They are Georgia soldiers.' "

On Longstreet's far right, yet another wholesale battle developed in the afternoon. The Rebels held the important Burnside Bridge, which crossed the Antietam, with a thin skirmish line. Some 2,460 Southerners were trying to keep 13,000 Federals in General Ambrose E. Burnside's IX Army Corps from crossing. The Yankees seemed to think that if they just kept coming they'd eventually get across because, surely, there weren't enough bullets in the whole Confederacy to kill them all. Lee acted quickly on seeing the danger here. He called up all the batteries he could, some from as far away as the Dunkard Church. Artillery shells soon hit the blue-clads straight on as they came everlastingly across the bridge. The Confederates added musket fire to the heavy shells. Still they came. Thirteen thousand men were a lot to contend with. If they got a sizable number across they could take over Sharpsburg and Lee would be cut off. He would be finished.

Then a cloud of dust could be spotted on the Shepherdstown road—A. P. Hill on his way in a hurry, in relief, from Harpers Ferry. Hill had on his red fighting shirt and was poking the pointed end of his saber at stragglers in his columns. Close up, close up! Hill saluted General Lee, and asked where he should go. Lee pointed to the Burnside Bridge, and Hill's Light Division, with no pause, went down the hill and into action. The Federals were establishing a position on the Confederate side when Hill's men, with no rest after their seventeen-mile march, flung themselves on the Federals. With that high-pitched unearthly yell.

The Union flag held, then began dropping back. The tattered gray line pressed them back and back until the bridge was cleared of the last bluecoat. And as the sun set, the South held the field.

Over the battleground whimpers of "Water, water" sounded. Men moved in a daze and in disbelief at the fury they'd been through and at the cost of that day. The whole war was moving into a new realm of madness. More than 10,000 Southerners lay dead or wounded. Perhaps it was miraculous that any had lived. And yet it was the same as at the beginning. The South held the same ground. And still more effort would be required if they were to keep it. Lee held a war council that night, and it was determined that if Little Mac still wanted to slug it out, he would have his chance tomorrow. In the dark the Rebels set up defensive positions in the time left from burying the dead and treating the wounded. Jackson slept in an open field. Men sat around campfires while bodies lay in piles nearby, the flames throwing shadows over their silent forms.

In daylight Lee and Jackson waited for Little Mac to show his hand, but no movement came from his direction. He had reverted to his true nature—he was hesitating. Lee himself did not relish the waiting game, and asked Jackson's advice. Should they keep waiting for battle—or move out. Jackson took a long hard look through his field glasses; he scouted enemy entrenchments. His advice, and one he hated to give: Retreat to Virginia. It had been a daring adventure to have invaded Maryland, but good sense said they should return home. Once more they all crossed the Potomac.

CHAPTER XVII

Back Where It Had All Begun

Through the night of September 18, 1862, the Army of Northern Virginia crossed the water into the Old Dominion. Major John Harman, Jackson's quartermaster, cursed a riveting, awesome streak—"Goddamitsonbitchingwhoremongerfrigger!"—enough to move mules by itself and leave Jackson with one perplexing problem he never solved. He never put the damper on Harman's tongue. Lee took up station on Traveller in the middle of the Potomac and was soon joined by Jackson. "Push on, close up, men!" They came through: caissons, foot soldiers, finally, as light broke, ambulances, the last on the line. Little Mac was left on the other side.

This army camped around four miles away, the troops just falling to the ground and into sleep. They awoke in the afternoon and began putting pieces back together, patching haversacks and penning letters, feeling lazy and secure for a change. As campfires blazed that night, the troops in bivouac, songs broke out and an occasional scuffle. At headquarters tent, Jackson was still at business at midnight when horse's hooves sounded outside and General Reverend William Nelson Pendleton burst in, completely shattered and nearly incoherent. He was out of breath and his words came in fits and starts.

"McClellan . . . the river . . . blue-clads got over. . . ."

Pendleton and his artillery had been stationed on a bluff by the Potomac to shower McClellan with shells should he attempt a crossing. Not only had Little Mac attempted a crossing, but he had been successful enough to have roped in all the Confederates' big guns. And he was heading this way! Jackson was thinking on his feet, and his first thought when trouble came was, as usual, A. P. Hill and the Light Division. Little Sorrel had been located and returned to duty, and Jackson galloped to the front of Hill's division, reconnoitering as he went. In early daylight Jackson sent Hill's infantry racing against the Union soldiers and their newly captured cannons. They raced into withering, shattering artillery fire—and just kept coming. They drove the bluecoats into the water, heading for the other shore. They then raised their muskets and downed one Yankee after another, and soon the river was clogged with bodies. The Confederates recaptured all but four guns, lost 261 as casualties, but saved the army. It was a near total disaster. Little Mac didn't try it again.

The Rebels went back to regrouping and getting their second wind. Not far from Martinsburg they swam in the clear cool water of Opequon Creek. They rid themselves of a goodly portion of lice; stragglers were located afield; and the sick and wounded got to doctors. And then, rested and regrouped, Lee took his army to new campsites at Bunker Hill, not far from Winchester. Lee's army now had two corps and two "wing" commanders: Jackson led the II Corps and Longstreet held command of the I Corps. Old Pete kept his own counsel and passed on a subtle word of disparagement about Jackson whenever possible, and Old Jack kept his counsel and went about his usual business.

Jackson brought back daily hard drills. He didn't soften his disposition any toward deserters—they should of course be shot. On the other hand, he was extremely concerned over the well-being of those who stayed in there to fight: He made sure his men had as good uniforms as possible and that campsites were near fresh clean water. He checked and kept checking and was the first sight his men saw in the morning, the last at night. Now in camp, promotions were handed out. Isaac Trimble, battered but unbowed, got his sought-after rank of major general. Major Elisha Franklin Paxton, Jackson's chief of staff, was elected to lead the esteemed Stonewall Brigade. Longstreet got promoted to lieutenant general. And on October 11, 1862, another was promoted to that high rank: T. J. Jackson, the erstwhile deacon and professor at V.M.I.

But some things did not change. Now in bivouac, at rest and relative peace, A. P. Hill went back to war with Jackson. He sent word to Lee that he had been treated with injustice by Jackson. Why, oh why, hadn't he been court-martialed? If Jackson had been correct in his charges, then he, Hill, should stand before the bar of justice. If the charges were in effect untrue, then the officer who made those charges (Old Jack) should be charged himself. Lee groaned. And Jackson and Hill began a set of formal communications whenever they had to do business together. Jackson would undoubtedly have loved to be back fighting in court, mulling over legal fine print, and pressing obscure points—but somewhere along the line he had come by a modicum of restraint. He let Powell Hill do most of the ranting and raving.

Then came a marvelous moment in the war. Major Heros von Borcke, the Prussian staff assistant to Jeb Stuart, arrived with a gift for General Jackson, compliments of General Stuart. Von Borcke laid on Jackson's camp bed a most marvelous uniform coat, the brass buttons sparkling. It had been turned out to perfection by a Richmond tailor.

Jackson wasn't used to this type of present. He felt the material. "Please give Stuart my best thanks, my dear Major—but the coat is much too handsome for me. I shall take the best care of it, and shall prize it highly as a souvenir. Now let's eat."

No, no, von Borcke would not be put off. "Please, General Stuart vould be disappointed if he didn't know coat fitted properly. Please, General."

Jackson did try it on, and it did look marvelous. He wore it out of the tent and on to the officers' mess for the evening. His staff had trouble recognizing him at first—what was the matter? He had worn the same old tunic since the start of the war. Now he was resplendent—and embarrassed. But he looked great. And it had been a gift from Stuart, for whom Jackson continued to have a weakness. Whenever the special jingle of Stuart's spurs sounded near Jackson, the general's face showed pleasure. There was something about the foolhardiness of Stuart, a zest of life, a recklessness and exuberance, that Jackson could never attain. He kept wearing the coat. And it became part of him.

But decked out in finery as he now was in the coat department, he mustn't forget humility and keeping things in proportion. He mustn't tempt fate or go beyond certain well-defined boundaries he always kept in mind. Loyal Anna wrote that his reputation was spreading far and wide, that Confederates wanted to know more about him. She didn't ask, didn't put it into words, but wasn't this what Jackson was after in great part—fame? Didn't he lust for such glory, to be a hero among his own people, to have them recognize him? General Dick Taylor, the president's son, had once caught that special glow of sublime ambition on Jackson's face, but this newly minted lieutenant general never lost his mountaineer suspicion, never ceased guarding, in effect, against a swelled head. Too many plaudits might turn him into a heathen. Anna wrote, asking if she might have an article written about him, furnishing tidbits of information about their nation's most daring and successful general.

He answered, "It is gratifying to be beloved and to have our conduct approved by our fellow-men, but this is not worthy to be compared with the glory that is in reservation for us in the presence of our glorified Redeemer. . . . I would not relinquish the slightest diminution of that glory for all this world can give. My prayer is that such may ever be the feeling of my heart. It appears to me that it would be better for you not to have anything written about me. Let us follow the teaching of inspiration—'Let another man praise thee, and not thine own mouth: a stranger, and not thine own lips.' I appreciate the loving interest that prompted such a desire in my precious darling."

A man of multiple contradictions. A man of many internal conflicts.

And now a man who was being showered with presents. He hauled in cakes and sweets, armchairs and socks. He especially liked a pair of socks an elderly woman from Tennessee knitted for him. But even here T. J. Jackson gave the credit to his Redeemer. "Our gracious Heavenly Father strikingly manifests his kindness to me by disposing people to bestow presents upon me." He was becoming a hero, a famous man—even in the North. Newspapers took him up, and column after column reported his ways. Even Europeans felt the pull of Jackson. There was something about his stubbornness, his plain simple style, and his unbending piety. There was no cant in him, the bugbear of the Victorian age.

As Jackson settled into camp life for the moment, visitors came in from the blue. They came from Winchester, Savannah, and England. Three Englishmen, one of them Lord Wolseley, who would later be commander in chief of the British army, came calling. Jackson impressed Wolseley with his firmness of character, but also, strangely enough, with his knowledge of architecture. The Confederate general began a discourse on the intricacies of Durham Cathedral, which he had visited on his sojourn in England. He segued into the history of the bishopric of Durham, too, which none of the Englishmen was ready for. They had come to learn, if they could, the secret of Jackson's military thinking, and here was this man with thin lips giving them a history and architecturel lecture. By doing all the talking himself—an unaccustomed role for him—Jackson avoided embarrassing questions. He kept the real secrets to himself.

The only time he let down his guard was around children. The army moved inexorably to Winchester once again, and Jackson stayed with Reverend Graham and his family. The Graham children adored this general who was so bloodthirsty on the battlefield. They climbed all over him; he was never patronizing, but entered wholeheartedly into their games. There was a bond between them that children understand. He had time for them, allowed them the freedom and liberties he never would his soldiers. He was about to become a father himself, for down in North Carolina his *esposita* was ripe with child—in fact, overripe.

Yet even with cold winter approaching, the war would not be stilled. Lincoln was determined to win, and he had for the moment replaced Little Mac and his caution with the bluster and aggression of General Ambrose E. Burnside, who had never quite got across that famous bridge at Antietam. Now the Army of the

Potomac, under Burnside, under pressure from Lincoln to take it
to them, was advancing on Fredericksburg. From there the Union
could press down on Richmond. Jackson got the call from Lee to
move his corps down there, and perhaps again the Confederates
could fling those people back to the Potomac. When, oh, when
would they have had enough?

Jackson and his men had had a revival spirit pass through
camp. The Reverend Dr. Joseph C. Stiles, chaplain of the Confederacy, had spread the gospel through camp meetings. One soldier
after another had fallen prostrate before the altar, begging God
to forgive his sins and asking Jesus Christ to be his personal
savior. Jackson couldn't have been more pleased by the religious
fervor and this spirit of religiosity in his men. Like Cromwell
now, he led his troops toward the enemy, an avenger. He wore
his resplendent coat and he had a new gleaming saber at his hip.
At Gordonsville a letter awaited him. Anna had given birth to a
daughter, a dark-haired, blue-eyed girl with the straight Jackson
nose. His *esposita* had been afraid that Thomas might be disappointed, that he might well have preferred a boy. Not Thomas.
He wrote joyfully, "Oh! How thankful I am to our kind Heavenly
Father for having spared my precious wife and given us a little
daughter! I cannot tell you how gratified I am, nor how much I
wish I could be with you and see my two darlings!"

Anna left the matter of naming the girl to Jackson, a husband's prerogative in the South. He chose the name Julia—after
his mother.

But Jackson was not to be beside his wife and new daughter
just yet. Burnside at Fredericksburg awaited him. The town was
a prosperous historic spot on the Rappahannock. Presidents had
stayed there; it offered lovely vistas and much charm in normal
times. It thrived in a valley that had protective ridges looking
down from above. Cautiously and determinedly the armies of the
North and South began gathering on opposite ridges above the
river and town. Jackson, setting his own pace and route, had come
down through the Wilderness—a seemingly endless forest. He
passed through an ordinary and insignificant-looking village
called Chancellorsville on the way.

It was cold. And despite the relatively good life back in
Winchester and the dip back into civilization, many of Jackson's

men were not in adequate clothing. In fact, quite a number could pass as ragamuffins for they were shoeless and in patched-over, skimpy clothing. An epidemic of smallpox had passed through their ranks; many hadn't had furloughs since the day they joined up; they stayed hungry and suffered continuously from diarrhea and lice. Still, they fought for Jackson. They marched twenty to thirty miles a day for him. They cheered and waved their caps, those who had caps, every time he rode past. And when he had been spied strolling toward a revival tent one evening, the word spread and his troops rushed slyly ahead of him so he would find a full congregation on hand. Many had been gambling at cards, aided by lighted candles stuck on bayonets, and they dropped the deck and ran in advance so Old Jack wouldn't be disappointed in the turnout. They wanted to please him. No matter the odds, no matter now the treacherous difficulties, they wanted to fight for him. He brought them glory—for no army was feared and respected more than Jackson's. He became for them what he had always needed and wanted—a father. They had Jackson. He made do with his Heavenly Father.

Now on the western heights at Fredericksburg, Lee's two corps took their positions. Longstreet's men dug in at Marye's Heights, which was directly in front of the town, while Jackson's corps was spread out thinly down below for many miles. The troops stamped their feet, flapped their arms, and breathed out in frosty white plumes. Burnside's troops were so close—across the Rappahannock—that often pickets of the opposing forces called to each other. After all, they spoke the same language.

"Hallo, Yank."

"Hallo, Secesh!"

"When you coming over, bluecoat?"

"When we get ready, butternut."

"What do you want?

"Want Fredericksburg."

"Don't you wish you could get it!"

Ambrose Burnside, the Federal commander across the Rappahannock from Lee, was a West Pointer, a Mexican War vet, and a failed businessman just before this war. He was tall, heavyset, gruff, and good-natured. His number had come up, his shoulder tapped by Lincoln—for the Great Emancipator was going down the line, trying to find fighting generals who had enough moxie to win once in a while. Burnside might eventually lose in battle, but he had won in the hair-on-the-head department. Hair meant a lot back then—why, we are not too sure today. To counter-attack the loss of foliage atop his head, he grew perhaps the most striking set of whiskers this side of the Potomac. It became his trademark: a row of fur from his ears, down over his chops, and up across his mouth like a rug. He shaved his jowls and chin and thus presented a one-of-a-kind in facial hair arrangement. He was hearty, a backslapper, a jolly good fellow—the type who would have been a booster in peacetime, who would in a later era have been at home with the Power of Positive Thinking of Dr. Norman Vincent Peale. Ambrose Burnside was going to take the war to Robert E. Lee, James Longstreet, and T. J. Jackson.

In the small hours of December 12 a frigid mist spread over the Fredericksburg scene. The moon shone through dimly, and Rebel pickets could not make out the Yanks across the way. But they heard something. It was a swish and a splash interspersed with low murmurs and sudden curses. The pickets strained their eyes, concentrated, and then they saw it: Burnside was putting down pontoons to send his army across. Brigadier General William Barksdale, a former U.S. congressman, commanded a brigade of Mississippi infantry in Fredericksburg itself and was given the task of slowing the crossing as much as possible. Lee didn't want Fredericksburg shelled. Unbeknownst to affable, can-do Burnside, he wanted the Federal troops to come forward—then, with the river at their backs, he could plow them into eternity back into the water.

Barksdale sent children and women up into the hills along with a few old men, and Fredericksburg became an armed camp except for a few civilians who took up quarters in their cellars. His Mississippi troops let the pontoon construction continue, keeping their muskets poised. When it seemed the pontoons were nearing their shore—and in the darkness—the Rebels opened fire. They aimed by ear, let off rounds, and then heard Federals scream and scamper for cover. A pattern soon evolved. The engineers raced out as far as the bridge went, worked frantically to extend

it, and then raced back when the musket balls became too hot.
The ritual lasted while the sun came up and the Rebels didn't
have to depend solely on their ears for guidance.

Burnside had had a bellyful of this kind of warfare, his men
being treated as sitting ducks. To hell with Fredericksburg and
landmark preservation. He called on his artillery to level the
goddamn town, and 147 heavy-caliber guns on Stafford Heights
opened up. Fredericksburg shook as if in the throes of an earthquake. Walls fell and floors exploded and rubble replaced streets.
But the Rebels, under Barksdale, held their ground through the
day of December 12. At seven that night, as darkness came, they
packed up and took to the heights to join their comrades. Come
on in, Yanks. Come on in and get cozy in Fredericksburg.

Fog covered the lowlands again the next morning, a vast gray
soup. Confident Burnside, sensing victory at his fingertips, sent
his men through the heavy mists, while artillery shells whistled
over their heads, heading for Fredericksburg. By noon the sun
had burned the fog away, and Lee observed the thousands upon
thousands of bluecoats who had crossed and were now on his
side of the river. Longstreet was on the heights facing them. Lee
called for all of Jackson's corps to come help. Burnside was
throwing a massed assault here, a major effort. Tomorrow Lee
would play his hand.

And so Union soldiers broke into Fredericksburg. They
ripped strings from grand pianos to make feed troughs for their
horses, and had unbridled fun in every dwelling they came to.
Bayonets ripped family portraits, gilt-edged mirrors were
smashed, and some bewhiskered Yanks, in a fine glow from captured spirits, put on women's lacy drawers that they came by in
the rubble. They wore crinoline gowns and got convulsive laughter from their buddies. But not everyone was drunk and wearing
ladies' underwear. A few wondered why the town had been
evacuated without a fight. "That's easy," a trooper said. "Old Lee
wants to show the world what heathens we are. He *wants* us to
shell Fredericksburg so he can get sympathy from all those Europeans. He wants to bring the Europeans in on his side. It's as clear
as night and day." "Shit fire," another said. "I'll tell you what he
wants. He wants us to get in here, yes, indeed. Getting out won't
be quite so smart and easy, though. You'll see."

On December 13 the ever-present morning fog clouded the sun and gave the landscape a luminous otherworldly glow. Lee and Longstreet conferred together on a forward hill that would become known evermore as Lee's Hill. Lee would never look finer than he did this morning: Perfectly groomed in his tailored gray coat and sand-colored planter's hat, he became, in the words of one of his aides, "the handsomest man in Christendom." Old Pete Longstreet didn't look bad either—deep-chested, burly, and sardonic, he projected an aura of great fortitude. He had made sure his cannons were well dug in so that they could protect his infantry. He was getting set for battle and it made his spirits rise.

Then Jackson rode up—and the scene lost whatever tranquillity it might have had. First, Jackson's uniform, the gift from Stuart. His new cap was bound with gold braid, his coat seemed to have popped from a storybook, and even his boots glistened. Jackson didn't do anything by half measure. And Longstreet could never leave Old Jack alone. He offered his usual rough banter, this time about the uniform. Jackson brushed it aside by mumbling something about its being "the doing of my friend Stuart," and then got down to business. After all, those people were down there, massed for assault. He asked permission to attack. No, Lee wanted those people to charge and be repulsed, get fagged out, and then . . . then they would be driven into the water.

Jackson saluted, and was about to leave when Old Pete spoke up. He simply couldn't leave Jackson alone. "General, do not all those multitudes of Federals frighten you?"

"We shall see very soon whether I shall not frighten *them.*"

"But, Jackson, what are you going to do with all those people over there?"

Stonewall began moving his horse out. "Sir, we will give them the bayonet," he said.

At ten o'clock the sun began to burn off the fog in patches, and the Federals down in Fredericksburg were revealed as if a curtain were being raised on a play. Church steeples, courthouse, rows of chimneys, and then blue lines of troops came into view. The troops were moving, and now that there was visibility, Federal batteries sent greetings. Their shells parted the thin mist, arched, and fell on the dug-in Confederates on the heights. And as Jackson sat on Little Sorrel, among his troops, massive Heroes von Borcke came charging up with word from Stuart. His general was concerned that Jackson might not be able to hold against this strong blue line. Jackson had no doubts. "Major," he said, "my men have sometimes failed to *take* a position, but to *defend* one, never! I am glad those people are coming!"

At 10:30 Lee brought his field glasses down, and said calmly, "Perhaps we should test the ranges on the left." Southern guns began to jump and belch smoke and fire from Marye's Heights and the shells went into clusters of blue-clads. Now the sun was bright, and gun smoke, not fog, swirled about the men and their weapons. A strange new sight was here, too—two huge yellow balloons floated over a Federal battery, the wicker baskets beneath rocking gently as the men aboard yelled sightings to gunners below. "Look at them Yanks! They're defying God Almighty goin' up in the air thataway!"

The distant batteries pounded one another, and then a three-division Federal corps began advancing in tight orderly lines, their brigade colors flashing in the sunlight. It was hard to believe so many men coming forward in neat array, no stragglers, no hesitation. Then Lee noticed something peculiar. Two horse-drawn guns, comic in their insignificance—like a circus-clown act—came rolling toward the Yanks' left flank, which held at least 18,000 men. It was not a clown but Stuart's chief of artillery, twenty-four-year-old Major John Pelham of Alabama. Long after the battles ended, after the resulting poverty and defeat, those who remembered what the Cause once was in its glory days spoke of John Pelham. He had left West Point on the eve of graduation in 1861 and joined the Confederate ranks. Handsome, tall, blond, a lad who had a way with the ladies, he reveled in daring stunts that took the fight to the enemy. Here he outdid himself. Before the Confederate high command on the hill—Lee, Jackson, Longstreet, and Stuart—he threw a rifled Blakely and a Napoleon against the whole might of the Federal advance. Right there, out in the open, a flyspeck of a target. The Blakely was immediately knocked out and Pelham turned full attention to the Napoleon, redoubling the volume. He was taking his turn throwing shells into the breech, and he wore around his head a necktie of red and blue, the colors of the Grenadier Guards. An English observer had presented him with the tie on the eve of battle and this was the manner in which Pelham put it to use.

The Federals didn't know what was happening. Was this war? Hell, they had been marching along at such a marvelous pace, ready to take on the world, and here was this pissant caisson flying all over the place, knocking them to pieces. Blue-clads fell like duckpins. And the whole advance halted. Stuart sent word to Pelham: "Retire!" Pelham sent back word to Stuart: "I can hold my ground!" And he did until he began running out of ammunition. From the hill, Lee said, "It is glorious to see such courage in one so young. If we had a Pelham on each flank we wouldn't need anything else."

When Pelham finally withdrew, the Federals caught their breath and then began throwing shells on the Confederate hill. They wanted to make the Rebels come out in the open and fight. It was very hard to fight people who stayed dug in and sent a little piece of horse artillery down to fight an army. After half an hour of bombardment, the bluecoats formed lines once again and came marching forward. It was a steady unhurried advance and the faces of the soldiers were set. At one thousand yards individual soldiers could be made out, but still the Rebels held their fire. A soft ominous quiet spread through the dug-in Confederate line. Jackson held his field glasses to his eyes, and then slowly lowered them. At eight hundred yards he waved his hand and the command spread in a chorus: *Fire!* Fourteen heavy guns blasted straight into the Federals and every musket opened up. The Federals had marched into a trap. Longstreet as well as Jackson was firing with every weapon at hand. It was a solid sheet of flame that came from the Rebel positions, and the bluecoats fell en masse, whole sections went down together. But their numbers were such, their courage so strong, that they kept coming. Burnside was a go-getter.

Finally the Federals reached a boggy wood that offered shelter and cover at last. Behind the wood, at the moment, Maxcy Gregg's South Carolina troops lay prone for protection against artillery. Their arms were stacked. When the Federals broke through in a wild, half-insane rush, Gregg, who was hard of hearing, thought they were exuberant Southerners and held out his hand. A minié ball immediately knocked him down. The

Federals seemed for a moment poised to rush over the whole
Rebel line when Jubal Early's division came running. "Hey, here
comes old Jubal! Let old Jubal straighten that fence!"

And Jackson watched Early's troops throw the Federals back
through the boggy wood toward an open field. Now it was the
Southerners' turn to become near mad and they flew toward the
horde in blue with the Rebel yell ringing. For a moment it seemed
to Jackson as if the Yankees, the whole Federal army, might be
run into the water. But the Federal artillery began showering the
rushing Rebels and at last the charge was halted. From the hill Lee
watched it all—the artillery duel, the blue-clad advance of thousands, the wild Rebel counterattack, and now a field with so
many dead Federals that it looked to more than one observer like
a blue carpet. A shell had landed at Lee's feet and didn't explode—a terrifying but strangely thrilling moment. Lee lowered
his glasses after a long look at these strange Federals who were
massing once again for an assault, prepared to step on the bodies
of their dead to go forward, and said to Longstreet, "It is well that
war is so terrible. We should grow too fond of it!"

The Federal attack sputtered, and then Jackson, of all the
commanders, in the midst of all the carnage, gave orders to continue. He wanted to wring the last advantage out of such a bloody
day. As twilight softened the field, Jackson's men advanced and
were beating the Federals back once more when heavy artillery
zeroed in and he had no choice but to retire. And as darkness
covered the battlefield, a mysterious light suddenly glowed, went
away, then flashed again and again. It was called the "Northern
lights."

It was the morning, though, that everyone was thinking
about.

CHAPTER XVIII

The Pause at Moss Neck

After the fury of Fredericksburg, which most of the generals in gray had seen from hilltops, a plan was made to meet Burnside head on if he chose to attack in the morning. Lee, the King of Spades, knew how to dig ditches, and he got his troops dug in during the chilly night for another bluecoated assault. But it didn't come. No more massed dark lines came forward. But a messenger woke Jackson at dawn. Could the general please come to call on General Maxcy Gregg, the South Carolina commander, who lay on his deathbed from the minié ball wound to his spine?

Gregg, forty-nine, a lawyer in peacetime, was representative of a certain type of leader in the Southern cause: civilized and highly cultured, broad-minded, but unswerving in his principal beliefs. He was a bachelor, who was much more at home with the works of Greek dramatists and philosophers than with the daily papers. In peace he reveled in the study of botany, ornithology, and astronomy. Like Jefferson of Virginia, he was a man of the eighteenth-century Enlightenment. He was extremely well-rounded; his private observatory in his hometown of Columbia was unsurpassed by any college or public one. He was not a West Pointer, as everyone else in high command seemed to be, but he lived by the code of a gentleman, which is a part of that time least easily understood today: Even in death, he must do the right thing. Dying, he remembered that he had earlier endorsed a paper that might somehow have given Jackson offense.

Jackson strode into the farmhouse where Gregg lay and immediately took a seat beside the deathbed. As a commander in battle Jackson had once screeched harshly in his high-pitched voice for Gregg to occupy a road and had come close to putting him and his colonels under arrest. Now he greeted Gregg in a low husky voice. Gregg apologized for the paperwork he had sent forward. Jackson told him to dismiss it from his mind; it had given no offense and he couldn't even remember it now. He took Gregg's hand in his own. "The doctors tell me that you have not long to live. I only ask that you turn your thoughts to God and to the world to which you go." Tears welled in Gregg's eyes.

"I thank you," he said softly, squeezing Jackson's hand in return. "I thank you very much."

Heretofore-jovial Burnside was beside himself in the aftermath of the fighting. Crazed might put it better. At first he wanted to renew the attack. All he could think of was attack, attack, attack. But General Edwin Sumner, who had never hesitated to advance before, said—no more. The other commanders voiced the same opinion—no more here. No more slaughter. Let's pack up and hand another one to the crazy Rebels. Even Fighting Joe Hooker said it would be suicide to renew in face of the Rebel positions and the wholesale bloodshed of the day before. The enormity of the situation was coming home to the go-getter. For one wild moment he decided he himself would lead his old corps against Lee's line and try to break the son of a bitch. Just haul the colors up and fling himself against Lee and then see who would break first. Go for broke. Then his emotions swung and he sank into deep despair. A general found him pacing back and forth in his tent like a madman. "Oh, those men! Oh, those men!"

"Those damnable Seceshes?"

"No, no! Those men over there," he said, pointing across the river to the field that was carpeted blue with the dead and dying. "Oh, God, I am thinking of them all the time!"

Instead of an attack, Burnside called for a truce wherein he could bury the dead and take care of the wounded and desperately ill. The adversaries who had thrown all their might and wits against each other the day before now waded together through the horror that a battlefield becomes. No one who trod the Fredericksburg battlefield ever forgot, even though he might live into the next century. They smelled the ripe, sweet scent of blood, heard the groans of men on the brink of death, and viewed those already frozen in grotesque positions. One account described corpses "swollen to twice their natural size, black as Negroes in most cases." They lay "in every conceivable position, some on their backs with gaping jaws, some with eyes as large as walnuts, protruding with glassy stare, some doubled up like a contortionist." An observer later wrote, "Here sprawled one without a head, there one without legs, yonder a head and legs without a trunk; everywhere horrible expressions, fear, rage, agony, madness, torture; lying in pools of blood, lying with heads half buried in mud, with fragments of shell stuck in oozing brain, with bullet holes all over puffed limbs."

War. A battlefield in the Civil War. But the panoply of Fredericksburg offered a new twist. The solid blue carpet showed white in spots. Federal corpses had been stripped naked in the night by roving Southern bands who were shivering from lack of clothing and were gathering warm clothing from those who no longer needed them. Naked bodies, bloated and cast aside, one atop the other in the sunlight, were a sight difficult to carry through the rest of one's life: another legacy of this war. In their avid quest for gear the Southerners didn't always check to make sure the owner might have need for it. A Rebel was pulling a boot that looked the right size from a "corpse" when it raised its head and looked sorrowfully at him. "Beg pardon, sir," he said, dropping the leg, "I thought you had gone above."

Lee and his lieutenants were furious when they later rode through the town of Fredericksburg and saw the vandalism there. The removal of britches and shoes paled beside the devastation of the old riverside town. It had been treated with cold wanton contempt. On the night of December 16 Burnside's army retreated from Fredericksburg while a storm raged and the wind howled. They took everything they could, even the pontoon bridges. It had been an unmitigated disaster for them—losing

12,653 to the Confederates' 4,201. It was, in its way, as bad a defeat as First Manassas. They had come with a mighty force, had a new team in command, and then had been hurled back without mercy. The Southerners were now so furious with these blue-clad uninvited visitors to their land that they fervently wished, one and all, that the punishment had been even greater. General Lee wrote to his wife, "They went as they came—in the night. They suffered heavily as far as the battle went, but it did not go far enough to satisfy me." Jackson was even more angry—and determined. "What can we do?" an aide asked, when he viewed the broken remains of Fredericksburg. "Do?" said Jackson. "Why, shoot every last one of them." Later he came to an attitude he carried to the end: "We must do more than defeat their armies," he said to a staff member. "We must destroy them."

The Yankees had vanished, Christmas was nearing, and many men instantly gave themselves furloughs. Jackson was bivouacked near Moss Neck at night, and he intended to sleep on the ground. His staff devoutly wished that he would ask to stay at the Corbin family home in the vicinity. It was cozy if not palatial, and it was quietly understood by all that Stonewall Jackson was a hero to the Corbins. But, no, Jackson was a soldier and soldiers slept on the ground. A great fire was made near a tall aged poplar and Jackson and his officers ringed around it. James Power "Jimmy" Smith, his recent aide-de-camp, the replacement for Kyd Douglas, who had got his wish to return to the front lines as a captain, rested by Jackson. Jimmy Smith was playful and energetic, brave to the core, the kind of aide Jackson liked to have around. "I say, Jimmy, do you happen to have any biscuits in your haversack?" The voice in the dark came from Jackson.

Southerners, one and all, love biscuits. No one knows why, any more than why New Englanders love chowder. Southerners long for a biscuit in moments of trial. "No, sir, I don't have any biscuits," Jimmy Smith replied happily. "You would find some certainly, sir, I believe, at the Corbins'."

"Thank you, very much, Captain."

The aged poplar, scorched by fire, took the occasion to fall, narrowly missing some reclining bodies. Everyone turned over once again; the wind howled. Then Captain Hugh McGuire rode up as the fire turned to embers, and Jackson called to him. "Captain McGuire, you know the neighborhood around here, I believe. This is your home territory, is it not?"

"Yes, sir, it is."

"Could I please prevail upon you to find some food. If it would not be too much of an inconvenience."

"Yes, sir, I believe I know where to find some."

He galloped to the Corbin estate and returned with a basket filled with ever-loving biscuits and half a ham for good measure. All sat up, ate, and lay back down. The fire died out. In the middle of the night Jackson woke. He had an earache. He said, "Captain McGuire, let's all just pack up and go to the Moss Neck house."

The Corbins were ecstatic to have Stonewall Jackson under their roof. The whole army could be housed there as far as the Corbins were concerned. Jackson fell into a featherbed that night and slept as he never had before. And he awoke to a way of life that for a short period of time was like an oasis amid storm and strife. He awoke first to a breakfast of sausage, pork steaks, waffles, and muffins—and although his sensitive digestive track could not accept all of this, his staff made up for him. Nothing was left on plates. And then everyone looked around. The house and hearth here were indeed palatial—almost too much for spartan Jackson. Also, it had a whiff of the Tidewater, and Jackson fundamentally, always, was the epitome of the mountain man, the frontiersman. He feared the seduction of luxury.

No, thank you very much, he could not possibly accept the offer to make his headquarters in the home, but, if agreeable, he would pitch his tents off in the side yard. On a sunny, warm December 17, Jackson's tents went up. Then, unfortunately, his earache returned while he was under canvas and he requested— if, of course, not too much bother and fuss—if he might set up quarters in an unused wing of the Corbin estate. Why, of course, General! To keep a rein on his sybaritic side he moved his small hard cot in, eschewing the featherbed, and placed his field desk close by. He moved in on Christmas Eve, and a guard from the Irish Battalion constantly paced back and forth before the door, twenty-four hours a day.

Richard Corbin, the master of the house, was actually a lowly private in the Virginia cavalry and he was home for the holidays. He almost melted in pride at having Stonewall Jackson as his guest—and all the large Corbin family threw themselves into making the moments now as far removed from war as possible. Jackson himself got caught up in the spirit of things and decided to throw a Christmas feast to which General Lee, Jeb Stuart, the Reverend General William Pendleton, and many on their staffs were invited. With great pleasure Jackson assigned the rambunctious Jimmy Smith to secure the food and arrange the seating.

It was a perfect success. From down the river came a bucket of oysters. From Staunton gifts of turkey, ham, and a big cake arrived. Jimmy hauled them in and got set. Even bottles of wine arrived. Jim Lewis, Jackson's servant, who never left his side away from the battlefield (and sometimes could be found close by while fighting raged), put on a starched white apron and bellowed orders. Jeb Stuart showed up in a plumed hat, with spurs and saber jingling. Lee wore a perfectly tailored uniform. The Reverend General Pendleton, grizzled and with rumpled clothing, took his eyes from the food only in order to pray. He steadily and methodically demolished food enough for ten grown men. There were jokes—at Jackson's expense. Stuart pointed out that the walls were decorated with prints of racehorses and gamecocks, and wondered if Jackson's moral character had gone into decline. They ate; they toasted one another; it was as if nothing bad could ever happen to these men with such a great jolly bond between them. It was Jackson's last Christmas.

As 1863 came in Jackson settled down to the chores of administration. He could hardly be bothered with what the incompetent Burnside might try. The unlucky but determined go-getter tried a flanking movement upriver on some of the gray garrison, but before he got near, the poor man was bogged down in mud. His whole army sank and could not move, and, to the fighter Lincoln, this was the last straw. He fired Burnside. Would the North ever find the talent it took to wage successful war?

Jackson bent over paperwork in his quarters, eyeshade on, scrawling one "T. J. Jackson" after another on documents. Sometimes he fell asleep in the middle of his signature. One thing e could never understand was why people coveted his—anyone's—*signature.* But nothing seemed to escape his attention, his need to give approval or rejection for what happened in his army.

Neither Christmas nor garrison duty softened his sense of duty. Six men had been convicted of desertion, three of whom had been sentenced to death. General E. F. Paxton, the new commander of the Stonewall Brigade, suggested that only one man be shot and that one chosen by lot. Paxton was a devout Christian, as was of course Jackson—but Old Jack sent the document off to Lee without listening to Paxton and losing a little respect for him to boot: ". . . One great difficulty in the army results from over lenient Courts and it appears to me that when a Court Martial faithfully discharges its duty that its decisions should be sustained . . ." he wrote to Lee.

Lee approved, but then Jefferson Davis overrode both Lee and Jackson and the men were saved.

In a pause from the war such as this, in bivouac, Jackson turned once again to the legal warfare between himself and A. P. Hill. Hardly anything of an administrative nature held so much interest for him. It all became highly technical. Hill now demanded a hearing on Jackson's charges. When his request passed through Jackson's hands, on the way to Lee, Jackson really settled down to business. At last, legal work. Jackson quizzed various officers about what Hill had said at various times, collected all instances where Hill had gone astray in a legalistic way, and then drafted a whole *new* set of charges and specifications against Hill. Once again Lee groaned and wondered if the Jackson/Hill skirmish would not get out of hand before the spring campaign began.

The Jackson/Hill conflict was not the only one now, unfortunately. Jackson found himself suddenly at odds again with General William B. Taliaferro. When Jackson assigned General Isaac R. Trimble over Taliaferro's head, to take command of Jackson's old division, Taliaferro fell into a deep dark funk. He became convinced—probably correctly—that Jackson had never forgiven him for his disruptive behavior on the Romney march. Win as many battles as he had, be brave enough to fight with three wounds and still hold his ground—it mattered not. Jackson remembered. He remembered that Taliaferro had been a skunk in Romney—and it didn't help that Taliaferro acted as if Tidewater aristocracy meant something. To solve matters, Lee transferred Taliaferro to duty in the Southeastern states, and Jackson made no comment when the courageous Taliaferro with the cocked hat rode off.

Litigation and transfers could not occupy all of Stonewall's attention. Another great revival swept the army—or perhaps, more accurately, the old revival of late 1862 had not quite ended. There were daily morning prayers and evening services twice a week. Sunday was filled almost entirely with worship. And Jackson resumed his quest to ban Sunday mail service. He brought in Lieutenant Colonel Charles J. Faulkner, a learned, cultivated man, to write the official accounts of the battles and campaigns of his armies. Jackson's men did not like an outsider coming in for such an intimate, important task, and they made life difficult for the erudite Faulkner at Moss Neck. Jackson was not an easy editor either. He passed on every word and looked constantly over Faulkner's shoulder as he penned the amazing saga. It was amazing that he managed as good a job as he did. Once finished, although he had been made chief of staff to Jackson, he found a way to be transferred. Not everyone loved life with Jackson.

One who did was five-year-old Janie Corbin, the youngest member of the Corbin clan. She had golden curls, bright eyes, and could not be separated from the general. He indulged her every whim, let her break into meetings, and set aside time to play games with her. The hero of Manassas and Sharpsburg learned how to cut out paper dolls in order to entertain the young girl, and once, as a lock of her hair kept falling over her eyes, he took the gold braid from his Jeb Stuart cap and tied it around her curls. "Janie, it suits a little girl like you better than it does an old soldier like me."

As spring hovered in Virginia Jackson made ready to be on the road, preparing to meet the enemy once more. Scarlet fever was spreading and, among others, Janie Corbin came down with it. As he mounted Little Sorrel his last words to Mrs. Corbin were "What is the latest news on little Janie?"

"Good news now, General. The doctors say she is out of danger."

"Praise the Lord, madam."

Now under canvas at Hamilton's Crossing on the Fredericksburg battlefield, he got startling news. Those he thought permanently by him and forever there were gone. Word came that

Pelham, who only a few months ago had saved the day at Fredericksburg, now lay dead, struck down in a charge at Kelly's Ford. Struck down as he urged his men forward. Also, a messenger from the Corbin family rode up one evening, solemn and distraught. Janie Corbin had grown worse, had sunk suddenly with no warning, and lay dead. Here on the battlefield where thousands had recently died Jackson wept. It was the lost innocence that struck him—the reverberations of tragic moments from his own life. He wanted his wife now; he needed to see his new daughter.

He left tent life and secured rooms at the home of the Yerbys. He wrote Anna that he had had a dream wherein she had come on a visit and he had at last seen his daughter. But after he had held his new daughter and kissed her, he woke and found it was all a delusion. Would his *esposita* consider leaving North Carolina and coming on a visit? Usually Thomas was giving her reasons not to come. It was as if he had a premonition.

Jackson rushed aboard the train when it arrived in a downpour at Guiney's Station. The cars were mobbed with soldiers, wives, hangers-on, sutlers, and politicians. Jackson hurried from car to car, in his rubber coat, water running down it, looking in face after face. Then he saw them—a dark-eyed woman holding a small baby. They clutched one another, but Thomas was afraid to hold the baby in his wet slicker for fear he might hurt her. They rushed off the train, onto a carriage, and off to the Yerby home—while soldiers who recognized Jackson began a series of wild yells.

Jackson held his baby in his private room at the Yerbys'. He observed their image together in a mirror. He put the baby down and then embraced Anna again. Next he began making plans to baptize the baby.

The rite took place in the Yerby parlor and all of his staff was in attendance. It went off with military promptness—up to the moment when Anna was due to arrive. Somehow she could never stick to her husband's strict schedule—a minor way of rebelling. Jackson however wanted baptism. Close up, press on! He marched out of the parlor, gathered the baby in his arms, came back before the Reverend Tucker Lacy, and the baptism was performed. Anna missed it.

But she was royally treated throughout her brief stay. Officer after officer came to call. Jim Lewis got to hold the baby. General Lee came, and nearly caused Anna Jackson to swoon. His very *name* struck awe in her and made her tremble. But she calmed and later wrote, "I was met by a face so kind and fatherly, and a greeting so cordial, that I was at once reassured and put at ease . . . and the call was greatly enjoyed." Thomas took her to church, which, in the army now, meant under a tent with thousands of soldiers around.

On Sunday afternoon there was no business and the couple spent time alone with their new baby. Anna wrote later, "He never appeared to be in better health than at this time, and I never saw him look so handsome and noble." He looked so fine indeed that his wife persuaded him to sit for a photograph—something he fought to the last moment. Anna thought the resulting picture all right but that it missed Jackson's "home-look."

Then one early morning in late April Jackson was awakened in his room at the Yerbys'. Jubal Early's adjutant was outside to say that Fighting Joe Hooker had *moved* and it looked as if he was going to cross the Rappahannock. Fighting Joe Hooker was Lincoln's new Jesus—the one he believed would save the Union and lead them all to victory. Jackson longed to meet Hooker on the field of battle. In his quick stride and lively manner, when battle was in the wings, Jackson rushed down the stairs, got information, rushed back up. It looked as if the spring campaign was ready to start. Anna should travel to Richmond with the baby, where they both would be safe. He seemed almost elated—happy that the waiting was over.

He kissed his wife and baby—and left for the front without breakfast.

CHAPTER XIX

Over the River and into the Trees

As Jackson rode to what would become the front against the enemy, he was blessed with a view of perfect Virginia springtime: peach and cherry trees were in full pink blossom; along the hills anemone grew; and the bright color of houstonia and bloodroot shone. It was a marvelous spring morning, April 29, 1863. The farms he passed were well tended, neat, seeming everlasting, permanent, secure. The air had a sharp heady quality to it, and its morning sweetness made one glad to be alive. Little Sorrel's hooves made a steady clack on the road's hard clay.

On the other side Lincoln had written to Fighting Joe Hooker, "Go forward, and give us victories." Hooker decidedly planned to do just that. He looked tough; he talked tough. "My plans are perfect," he announced, "and when I start to carry them out, may God have mercy on Bobby Lee; for I shall have none." All of these West Pointers knew each other—had their old scores to settle, their memories of having once been comrades-in-arms. Hooker and Jackson and Lee had served in Mexico and had formed notions of one another's character from that period. Lee referred to him as *Mr.* F. J. Hooker. He was a dapper man, as physically brave as any of them, and more outspoken and critical of superiors than most. He was a soldier's soldier in many ways: He took care of his men (shoes, socks, and warm food a must in his army), and he fully realized how soldiers' minds worked without reference to cant. Women and liquor were available around his camp. The sobriquet for a prostitute in some circles today is a "hooker," and to take a shot of whiskey is more colorfully put as to take a "hooker." Thus, Mr. F. J. Hooker lives.

In that late April of 1863 he had 130,000 men at his command. His plan simply, and apparently wisely, was to cross the Rappahannock upstream from Fredericksburg, move swiftly through the Wilderness, and get between Bobby Lee and Richmond. If he was successful—and how could he fail with such a force?—old gray fox Lee would finally have to fight where Fighting Joe wanted, not where Lee directed. When he himself crossed the Rappahannock on April 30, he told a newsman: "The Rebel army is now the legitimate property of the Army of the Potomac. They may as well pack their haversacks and make for Richmond; and I shall be after them. . . ."

When Jackson heard that Yankee pontoons had gone across the Rappahannock he scribbled a note to Anna and asked his brother-in-law, Lieutenant Joe Morrison, now on his staff, to deliver it and make sure she and the baby got safely to Richmond. No, pleaded his brother-in-law, let him stay in the war; send Chaplain Lacy, whose line of work was more in that direction. Jackson was going to need every hand he could get now. Let him stay at his side. Jackson was touched and agreed. Lacy carried out the mission—and, assured of his wife and baby's safety, Jackson turned his full vengeful attention on Fighting Joe, who had taken the initiative.

On the twenty-ninth Jackson stayed under canvas at Hamilton's Crossing, his old familiar spot, a short distance from the Rappahannock. He was up well before dawn on the thirtieth, breaking camp, ready to move out. Immediately before his tent was struck, he went in and closed the flaps. His shadow, Jim Lewis, stood guard outside, and when anyone came near, he hissed, "Shut up, the general is praying."

At the front line Jackson met up with Lee. Now was the time for them to put their heads together to come up with a way of impeding, if not crushing, Hooker. It was a large order. They were outnumbered about two to one, and in place of manpower they would have to come up with ingenuity. They would have to outguess Hooker and anticipate what he was going to do. They gazed toward Stafford Heights and took in the woeful Federal batteries, and then the blue-clads who had crossed the river and were entrenched on the west bank. Lee was in favor of letting the enemy come to him. Jackson saw bluecoats and his reaction was immediate. Attack them!

Lee listened, as he always did now to Jackson. "If you think it can be done, I will give orders for it." Like that.

Jackson asked time to make a reconnaissance. In a steady light rain, his slicker buttoned to the throat, Jackson rode Little Sorrel down near the enemy line, dismounting now and then, taking long hard looks. He made judgments about artillery range, about the ground his men would have to cross before hitting the Yankees, about lines of retreat. The moon was out when he rode back to Lee. Lee was right. "It would be inexpedient to attack here." Lee was now ready for what then should be done. He snapped his field glasses shut in their case. "The main attack will not come here—but above," he said.

His intuition said that General Hooker would strike through the Wilderness to try to turn the Confederate left. The main action would therefore be upstream. Lee would keep a skeleton army where he now stood to guard against a frontal assault, but Jackson should go upstream to join General Dick Anderson and his division, who had taken a position four miles east of Chancellorsville, along a fringe of the Wilderness. Chancellorsville hardly deserved eminence as a town; it was more a crossroads. The Wilderness, however, was aptly named. It was a forest of scrub oak and pine, twenty miles long, fifteen miles broad, crossed by a pike and an old plank road. Little of civilization penetrated it—the perfect place for Jackson to hide his army and surprise Fighting Joe.

Around midnight on the first of May Jackson was up, dressed in his resplendent uniform and ready to fight. He had his men on the road by three o'clock and heard the crack of musket fire toward the west as dawn broke. By eight he had joined up with General Anderson, who had formed a line guarding the Old Turnpike and the Plank Road. From Hotchkiss's maps Jackson knew these roads came together, four miles away, and formed what was known as Chancellorsville.

Anderson filled Jackson in. The Federals were moving now through the Wilderness on Chancellorsville. Jackson could hardly restrain himself. With scarcely any sleep the night before, after moving his army through the dark and early dawn, he wanted to fight. Hooker must be attacked while still in and around a primitive woodland, where it was hard to see a hand in front of you. General McLaws was to move his force down the Turnpike while Jackson and Anderson took to the Plank Road. The Rebel soldiers went forth in battle lines, skirmishers spread out, advancing. Everyone's ear was primed. They smelled gunpowder; they smelled Yankees. Suddenly a crack of rapid fire. McLaws had met the enemy.

Jackson ordered McLaws to hold, and then brought up artillery to shell the Federals from the Plank Road as they deployed. Always thinking, always pressing. Just then a courier rode up from Jeb Stuart. His cavalry, Stuart reported, had circled Hooker and now stood in a position to protect Jackson's left flank. "I will close in on the flank and help all I can when the ball opens," he wrote. Then a prayer from the cavalryman: "May God grant us victory." Jackson took time to scrawl on the back, before returning it, "I trust that God will grant us a great victory. Keep closed on Chancellorsville."

Because of Jackson's bluster, perhaps because they overestimated his strength, or maybe because they were just plain tired and didn't have their hearts in it, the Federals retired before Stonewall's pressure without making a stiff fight. A strange sort of rhythm developed in the vast woodland. Rebel skirmishers, followed by a battle line, pressed forward; the Federals would send off a volley or two and then fall back deeper into the brush. Jackson improvised. When his men came to a particularly thick patch of woods he would halt them and take cover; they were protected. Then he would order the area immediately in front of them shelled. Press on! And always by his side went Lieutenant Joe Morrison, his brother-in-law.

Jackson caught up with Jeb Stuart on a small crested hill and there was a warm greeting. Then, business. Jackson wanted to know what roads led to Hooker's rear. Stuart pointed out those he knew, but the woods around them were so thick that Jackson could get only a vague idea. Somewhere in there, though, were Hooker's troops. Would that Divine Providence might point them out! Back on the Plank Road he ran into A. P. Hill. Hill wore his red battle shirt, and now, in combat, the friction of garrison life was left behind. The look between the two men, who knew each other so well, was elation. Action was at hand. Hill and Jackson rode together toward the sound of heavy firing, serious action, at a point close by. They found that General Heth had been stopped in his tracks by concentrated enemy fire; McLaws had determined that they would never break through, had set up a defensive line, and had ordered a bivouac for the night.

Jackson still wanted to know how strong the Federals were and where they were concentrated. As he spurred Little Sorrel down the road, he saw a lone Confederate officer galloping toward him. The man had pure bliss on his face when he recognized General Stonewall Jackson. Captain Alexander C. Haskell, from South Carolina, reined in and said, "General Jackson, ride up here with me if you will, sir. You'll find something that should be quite interesting."

The captain took him off the road to the right and up a narrow path. On top of a little hill they halted and Haskell pointed. Old Jack took out his field glasses and swept the land in front. There they were! Spread out before him, quite close, were three Yankee battle lines, dug in behind heavy earthworks. He left Captain Haskell to guard the observation spot and galloped back toward his men. At sundown he met with Lee who had journeyed up from Fredericksburg. They met on the Plank Road just over a mile from Chancellorsville, and had an immediate war council. As some Yankee sharpshooters began peppering cannoneers nearby, they left the road and took refuge in a piney wood, finding a log to sit on. Here their war council continued. They drew lines on the dirt in front of them. Why were Hooker's men falling back? Jackson was of the opinion that they would all be gone the next morning. Lee was not. Fighting Joe would fight. All right, if he held his lines tomorrow, then he must be attacked himself. What flank, which position? Where?

There was fury and mad dashing to and fro by cavalry, shouts and shrieks from the woods, skirmishers rattling off their rounds. Then came a special jingle, a certain clank of a saber: Jeb Stuart swung down from his mount, the plume on his hat bobbing. He had a report from Fitzhugh Lee, who had swung far west and come back to report that Hooker had not anchored his right flank on any natural or artificial barrier. It was, as they put it at West Point, a battlefield "in the air." Two scouts then rushed up to report that an attack now, to Hooker's front, would be suicidal. He was fortified, entrenched there. His men were swinging in cannon and digging deeper even as they spoke. They would all die if they rushed forward. Now, by candlelight, these men looked at a well-worn parchment map. Lee traced his finger over it. "How, oh, how can we get at those people?"

Jackson said, "You know best. Show me what to do, and we will try to do it."

Lee seemed to go into a trance, tracing and retracting a line with his finger. It did not follow a road or path, merely a general route around Hooker's right flank and rear. "You will go there, General Jackson. General Stuart will cover your movement with his cavalry." He didn't say how or when—that was up to Jackson and that was the only direction Jackson needed. Old Jack rose, saluted, and said, "My troops will move at four o'clock."

He went back among his men and did not give the marching order; it was his secret and they, as well as Hooker, should be kept in the dark as long as possible. All his commanders learned was that they would move out very early—where, he didn't say, to anyone. Even Lee did not at this moment know exactly what his most trusted lieutenant had in mind. Jackson slept badly during what little time he had. He was shivering from the cold; Sandie Pendleton gave him the cape from his greatcoat to roll up in. It did no good. He awoke well before his men, a nasty head cold coming on. He took the cape and spread it over the sleeping Pendleton, and went to a picket's fire. It crackled and popped, and Jackson warmed his hands. Soon Chaplain Tucker Lacy was stirring and joined the ex-deacon by the fire.

Usually Jackson talked of spiritual matters with the pastor. Now he asked, with scant preamble, if the minister knew of any usable roads around either Federal flank. Reverend Lacy had preached in this section of Virginia and might know routes that weren't on maps. Jackson took out one of Hotchkiss's maps and asked him to trace any roads not shown there. "Roads, Reverend Lacy, that would support artillery."

Reverend Lacy came up with a road or two. No, no, they wouldn't do. Too close to enemy positions. Jackson wanted to get well around Hooker, to his rear, without being observed. He would be marching many thousands of men to get at Hooker's rear. Lacy did not know of such a road, but he did know some people in the area who *might* know. Jackson didn't waste a moment. He told Lacy to wake Hotchkiss; the two of them should ride to anyone who might give them the sought-after directions, the hoped-for road or path. In no time Lacy and Hotchkiss were in the saddle and plunging into the black night. They returned at the gallop just as Lee had arisen and joined Jackson by the picket fire.

They had found the road! Hotchkiss busily spread out parchment and began to sketch, pointing and drawing as he did so. Jackson stood immobile, his eyes narrowed, silent. Every time Hotchkiss explained geography Jackson went into a kind of trance. In his way he drank in the lesson whole, remembering it exactly from then on. Jackson had satisfied himself that he could now get to Hooker's rear and, the good Lord willing, not be seen by Hooker. No matter, there were still great problems facing the Army of Northern Virginia. It was not massed; it was split. Hooker had an overwhelming force wherewith he could crush Lee head on here and swing down and annihilate Early's troops at Fredericksburg. All the cards were in Hooker's hands. All he had to do was play them.

Lee had understood Hotchkiss's geography lecture, too. Now he said, "General Jackson, what do you propose to do?"

"Why, follow the route Hotchkiss and Lacy have found. Get at Hooker's rear."

"Tell me, General. How many men do you propose to take from this army?"

"My whole corps."

Lee blinked. "What will you leave me?"

"Anderson and McLaws." In other words, down in black-and-white, Jackson would take 28,000 troops, circling behind Fighting Joe Hooker while the immaculately dressed, kindly-eyed general would be left with all of 14,000. Lee would be left with, in effect, an actor's job. He would have to make Hooker believe the main army was here, that his 14,000 might be closer to 60,000. He would have to have sharpshooters racing around trees, making one man appear to be a company. He would have to shift batteries on the fly, confusing Hooker about his position. He would have to hold the might of the Federal army with his 14,000. Lee didn't have to consider long. "Well, General Jackson," he said, "move on."

Jackson's troops moved early, but not at the expected four o'clock. Tangled brush and stray felled trees delayed his march, and it was not until eight that the flank march got under way. It was a warm spring morning and the recent rain had mercifully dampened the dirt road so that dust clouds did not appear. Jackson had given strict orders for no unnecessary jabbering, certainly no cheering. As he trotted Little Sorrell toward the lead column his troops stifled deep urges to bellow. They saw the fierce glint in his eye, his determined manner, and knew he was taking them to battle—but where, with the exception of Hotchkiss and Lacy, they knew not. To pass the time they teased Jackson's young staff officers who trotted on their horses near him. "Say, hyar's one of Old Jack's little boys, let him by, boys." And, "Don't let him begin the fuss till we get thar!"

Unexpectedly they came to a hill bare of cover, out in the open, unprotected by the Wilderness. There was no time for scouts to probe, no time to make sure they could travel it safely. Jackson called up Hotchkiss. Was there an alternate road they could use for this stretch? Yes, one was found after a furious search. But it would take too much time for the whole army to backtrack and use it. Jackson, sent caissons and supply wagons over it and ordered his foot soldiers to cross the uncovered hill on the double. A Yankee battery indeed spotted this weird line of Rebels route-stepping over the crest of the naked hill, then plunging back down into the morass of the Wilderness. The battery began lobbing shells, testing the range. Jackson did not allow any delay. He fought stragglers, almost with his bare hands, and his muffled cry became a litany: "Close that column. *Press on!*"

Jackson rode at the front, and soon was joined by Generals Rodes and Colston and by Colonel Tom Munford. For this small moment in time it could have been part of a V.M.I alumni gathering. Jackson, Rodes, and Colston had taught at V.M.I.; Munford had been a cadet when Jackson had arrived to teach. In fact, Munford had been the cadet adjutant who had welcomed the stranger Jackson, in his oversized boots and funny-looking uniform, his first day at the Institute. They reminisced about the old days and recalled shared memories. Like all men who shared a past, they spoke in clipped sentences, not having to finish thoughts or explain more than the minimum. "Remember when Crutchfield—" and "How about the time Lindsay Walker went into town and—" The sun beat down, and the horses moved steadily. It had only been a few years back, but how the world had changed—had changed more than any man could possibly drink in.

But Jackson had no time now for philosophizing or for nostalgia. He said abruptly, "I hear it said that General Hooker has more men than he can handle. I should like to have half as many more as I have today, and I should hurl him in the river! . . . We have always had to put in all our troops and never had enough at the time most needed."

But Confederate luck held here and that might have been just as important as an excess of troops. Hotchkiss's road had proved to be all Jackson had hoped for. He was moving beyond Federal spyglasses and he was inexorably gaining Hooker's rear.

After lunch and a short rest the troops were back in stride, and then Fitz Lee came riding up in great excitement. Please, if the general permitted, he would like a private word. "General," he said, "if you will halt your columns here, out of sight, I will show you the enemy's right."

Jackson took off at once with Fitz Lee, along a trail running above and parallel to the Plank Road. Lee plunged forward without pause or explanation, pushing aside tangled vines, scraping aside low brush from his face. It seemed he was leading Jackson into solid prehistoric vegetation. Then all at once they gained a slight rise, and there spread out was the Army of the Potomac. The poor lambs were at complete unworried rest. Steam rose from pots where cooks were preparing supper. Arms were stacked. Men lay on their backs, legs crossed, some playing the harmonica or lazily gabbing. Above them, a few hundred yards away, stood

the avenging angel for their march into Virginia. Jackson went to
work. By eye he measured the length of the flank and what it
would take to attack here. Better, he judged, to catch them from
the Old Turnpike. A courier was with him, and he wasted not a
second: "Ride to General Rodes and tell him to move across the
Plank Road. Tell him to halt when he gets to the Old Turnpike.
I will join him there."

By the time Jackson got to the Old Turnpike the afternoon
was half gone. He encountered Munford and said cheerily, "The
Virginia Military Institute will be heard from today!" He did
things now in rapid-fire order, his thoughts and plans a slight step
ahead of his spoken commands. Rodes's troops should move
forward. The Stonewall Brigade should guard the crossing of the
Plank Road. Munford was to seize the Ely's Ford Road, hold it,
and keep Jackson posted. Columns must move smartly now, ammunition be brought up front, straggling brutally stopped. Not
much time—for he had the Yankees now.

At four o'clock the order went out to deploy: Form a battle
line and get skirmishers ready. Each brigadier understood immediately Jackson's attack plan. The whole battle line would sweep
as one, first for a clearing called Talley's field on the map and next
toward a small spot, called Melzi Chancellor's farm, on a crest
nearby. Should the enemy stop to fight, Jackson had arranged for
artillery to shell them. If any Federal reserves appeared, General
Dodson Ramseur, West Point '60, and a brigadier general now at
age twenty-six, was to hold them back. Above all, and most
important, Jackson wanted it understood that positively, absolutely, under no circumstances, would there be any pause what-
soever in the advance.

The picture now was this in this obscure piece of geography
in Virginia, on the fringe of the Wilderness: Thousands upon
thousands of gray-clad men were lined up ready to attack an
unsuspecting Northern army. In the forest these men with their
multiple guns, wagons, and animals made last-minute prepara-
tions, keeping their voices to a whisper.

While the blue-clads down below began innocently to line
up for chow, indulging in a little horseplay, enjoying the soft
Virginia springtime. Just as innocent was Mr. F. J. Hooker, who
was lounging on the veranda of nearby Chancellor House, which

was often used as an instant tavern for the weary traveler. Fighting Joe was just such a traveler, although for the past few weeks he had sworn off hard liquor. He had just finished inspecting troops and he was bushed. But he was elated. He considered his troops the finest in the world and the most prepared. He had given them meticulous inspection. They were spick-and-span, healthy and alert. On their own they had thrown up elaborate fortifications at their front. Bobby Lee would have to use every man, woman, and child in the Confederacy to even make a dent in it. Hooker was especially pleased with his men on the right. They might speak funny, but they knew how to put their shoulders to the wheel. Hooker was pleased to see with what meticulousness these Germans had set out their line and put up breastworks. And the regard had been mutual. That day, at inspection, Hooker had seemed the very picture of a confident warrior chief: tall and ramrod straight in the saddle, cheeks flushed, spiffily clad in tailored dark blue, riding a big white prancing horse, with a line of staff behind him that disappeared in the distance.

Now on the veranda in late afternoon he unwound. Sun's setting, time for a little snort, but since he'd given up the sauce for the present he could only indulge in his pride of fortitude. Tomorrow or the next day Lee would attack, attack him in the center most likely, and Hooker was going to mow him down in a reverse Fredericksburg. Lee would come forward; wily old Joe Hooker would cut him down, line after line, until the whole shooting match was over. Lee would shit green corn. Lincoln might too. He was going to end this war. He'd drink to that except he wasn't drinking.

It was 5:15 and the sun had passed the yardarm. In the woods Jackson took out his pocket watch, noted the exact second, then said, "Are you ready, General Rodes?"

"Yes, sir, I am."

"You can go forward then," Stonewall Jackson said quietly, as if he'd just told him to pass down the aisle with the collection plate.

A bugle rang in soft evening air, a strange sharp blast at that hour. Then a series of bugle calls came, from brigade after brigade, left and right. Then an etched moment of pure silence. The Federals looked over their shoulders, still holding their mess gear absurdly in their hands. First the skirmishers rushed forward, then came the battle line, gathering speed, like a locomotive coming down the tracks. Deer and rabbit, frightened as much as any man, led the way and came wildly charging in on the Federals. The Rebels held their red battle flags out front and unleashed their high and eerie yell. As the skirmishers tore through the brush and briars their clothes were often torn right off. They ran anyhow, in tatters, near naked. Then the skirmishers, then the line hit the clearing and fell on Federals—bayonets out, shots ringing.

The Federals did what any humans would have done—they ran. At some moment they ceased being an army, too. They became as wild and crazy as the rabbit and deer. They threw rifle and gear away. They abandoned as useless the carefully laid breastworks that ludicrously faced the wrong way. It was as if the end of the world had come—here, at twilight, while somehow the smell of evening mess still lingered in the air. Many fell; some cut knapsack and gear from their bodies and tore out with knees pumping high, like track stars. Jackson rode just behind the first wave of troops—exultant. "Push right ahead," he said, jerking his hand forward. A lieutenant cried, "They are running too fast, sir. We can't keep up with them." Jackson said, "They never run too fast for me. Press them, press them."

One thing Jackson hoped for was to strike deep enough to cut off Hooker's retreat across the Rappahannock. If he could do that, he just might kill them all before they knew what had happened. Indeed, on the veranda, in the sunset, Hooker and his staff did not know what was happening. The heavy growth and vines in the Wilderness forest muffled the firing and shrieks. It wasn't until one of his officers chanced to stroll onto the road in front of the veranda that the news arrived. "My God—here they come!"

Those on the veranda, Hooker included, rushed to see. From down the road to the west came a wild mob of crazy-eyed men, without firearms, some falling and being trampled on, others falling from fire. The noise soon became deafening. Hooker was a soldier and jumped right in to fix things. He called for a reserve division. "Receive them on your bayonets! Receive them on your bayonets!" It was unclear whether he meant the Rebels or the flying Dutchmen. The Dutchmen were screaming to get out the way! Out of the way! "Vere ist der pontoons! Vere is der pontoons! Ve must cross der riber!"

Hooker swung onto his fine white mount, drew his saber, charged, and was lost for a while in the melee. The rout passed right by him and he didn't stop anyone. He became so engulfed that no one captured him, no one shot him. The Rebels chased the mob until blackness descended and a maze of tight woods engulfed them. Organization then vanished and Rodes called a halt—reluctantly. He would have to regroup. His men had sprinted for miles and now needed a breather. He had the presence of mind, though, to call for A. P. Hill's fresh troops, which had been held in reserve, to continue the pursuit. They could do it in the moonlight.

Hill reported to Jackson in his red battle shirt, and Jackson said, "Good, good. Press them. Cut them off from the United States Ford. Press them, Hill!"

Now was Jackson's main chance; he was not going to let it slip, not for time of day or night or condition of men. In the silvered light he watched Hill's men moving out on either side of the pike. Jackson must know more about the enemy. He asked a courier named David J. Kyle if he knew the countryside roundabouts. "Yes, sir, reckon as how I do."

"Then stay with me. I'm going to find the enemy."

Kyle joined Jackson and a few of his officers, including the ever-present, loyal Joe Morrison. They rode east on the Orange Plank Road until they came to an old schoolhouse. Some Confederates had just arrived there and couldn't tell him much. The area had the smell of Yankees, but they couldn't be sure where they were. Farther down the road he came to some Confederate infantrymen who had formed a line across the road. These turned out to be A. P. Hill's troops. General James Lane was happy to find Jackson. He said, "I've been looking for Hill, sir. I'm waiting for him to give the attack order. Will you give it, sir?"

"Yes, indeed! Push ahead, Lane! Don't let these Yankees get set. Terrorize them, make them panic—now's our chance!"

Jackson, still excited, must know more. He determined to

ride out to the skirmish line to get better understanding. It was slow going, in patches of pale light, on weary horses. Jackson let Kyle lead the way. All at once the air was quiet. They had passed the Confederate picket line surely, although they hadn't encountered any Rebel soldiers. "General," said one of his staff, "don't you think this is the wrong place for you?"

The General said, "The danger is all over—the enemy is routed!—go back and tell A. P. Hill to press right on!"

Kyle led the way, as guide, and Jackson drew alongside impatiently. Then from the stillness came sound, the sound of chopping and brush and trees falling. Voices came, too. Yankee voices, grating and afraid. They were putting up a line of defense here. He must now hurry back to Hill and give him this information. Even though it was night the Light Division under Hill could cut off the Federals from United States Ford and seal Hooker's doom. Silently, lost in thought, Jackson rode until he came near a weather-boarded house in the woods by the roadside. Suddenly, from a southern direction, came a shot. Then another. Finally a volley broke.

These were Hill's men, for here came Hill's voice: "Cease firing, cease firing!"

Jackson felt Little Sorrel break into a panic; it hadn't happened before in the midst of heavy battle; it did now, in the woods. Jackson held reins with his left hand and brought his right up to protect his Jeb Stuart cap and his face from low boughs.

"Cease firing," Morrison yelled, leaping from his horse and running toward the line. "You are firing into your own men!"

"Who gave that order?" a gruff Southern voice said. "It's a lie! Pour it into them, boys!"

A kneeling line of the 18th North Carolina, troops under General Lane, opened up with a long hot flash. Jackson was hit at once. His left arm fell and the horse went out of control. A bullet struck his upraised right hand, and it dropped from holding his cap and warding off branches. Little Sorrel, still spooked, wheeled and took off toward the enemy line. With great effort Jackson turned the sorrel and weaved in the saddle. A strong pair of hands then came out of nowhere, grabbed the reins, and a rough voice talked soothingly to the horse, calming him. Captain

Wilbourn, aided by another, had stopped the horse. Men yelled and bullets sang; it was hard to tell what was going on. And here was General Jackson, who was in charge of the battle, wounded in the saddle and almost falling from it.

"They certainly must be our troops," Wilbourn said, glancing about. To no one. To Jackson. It was all he could think to say.

Jackson nodded and looked toward his own line, as if he had trouble understanding that his men had fired on him. Actually he was in the first stage of shock.

"General, can you move your fingers?" said Wilbourn. Again, all he could think to ask.

Jackson tried, but it was impossible. He weaved. Wilbourn tried to lift Jackson's left arm, examine it, but Jackson said quietly that the pain was too much to bear. Until that moment, although starting into shock, weaving, he was in the saddle. He was in command of his army—as Captain Wilbourn wished him to be. "Please," Jackson said, "you had better take me down."

He tried to help but his foot got caught in the stirrup; Lieutenant Wynn of the signal corps, who identified himself to Jackson, helped free the foot and Jackson was brought down. The men supported the general and walked him ten or fifteen yards off the road, staggering. Wilbourn, outranking Wynn, sent the lieutenant off for a surgeon—Medical Director McGuire, anyone with medical skill, but with a warning: Do not tell anyone that Stonewall Jackson had been wounded. Under a tree Wilbourn removed Jackson's field glasses and haversack and put them over his own shoulder for safekeeping. Then he ripped off the layers of clothing covering Jackson's wound—the sleeve of Jackson's gum coat, Jeb Stuart's uniform jacket, and two shirts the general wore beneath, one atop the other.

As Wilbourn, a battlefield expert, worked, horses hooves clacked up and General A. P. Hill arrived. His voice was anguished: "I've been trying to make the men cease firing," he cried, in deep pain himself at the sight of Jackson, wounded beneath the tree. He knelt by the man and asked, "Is the wound painful?"

"Very painful, I'm afraid. My arm is broken."

Powell Hill, as gentle as the gentlest nurse, removed Jackson's large gauntlets, blood pouring from them. Then he ever so carefully took off Jackson's sword and belt, the symbol of command. "Give General Jackson some whiskey. Is there no whiskey here?"

On the battlefield there was always whiskey. A bottle materialized. Jackson took in a large mouthful, swallowed, then asked for water. Hill tenderly held Jackson's head, feeding him the liquid. Jackson realized all too well what was going on. So many in like position he had seen. Now he was one. He wondered how long it would take for a surgeon to come. One was coming, one was coming—reassurance, what the wounded and sick want to hear. Good, very good, Jackson said. In a whisper to Hill, whom he would trust with his life any day, he asked if the surgeon on the way was competent. He knew battlefield medicine; it could be more dangerous than enemy fire. "He's a good surgeon," Hill said, knowing how to be reassuring once again.

The surgeon who galloped up in the dark was brisk and alert. He examined the tourniquet that Wilbourn had put on and announced it adequate. The blood was clotting, thank God. Now the question was whether to leave the general here, making sure new bleeding didn't start, or risk it and remove him behind the line. While the debate went on among the small knot of men now around their commander, a cry sounded from the moon-streaked road: "Halt! Surrender! Fire on them if they don't surrender!"

Yankees coming!

Ever so gently, as always, Powell Hill removed the arm that cradled Jackson's head and put him in someone else's care. He drew his pistol and started off, saying over his shoulder that he would do his utmost to keep the news of Jackson's wound from the men. "Thank you," Jackson whispered.

Hill reached the front line and, as the crescendo of noise descended and a sheet of white fire spread, he felt the top of his boots take a hot shell fragment. The blow knocked him down, and he feared that his feet might have been severed—but, no, somehow the flesh hadn't been mangled or cut. He could hardly stand, though, couldn't move. He couldn't command now either. The II Corps of Lee's Army of Northern Virginia must now pass to Jeb Stuart, who was a wonderful cavalryman, a marvelous leader of men, but who knew nothing of infantry.

Jackson was now in no-man's-land. Joe Morrison, huddled

over him, saw the outline of two Union soldiers with their hands up, being taken prisoner. The two forces were becoming mixed. He raced off, raced back, and shouted: "The enemy is within fifty yards and advancing; let's take the general away!"

"Let's take him in our arms," Wilborn cried.

"No," Jackson whispered, "help me up, and I'll try to walk."

The younger men held Jackson and he stumbled forth, gaining the road. Almost at once, as if in greeting, a barrage of shells burst around them, whining over and then landing with a resounding blast. Dirt and hot metal flew. Wilbourn was holding three horses, keeping them from running toward the enemy and using them as protection from the firing. Jackson staggered. And here now came Confederate soldiers, running forward as Old Jack had taught them to do, off to fight back the enemy and send them again into retreat. On the dim road they saw the attention and care being given to a lone man. Odd. Usually soldiers simply fell and then waited for the surgeon or an ambulance or a fellow soldier or death. All this attention! They looked excitedly at the scene, for in battle soldiers are most curious when they have a notion that someone of high rank may have been killed or wounded. "Who's that?" one asked, slowing. "Who you got there?"

"Just a friend," an officer said.

As they resumed rushing forward, Jackson whispered, "When asked, say it is a Confederate officer."

But one soldier got close, and in the moonlight, saw very well who it was. His moan was animallike, tender and bereaved: "Great God, that is General Jackson!" And then he was off, lost in the darkness and gunfire.

Jackson could walk no farther, and a litter was called for and miraculously found. As firing increased, Jackson was lifted onto canvas supported by two poles, and four young soldiers each grabbed a handle. They shifted weight, took a step, and the woods and road became a nightmare of flashing fire and flying metal. Every weapon of war seemed to fall: canister, grape, minié balls. One litter bearer took shots in both arms and keeled over; the man next to him caught the handle and saved Jackson from pitching over. But another soldier on the litter detail saw this and something happened behind his eyes: He lowered his end to the ground and walked mutely into the woods to escape. Jackson lay on the ground, and the previous sheet of fire paled then in what followed. Projectiles of all description flew over Jackson's head, landing a few feet away. Branches fell; saplings were blown from the earth. Whine and bang, whine and bang. The horses Wilbourn held reared and bucked and he was lifted off the ground at times. Then the three remaining litter bearers, without discussion, wrapped themselves around Jackson to protect him. If metal came, it would strike them first. In a daze, confused, Jackson tried to rise. Jimmy Smith laid himself across Jackson's body. "Sir, you must lie still; it will cost you your life if you rise!"

At last the Federal artillery range passed them and they could move. "I can walk," Jackson said. But he couldn't. He took a few steps and then had to be lowered. He asked for spirits, and Wilbourn left the care of the horses to someone else and took off for it. Whiskey was important; so were horses. But now there were but three to aid the general. One held the horses, the other two carried the litter. What would happened if the range found them again? They needed more hands, and the only way to get them was to ask the soldiers racing about in the woods. The dilemma was that they didn't want to say it was Stonewall Jackson they carried. The cry went out, "Someone help. We have a wounded officer here. Please give us a hand." And one after another soldier turned his head, didn't answer, walked off. It was safer in the woods than, exposed, on the road, toting a litter with a dadburn old officer on it!

Jackson's men could take it no longer. Their pace had slowed, and the Yankees might find the range again. His wound might bleed again. Throw caution to the wind! "Hey, you men there, we have General Jackson on this litter and we need help getting him to safety!"

They then had more than enough volunteers. Everyone within earshot came running to help. They stumbled forward once more with the litter, and up ahead suddenly ran across General Dorsey Pender. He was wounded himself, although not crippled, and he said, "Ah, General, I am sorry to see you have been wounded. The lines here are so much broken that I fear we will have to fall back."

It was apparent—the shelling, the chaos, the disorganization.

But then the old Jackson came back briefly. He raised his head from the litter and barked, "You must hold your ground, General Pender; you must hold your ground, sir!"

Then the litter bearers plunged forward into the moon-swept night. For safety they veered into the woods, leaving the road. Firing would undoubtedly break out again on the road, and they carried the general easily, the litter ends on their shoulders. Where was Wilbourn? Jackson wanted to know. Where was the whiskey? Soon, soon, he was reassured. And then a litter bearer caught his foot in a vine and toppled over headfirst. He cursed; Jackson fell from the height of the men's shoulders to the ground—fell on his shattered arm. He gave then his first groan of pain. He was put back on the litter and hefted up again.

"General," Jimmy Smith asked, "are you much hurt?"

"No, Mr. Smith," Jackson said in a steady voice, composing himself, "don't trouble yourself about me."

At long last they spotted an ambulance. Already inside were two other patients: Jackson's chief of artillery, Colonel Stapleton Crutchfield, and a captain. Crutchfield's leg was torn up. The captain, who was not severely wounded, gladly gave up his place to Stonewall Jackson. The ambulance had a plank floor and few springs, but it beat litter bearers and could move faster to the rear. It went back along the way Jackson had so furiously charged only a few hours before. Joe Morrison, the devoted brother-in-law, sat beside Jackson on the trip, holding his wounded arm to lessen the shocks of the road. A rider went ahead of the ambulance, yelling out when bumps and ruts approached. Jackson asked again about whiskey. Others had been sent for it beside Wilbourn, but none had been successful. In the heady fighting the Rebels were drinking their supply up fast. Empty bottles everywhere.

As the ambulance rolled up to the Reverend Melzi Chancellor's house, Jackson's luck changed for the better. Dr. Hunter McGuire was there to take care of him, and, almost equally important, he got whiskey. McGuire added a dose of morphia, and the tenseness in Jackson's face faded. "I hope you are not badly hurt, General," McGuire said, as he knelt by Jackson.

"I am badly injured, Doctor; I fear I am dying," he said faintly; then added courteously, "I am glad you have come."

Jackson needed now to be in a field hospital, and he was put back in the ambulance. Inside McGuire kept his finger on Jackson's severed artery so there would be no chance now for bleeding. Mercifully they were now well behind the lines and beyond shelling, and torches were used along the road to warn of rough patches. Along the way Jackson motioned to McGuire to lower his head. "Is Crutchfield dangerously wounded?" he whispered.

"No," said McGuire, "only painfully hurt. His leg is broken."

"I am glad it is no worse."

Not much later Crutchfield pulled McGuire's head down in the same fashion. "What are General Jackson's wounds?" he said softly.

"I am afraid the general is very seriously wounded."

"Oh, my God!" Crutchfield screamed.

And Jackson, thinking Crutchfield could bear his pain no longer, asked that the ambulance be halted for a while to alleviate his suffering.

At long last, toward midnight, the ambulance pulled into a field on the fringe of the Wilderness where the II Corps hospital had been set up. The supervising surgeon, Dr. Harvey Black, had already received news about Jackson and had warmed the tent for his arrival. Jackson got more whiskey, several blankets placed over him, and he seemed much improved. But his pulse was weak. McGuire waited. A whippoorwill called sadly across the field, and in the distance came the sound of firing, the rumble of artillery. But around the field all was peaceful save for the whimper of wounded men and the rasp of a surgeon's saw. At two o'clock McGuire strode into the tent with Dr. Black and two other doctors. McGuire said that chloroform would be administered, an examination made; if amputation seemed necessary, should they proceed immediately?

"Yes, certainly, Dr. McGuire, do for me whatever you think best."

One surgeon folded a cloth into the shape of a cone and poured a healthy amount of clear chloroform on it. The chloroform had come courtesy of a blockade runner who had reached a Southern port from abroad. The surgeon bade Jackson exhale fully and, as the general drew in his breath, the man held the wet cloth a few inches above Jackson's nose and mouth; he kept doing this, time after time. Jackson drifted off, saying, "What an infinite blessing! Blessing . . . blessing, blesssssing, bless . . ."

His right hand was taken care of first, and a round ball was found to have entered the palm, breaking two bones and lodging under the skin at the back of the hand. McGuire removed it, and saw at once that it came from a smoothbore Springfield musket. It was a Confederate ball, not a Federal bullet. Here was absolute proof that his own men had shot him.

Now the general's left arm. A ball had entered about three inches below the joint of the shoulder, had severed the main artery, had broken the bone, and exited. A third ball had struck the forearm about an inch below the uplifted elbow and had come out just above the wrist. Here was a classically shattered arm from battle. To save his life it must be removed. The possibility of gangrene setting in was extremely high. All the surgeons agreed.

The operation itself was routine, one these doctors had performed often on the field, and not considered dangerous. As one doctor kept the chloroform flowing, Dr. Black kept watch on Jackson's heartbeat. Dr. McGuire did the surgery. He made a circular incision and sawed off the bone with an appliance quite similar to a household saw. Little blood was lost. Dressings went on, and the anesthetic was stopped. They had completed a successful operation; now it was up to the patient and the Almighty.

When Jackson came around in half an hour he drank a cup of coffee and then he was scheduled for a long, uninterrupted sleep. It was not to be. An hour later Sandie Pendleton came in, and Jackson woke, at first brightly. He said, in a full voice, "I am glad to see you; I thought you were killed."

Pendleton believed that the old Jackson was before him now—Old Jack minus an arm, that was all. So much had happened this day. He began filling his general in—Hill injured and out of action; Stuart now at the front and taking charge. But Stuart was unaware of the overall plan and needed help. What instructions should he take back? Again, it seemed as if the old Jackson was back in business. He asked quick brisk questions about troop movements and the front. Then he got set to lay down some directions. His brow narrowed and his lips became set; his nostrils dilated and his eye flashed as usual. But all of this was but for a moment. He struggled with his mind, and then the light went out in his eye. "I don't know—I can't tell; say to General Stuart he must do what he thinks best."

Pendleton left, and Jackson moved into a further realm. He lost his reticence, his hold on secrecy, and became gabby—letting go. He called good Jimmy Smith over and began lauding the wonders of chloroform. The vapor had stolen inside his brain, numbing all pain, and what he remembered while in its twilight limbo was hearing the faint sound of delightful music. "I believe, Jimmy, it was the sawing of the bone." Smith looked at Jackson out of the corner of his eye; this was not quite the man he had known. Now Jackson was stating that he would not like to meet death under chloroform, for a person's mind should be clear then; barring that situation, the experience was on the positive side. Jimmy Smith thought perhaps the general should try to return to sleep; Dr. McGuire had recommended sleep. Ah, well, Jackson would try. He fell into a deep sleep immediately.

He awoke late the next day, at nine in the morning. It was the Sabbath and a stupendous morning. A heavy dew still lay on the grass. Around the countryside the fruit blossoms moved in a gentle sweet breeze. Birds sang—especially the robin. And far off came the rolling thunder of artillery and the dim pop of muskets, which receded by the minute. Jackson woke hungry and very much alive. His old military persona took charge and he dashed off a quick message to Lee, informing him of his wound and of the transfer of command to Stuart. He directed that all his staff save Jimmy Smith go directly to the front. They were more needed there than around a sick bed. Jimmy would keep him company, and Joe Morrison would go to Richmond to inform Anna of the wound and to bring her to him if possible.

The doctors were optimistic and all smiled. Ah, in a short time old Stonewall Jackson would be back on the field. Then Reverend Lacy rushed in and, minister and comforter of the ill though he was, he lost his composure. He couldn't keep his eye from the bandaged stump where once Jackson's arm had been. "Oh, General," he blurted out, "what a calamity."

Softly Jackson comforted the minister. The will of God had taken his arm from him. There was always a *reason* for what God did; it might seem unreasonable now but later we all learn God's wisdom. In the world to come—or later in life—Jackson would understand why his arm had been taken from him. (Actually it was buried nearby, complete with a religious ceremony, and a marble marker placed over it; God watched over all.) As he warmed to the subject, he recounted that when the litter bearer tripped and dropped him, he had, at that moment, given himself up to his Creator. He had felt perfect peace, not fear, and despite the pain it had been a precious experience.

Still there was this ache on the right side where he had landed. Perhaps he had hit a stone or a gnarled root. Dr. McGuire made a thorough examination of his chest, abdomen, and back. He went over him carefully. He could find no broken rib, not even a bruise. Everything was most encouraging. McGuire smiled, and so did the other doctors. Still Jackson felt the ache.

Kyd Douglas rode in from the front and brought news. Paxton, the latest leader of the Stonewall Brigade, had died in the battle. He had been summoned to attack the enemy while reading the Bible. He had closed the book, climbed in the saddle, and an hour or two later had been shot dead. Captain Boswell had been shot through the heart; so had so many others. General Stuart had himself led a charge by the Stonewall Brigade, exhorting the men to remember their first commander. As they made their last grand charge at Chancellorsville, they began a Rebel yell that carried over the musketry. They had cried, "Remember Jackson!" and won the field.

Jackson's eyes watered, and he said with a quiver to his voice, "It was just like them, just like them. They are a noble set of men. The name of Stonewall belongs to that brigade, not to me."

Jackson became expansive in the extreme. He praised subordinates whom he had reprimanded only days before. He forgave all. He even had a good word to say for Mr. F. J. Hooker. Hooker had had an excellent battle plan, would certainly have won at Chancellorsville except for not having a line of cavalry on his right flank. If cavalry had been there Jackson could not have ridden around and attacked his rear. Hooker was a good general. Lee sent a message: "Could I have directed events, I should have chosen for the good of the country to be disabled in your stead. I congratulate you upon the victory, which is due to your skill and energy." Jackson turned his face away from Smith, who had delivered the message. "General Lee is very kind, but he should give the praise to God."

Somewhere out there quite close the fighting still raged, and good judgment said that Stonewall Jackson should be moved many miles to the rear. He was too close to the front. Lee sent word that troops should guard the hospital tent at all hours. The enemy must not capture Stonewall. But Jackson brushed off the idea, and showed no fear or concern. "I am not afraid of them; I have always been kind to their wounded, and I am sure they will be kind to me."

But Lee persisted. Jackson must not be captured; he must be moved. He further ordered that McGuire stay with him at all times. "General Lee," Jackson said, as evening fell, "has always been very kind to me, and I thank him."

Where he would go to recuperate was left to Jackson. He thought immediately of the home of the Chandler family near Guiney's. He had visited there while at Moss Neck, and it had impressed him as a happy home. If the family was willing to have a wounded soldier for a while, the Chandler home was where he wanted to be. They sent back word they would be delighted to have him. Jackson began to think of life away from the army now, away from war, looking forward to eventually going back to Lexington and seeing old friends.

He slept well the night of May 3 to 4, and took eagerly to the ambulance ride to Guiney's. Hotchkiss mapped out the route, choosing the smoothest and shortest way. Inside the wagon went Chaplain Lacy, Dr. McGuire, the ever-present Jimmy Smith, and once again Crutchfield, who was greatly improving. It was a twenty-five-mile trip, and it was much more pleasant than the previous ride from the battlefield. They all talked in the ambulance in a tone usually reserved for veterans after a war has ended. Jackson explained his strategy at Chancellorsville—how he had been trying to cut Hooker off from the United States Ford, how he planned to then form a strong defensive position and cut down the Federal troops when they attacked. He spoke as if Chancellorsville had already received a place in history.

Toward the end of the ride Jackson became nauseated, and Dr. McGuire applied a wet towel to his abdomen. This was Jackson's own cure, but McGuire had no objection and it seemed to do no harm.

At the Chandlers' Jackson perked up. Everything was prepared and ready for him—the gracious hospitality of Virginians. Around the home spread a long green lawn. Jackson was given a small separate dwelling—an office—off to the side. On the left as one entered was a small room, and at the back two chambers, in one of which Jackson was placed on a bed. Upstairs were two very small rooms, for doctors and visitors. Out front were two tall oak trees, and a well to the side, the kind of country setting Jackson relished. The walls of his room had been recently whitewashed, and he could see a garden of flowers outside his window. He took some bread and tea, and McGuire found that the wound was healing nicely. Voices buzzed around the Chandler home, everyone happy and busy. Army officers bustled about, but Stonewall lay in bed and fell asleep.

On Tuesday morning he awoke to ask McGuire how soon it might be before he would take the field again. McGuire gave him a doctor's noncommittal answer but his face indicated optimism. Jackson spent the day doing what he enjoyed as recreation: arguing Scripture and theology with Reverend Lacy and Jimmy Smith. He sprang questions on Smith in a professorial manner: "What were the headquarters of Christianity after the crucifixion?" Smith rubbed his head, and began a learned answer on the Christian centers at Jerusalem, Antioch, Iconium, Rome, and Alexandria. It was not enough to please the professor. "Why do you say 'centers of influence'? Is not 'headquarters' a better term?" Nor was Dr. McGuire safe. He asked if any who had been healed by Jesus ever again suffered from the same illness? McGuire had no answer. "Oh, for infinite power!" said Jackson.

Lee continued to worry about his lieutenant. He sent Dr. S. B. Morrison, a relative of Anna's and the family doctor, to help in the care of Jackson. He sent also this message: "Give him my affectionate regards, and tell him to make haste and get well, and come back to me as soon as he can. He has lost his left arm; but I have lost my right arm."

"Many," Jackson said to Smith, "would regard my injuries as a great misfortune; I regard them as one of the blessings of my life."

Jimmy Smith came in on the beat. "All things work together for good to them that love God."

"Yes, that's it, that's it."

Wednesday night, May 6, McGuire believed Jackson had shown enough improvement to warrant not being watched closely by a doctor. He decided it was time that he himself got a good night's sleep in the upstairs room. Jim Lewis was more than happy to stand vigil. At one in the morning Jackson woke, sick to his stomach. The pain was grinding away at his right side. Jim Lewis was close by the bed and wanted to call McGuire. No, no, simply get the wet towel and once again bathe the stomach. That always helped. This time it didn't. At dawn, as Jackson clutched his side with his one hand; he could postpone no longer. Call McGuire.

Dr. McGuire went to work quickly with all that he had in his medical tool chest, and he forbade the use forever of the wet cloth. He used cupping, mercury, antimony, and opium. Drugged now, a high fever developing, Jackson began his slide into delirium. Anna and his baby Julia, along with nurse Hetty, arrived that day in a flurry. Anna gasped as she stepped from the Richmond train and beheld the pained expression of the staff officer who met her. She could not go in immediately to see Thomas, for the surgeons now worked over him. She passed time on the Chandlers' porch, walking up and down. All at once she noticed digging in the family graveyard. It was a coffin being raised for shipment elsewhere. She was told it contained the body of General Paxton. She had not known that Paxton, a Lexington neighbor, had been killed. Anna could hardly keep her hands still, and when she was asked if she wanted to prepare lemonade for her husband, kept putting in spoon after spoon of sugar. He was given the drink just as she entered his room. "You did not mix this, it is too sweet; take it back." And he faded into delirium as Anna stood by his bed.

Anna Jackson later wrote, "Oh, the fearful change since last I had seen him! It required the strongest effort of which I was capable to maintain my self-control. . . . Now, his fearful wounds, his mutilated arm, the scratches upon his face, and above all, the desperate pneumonia, which was flushing his cheeks, oppressing his breathing, and benumbing his senses . . ."

She stood there patiently, and he came back finally into the world. Why, it was Anna! She looked so sad. "My darling, you must cheer up, and not wear a long face. I love cheerfulness and brightness in a sickroom." He passed in and out of consciousness, to say, "My darling . . . you are very much loved!" and "You are one of the most precious little wives in the world."

She wondered if he might like to see Julia. He answered, "Not yet; wait till I feel better."

She waited for further words. Suddenly he said, "Tell Major Hawks to send forward provisions to the men." Then, "Order A. P. Hill to prepare for action. . . . Pass the infantry to the front."

The war, back to the war.

The routine of the sickroom continued—busy steps, anxious words, soft voices. Jackson came to suddenly to see a great number of doctors around his bed. He said evenly, "I see from the number of physicians that you think my condition dangerous, but I thank God, if it is His will, that I am ready to go."

In the Confederate army the troops could not believe that Stonewall Jackson could be struck down. Impossible. He was charmed. As General Dick Taylor had once said, "A bullet which could kill Stonewall hasn't been molded." To lose Stonewall now, to these men, was to lose one's father. General Lee worried most of all: "Surely, General Jackson must recover; God will not take him from us, now that we need him so much."

Jackson stopped calling for Hill to listen to Dr. Morrison say that he feared the disease might not be overcome. Pneumonia was too fierce an enemy now. He told everyone in the sickroom: "I am not afraid to die; I am willing to abide by the will of my Heavenly Father. But I do not believe that I shall die at this time; I am persuaded the Almighty has yet a work for me to perform." Jackson asked for McGuire to come and give an opinion. This doctor shook his head and admitted doubt concerning Jackson's recovery. Still the general insisted he would make it through.

He called for Chaplain Lacy and plowed into a theological discussion even though his attendants tried to dissuade him from getting worked up. He wanted to know if Lacy was promoting Sunday in the army. Yes? Good, very good. He shut his eyes, seeming to pray. Then he opened them, calling, "Order A. P. Hill to prepare for action. . . . Pass the infantry to the front."

On Saturday night Anna read the Psalms of consolation to him. His breathing was rapid and labored, but he listened and understood. He asked for a hymn, and Joe Morrison, who stood beside his sister, steadying her, joined with her to sing his request:

> Show pity, Lord; O Lord, forgive;
> Let a repenting rebel live;
> Are not thy mercies large and free?
> May not a sinner trust in thee?

Jackson's face was given a cold sponging, which seemed to help. But he continued to sink. One physician tried to get him to take a drink of brandy. Jackson put it to his lips and said, "It tastes like fire and cannot do me any good."

Sunday the tenth of May broke in glorious full sunlight. Early Dr. Morrison motioned for Anna to step from the sickroom and speak privately with him. "The end is coming," he said. "Thomas cannot live through the day."

Anna composed herself, drew back her shoulders, and moved to his side. "Do you know," she said gently, "the doctors say you must very soon be in Heaven."

His mind was elsewhere—in battle, seeing to the welfare of his men. He could not hear her. She repeated the sentence. Then said, "Do you not feel willing to acquiesce in God's allotment, if He wills you to go today?"

"I prefer it," he said.

"Well, before this day closes, you will be with the blessed Saviour in His glory."

Then she asked him practical matters. Where did he think she and Julia should live? She should go to her father in North Carolina. Where did he want to be buried? "Charlotte." She must have misunderstood. Charlottesville? Surely not there either. He didn't know anyone there. She mentioned Lexington. "Yes, Lexington. Lexington would be fine." But he seemed to have lost interest in that subject.

In that day one said good-bye to those near when the end approached. His baby Julia was brought to him. She did not seem at all unhappy or alarmed—in fact, the scene around the bed had the appearance of people at play. Jackson recognized his daughter and was happy to be able to leave off the subject of a burial plot. "Little darling," he said. ". . . sweet one!" His daughter smiled.

Jackson called for Dr. McGuire. "Doctor, Anna informs me that you have told her that I am to die today; is it so?"

"I'm afraid, General, medicine has done its utmost."

"Good, good. Very good; very good; it is all right."

Dr. McGuire offered a glass of brandy and water. "No, it will only delay my departure, and do no good; I want to preserve my mind, if possible, to the last."

Outside the room Sandie Pendleton lowered his head and wept. Jim Lewis was crying openly in the room itself. Jackson's breathing became choked. Prayers were being said softly. . . . "Our Heavenly Father, please take your servant forward. . . . Send for Major Hawks. . . . These men must be fed!"

McGuire was reminding him that the sands of time were running out, that he might not have more than two hours to live. It was 1:30 on this Sunday.

"Very good; it is all right!"

Further orders for Hill and commands for deployment of infantry, and then a pause. A long, drawn-out pause. The spirit that had been somewhere within him through all his life, that had determined how he would act in all of life's situations, was leaving. Where it would go no one in that room knew. He said, as if inviting them along, "Let us cross over the river, and rest under the shade of the trees."

Afterward . . .

Ewell, minus the leg he had lost at Second Manassas, came back to fight at Gettysburg and lead Stonewall Jackson's troops. At the beginning of the fight Lee suggested that Ewell overtake a slight rise of earth called Cemetery Hill, a most strategic piece of terrain. If Ewell could take it, the whole line of Federals on Cemetery Ridge might be wiped out. Jackson would certainly have understood Lee's strategy and somehow have taken Cemetery Hill —"marching around Washington if need be," someone once observed. Ewell, in a strange lassitude, did nothing. Stonewall's men didn't move. Cemetery Hill remained in Federal hands during the crucial early moments of Gettysburg, when cunning and alacrity might have won the day. On the third day—July 3, 1863—came Pickett's Charge and the South lost the battle. It was downhill after that and only a matter of time until the South should lose the war altogether.

After Appomattox several Rebel commanders went to prison. Ewell served a short stretch. He had married in his autumn years and, after release from behind bars, retired to his wife's farm in Tennessee, where he became a devout Christian who shunned public view and ceased taking the name of the Lord in vain.

Kyd Douglas went to a penitentiary in Washington, D.C. He returned to Maryland to become a successful lawyer and later to serve as a highly respected judge on the circuit court.

Longstreet became a successful businessman in New Orleans soon after the war. He became a Republican too, thus ensuring his ostracization by many former comrades. He gained one federal appointment after another, dying in 1904 at age eighty-three.

Shanks Evans ended as a high-school principal in Alabama.

D. H. Hill worked as a newspaper and magazine editor before becoming a college president.

A. P. Hill did not live out the war. He was shot through the heart in the final days while seated on his dapple-gray horse, extending his gauntleted left hand toward two blue-clad skirmishers, calling upon them to surrender. He was dead before he hit the ground.

Anna Jackson took her daughter, Julia, to Charlotte, North Carolina. Jackson's daughter married a Richmond newspaperman, William Edmund Christian, and they had a son and daughter. Julia died at twenty-seven, and Anna reared the grandchildren herself, both of whom married and have descendants. Anna Morrison Jackson was affectionately known as "Cousin Anna" and her home on West Trade became a shrine to which Confederate veterans paid their respects. She kept General Stonewall Jackson's saddle on a post in her front hallway. She died at age eighty-four in 1915, and friends remember her beauty of character as a little old lady dressed in black with her face framed in curls.

STONEWALL JACKSON'S WAY

Words: John W. Palmer
Music: Anonymous

This song is based on a poem that was written during the battle at Antietam. The poet, John Palmer, was also a playwright and newspaper correspondent. Legend has it that the original copy was lost, then discovered on the body of a Rebel sergeant of the Stonewall Brigade while fighting raged at Winchester.

Come, stack arms, men, pile on the rails;
    Stir up the campfires bright;
No matter if the canteen fails,
    We'll make a roaring night.
Here Shenandoah brawls along.
There lofty Blue Ridge echoes strong,
To swell the Brigade's roaring song
    Of Stonewall Jackson's way.

We see him now—the old slouched hat,
    Cocked o'er his eye askew;
The shrewd dry smile—the speech so pat,
    So calm, so blunt, so true.
The "Blue-Light Elder" knows them well:
Says he, "That's Banks—he's fond of shell;
Lord save his soul! we'll give him _____" well,
    That's Stonewall Jackson's way.

Silence! ground arms! kneel all! caps off!
    Old Blue-Light's going to pray;
Strangle the fool that dares to scoff!
    Attention! it's his way!
Appealing from his native sod,
In forma pauperis to God,
    "Lay bare thine arm—stretch forth thy rod,
    Amen!" That's Stonewall's way.

He's in the saddle now! Fall in,
    Steady, the whole Brigade!
Hill's at the Ford, cut off!—we'll win

His way out, ball and blade.
What matter if our shoes are worn?
What matter if our feet are torn?
Quick step! we're with him before morn!
   That's Stonewall Jackson's way.

The sun's bright lances rout the mists
   Of morning—and, by George!
There's Longstreet struggling in the lists,
   Hemmed in an ugly gorge.
Pope and his columns whipped before—
"Bayonets and grape!" hear Stonewall roar;
"Charge, Stuart! Pay off Ashby's score!"
   That's Stonewall Jackson's way.

Ah! maiden, wait and watch and yearn
   For news of Stonewall's band;
Ah! widow, read with eyes that burn
   The ring upon thy hand.
Ah! wife, sew on, pray on, hope on,
Thy life shall not be all forlorn;
The foe had better ne'er been born
   That gets in Stonewall's way.

Index

ABOUT THE AUTHOR

John Bowers was born and educated in Tennessee. He is a free-lance writer and also teaches writing part time at Columbia University. He lives in New York City with his wife and their two young sons.

DATE DUE

OCT 30 '89			
DEC 1 '89			
FEB 27 '90			
MAY 21 '90			
MAR 27 '91			
JUL 8 '91			
JUL 17 '91			
JAN 20 '98			
GAYLORD			PRINTED IN U.S.A